To
Lacey
May 2013
xo Kathi + Press

SISTER

SISTER

THE LIFE OF THE LEGENDARY
AMERICAN INTERIOR DECORATOR
MRS. HENRY PARISH II

Apple Parish Bartlett and

Susan Bartlett Crater

ST. MARTIN'S PRESS

NEW YORK

SISTER. Copyright © 2000 by Apple Parish Bartlett and Susan Bartlett Crater. All rights reserved. Printed in the United States of America. No part of this book may be used or reproduced in any manner whatsoever without written permission except in the case of brief quotations embodied in critical articles or reviews. For information, address St. Martin's Press, 175 Fifth Avenue, New York, N.Y. 10010.

www.stmartins.com

Book design by Gretchen Achilles

Frontispiece: Sister with Yummy.

Illustration credits appear on page 358.

Library of Congress Cataloging-in-Publication Data

Bartlett, Apple Parish.
    Sister: the life of legendary American interior decorator Mrs. Henry Parish II/Apple Parish Bartlett and Susan Bartlett Crater.
        p.   cm.
    Includes bibliographical references and index.
    ISBN 0-312-24240-9
    1. Parish, Henry, II. Mrs.   2. Interior decorators—United States—Biography   I. Crater. Susan Bartlett.   II. Title.
    NK2004.3.P365   B37   2000
    747.213—dc21   00-027968

10 9 8 7 6 5 4 3 2

IN MEMORY OF

SISTER AND HARRY PARISH

Acknowledgments

➤➤ ── ◄◄

FIRST AND FOREMOST, my mother and I would like to thank all of Sister's friends and the members of her family, many of whom we interviewed for the book. Each and every one gave generously of their time and frequently put up with such disturbances as barking dogs and the mechanical failures of my tape recorders. What struck me immediately was the degree of affection they all felt for Sister and how each interview produced a lot of laughter—something a conversation with Sister was bound to produce, as well. I also want to thank them for their honesty and courage in remembering Sister and commenting on the many facets of her life and personality. She was many things to many people, and I hope that the diversity of their contributions demonstrates this.

When we began the project, we saw it as a traditional biography, which would include Sister's autobiographical sketches. As we began to talk to her friends, however, the richness of their stories gave us the idea of presenting this as an oral biography. I was also greatly influenced by *Edie,* the oral biography of Edie Sedgwick by George Plimpton and Jean Stein. I thank them for the inspiration their book provided. One of the advantages of compiling an oral biography was that my mother and I were, we hope, able to avoid judging Sister. We knew that she was her own best narrator, and the use of her family's and friends' words gave her story a context and honesty we could not have achieved through our words alone. My mother deserves special credit for writing a book about her mother, something few people would attempt.

I would also like to thank our agent, Faith Childs, who was with the project from the very beginning and guided me every step of the way. Her suggestions were invaluable. I would like to thank the following people at St. Martin's Press: Sally Richardson for believing in the project, Bob Wallace for his help and enthusiasm in the early stages, and, most especially, my editor, Charles Spicer, for his never-ending support and enthusiasm. Charlie's insights and comments helped shape the book; I couldn't have done it without him. I would also like to thank Steve Snider and David Berry of the St. Martin's art department, for their beautiful work on the jacket, and Gretchen Achilles for her work on the book's overall design. I am also grateful to Carol Edwards for her extraordinary copyediting.

For help in my research, I would like to thank Cynthia Cathcart at the Condé Nast library. I would also like to thank everyone who worked at Parish-Hadley and made it the amazing place it was, both those who worked there during my grandmother's time and those who were employed there later. From the time I could walk, I felt a visual delight in being at the office, and I remember the kindness and courtesy that everyone there has always shown all members of my family. When we began the book, every effort was made to help me, and I couldn't have completed it without the help of those people. Nancy Porter, Carole Cavaluzzo, and Britt Smith gave generously of their time, and Libby Cameron was enormously helpful, as well. Very special thanks go to Albert Hadley, who truly is an integral part of this book and certainly helped make it a reality.

I am eternally grateful to Deborah Dalfonso, who contributed an extraordinary amount of time, energy, and editorial assistance in helping to parse together the interview transcripts and to bring the book to completion. Her research assistance and the interviews she did with the Islesboro year-round residents were also invaluable. We offer special thanks to Elenita Lodge, Jennifer Maguire, John and Sandra Kramer, Sarah Wadsworth, and Joan MacDougal, who read the early drafts of the manuscript, and Liza Dalfonso, for help in transcribing the interview tapes. I am also grateful to my brother Harry for taking pictures of the Summer House, to my father for his help and encouragement, and to my brother Charlie for his always-appreciated humor. We would also like to offer thanks to Eddie Parish for his time and energy, to Maisie Houghton for her ideas and encouragement, and to Joan de Mouchy and KK Auchincloss for their help and support.

My husband, Doug, and our children, Eliza and Tucker, all had a hand in the creation of this book, and I certainly couldn't have done it without their thoughtful suggestions and unlimited patience and humor. In addition, I would like to thank all of those unnamed friends who gave us their support, and, of course, Sister and Harry for giving us an opportunity to tell their story.

SUSAN BARTLETT CRATER

A SPECIAL ACKNOWLEDGMENT to Susan, my daughter. Without her tireless efforts, this book would never have come to fruition. I know that both her grandmother and I are very proud of her.

APPLE PARISH BARTLETT

The kiss of the sun for pardon,
The song of the birds for mirth
One is nearer God's heart in a garden
Than anywhere else on earth.

DOROTHY FRANCES GURNEY

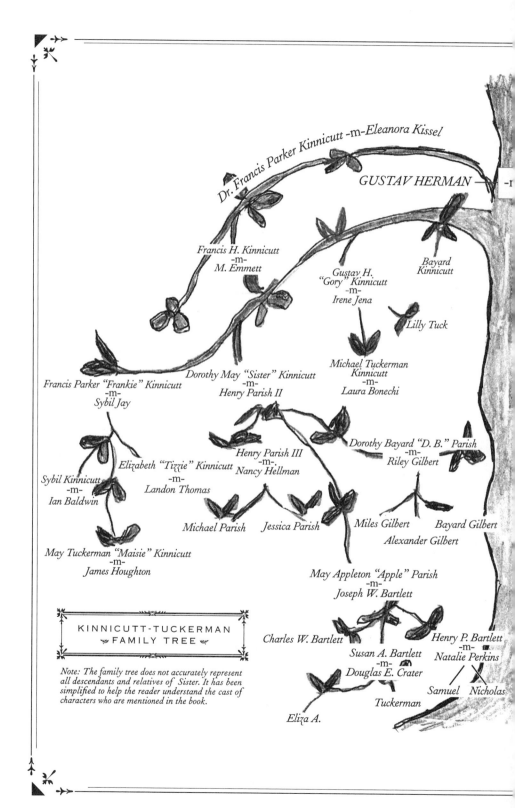

Dr. Francis Parker Kinnicutt -m- Eleanora Kissel

GUSTAV HERMAN — -m

Francis H. Kinnicutt
-m-
M. Emmett

Gustav H.
"Gory" Kinnicutt
-m-
Irene Jena

Bayard
Kinnicutt

Lilly Tuck

Michael Tuckerman
Kinnicutt
-m-
Laura Bonechi

Francis Parker "Frankie" Kinnicutt
-m-
Sybil Jay

Dorothy May "Sister" Kinnicutt
-m-
Henry Parish II

Henry Parish III
-m-.
Nancy Hellman

Dorothy Bayard "D. B." Parish
-m-
Riley Gilbert

Elizabeth "Tizzie" Kinnicutt
-m-
Landon Thomas

Sybil Kinnicutt
-m-
Ian Baldwin

Michael Parish   Jessica Parish

Miles Gilbert   Bayard Gilbert

Alexander Gilbert

May Tuckerman "Maisie" Kinnicutt
-m-
James Houghton

May Appleton "Apple" Parish
-m-
Joseph W. Bartlett

KINNICUTT-TUCKERMAN
⇝ FAMILY TREE ⇜

Note: The family tree does not accurately represent
all descendants and relatives of Sister. It has been
simplified to help the reader understand the cast of
characters who are mentioned in the book.

Charles W. Bartlett

Susan A. Bartlett
-m-
Douglas E. Crater

Henry P. Bartlett
-m-
Natalie Perkins

Samuel   Nicholas

Tuckerman

Eliza A.

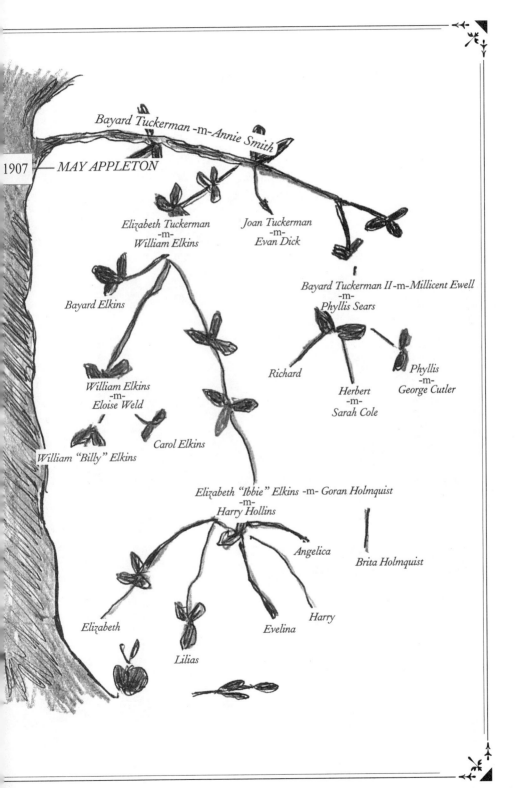

Bayard Tuckerman -m- Annie Smith

1907 — MAY APPLETON

Elizabeth Tuckerman
-m-
William Elkins

Joan Tuckerman
-m-
Evan Dick

Bayard Elkins

Bayard Tuckerman II -m- Millicent Ewell
-m-
Phyllis Sears

William Elkins
-m-
Eloise Weld

Richard

Phyllis
-m-
George Cutler

Herbert
-m-
Sarah Cole

Carol Elkins

William "Billy" Elkins

Elizabeth "Ibbie" Elkins -m- Goran Holmquist
-m-
Harry Hollins

Angelica

Brita Holmquist

Elizabeth

Harry

Evelina

Lilias

Contents

➤➤————————————————————————————◄◄

	Foreword by Albert Hadley	*xvii*
	Prologue	*xix*
1.	Beginnings: 1910 and Earlier	1
2.	Mayfields: 1917–1925	25
3.	Education and Coming Out: 1926–1928	35
4.	Marriage: 1930	45
5.	Long Lane: 1930–1940	53
6.	The War Years and Return to New York: 1941–1952	67
7.	Jackie: 1953–1960	77
8.	The White House: 1960–1963	87
9.	Parish-Hadley: 1963–Onward	114
10.	On Decorating	134
11.	A Day at the Office	159
12.	At Home	181
13.	Clients	203
14.	The Jock Whitneys	219
15.	The Charles Engelhards	236
16.	The Thomas Watsons	251
17.	The William Paleys	261
18.	Coolidge Point	266
19.	The Duke and Duchess of York	273
20.	Family	280
21.	Maine	292
22.	Continuity	325
23.	We Gathered in Dark Harbor: 1994	334
	Epilogue	*340*
	Notes on the Contributors	*343*

APPLE BARTLETT AND Susan Crater have written, lovingly and with considerable flair, the story of their mother and grandmother's remarkable life. They have accomplished the almost impossible task of capturing in words the essence of Dorothy May Kinnicutt Parish's long and colorful journey.

Sister Parish, as she was known to her family, her friends, and the outside world, was raised in an atmosphere of privilege and luxury. The circumstances of her birth afforded her the background against which to play the varied scenes that were hers to explore and project.

Susan and Apple have masterfully focused not just on the private life of family and home, which was Sister's paramount concern, but they have also drawn vivid images of the creative artistry of her public and professional life. In addition to her intuitive sense of style and her knowledgeable taste, underlying all she created were the values about which she was passionate—especially her love of family and home.

The beauty and harmony of her own surroundings were expressed with conviction and clarity in the environments she helped to create for others. At the core were all the elements of refined taste, but taste flavored by a sometimes wicked wit and a degree of jovial irreverence that possibly explains the magic of her creative genius—her genius for the art of living, the art of home.

Sister's devotion to family was extended to those whom she chose as friends. Her loyalty was legendary, as was her code of ethics. Her astonishing self-discipline was also something she demanded of others.

I applaud Apple and Susan for the many-faceted reflections they have compiled of a remarkable woman, their mother and grandmother, Mrs. Henry Parish II, who was to her many admirers, simply Sister.

ALBERT HADLEY
New York, New York
March 1999

WE CALLED HER "Poppop." My California cousins called her "Poppops," with the emphasis on the second syllable. Her children—Harry, "D.B.," and my mother, Apple—called her Mummy. To the rest of the world, she was Mrs. Henry Parish or Sister, the famous interior decorator.

Sister was born in 1910 into the privileged and rarefied world of New York society. At the time of her childhood, Sister's world was circumscribed by certain boundaries or guidelines that were established at birth. Young ladies, such as Sister, came out and then married into the appropriate family, keeping the circle intact. At their boarding schools, they learned to pour tea and serve sandwiches. They learned from their mothers which weekend was customary to open one's summer house in preparation for the season. They also knew that one spoke with a certain clipped accent in sentences spiked with Anglophile words such as *motor* and *chemist*. Certainly one did not refer to pants as "slacks" or to curtains as "drapes."

Admission into the correct schools and clubs was preordained by the previous generation. It similarly was accepted that friends' births, marriages, and the names of summer houses, yacht clubs, and other clubs were duly recorded in the *Social Register*. Sister was a product of this tiny, insular world, but she was also a quick-witted charmer who could enthrall a roomful of people at the drop of a hat. This, along with an amazing talent for decorating houses, took her far.

Compelled to work because of the lean years of the Depression, Sister used her privileged background to promote her decorating career and her work, and her blue-blooded client list reflected her patrician roots. She was influenced by her family's summer house on an island in Maine, which inspired the "American country" look, which she is credited with inventing. This unique American style also reflected Sister's Yankee roots, which ran deep and were an integral part of her personality.

Sister was also a teacher. She and her partner, Albert Hadley, trained a talented, and now-renowned group of decorators, and the published work of their firm, Parish-Hadley, influenced a generation of designers.

Sister had wanted to write her autobiography and had attempted it twice without conclusion. A few years after her death, my mother and I decided it was time to tell her story, in her words and those of her family and friends.

She was an American icon as well as being my grandmother. This is her story.

SUSAN BARTLETT CRATER

NEW YORK TIMES OBITUARY, SEPTEMBER 10, 1994

Sister Parish, the acclaimed and enduring American interior decorator who began her career when she was a young Depression-era mother and later came to redesign rooms of the White House during the Kennedy Administration, died on Thursday at her home in Dark Harbor, Maine. She was 84 and also had a home in New York City.

She had suffered a lengthy illness, said Dorothy B. Gilbert, one of her daughters.

Mrs. Parish's six decades of decorating epitomized the rise of women in her own and other professions in 20th-century America. The one-room business she founded in 1933 in Far Hills, N.J., evolved into the noted decorating firm of Parish-Hadley Associates, based in Manhattan, whose designs consistently exuded quality.

The anxious 23-year-old of 1933—whose nursery nickname had replaced her seldom-used given name, Dorothy—went on to become a force in forming and articulating tastes in interior design. Vogue magazine once said she was "the most famous of all living women interior designers, whose ideas have influenced life styles all over America."

John Richardson, an art historian, wrote in 1989, "No one else in America does a room with such patrician aplomb, such life-enhancing charm, such a lack of gimmickry or trendiness."

With a profile that seemed carved from the Maine coastline, her long-time home and design influence, Mrs. Parish was a strong traditionalist. "What seems important to me is permanence, comfort and a look of continuity in the design and decoration of a house," she once observed. "The happiest times of my life are associated with beautiful, familiar things and family."

She and her firm became known for the low-keyed handsomeness of their work and for their well-heeled and relatively conservative clientele. It included President and Mrs. John F. Kennedy; the philanthropists Brooke Astor and Enid Annenberg Haupt; William S. Paley, the chairman of CBS; and members of the Bronfman, Getty, Mellon, Rockefeller, Vanderbilt, and Whitney clans.

Mrs. Parish stayed on as a partner in the firm into her 80's proving to be a notably durable member of a pioneer cohort of American women who came to prominence as interior decorators between the two world wars.

Mrs. Parish is widely considered to have originated, in the 1960's, the decorating idiom that became known as American country style: she was an early and influential champion of the humble striped cloth called mattress ticking, which had traditionally covered mattresses, using it for slipcovers and on throw pillows.

She saw no conflict between innovation and traditionalism. As she wrote in HG magazine in 1990, "Years ago, my partner, Albert Hadley, and I were delighted when patchwork quilts, four-poster beds, painted floors, knitted throws, rag rugs and handwoven bedsteads were first listed among the 'innovations' of our firm.

"The list sounds old-fashioned, and no decorator wants to be that," she continued, "but Albert and I understood that innovation is often the ability to reach into the past and bring back what is good, what is beautiful, what is lasting."

Mrs. Parish's own girlhood was, if not regal, at least baronial. She was born Dorothy May Kinnicutt on July 15, 1910, in Morristown, N.J., the daughter of G. Hermann Kinnicutt and the former May Appleton Tuckerman, who had homes in Manhattan, Maine, and Paris, as well as New Jersey.

Mrs. Parish's father was a collector of antiques (as was a cousin, Dorothy Draper, who also became a renowned decorator). Much later she would recall the distaste she felt as a child for the furniture her father collected, "that awful English brown," as she put it.

As a teen-ager, she saw painted French furniture in Paris—and experienced a revelation.

She went to the Chapin School in Manhattan and to the Foxcroft School in Middleburg, Va., made her debut and was married to Mr. Parish in 1930 in

Manhattan with, as the New York Times reported at the time "a representative gathering of old New York families on hand."

After her marriage, she and her husband had a home on East End Avenue in Manhattan—which had been done by a decorator—and a farmhouse in Far Hills, N.J., which Mrs. Parish herself decorated, with gusto.

Her handiwork was admired, friends began coming to her for help with decorating, and she later confidently recalled that "it never occurred to me that I wasn't qualified to give it."

It was four years after the Wall Street crash of 1929 that Mrs. Parish, who had never received a high school diploma, opened her first office. Hard times were coming upon her husband and her father, both blue-blooded stockbrokers. She called her business "Mrs. Henry Parish 2d Interiors" and placed it in Far Hills.

The success that followed was fueled by her taste, talent and strength of will. Mr. Hadley, who joined forces with her in 1962, said in 1991 that "Sis always knows when a room is right and a room is not." She was famed for creating a homey "undecorated look."

In some ways, Mrs. Parish's rise was made easier by her upper-crust roots, and her earliest work was decorating the houses of friends.

Decorating by Mrs. Parish and her firm also acquired a reputation for being expensive. The New York Times columnist Charlotte Curtis wrote in 1985 that Parish-Hadley work "costs money, big money."

But Mrs. Parish also had an economical streak. In the mid-1960's, she acquired a batch of turn-of-the-century golden oak furniture at a bargain basement price, the story goes, then painted it white and used it in decorating a house that she and her husband had bought in Maine.

As the design editor Elaine Greene wrote later in The New York Times, "when shown in the January 1967 issue of House & Garden, the house dazzled decorators the way Christian Dior's 1947 New Look did the fashion world."

The white furniture and other furnishings in the house—including soft-hued chintz, needlework, hand-crafted cotton rugs and paintings of dogs—became staples of the style.

Mrs. Parish met Jacqueline Kennedy socially in the late 1950's and helped her decorate the house in the Georgetown section of Washington where she and her husband, John F. Kennedy, lived while he was a Senator. After Mr.

Kennedy was elected President, his wife made Mrs. Parish a consultant in her redecorating of the White House.

Mrs. Kennedy also named her to a committee that was formed to help furnish the White House with authentic pieces from a century and a half earlier.

Speaking of Mrs. Kennedy's plans for redoing the family quarters in the building, Mrs. Parish said early in 1961 that the nation's new First Lady was a person of "simple tastes who wants to create a home."

The walls of the family quarters were done in pastel tones—the private drawing room was eventually done in yellow and white.

In the years since, there have been persistent reports that Mrs. Kennedy and Mrs. Parish—who could be blunt and acerbic—had a falling-out over the White House. As Town & Country magazine recounted in 1988, the First Lady "fired Sister for telling little Caroline to keep her feet off the upholstery. Sister would later describe the experience in explicit, harsh terms."

But Mrs. Parish could go to enormous lengths to please a client. Sally Bedell Smith wrote in her 1990 book "In all His Glory: The Life of William S. Paley" that in a single bedroom Mrs. Parish and Mr. Hadley did in the 1960's in Mr. Paley's Fifth Avenue duplex, "a painter worked for five months applying 18 coats of paint—six different shadings just for the base, plus glazing."

Mr. Parish died in 1977, having spent 34 years with the Wall Street securities firm of Loeb Rhoades & Company.

Mrs. Parish is survived by her daughters, Mrs. Gilbert of Hot Springs, Ark., and May Appleton Bartlett of Boston, eight grandchildren, and four great-grandchildren.

ERIC PACE

SISTER

Opposite page: Frankie, Bayard, Gory, and Sister Kinnicutt on the steps at Mayfields.

Chapter One

Beginnings: 1910 and Earlier

They were interested in a life just beyond the square box.

MAISIE KINNICUTT HOUGHTON

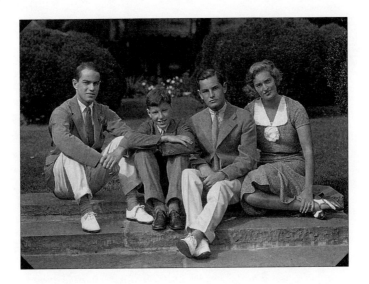

NEVER IN LIFE has there been such a hideous baby. After staring for days at my scrunched-up face, my sallow skin, my straight brown hair, Father finally pried my eyes open—only to discover that they were a dull brown.

"We'll always dress her in brown," Mother is reported to have said. "It's our only possible hope."

Even my aunt Joan, hopelessly sentimental about every member of our family, admitted that I was hideous.

My birth certificate read Dorothy May Kinnicutt, but, lest you think that the name "Sister" has any ecclesiastical significance, let me hasten to point out that it was immediately hung on me by my three-year-old brother, Frankie. It has not been an easy cross to bear. It has caused considerable confusion. My husband constantly complained about the awkwardness of being married to a woman whom he called Sister. People who don't know me lower their eyes in embarrassment when the Lord's name is taken in vain in my presence. I often receive calls from religious groups asking me if I'd meet refugees at the dock. And when I was asked to help "do" the White House, a newspaper headline announced "Kennedys Pick Nun to Decorate White House." It has not been an easy name, yet it has brought me many a laugh.

I was born by mistake in our house in Morristown, New Jersey. I was supposed to have entered the world properly in our New York house, but Mother and I didn't have time. The date was July 15, 1910, and my premature arrival was one of the last occasions when the timetable of our lives would be interrupted for many years to come.

Fifteen days later, I was aboard the Bar Harbor Express, heading toward the first of my summers at Dark Harbor on the island of Islesboro, Maine. The windows of the children's stateroom were draped with white linen sheets, so we wouldn't be contaminated. I traveled in a white wicker bassinet with pink ribbons— the same bassinet that had carried my mother and her mother, the same bassinet that would carry my daughter and her daughter. I was receiving, quite unconsciously, my first lesson in good things. Even the simplest wicker basket can become priceless when it is loved and cared for through the generations of a family.

Ours was a close family, physically as well as emotionally. I grew up surrounded by grandparents, aunts and uncles, and, in our family, even second cousins were important. My maternal grandparents, the Bayard Tuckermans, lived just two blocks from us in New York. My paternal grandparents, the Francis Kinnicutts, had a house next to ours in Morristown, around the corner from us in New York City, and we spent the summers in their Dark Harbor home until my younger brothers, Gory and Bayard, came along. When we moved on the island, it was to a house just a few yards away.

A strong sense of family tradition was instilled in me from the beginning. Our American forebears included Cotton Mather and Oliver Wolcott, who signed the Declaration of Independence, and we were told that a strong wire of character stretched from them through all generations of our family. If the wire was strong enough in us, anything we might do would turn out all right.

SUSAN BARTLETT CRATER (Sister's granddaughter): Family and tradition were of the utmost importance to Sister. Her unspoken message was that the family—specifically, the Tuckermans, from her mother's side; the Kinnicutts, from her father's side; and the Parishes, from Grandpa's side—mattered more than anything.

Family was at the heart of our life during the summers in Maine, where everyone was a cousin of some sort. In Dark Harbor, there continue to be generations of Kinnicutts, plus Tuckerman and Kissel cousins, as well. In the Victorian front parlor at Sister's house, the Summer House, with its brightly painted blue floor and mishmash of faded chintzes, Sister and Harry's history seems to seep out of the walls. Black-and-white photographs of generations of weddings, christenings, and picnics are everywhere. Because the images made one hundred years ago were taken on the same familiar rocky beaches of today, past and present seemed forever intertwined.

Likewise, family names have repeated with each generation. The name Appleton has been carried down from my great-grandmother to my daughter, Eliza. Mum's real name is May Appleton, and when Sister knew Eliza's middle name was to be Appleton, she told us to call her "Little Apple." We ask, "Was it Big Harry or Little Harry? Do you mean Bayard Elkins or Bayard Kinnicutt?" The wire Sister spoke of twists through the names we carry and the places where we live. It was always Sister's hope that this wire would be carefully fostered by each passing generation.

My maternal grandparents, the Bayard Tuckermans, were very social. Annie Tuckerman was a pretty, frail woman of enormous charm. Her house at 118 East Thirty-seventh Street was a perpetual drama. Her friends and family would flock to call on her, and she would reward them with the latest gossip, delivered in her own witty, biting manner. My mother, who was to inherit her charm—and her sharp wit—was the object of her more notable remarks. On one occasion, Grandmother Tuckerman introduced her to President Cleveland by saying, "I'm sorry, but today May looks like a piece of tissue paper." Another day she explained, "May is rather plain, but she always has a pure heart and a clean handkerchief."

I often visited Grandmother Tuckerman at teatime, and I remember that she would always be found lying on the sofa, exhausted. Being exhausted at teatime has become a family trait.

Bayard Tuckerman was a gentle, adoring husband, whose occupation was first to minister to his wife's real or imaginary needs—principally the latter— and second to write books of narrow historical significance. He was a lecturer at Princeton until Grandmother made it quite clear that she couldn't bear living there. He deeply loved all his grandchildren, and he took a real interest in how we were doing at school, in our trips to the dentist, and even in our silliest observations of the world. We loved him back fiercely. I would sit on his knee for hours, listening to the Westminster chimes in his gold watch, trying to figure out, usually unsuccessfully, what time the bells were tolling. He died when I was only ten, and this is my first remembered sadness. Like most of the families in this area, they were very social. Their house was in Murray Hill, one of the most fashionable sections of New York prior to World War I.

SUSAN: Bayard and Annie Tuckerman lived with their four children—Sister's mother, May, and Elizabeth, Bayard, and Joan—at 118 East Thirty-seventh Street in New York in the winter and at their house "Sunswick" in Ipswich, Massachusetts, in the summer. Sunswick was a classic gray clapboard summer house with a large porch for lounging, tennis courts, and barns for the Tuckermans' horses and other animals.

Twenty-nine miles north of Boston, Ipswich is the site of Appleton Farms, a one-thousand-acre farm that has been owned and farmed for three centuries by Annie Tuckerman's mother's family, the Appletons. There were two Tuckerman-Appleton marriages, so the families were closely intertwined. Three estates were built along the north side of Waldingfield Road by grandchildren of Gen. James Appleton. "Waldingfield" was built by Randolph Morgan Appleton (Cousin Budd). Sunswick, next door to the west, was built by Sister's maternal grandparents, Bayard and Annie Tuckerman. "Applegate," to the east of Waldingfield, was owned by Ruth Appleton Tuckerman and her husband, Charles.

It was an insular world, where the cousins played together—hunting with the Myopia Hunt Club, having lunch and supper dances, playing tennis, and roaming the countryside. Apparently, they did not venture far from the family circle that dotted Waldingfield Road. Bayard Tuckerman's niece, Cousin Annie Appleton Flichtner, vented her frustration in her teenage diary: "I've been fighting against it but there's no use, I'm depressed tonight. The reason, at present, is that we are not able to go to West Beach and Beverly and get to know those attractive people. It does seem hard and there's not one boy who isn't a cousin. The grown-ups are beginning to appreciate this and Aunt Violet says, 'Well, I've done my best to get them over here.'"

The only other decorator the family produced came from the Tuckerman side of the family. She was Dorothy Draper Tuckerman, my mother's first cousin. As Dorothy Draper, she wrote, "Decorating is Fun," did a newspaper column for young homemakers, and is reputed to be the culprit who turned the noun fun into an adjective by coining such phrases as "Fun City," "Fun Cottage," and "Fun Weekend." Having seen her trademark, giant red roses splashed over wallpaper and curtains, I wouldn't be at all surprised if the rumor were true.

TILLIE TUCKERMAN CUTLER (Sister's cousin): The Tuckermans lived in Ipswich in the summer and New York in the winter. At Sunswick, Bayard Tuckerman built a little shack because his wife talked too much. It was a separate place, a studio where he went to write. Annie was his wife, my Granny Tuckerman. She was wonderful. The Tuckermans didn't have much money, but they married very rich people, as arranged by Grandmother Tuckerman. She arranged them all. So Granny Tuckerman was arranging marriages while Grandpa was down in that studio writing books.

Aunt Joan was the youngest daughter. She wasn't as rich as the other ones. Her husband went broke the day before they got married.

When Aunt Joan went to a funeral and was put in the wrong place, Granny Tuckerman said, "There's always something that ruins a good funeral."

SUSAN: Aunt Joan was a favorite of Sister's and of the whole family. At the end of her life, she wrote a slim novel called *What We Remember and What We Forget*, chronicling Sister's mother's and her Ipswich and New York childhood.

JOAN TUCKERMAN DICK (Sister's aunt): Mother often spoke in hyperbole, taught to her by an Irish nurse. I remember such phrases as "It's enough to make the angels weep" and "You must feel like a giant refreshed." When she saw me smoking, she said, "I expect a bolt from heaven will fall on you." Her father, who was the minister of the Church of the Ascension in New York, brought down fire from heaven in the pulpit on Sundays. He was very fastidious, and he had the houseboy draw on his boots and put eau de cologne on his handkerchief. He did not allow his daughters to dance, and he always accompanied his wife to the shoe store. When Grandma told him their eldest daughter was having a baby, he said, "We don't speak of such things."

Sunswick smelled so good when we arrived in the spring—the straw matting on the floors and the apple blossoms out the window. The wallpaper in

Sister's uncle Bayard Tuckerman (left) hunting with the Prince of Wales.

my bedroom was bright yellow, with nymphs wading in blue pools, and the cheerful rhyme like a garland: "Oh, who would not live with the water fays. In the glad sunlight of the summer days!"

When my older sisters had their friends to stay, I had to move out of my room, yet I was very proud of them and considered them an asset. They gave me ascendancy over my cousins, as I was the only one with older sisters. My brother Bayard became a character very young. He lisped, and everyone laughed at whatever he said.

I would keep my light on long after I had been told to put it out, reading forbidden books like *Portrait of a Lady*. During my adolescence, I would faint occasionally. I remember looking through the slats of the banister while my anxious parents dosed me with ammonia. I have never had a drink so satisfying.

I handed out books of rules, rather like Benjamin Franklin's, where week by week we recorded improvements: a compliment we had received, or the fact that we had talked to a boy without a moment's pause in the conversation.

I had rules for God, too. Never let me fall overboard and be drowned from a steamer, a ferryboat, the fishing boat *Carlotta*, a rowboat, or a canoe. It would be so awful if there were any kind of boat that I had left out.

SUSAN: In the Tuckerman's Murray Hill neighborhood, as in Ipswich, they were surrounded by cousins, Aunt Joan remembered: "On Thirty-sixth Street, opposite where the Morgan Library is now, lived Uncle Fuller Appleton. His yard was so big that he kept a cow, and during the great blizzard of 1888, he provided milk for the children of the neighborhood. His cousin Gerard, when asked about his recent trip to Paris, said, 'It was just like Ipswich—hot as hell and full of Appletons.' "

TILLIE TUCKERMAN CUTLER: My father, Sister's uncle Bayard, never worked; he just went riding. He was a jockey, and he hunted. He went to England and met the Prince of Wales, whom he later entertained in Ipswich in 1921. He started Suffolk Downs, the racetrack in Boston.

APPLE BARTLETT (Sister's daughter): Uncle Bayard was furious when Joe and I got married on the same day as the Maryland Hunt Cup. I remember that he swore and demanded, "How dare you?"

My paternal grandfather was Dr. Francis Kinnicutt, head of Presbyterian Hospital in New York and one of the foremost physicians in the country. He used to visit the wards in his morning coat every day, with the nurse preceding him. Occasionally, he would drag my brother and me along "to encourage the patients." We would dress in ermine coats and brown velvet leggings, and I doubt that we raised many spirits. But, in another way, we learned what sadness meant and how lucky we were.

When patients summoned him to their bedside, they often sent their private

Dr. Francis Parker Kinnicutt with his wife, Eleanora, sailing in Maine.

railway car to ease the trip. When he wasn't curing them, he was likely to be off
hunting with them. One of his patients and closest friends was Edith Wharton,
who managed to include him as the distinguished doctor in almost every book
she wrote.

SUSAN: Sister's paternal grandfather, Francis Parker Kinnicutt, was born in
Worcester, Massachusetts, in 1846. He went to Harvard and Columbia
Medical School, then did graduate work in Vienna, Heidelberg, and London.
Dr. Kinnicutt was one of the earliest doctors to treat the mind as well as the
body. After treating Teddy Wharton [Edith's husband] for years, he was convinced his problem was a mental one, stemming from melancholy, insomnia,
and nervousness, and possibly caused by Edith's increasing success. Maisie
Kinnicutt Houghton, Sister's niece, did her dissertation on Edith Wharton at
Radcliffe College, and she told us that one of Kinnicutt's best pieces of advice
to Edith was for her to stop spending summers with her mother. His obituary
in Boston's *Medical and Surgical Journal* described him as being a gentle man:

In dress he was very soigné, without being otherwise conspicuous. His good manners, in no way studied, were the outgrowth of his nature. Always considerate of others, even of their failings, he had a sweetness of character almost feminine in kind and degree. His gentleness, tact and sympathy kept him unspoiled of the world. These are qualities that we sometimes see in men who are thereby unfitting to cope with the world and its marketplaces. Not so with Kinnicutt, who combined harmoniously therewith an equal degree of manly strength and the power to control emotion and impulse by reason. To the poor and outcast he was the same courteous gentleman that he was to the more fortunate in life.

My paternal grandmother, Eleanora Kissel Kinnicutt, was a woman of distinct character and frozen expression—all bust, bustles, and severity. Her principal charity work was placing NO SPITTING signs in subways. I'm afraid that the Kinnicutts had appalling taste: polar bear rugs, moose heads, and antlers everywhere, golden oak furniture and dreary pastoral paintings. Their houses in New York and Morristown were large, dark, and musty. The party rooms were always closed.

SUSAN: Eleanora's family, the Kissels, were a distinguished German banking family, who settled in New York. She was accomplished in her own right, for her efforts on behalf of the New York Sanitation Department, the State Lunacy Commission, and the founding of Barnard College. Eleanora often wrote articles for periodicals and letters to government officials expressing her views. I came across a reply from Teddy Roosevelt that was sent to her from the White House in 1902. "Dear Mrs Kinnicutt, I wish I often received a letter half so interesting as your private one. All that you said, from national health to triumphant democracy in England, greatly interested me. . . ."

Dr. Kinnicutt and his wife, Eleanora, had two children—Sister's father, Gustav Hermann (called Hermann), and Francis. The Kinnicutt houses that Sister said were filled with polar bear rugs and dreary pastoral paintings were in Morristown, New Jersey; Dark Harbor; Lenox, Massachusetts; and New York.

My father was Gustav Hermann Kinnicutt. He went to Harvard and, several years after graduating, formed with his uncle Gustav Kissel the brokerage firm of Kissel-Kinnicutt, the forerunner of Kidder, Peabody & Co. My father ran the firm for many years, surviving the Depression and recessions, and they managed to survive two crashes. He worked hard and he lived well until he died of a heart attack on Pearl Harbor day.

He joined eminent dining clubs here and abroad. He was an avid sportsman—polo, tennis, coaching, golf—and a crack shot. He had a shooting lodge in Havre de Grace, Maryland, where, during duck season, he would invite his men friends. They included some of the best-known people in the financial world.

One of my earliest memories of my father is sitting beside him in the two-wheel Hempstead cart that drove him to the train in Morristown. If I met him at the train upon his return, the coachman and horse would have to wait patiently while he went to the candy store and bought me a Tootsie Roll. If I was sick, he would always bring me a bouquet of flowers. On Valentine's Day, I could count on receiving cards, candy, and flowers from a mysterious admirer. He encouraged Mother to buy me beautiful clothes, and he often went shopping with us. One of the great joys of being his daughter was that he treated me as a person, as an adult.

My father had a dimension beyond the business, sporting, and social life that was common to most successful men of that time. Father was a learned man, and a well-traveled one. He became a collector and connoisseur of English and American antiques. I'm sure that much of my knowledge originates with him. We used to bicycle all over the New Jersey countryside, exploring out-of-the-way antique shops. And whenever we tinkled the bell on an antique shop's door, Daddy would invariably buy me a Staffordshire figure. Thus collections are born.

My father had good taste in a scholarly sense. A thorough knowledge and love of good furniture is essential to decorating. I am sure that it helps to be the only daughter of a known authority on antiques.

My mother, May Appleton Tuckerman, had instinctive good taste. My father would find a magnificent eighteenth-century desk. An important one. My mother would instinctively know that the charcoal sketch of my brother should go above it and that the crystal candle stick should go on it, that this figurine and that precious Chinese bowl would nicely balance the framed family photographs that brought the desk to life. She knew exactly how that desk should look in a morning room, and precisely how it should look in a study. Taste is instinctive, and I think that possibly it is inherited. If it is, mine came from Mother.

A decorator's taste, a decorator's eye, the personality that any decorator

Dr. Francis Parker Kinnicutt, Eleanora Kissel Kinnicutt, and their son G. Hermann at their house in Maine.

expresses in his or her work comes from deep within, some of it inherited, some of it experienced, some of it acquired. I have no doubt that much of what I do today as a decorator comes, in some way, from my parents.

Mother was gentle but strong-willed. She never raised her voice to make her point. More often than not, she would say nothing at all. She spoke slowly, and very softly, pausing between sentences.

She had a way of looking at a spoon, and the maid would instantly whisk it away and get out the silver polish. She would turn her gaze to a corner of the garden, and Angelo would know exactly which rose to prune. When she thought a table needed dusting, she would run her finger idly along the edge. No more needed to be said. The servants adored her, and there was no question who was in charge.

Mother, who was famous for many of the things she said, once denied any interest in society. "It just happens," she explained, "that I only like a certain type of person, and they all just happen to be socially important."

Her innate sense of a well-ordered, properly regulated life was documented at a very early age. She was passing a neighbor's house in Murray Hill and she noticed black crepe on the door. She explained to her sister, Aunt Elizabeth, with absolute childlike certainty, that the death had occurred because "they haven't been properly regulated in going to the bathroom."

Everything in its place was almost an obsession with Mother. When she came home from the hospital just before she died, she had the hospital orderlies carry her on a stretcher from room to room, and wherever she went, she would find something an inch out of place and put it back. That is perfection.

My mother strived for perfection in her clothes as well as in her housekeeping. She was by no means a great beauty, but she always made a striking appearance wherever she went because she was beautifully dressed.

"Just have a basic black dress" was her motto. Though perfection was her own personal goal, she had a loving heart and was enormously understanding of others. If the trouble was personal, she would show her concern in a helpful, personal way. If the trouble was financial, out of the blue she would be there.

I did not inherit her obsession with neatness, but, to this day, one of the things I dread most is walking into a house that has not been properly cared for. I sense a lack of love in an unkempt house. It has nothing to do with money or maids. Certainly if you have a staff, that helps, but what it really takes to care for your house is love. I admire perfection and people who strive for it.

SUSAN: Sister's parents, May Appleton Tuckerman and Hermann Kinnicutt, were married on April 18, 1907. One newspaper account began: "One of the largest weddings of the season took place yesterday afternoon at 3:30 when G. Hermann Kinnicutt and Miss May Appleton Tuckerman were married in the Church of the Incarnation at Madison Avenue and Thirty-fifth Street. The bride wore a gown of chiffon and lace with a satin coat train and a long tulle veil caught with orange blossoms. She carried a shower bouquet of Lillies of the Valley and wore a diamond and pearl clasp at her throat."

Town Topics reported, "About five hundred persons crowded the Church of the Incarnation on Thursday afternoon. . . . The ceremony was performed by the Reverend Roland Cotton Smith of Washington, an uncle of the bride, and the guests included the Morgans, the Cuttings, the Harrimans, the Havermeyers, the Iselins and the Burdens."

D. B. GILBERT: (Sister's daughter): I remember Grandma . . . her bathroom . . . so beautiful . . . glass doors that opened up and all of these lovely negligees. Well, they didn't call them that then. They had the most beautiful scent. The most fragrant sachet. You feel so luxurious to smell like that.

I remember Grandma smoking cigarettes. Wonderful holders. Also, her cigarettes were in lovely silver cups everywhere around the house.

May Tuckerman Kinnicutt
and G. Hermann Kinnicutt
at Mayfields.

SYBIL KINNICUTT BALDWIN (Sister's niece): I associate Grandma Kinnicutt
with beige cashmere sweaters and long, beautifully manicured fingers with
pink nail polish. In my memory, she wasn't a bit pretty, but she was so elegant,
so glamorous. She exuded glamour. I also associate Grandma Kinnicutt with
fur coats and with the Ritz in Boston. Something about the smell in the elevator there reminds me of her perfume. It was an aroma that she had about
her, rich and comfortable.

IRENE KINNICUTT (Sister's sister-in-law): Mr. Kinnicutt had lots of interests.
Like everybody, he lost lots of money in the crash, but he made it all back. He
was intelligent and a very good investment banker. He collected all of the furniture from France; all the good things we all have were from Mr. Kinnicutt.
Mrs. Kinnicutt was charming; she got along with people very well. She had

Hermann with his eldest son, Frankie, and Sister, c. 1914.

good taste. There were always flowers and the best food and a wonderful household. At Mayfields, there were many to help—a butler, gardeners, cooks, maids—the whole works. Everything was perfect.

Mr. Kinnicutt was not too social. He had an orchid garden where he spent a lot of time alone. He was up in the morning at five, you know, working on it. I don't know if he ever got it or not. He rode and hunted. Mrs. Kinnicutt was not what you'd call sportive, but everybody loved her. She had a very good sense of humor. Sister inherited lots of things from her father, especially the taste and buying of good things. They had an apartment in Paris at 23 quai d'Orsay.

MAISIE KINNICUTT HOUGHTON (Sister's niece): My grandfather was a very disciplined and hardworking man. Grandma Kinnicutt was always beautiful-ly dressed and had that famous dry way of speaking; the way they all spoke, the way Aunt Sister spoke. I remember sitting with her on the porch at the "little inn" in Maine, and she seemed very old to me, although she was only in her early sixties. I remember her saying to me to go upstairs. "I want you to bring down a little present wrapped in tissue paper," she told me. I opened it, and it was a little silver knife and fork that was marked MK. As you know, we had the same initials. My father adored her, and they had the same sense of humor, as he was the oldest son and good-looking and fun.

I think the Kinnicutts were interested in a life just beyond the square box. They could laugh at themselves; they had a sense of humor. They liked to have nice things and they liked interesting people. They cared about the fam-ily, which were the values that Sister had. Imagination was what she valued—in herself and in other people.

The children's looks came from the Kinnicutt family. Grandmother Kinnicutt was not a great beauty, but she had great style. The best-looking one was Grandpa Kinnicutt; he had that incredibly strong face.

TILLIE TUCKERMAN CUTLER: We used to go to Far Hills and stay with Aunt May. She was funny and she was wonderful. One time, she came to Boston. She got in a taxi and she wanted to go to this particular address. The driver asked, "Where's that?" She said, "I know, but I'm not going to tell you." She said things like that all of the time.

MARY HOMANS (family friend): I visited Sister's parents in Far Hills when I was young. I was staying with them while I went to a coming-out party. It was her father, everyone said, who had all the taste. Mrs. Kinnicutt was something.

She talked very slowly. Once, Mr. Kinnicutt allegedly had the hiccups, and, as you know, there are so many theories about how to get rid of the hiccups. One theory is to scare a person. Apparently, Mrs. Kinnicutt got behind the couch and stood up slowly and said, "Boo, Hermann. Boo."

MRS. ETHAN HITCHCOCK (family friend): Mrs. Kinnicutt was killingly funny. She was unbelievable. She had this slow, dry sense of humor and never cracked a smile. Her husband, Hermann, was kind of a stuffed shirt. He had no sense of humor, but he was very, very attractive.

NED SUNDERLAND (Sister's cousin): May Kinnicutt was delightful. She had a tremendous sense of style. She was the smart one. People who didn't like her said she was a snob and that all she cared about was to have her children hang around rich, smart people. At that time, you could make that accusation against Frankie and Gory when they were young. But anyway, that was years ago.

Her character really came out when her best friend, Gertrude Whitney's husband, Richard, went to jail and she invited Gertrude to come and live in the farmhouse on the Kinnicutt place. May Kinnicutt stuck by Gertrude, and that does say something about her. She was wonderful that way. Richard Whitney went to jail in 1938 for embezzlement. This was a huge scandal because Richard Whitney was the brother of George Whitney, J. P. Morgan's partner. Richard Whitney had been Morgan's broker. If Mrs. Kinnicutt was invited to tea, she wouldn't go unless Mrs. Whitney was invited, too. Alexander Aldrich is writing a book about this, in which he tells how one morning he was going in to say good morning to his father before school and the butler said, "You are not to go in." By this time, he had opened the door, and there was Richard Whitney asking Winthrop Aldrich to persuade Winthrop's brother-in-law, John D. Rockerfeller, to lend Richard Whitney a million dollars. Then Richard Whitney ended up going to Sing Sing, and the warden said, "Now, Mr. Whitney, I have a few investments. Maybe you could advise me." He was given a phone in the prison library, and he made the warden a millionaire.

SUSAN: Sister saved every letter ever written to her, as well as those of her parents and grandparents. They are on that luxurious heavy writing paper with the names of grand European hotels embossed at the top or the names of friends' houses, such as Morelands or The Knoll, printed simply in block letters. Many are from ocean liners on which they were traveling, with enclosed menus detailing ten-course dinners and the evening's entertainment. The absence of street addresses and zip codes contrasts sharply with the exotic stamps from cities such as Peking and Cairo, which cover the envelopes.

In these letters, Sister's parents' devotion to each other is chronicled in minute detail. Despite their formal appearances, the letters from Hermann to May are informal and loving. He addressed his letters to May, "My dearest little Maybird," and, in her return letters to Hermann, May signed, "Your little girl." It appears that they wrote every day that they were apart, and the letters are filled with gossip, menus, details of their various houses, and news from the different European cities where they were visiting, or little bits about the children's progress at home. The accounts of the running of the house are exhaustive. Letters, with enclosed lists, three typed pages long, detail the inventory of silver, which was being transferred from one house to another.

The breadth of my great-grandparents' world geographically, and the scale of luxury they enjoyed, is sweetened by their simple devotion to each other and their children.

Mother had her own special way of running a household, and it worked. On occasions when she wanted to use leftovers for dinner, she would ask the cook what he had in the kitchen, and he would invariably answer, "Nothing."

She would say, "Then make something very, very good out of it." And he would.

When Daddy tried to cut down on household expenses, he asked her for a strict accounting of costs. After a month, he asked her where she had economized.

"Didn't you notice?" she asked. "No chocolate peppermints in the front hall."

PETER GATES (family friend): That was a magic generation, and my parents were part of it. It struck me as being very small at the time. There were maybe 150 people worth knowing. There may have been twenty in Philadelphia, twenty in North Shore, Long Island, fifty in New York, twenty in Boston, ten in Greenwich, and maybe an occasional fortunate one in Grosse Point. Very snobbish, and very inbred in the sense that they all knew one another at school or college.

Our New York neighborhood for the first six years of my life was Murray Hill, an area that could be roughly defined, socially, if not geographically, as between

Thirty-fourth and Thirty-eighth streets, and between Lexington and Madison avenues. In those days, it was considered "uptown." The houses were mostly large comfortable brownstones, but with the exception of J. P. Morgan's, there were few mansions to rival those on Fifth Avenue. When I roller-skated around the block, I knew the families that lived in each house. And I didn't have to venture more than two blocks in any direction to find a treat at one of my grandparents' houses. If not the most fashionable neighborhood, it certainly was the friendliest. It was social in a very special way. Everyone knew everyone else, and on more than a nodding basis. The parties were grand, top hats were still common, and footmen helped ladies down from their carriages.

The memory that emerges most strongly from my childhood is the strict, reassuring pattern of family life. It worked like clockwork. We would leave Dark Harbor for Morristown the day after Labor Day. No questions. We would leave Morristown for the house in New York City the Monday after Thanksgiving. No questions. We would leave New York to return to New Jersey on the Thursday before Good Friday. No questions. We would leave the country to board the Bar Harbor Express for Maine on July 2. No questions. We moved a lot and traveled a lot, but there was a clear, reassuring pattern to our lives. We children never had to wonder what would happen next, and this gave us a feeling of security and confidence. That is something that stays with you for your whole life.

There was a definite continuity to my life. Year after year, nothing changed, and yet the excitement was intense. It was like another Christmas every time we moved. Each fall, on the way back from Dark Harbor, I couldn't wait to see the red apples on our favorite tree, to see the cherries bursting with ripeness, ready to be devoured. I knew that the Seckel pears would still be green, but we could pinch them and tell if they'd be ripe in one week or two. There would be white peaches in baskets, ready to be placed in big Lowestoft bowls in the front hall, and the fresh smell would follow us from room to room. The greenhouse would be bursting with chrysanthemums almost ready for the pots on the winding staircase. Angelo, our devoted and always-present gardener, would have his rake ready to catch each falling leaf. The elms and maples around the house would be starting to turn and soon tinges of yellow, gold, rust, and flaming reds would be giving me wonderful lessons in color.

Upon returning each fall, our only fear was that school would soon be starting. But at least that, too, was a certainty. Every morning, Mademoiselle would sponge the "Boston waterproof" around the soles of our shoes so they'd be black and shiny when we went off to school. Mealtimes were sacred, and if you weren't on time, you didn't eat. No one ever picked up a fork until the first bite was between Mother's lips. We never reached across the table. Manners, of course, were always correct. When an adult entered the room, we stood up. When someone was introduced, the boys bowed and I curtsied. The five most important expressions in our vocabulary were: "Sir," "Madame," "Please," "Thank you," and "Excuse me." Elbows were never on the table. We would start each day with our hair combed, our teeth brushed, our faces scrubbed shiny, and that's how we'd be when we climbed into our beds at night. Bedtime was always on the dot, with a half-hour privilege for the eldest. These things were inviolable. Ours was an orderly, organized household in every way, and family tradition was instilled from the beginning.

Self-discipline is one of the continuing threads that run through the generations of my family. It is what made my grandfather Kinnicutt a superior doctor, and what enabled my grandfather Tuckerman to be a serious historian. It was what made it possible for my father to steer his brokerage firm through two crashes, and to pay the firm's debts with his own money. It carried my mother and father through many heartaches, including the sudden death of my younger brother at a baseball game at St. Mark's School.

Although I'm sure that many of my strengths, weaknesses, and idiosyncrasies can be traced to Cotton Mather and beyond, the real influences on my life came from the family that surrounded me on Murray Hill.

SUSAN: Hermann and May Kinnicutt had four children: Francis Parker ("Frankie"), Dorothy May ("Sister"), Gustav Hermann ("Gory"), and Bayard ("Bydie"). The children all had striking looks—dark hair, piercing eyes, and fantastically seductive smiles.

IRENE KINNICUTT: They had quite a childhood. They traveled to Europe, always with a chauffeur and their nurse, Mademoiselle. They had the most beautiful car—a Mercedes Daimler—and once they all went on a family outing with Mademoiselle and the car tipped over with all of them in it.

I do not think any four children fought as much as we did. It never ended— morning until night. I was closest to my middle brother, Gory, who would occasionally give me a small break—of course I would have to do a lot for him in return. Such as stealing from the pantry for him and his horrid little friends. Thus to make him a hero.

Bayard Kinnicutt.

APPLE: Mummy's brothers Frankie and Gory were completely different in character. Frankie was a real intellectual and very knowledgeable in the field of modern art. He was more of a man's man. Gory was far more easygoing and accessible, the leader of Dark Harbor's Tarratine Club for many years.

IRENE KINNICUTT: Gory, Bayard, and Frankie all went to St. Mark's. Bayard died there, and there is a fountain in his memory on the campus. When Bayard died, it was terrible. Mr. Kinnicutt wrote a beautiful letter saying that Bayard didn't use his sword in life. They were crushed. He was fourteen.

JOHNNY PYNE (family friend): I was walking my bike when I was about thirteen. I was going to the lake, when Kenny Schley and Bayard came by. Bayard had that slow way of talking. We used to go to the movies together in Bernardsville. Our driver, whose name was Smart, would take us there. Bayard died when he was playing ball at St. Mark's. I still miss him, and I think of him every now and then.

My youngest brother, Bayard, was already a real character by the time he was seven years old. Marvelous-looking, a great sportsman, and a joy to all. When he died playing baseball at St. Mark's, it was a loss to young and old. I will never forget as the school lined up to say farewell to him. The voices of those two hundred boys shouting, "Let's give a long cheer for Kinnicutt," and then the St. Mark's hymn was sung. Not a dry eye could be seen, and as the door of our car was closed, I could see each boy wander off alone in sadness.

SUSAN: I think that one of the reasons Sister was so determined to be strong was that many of the men in her life died young, beginning with Bydie and ending with her own son, Harry. All three of her brothers and her son died prematurely of heart attacks.

IRENE KINNICUTT: Sister, Gory, and Frankie all had very good judgment of people. Their comments were sometimes strong, but always honest. They were not rude, but they didn't beat about the bush. People liked the way that they were straightforward. They got their looks from their father. Sister was very handsome-looking.

Frankie always came over to our house because we had the house on the water where he had lived as a boy. We got it when Mr. and Mrs. Kinnicutt died, as Sister and Frankie already had houses. Frankie came over in the

Frankie Kinnicutt (left) and Gory Kinnicutt (right).

evening and told me about his life. He was more sophisticated, you know. He loved modern art.

MAISIE KINNICUTT HOUGHTON: My father, Frankie, was very proud of Sister. I remember she came over with Uncle Harry and said she had gotten this big offer to go to South Africa and to do this big job. I remember hearing the buzz of grown-ups talking, and I remember Daddy saying, "Go. It's a fantastic opportunity." Sister said she didn't know if she could do it. She told me years later that once he came over to the house and he was walking around with a cane—this was at the end of his life. He began gesturing in the little pink-and-white living room and saying, "What's this? What's that? Everything here is goddamn junk except—who did this?" And gesturing to this little picture, Sister said, "I did it." It was a collage that she had done, and later she gave it to me. When we moved into the new house on the water, she said, "I am going to give you a present." When I came home, there was this picture on the front step, just there. It wasn't wrapped or anything. I lifted it up and turned it over and, on the back of it, it said, "It has a story."

And that was the story. It had meant something to her that he had admired it. She admired his eye. He was very interested in modern art. In the forties, the whole idea of modern art was something very new and exciting. And, of course, it wasn't her taste, but she recognized that he had an eye in a whole other field.

MICHAEL KINNICUTT (Sister's nephew): When I say my name, often the first thing I hear is, "Oh, any relation to Frankie?" His reputation seemed to have been widespread, but basically my understanding is that he really did very little as far as earning a living, although he was very creative. He had artistic instincts and he recognized Abstract Expressionists like Jackson Pollock before they were popular.

He always had some kind of prop. I remember when he had a cane. He was very theatrical. He had this beautiful sailboat—the *Windsong*—a wooden boat that sparkled. He was independent and liked to go out on the boat on his own. He liked to have a good time.

FRANCIE TRAIN (family friend): Frankie told me a wonderful thing once. He said, "Francie, whenever you go to a party, if you see a really unattractive person sitting all alone, whom everyone's ignoring, go up and talk to them, because nine times out of ten, they'll be the most interesting person there."

JOSEPH BARTLETT (Apple's former husband): The secret of Frankie's success with people is clear to me, on reflection. A close friend of mine died recently, and his son said something at the funeral that rang true both vis-à-vis Peter and, as I think of it, Frankie. They treated everyone alike, from the lowest to the highest. This is a precious commodity, an attribute found, in my experience, in men and women entirely secure in themselves. Frankie was a natural "aristocrat" and, like all real aristocrats, sure of himself, sure of who he was and what he wanted to do in life. Accordingly, lacking the insecurities and anxieties that plague most of us, he was able to be natural, open, and friendly, almost childlike, with everybody from the Duke of Devonshire to the proverbial cop on the beat. This is a rare achievement, I have found. It only comes naturally, and too few of us have it.

Frankie was one of the two or three most attractive men I have ever met. His conversation was interesting, his interests eclectic and informed, and, most important, one felt immediately and entirely comfortable in his presence.

Gory, Frankie's brother, was both like and quite unlike Frankie in certain very important ways. He was like him in that he was a member of the

Porcellian Club, a man without affectations who was not uncomfortable in anyone's company. He had the same God-given sense of humor and ability to entertain at the drop of a hat. His wife, Irene, was and is a great beauty.

One part of the Kinnicutt charm with both Frankie and Gory was that both were living in the past, in a New York closer to Edith Wharton than to Thomas Wolfe.

With both men, of course, friendship was key . . . within an extended family (which included me) and with people who (as Jack Kennedy once put it) were around when the "sap was first rising."

When I think of the two of them, I think of that short and sweet toast that economically expresses complex emotions: "To absent friends."

Opposite page: Friends and family on the lawn at Mayfields. Frankie Kinnicutt on right.

Chapter Two

Mayfields: 1917–1925

Every time I smell boxwood, I remember Mayfields, with its incredible
boxwood hedges going down to the swimming pool.

SYBIL KINNICUTT BALDWIN

WE HAD MONEY, *but not "real" money, as it was known in those days. No sec-*
ond butler, no footmen—but a series of nannies, maids, and cooks. Neither my
grandmother nor my mother ever knew where the kitchen was.

My own first conscious recollection of a room was one that was taken away
from me when I was six. It was my family's sitting room in Morristown, New
Jersey. I can remember every detail as though it were yesterday.

The walls were white, the floors covered with pale yellow matting and a
needlework rug of strewn white roses, tattered and worn. The furniture was
wicker, painted white, upright and stiff. Some of the wicker tables were covered
in lace to the floor; others were just bumpy. The backs and seats of the chairs had

hard cushions, padded and buttoned. I remember the buttons would pop off, leaving little strings. I felt sorry for those buttons and tried to put them back on. The material of the cushions and curtains was a heavy white cotton printed with vines and roses. The window seat was cushioned with the same material, with white borders, starched and fluted. The bowls of flowers, filled every day with roses from the garden, looked like the curtain and cushion material. Family pictures in silver frames were everywhere, especially on top of the eye-level bookcase. The wood basket with a big hoop handle was always full; the doorstop was an painted iron dog.

The white mantel had a deep organdy-and-lace ruffle that extended beyond the edge of the shelf. On the mantel was a gold clock, with two heavy columns, under a glass dome. I remember that it struck on the half hour. On each side of it were white candlesticks with angels clustered at their bases.

The desk was a white table. I can see every object that was on that desk: a big green blotting pad with silver corners, an upright silver paper-holder with three partitions, ribboned bookmarkers, silver scissors, sealing wax, a glass inkstand with a silver top like a shining ball, and pen holders of ivory, tole, and gold, the quills lying alone beside them. The desk chair was white, too, but made of cane and garlanded with flowers around its curved back. On the end table next to the stiff sofa was a silver bell. To this day, I can see and hear it, summoning someone in the house. Maid or child, we came.

There was a tea tray of white wicker on a two-wheeled cart. The tray had a glass top, with the same cotton curtain material underneath.

To my utter amazement, the silver kettle on its stand could be tipped forward to pour. The china was white, with a gold rim; the food, bread and butter with a little jam. The smell of that room was a potpourri of lavender in a bowl.

The lamps—the feature of the room—were twisted glass, with shades made of paper. My father had them made with cutouts of lacy designs of flowers, birds, and clouds. I remember my mother saying, "Please put a wash of pale pink inside them."

Years later, in Paris, I was to hear those same words of advice echoed. Madame Ritz herself was conducting me on a tour of the Ritz Hotel. She said to me, "In doing a room, you have only one rule to remember—always line your lamp shades with pale pink."

I shall never forget the "change"—the day my beloved room and everything in it dear to me was destroyed. The wicker was replaced with American antiques, overstuffed sofas and chairs appeared, and new ornaments infiltrated the room—wax flowers, Staffordshire animals, loving china couples, tufted flower pictures, and oil paintings of valleys and streams.

It had been transfigured for the wonder of all to see, and I had received my first lesson in the trauma of redoing a room.

The feeling for that sitting room, the way it was, has never left me. White wicker crept back into my life when I decorated my first house, when I was nineteen. And today, the house in Maine feels like home to me because it looks like the first room that I remember. Without my even trying, it just came back, the white painted furniture, needlework pillows, white wicker everywhere, the white organdy ruffle on the mantelpiece, bowls of roses from the garden. I realize how much that first impression meant to me.

APPLE: Shortly after redoing the Morristown house, Grandpa Kinnicutt's business flourished, and they decided to move their New York home from Thirty-sixth Street to a townhouse at 65 East Eighty-second Street. In those days, people "did" their own houses and decorators were not in evidence. If the job was a large one, they enlisted the help of upholstery shops such as Lenygon and Morant, Schmidt Brothers, Mrs. Hooper, or French and Company. For their move, the Kinnicutts hired Schmidt Brothers.

I was seven years old when this move was made, and though not deeply touched by this house, I was impressed. It was a six-story town house with an elevator, paneled rooms, Adam mantel, a great curving stairway winding upward, free from the walls, and banked, step by step, with flowering plants. The people from Schmidt installed the pine-paneled library from England, the white-and-gold-paneled drawing room, the mahogany doors, the old parquet floors, the Queen Anne mirrors. My father traveled to England to inspect the various paneled rooms that the Schmidt Brothers or their agents had found, and he would have to give his approval to nearly every board before it was marked, dismantled, crated, and shipped for the perfect reassembly on Eighty-second Street.

I suppose that we were part of the beginning of the slow but sure dismantling of England's architectural treasures. In our case, the result was a house filled with history. "English, all English" were the words I was to hear so often from my father. And across the sea they came—gorgeous inlaid sideboards, a magnificent breakfront secretary, lacquered consoles, drum tables, beautiful porcelains, four perfect Adam chairs that stood around a very old card table. Even all the paintings were English. From their own custom workshops, the

Schmidt Brothers provided the damask curtains, the needlework rugs, the chintz from England. My mother and father were consulted on every detail, and if there was any doubt at all on any matter, my mother's opinion would carry.

The only exception to my father's "English, all English" command was my bedroom. I had two canopied beds and a fine highboy, which were distinctively Early American. They are in my granddaughter's bedroom in Boston today, looking as warm and beautiful as they did when I was a child. The curtains and chairs in my bedroom were covered with an English chintz, which I recently discovered, to my delight, in a New York wholesale house. It has suddenly become a very popular chintz, reaffirming my belief that good taste can survive the whims of fashion.

At night, when I was tucked into my bed in our house on Eighty-second Street, an old-fashioned quilt would be pulled up to my chin. This was the beginning of my love for quilts, and the origins of "the quilt thing" in my decorating life. Parish-Hadley is credited with the revival of the quilt, but the real credit should go to my mother, who knew instinctively that the most important things in decorating are the little things that add to the warmth and love and well-being of the family.

SUSAN: In 1920, when Sister was ten, she moved with her family from the weekend house in neighboring Morristown to Far Hills. Their new house, which was built for Grandpa Kinnicutt, was called Mayfields, after his wife, May, and it was this house that inspired Sister for the rest of her life. It was not only her memories of the house itself but also the way in which her mother ran it that stayed with her and that she returned to again and again. It was her knowledge of such a house, and her ability to re-create it in various forms, that later drew clients to Parish-Hadley.

The most momentous event of my life occurred in 1920, when I was ten. It was the day we moved from Morristown to Mayfields, our new and wondrous stone house set on miles and miles of rolling country in Far Hills, New Jersey.

It had taken three years to build, and Daddy was absorbed by the project. We had a swimming pool and a tennis court, a bathhouse and a tennis house, and a barn.

The big stone country house had a waving slate roof and freestanding staircases, a magnificent paneled library, impressive living and dining rooms, wide, stately halls, and warm, cheerful bedrooms. John Cross was the architect, and

Mayfields.

Daddy worked closely with him. He took a vital interest in every inch of it, poring over blueprints, adding, taking away, always watching where the sun would be at the important house.

The result was perfection. A distinguished house, and a wonderful home. It was set on beautiful land, miles and miles of rolling country and well-fenced farmland. The only neighbors whom we regularly saw were the herds and herds of deer, milking cows, chickens and geese, guinea pigs, horses, and, best of all, ponies.

My own room was the only French one in the house. It was done in yellow flowered chintz and painted furniture, gay, but very sophisticated for a ten-year-old. I had white wallpaper with little gold stars and a parquet floor from Paris,

Sister's bedroom at Mayfields.

glowing with ash and age. Before the fireplace was an Aubusson carpet, brown, with pale flowers and blue ribbons. When my parents showed the room to me with pride and joy, I hurled myself on the bed and sobbed, "You promised me pink!" I think it was the only time I ever saw Mother cry. But, of course, I did learn to love the room, especially when I noticed that there was something in it especially for me. I had a window seat to remind me of the old sitting room in Morristown that I lost when I was six. Almost everything that was in it remains with me today, and each piece, regardless of value, is a priceless treasure.

Mayfields was to be my parents' last and most important home, the ideal house for Daddy to express his love and knowledge of good furniture, for Mother to show her superb taste, for them both to fulfill their fondest dreams of the most beautiful gardens, the most fulfilling house, and the ideal setting for themselves and their children.

SUSAN: John and Eliot Cross, of the architectural firm Cross and Cross, were themselves members of New York society. This made their firm a natural choice for Grandpa Kinnicutt. For their clients, a country house for use on weekends to relax and to entertain was a necessity. Cross and Cross was also responsible for many buildings in New York, including Tiffany & Co.'s building, the Art Deco RCA Tower (now the General Electric Building), and 1 Sutton Place.

Mayfields still looks much as it did when Sister was a child. When I first saw the house, I felt her presence strongly, as she had spoken with such love for it and the land. It is an English Tudor house made from materials that give it the look of a house that has stood here forever. Slate and fieldstone, combined with the generous use of mortar and brick, make Mayfields appear to be an elaborate meandering cottage with a roof that undulates.

Mayfields sits at the end of a long, winding drive. When Sister lived there, it was surrounded by three hundred acres of manicured lawns and gardens, dense forest and rolling hills, in what is known as "horse country." Looking in every direction from the house, you can see miles and miles of untouched land. The driveway, which ends in a great pebbled circle in front of the house, is shaded by huge elms.

APPLE: At Mayfields, we children ate in the breakfast room, with John Glanville, the butler, keeping track of us. He was our friend and never got cross even when we threw our Jell-O up to the ceiling, where it got stuck. He taught me how to shine shoes the proper way: Polish all over, including the instep, let it dry for a while, then brush and finally rub with a very soft rag. He also made ice cream in one of the small rooms off the kitchen.

I remember the tea parties at Mayfields. The secret of the tea sandwiches was thinly sliced bread. Each slice of this homemade bread had a thin layer of butter and another of mayonnaise, pronounced "myonaise." The fillings were very finely cut cucumbers, chicken, tomato, or watercress. Each was wrapped with waxed paper or a slightly dampened kitchen towel. We also had tiny tea cakes, sitting on a three-tiered tray. When they were passed, each tier could be taken out individually.

I remember Grandpa Kinnicutt bringing houseguests home for the weekends. When they would go down to the pool for a swim, D.B. and I would spy on them from the roof of the bathhouse. Afterward, they would come back to the house for martinis under the elm trees. I remember they had small, almost square martini glasses and Cheez-Its. There was a lake, and I would go there with my brother, Harry, while he fished. We had a barn filled with roosters and chickens. One of the hired men about the barn would wring a chicken's neck and chop its head off with a hatchet whenever the cook wanted a chicken.

SYBIL KINNICUTT BALDWIN: At Mayfields, Maisie would eat the butter balls right out of the dish. I can remember incredible comfort. I had never seen a butler in my life, and there was John, the butler, remembering everything about me. I was a tricky little girl who wouldn't touch milk, so the next time I was there, John remembered and had chocolate milk for me. But I wouldn't touch it, and even I was embarrassed for myself. I remember beautiful flowers and gleaming mahogany tables.

D. B. GILBERT: Mayfields was a beautiful place. It was a beautiful place more than a beautiful house. It was grand, unlike Mummy's later houses. The house and the furniture, I thought, were sort of cold. It wasn't a cozy house. The living room was very grand and cold.

APPLE: The driveway was always raked. We also had enormous vegetable gardens and three greenhouses; one was just for orchids. Mayfields was always filled with flowers from the cutting gardens. I remember standing nearby a huge white mulberry tree and eating its berries and curling up on a tiny seat

The cocktail hour. Sister with Apple and D.B. at Mayfields.

that was nearly obscured by grapevines. It was near the tennis courts and just up from the pool. I remember sitting there with Daddy and asking him what brand of cigarettes I should smoke when I grew up. He suggested L&M's.

SUSAN: The gardens at Mayfields were the creation of Ellen Shipman, the famous landscape architect, who was known to design gardens with the most "demanding perennials for the most demanding clients."

DeWitt Chatham Hanes, who was a good friend of Sister's and whose parents hired Mrs. Shipman in 1929, remembers Mrs. Shipman's strict rules for the garden: "Don't ever plant one thing outside the garden wall that isn't native, but you can plant anything you want inside it." She also taught Mr. Hanes how to prune. "There are only two things that man can really control. One is a tree and another is a vine. Always cut out anything that grows up, and make sure you don't leave any nubbins." Even in her largest gardens, she stuck to her simple design formula: "A path, a coping around a bed, a tree, a place to sit—that is a garden."

Sister was greatly influenced by the gardens at Mayfields and spent her happiest moments designing her own gardens in Maine. The garden bench she and Harry bought together and placed in her garden under the apple tree harks back to Mrs. Shipman's simple formula.

But if my parents were striving for perfection in their only daughter, I'm afraid that they were desperately disappointed. They discovered that, by the second grade, I was a hopeless child, untalented, uninteresting, and not at all graceful. Together, they did everything in their power, and in the power of the most expensive tutors, coaches, and teachers, to salvage what they could of me. Nothing went untried, but every attempt was doomed to failure.

The first and only time that I was a heroine occurred on one of our first family trips to see Mayfields. We had a large canvas-topped touring Cadillac. On this occasion, my mother and father, all four children, my grandmother and grandfather Tuckerman, and the chauffeur, Andrew, were rounding the corner at the entrance to Mayfields, where a small pond existed. Andrew somehow lost control of the car and we rolled over and into the pond. I was the only one thrown free. My instinct was to rush to the main road and lead people to the rescue. I can still hear the praise I got for being completely under control.

"That's the first time," my father said, "that Sister has ever had to use her head."

And of course it was true. When you grew up as I did, in Far Hills, on Eighty-second Street, and in Dark Harbor, you were as far removed from the terrors, the surprises, and the needs of this world as a person could possibly be. There were few occasions when you were called upon to use your head.

Opposite page: Sister and Foxcroft classmate Ellie Weld Choate and cousin Ibbie Elkins Holmquist.

Chapter Three

Education and Coming Out:
1926–1928

*Once there and for the rest of their lives, the young women
became labeled "Foxcroft girls."*

SUSAN BARTLETT CRATER

BY THE TIME *I was sixteen, I'd hardly used my head at all, and I'd exhausted
almost all of my parents' hopes for me.*

*My father should have had a hint when I finished first grade. He asked me
what I had learned in school that year, and I answered, "George Washington
is Jesus' father." That should have been the clue, but it wasn't until I was ten
that they went to work in earnest to salvage what they could of their only
daughter.*

Nothing went untried—fencing lessons, ballet class, sewing instruction— but every attempt was doomed to failure. Then a large piano was moved in. A master teacher was hired, only to prove conclusively that I was tone-deaf.

I fared no better when they sent me to ballroom dancing. The fox-trot and the waltz eluded me. Modern dances like the tango and the Charleston were way out of my league. When I started going to parties, I became highly adept at "sitting this one out." It was quite apparent that I'd never be a student, a dancer, a pianist, or an artist.

The most wasted efforts of all were the journeys to Europe "for education." We traveled in great style aboard the great steamships and stayed in luxurious cabins. Other times, we chose the best hotels in Europe or visited lovely country houses owned by friends of the family. Once we toured in a Hispano-Suiza, followed by a second car bearing our luggage. We visited all the great palaces and museums, but I never learned anything. I kept my eyes closed tight in every cathedral.

My only clear memories of those childhood trips to the Continent are the troubles my brothers and I got into. One evening at the Ritz in Paris, my parents left us in the room to order our own dinner. We ordered bowls of plover's eggs (even then a rare delicacy) and were apprehended after we had fired them all out the window, splattering the doorman and a party arriving in evening clothes. I recall an embassy lunch at The Hague when my cousin and I had to be removed from the table after developing an uncontrollable fit of giggles.

Of course, my parents laid their greatest hopes in the schools they sent me to, and this must have been the most bitter disappointment of all. If I have very few memories of my first schools, it is because I allowed so few thoughts to enter my head there. In New Jersey, I went to Peck School in the spring and autumn. During the winter, I went to Miss Chapin's School, in New York.

Somehow, I managed to make it through until it was time for Foxcroft. No other boarding school was considered. My principal accomplishment at Foxcroft was the method I developed for avoiding exams: All I had to do was press a tender spot on the bridge of my nose and I would get a nosebleed. I won a prize for punctuality and was runner-up for the good manners prize. But no diploma, not even a certificate.

At some point, the school became so alarmed at my utter lack of progress that they took a step unheard of in those days. They suggested that I be analyzed by a doctor. Mother took me to Dr. Draper. He was a psychiatrist, but he also was a relative, so that made it all right. He asked me, "Do you like school?" and Mother answered, "No." He asked, "Do you like riding?" and Mother answered,

Photo of Sister taken for her father.

"Yes." He asked, "Do you believe in God?" and Mother answered, "No." Finally, he told me that I could leave. He asked Mother to stay.

SUSAN: Girls from socially prominent families attended Foxcroft School, which was founded by Charlotte Haxall Noland in 1914. Only twenty-nine years old at the time, she founded Foxcroft School in the heart of hunt country in Middleburg, Virginia. A so-called finishing school, it reflected Miss Charlotte's love for riding and the outdoors.

In Miss Charlotte's biography, the beginnings of the school were described:

Before opening, the Brick House saw some feverish preparations. A prospective parent and daughter arrived at the Plains unannounced. Brick House was only partially finished when they telephoned from the railway station. While they were being driven out in a barouche and pair, Miss Charlotte, who knew the value of a first impression, borrowed a butler from a neighbor, tacked chintz over extra chairs and frosted a sponge cake. Pleased by the Virginia hospitality and Miss Noland's dynamic personality, the parent enrolled her daughter.

When another student arrived at the station with eight trunks and a maid, Miss Charlotte asked which of the trunks contained underclothes. The one so designated was loaded into the wagon, and the maid directed to return from whence she came, with the other seven.

Foxcroft was not for the faint-hearted, and Miss Charlotte probably had little time for girls who hid out in the infirmary, like Sister, who told me that she had continually picked at some spot on her nose so that she could live in the infirmary, where it was "more comfortable." Although Sister left before graduation, her closest friends and many of her cousins had been at Foxcroft with her. Her best friend, Tootsie Todd, mother of Governor Christine Whitman, was later responsible for Foxcroft bestowing an honorary degree on Sister. She was so proud when she received this "certificate," as she called it.

Mom and I both went to Foxcroft, as well, and it was very important to Sister that this "Foxcroft girl" tradition continue, despite her having fled after a year.

When my mother and grandmother were there, girls slept on unheated sleeping porches with flannel sheets and canvas coverings to keep the snow from seeping in. All of this was meant to develop character.

APPLE: Mummy would not consider any other school for D.B. and me. We were supposedly on a boarding school tour of Garrison Forest and Foxcroft. We drove in through the gates of Garrison Forest, turned around, and continued on to the two-hour drive to the Foxcroft gates. At that point, she turned to me and said, "This is where you will go."

PHYLLIS DILLON COLLINS (family friend): Once, everyone in our class got drunk. They got into the teachers' cocktails. Miss Charlotte found out about it, and they all thought they were going to be fired, of course. So she asked everyone in the guilty group to come to her house. When they arrived, she said, "Girls, the bar is over there." They didn't know what she meant.

"Do you want a drink?" she asked. "Go get yourself a drink and come back and sit down." Well, of course, nobody moved. Miss Charlotte said, "Well, I'm glad this happened to you in a safe place like this instead of off in some dangerous place where there a lot of boys and goodness knows what might have happened. I know all young people are going to experiment like this. I think some of you are rather sick, but if you really don't think you've

Charlotte Haxall Noland.

experimented enough and want to find out what it really is, you just come right here to my house and there's the bar and you just drink."

Miss Charlotte had this properly done white hair, and she used to wear brightly colored suits, usually bright blue or bright green.

The men were enchanted with her. The Marine Corps used to come out and review drills. All these famous people from Washington came to look at these silly girls wandering around a drill field. Once. Gen. George Marshall came out and reviewed our drill.

Miss Charlotte was just an amazing character. She used to fancy herself a preacher. I remember one sermon of hers that had to do with sin. She said that each time you commit a sin, you've got to hammer a nail into this board. And later on, when all the sins are forgiven, well, you could take the nails out of the board. All the nails come out of the board, she told us, but she said, "Now, look, the holes are still there."

We all went to church in the back of these open trucks. In order to keep warm, we'd sing songs. We got these little envelopes. It was either twenty-five or fifty cents for the collection. We caught on, after being there for a few years, that if you didn't feel you were good enough to take Communion, then you could go out. Well, we'd step out with our church money and go buy an ice-cream cone, then show up and get back in the truck.

SUSAN: St. Mark's and St. Paul's schools were the traditional schools for boys in the family, and Foxcroft was the only acceptable school for the girls. Dark Harbor is chock-full of Foxcroft graduates. My mother's friend and classmate Joan Dillon de Mouchy remembered when Miss Charlotte came to Dark Harbor.

JOAN DILLON DE MOUCHY (family friend): The sailing instructor, a brother of a Foxcroft alumna, was at the tennis courts on the morning of a Foxcroft lunch given in honor of Miss Charlotte. The place was deserted except for a few people, who were newcomers on the island. They asked the instructor what was happening to cause the lull that day. He answered, "Miss Charlotte is coming and all of the Foxcroft girls have gone up to the ferry landing to watch her walk across the water from Lincolnville."

It was quite apparent that I couldn't possibly be a dancer, a pianist, a sports woman, an artist, a student, or a fencer. I have found that girls who do poorly in school, and who can't fence, usually make up for it by having enormous success with boys. I cannot say that the theory proved true in my case. In those days, of course, sex came later in life and wasn't discussed at all.

My brothers invariably tried to make any relationship with boys twice as embarrassing. When I was invited to my first dance, I wasn't sent flowers, so I sent them to myself. Unfortunately, my brother Gory spotted my handwriting on the card and off he ran, gleefully announcing to the entire house, "Sister sent herself flowers!" Girls weren't supposed to know anything, and that was confusing. The first time I was kissed, I immediately informed my parents that I was going to have a baby.

By the time I was seventeen, nature had begun to change its mind about me. I was beginning to look somewhat attractive, and a series of beaux paraded through my life. Mother and Daddy, who were horrified at my seeing a Yale man, decided, without much confidence, I suspect, that the time had come to introduce me to society.

This was a time of the great parties, one grander than the next. In New York, they were usually held in the ballroom of the Ritz. In Philadelphia, they were given at the Barclay, and on Long Island, enormous striped tents created rooms larger and more beautiful than any ballroom. Party after party, the young men in white tie, the young women in white satin. Always the same people, the same Cole Porter, Rogers and Hart, and Gershwin tunes, the same champagne, the same small dinner before, the same scrambled-egg supper at dawn, the same gossip the next day. There was no tomorrow, except for what to wear tomorrow. It was a dizzying time.

My coming-out party was held in New York at the Pierre Hotel during the Christmas holidays. We had Lester Lanin at one end of the ballroom and Meyer Davis at the other. Predictably, quite a few of the guests arrived slightly drunk after the 1927 Harvard-Yale game festivities, but my brothers were effective bouncers.

My mother and her social secretary had planned the party for months. It was a huge success, except for the fact that I spent much of the night out on the street with my boyfriend, George Munson. His grandmother had just died and he was supposed to be in mourning, so he couldn't come to the dance.

I finally had enough of the dances, and the next summer I went again to Paris, this time with a close friend. My parents had an apartment at 23 quai d'Orsay. I'd seen the apartment before, of course, but when I entered it this time, eighteen years old and feeling very grown-up, something stirred inside me. I marveled at the delicately carved Louis XV and XVI fauteuils covered in

Sister prior to her marriage in one of the Mayfields gardens.

exquisite stripes and damasks. I began to feel the love of painted furniture that has followed me through all my decorating. I knew I was discovering something important, but I didn't know why. The rest of the trip was spent touring French houses. This time, my eyes were open, and so was my heart. I was at last beginning to understand beauty and the role it would play in my life.

I have a photograph taken of me at that time. I hardly recognize the girl in the picture. She looks, surprisingly, quite pretty. She is wearing a simple, beautifully cut summer dress. Her expression looks bright and cheerful; her eyes look confident. She looks very much like my own daughters looked when they were eighteen, and very much like my mother looks in a small yellowed photograph that was taken of her at about the same age.

I'm sure that my head was filled with inconsequential thoughts when that picture was taken, but I am quite certain that deep down I was conscious of a strong sense of family tradition. A sense of the past as it relates to the present had already been subtly imbued in me as I grew up. Already, at eighteen, I had a deep, abiding belief in all things inherited, and all things of real lasting quality. I was not afraid of change, but I firmly believed in the continuity of values that I had learned while growing up. A sense of family and of home were the strongest values of all, and perhaps the look of confidence in my eyes that the photograph reveals sprang from the knowledge that the values I had learned would be with me no matter what lay ahead.

My parents' goal for me at eighteen was marriage, as quickly and as honorably as possible. Honorably did not include any of the Yale sophomores I had been seeing. Mother became more convinced than ever that Yale was not really a college and that those who went there had little justification for being alive. She felt the same way about Princeton. The only man for me would be a Harvard man, and then only if he were a member of the Porcellian Club. The Porcellian Club elected fewer than ten members a year, so this considerably narrowed my prospects. With that in mind, Mother sent out invitations to a black-tie dinner party. I didn't have to ask where they had gone to college or what club they had joined. They were all at least three years out of Harvard and settled in good jobs in either banking or finance. I thought they were ancient. They thought they were gods.

Before the party, my mother asked my father, "Do you think we should have a trick man to get things going? Someone to pull a rabbit out of the hat?"

Father reminded her sternly that this was not a children's party, that these were businessmen. For the first hour of the party, I wished that we'd had a "trick man."

We girls were all in a state of excitement and dread, and I doubt that any of us would have said more than two intelligible words to the men if one of them hadn't been so innately polite that he saw his duty to make an effort with us. His name was Harry Parish.

Opposite page: Sister and Harry.

Chapter Four

Marriage: 1930

Harry was a very loved person. He had a sweetness that wasn't sappy;
it was a decency.

VOLNEY "TURKEY" RIGHTER

HE WAS WONDERFUL-LOOKING, with bright blue eyes and broad shoulders,
and I soon learned that he was gentle and sweet as well as perfectly mannered,
and, best of all, we had Benny Goodman in common.

This led naturally to dancing to the bands at the Casino in Central Park off
Seventy-second Street, where Benny Goodman played. Soon we were dining there
two and three times a week, always the same table on the same huge veranda that
went all the way around the Casino. Our song was "This Can't Be Love." This
had to be played over and over for us. I was bound I was going to marry him.

Another family trip to Europe had been planned for that summer, and I was
miserable about leaving. But to help take my mind off Harry, I did have Paris
and trips to Versailles and country châteaus and our lovely apartment on the
quai d'Orsay, and my new interest in French painted furniture and all the beauty
it offered. I vowed then that I would have a canopy bed someday and curtains with
pelmets, cords, tassels, and bells, and hopefully an Aubusson rug with garlands

of flowers in soft pastel colors. When I came across anything especially pretty, I would imagine it in "our" house. I would wander past the shops, slyly buying small flower drawings, a teacup, or a porcelain bowl with garlands of roses and ribbons. To this day, I cannot resist a rose or a ribbon.

We returned home on September 7 and I was allowed to have a large house party before the coming-out party of one of my best friends, Eleanor Todd. Of course Harry came, and I was so proud of him. From then on, Harry and I were hardly ever separated. It became apparent to both of our families that formal discussions would have to be held soon.

Harry's mother and father, Mr. and Mrs. Edward Parish, were older than my parents and of another world. They had been brought up in a serious, ponderous way in enormous houses. One is now Bendel's [the New York department store]. My mother and father were racy by comparison. At the time I was falling in love with Harry, his family was living with his grandfather, the banker Henry Parish, whose house on East Seventy-ninth Street was one of the grandest in New York. Most of the furniture came from Paris in suites made to order, and the Parish children learned to roller-skate on an Aubusson rug that I later inherited.

Henry Parish was president of the Bank of New York. He didn't believe in telephones. He considered them too impersonal for business dealings. For the forty-four years that he was president of the bank, all business was transacted in person or through messengers.

When it came time for the two families to talk seriously about our marriage, my mother met Mrs. Parish at the Tea Court of the Plaza. Mrs. Parish wore pearl gray; my mother had her new mink. As soon as the tea arrived and the waiter was gone, Mrs. Parish, with a trembling voice, announced that she had a confession to make that might stop our wedding. Mother waited with dread to hear her out, fearing syphilis, insanity, or worse. With tears in her eyes, Mrs. Parish confessed that her daughter Eliza was "contemplating divorce." She added that she would understand completely if Mother didn't want such a thing in her family.

Despite other hurdles, Harry and I were married in St. George's Church near Gramercy Park on Valentine's Day, 1930. Dr. Drury, the famous headmaster of St. Paul's School, came down from New Hampshire to marry us. Everyone I cared about was there. The church was filled with white flowers, and one of the greatest choirs that has ever sung provided the music. I remember my mother asking my father at the last moment, "Do you think it would be worth it

Harry Parish shortly after his marriage to Sister.

if the choir added 'Oh Perfect Love'? It will cost a thousand dollars." My father shrugged and held out his hands. "At this point," he said cheerfully, "anything."

Everything would have been perfect if I hadn't come down with a serious case of chicken pox on the day of my wedding. I broke out head to toe, developed a 102-degree fever, and as I walked down the aisle, my only thought was, Thank God for my veil. Throughout our honeymoon in Nassau, poor Harry had to handle a sick patient instead of a happy bride, but we were both radiant upon our return.

SUSAN: We were told that Harry's family had been very grand. Sister used to drop little details of the past to instruct us on our heritage. Once when we were driving through Riverdale, New York, she turned to me with a loud sigh and said, "Look out there, Susan. This was once all Parish land." I never knew whether it was true or not.

Harry's father, Edward Codman Parish, graduated from Columbia College in 1896 and entered the practice of law in New York in 1898. The Parishes were very philanthropic and served on many boards in New York, as well as belonging to all of the clubs that served the city's old guard. Harry's brother, Eddie Parish, remembers his family's move from Fifty-seventh Street in New York to a four-story brownstone on East Seventy-ninth Street. Many of the furnishings brought from Paris by his grandfather Parish were incorporated into the new house. Grandpa Parish had lived in Paris for a number of years in the house previously lived in by Victor Hugo.

EDWARD CODMAN PARISH II (Harry Parish's brother): My parents, the Edward C. Parishes, and their four children—Eliza, Harry, Marie, and myself—lived in New York at 18 West Fifty-seventh Street. We spent summers in Elberon, New Jersey, a summer resort on the coast, a short trip from New York.

Later, we moved to a brownstone on East Seventy-ninth Street. There was a ceiling mural depicting lady Aurora at dawn dropping crystal beads from a broken necklace. This scene was meant to portray raindrops coming from the sky. The floor was covered by an Aubusson carpet that, much to my father's consternation, proved to be a great surface for roller-skating.

Harry, who was eight years older than I, was at St. Paul's School in Concord, New Hampshire, and was seldom home, even during school vacations. While I toured the United States in 1920, Harry opted to spend the time with our cousin, Teddy Sparrow, on a ranch.

We later went to Rome and had an audience with Pope Pius, as well as visiting the Italian Senate, which was in session, with Mussolini presiding. I will never forget watching Mussolini, who, as we sat and watched, held a rose in one hand and systematically picked its petals off, one by one, until none was left.

VOLNEY "TURKEY" RIGHTER (family friend): Harry and I met at St. Paul's School as third formers. We had very, very happy times. Harry was always popular, and he had very good manners. I was well brought up and went to St. Paul's with good manners, but I learned a lot from Harry. I remember his sisters, Marie and Eliza, as well. They all had charm. You couldn't beat that group.

We went to Harvard together. In those days, all you had to do was pass your college boards and you could go to the college you chose. This was the

Portrait of Sister by Ned Murray.

class of 1926. At St. Paul's and Harvard, Harry was a very loved person. He had a sweetness that wasn't sappy; it was a decency.

I had met Sister's cousin Ibbie Elkins at a party in Newport. We had a summer romance, a perfectly lovely time. She said we would have to go to Far Hills, so Harry Parish and Charlie Harding and I stayed at the Kinnicutts'. It was there I got to know Sister, Gory, and Frankie. Frankie became an intimate friend of my brother, Brewster. Those two would stay up until 3:00 A.M. nursing a bottle of scotch. Frankie loved to talk and Sister loved to talk. It was in the Kinnicutt family. Sister had a sharp tongue, so did Ibbie, and they were cousins, so I think it grew up from deep roots. At that time, they were young and pretty excited about the boys they had around. That was the fall that Harry met Sister.

SUSAN: Harry's family was related to many of the old families of New York, including the Roosevelts. This connection was by marriage, through Harry's uncle Henry Parish, who was married to Eleanor Roosevelt's cousin Susie. In fact, Franklin and Eleanor were married at the Henry Parish house.

Harry had an uncle named Henry Parish; thus, Harry became Henry Parish II. Uncle Henry did not have any children, so he and Aunt Susie (who brought up Eleanor Roosevelt) took up Harry almost as a son. Eleanor Roosevelt had not yet become the First Lady, and so Aunt Susie wailed, "Had I known, I would have had her teeth straightened." When Harry married me and I went "into trade," it was too much for Susie, and we did not receive the fortune, which went to Eleanor instead. It must have been a difficult decision, but they concluded that even marrying a Democrat was preferable to marrying a woman in trade.

APPLE: Grandmother Parish seemed at first to be extremely kind and gentle, but I think she was actually terribly tough. D.B. and I used to go stay with her in Tyringham, Massachusetts, each summer for a week. She was very religious and proper, and extremely strict with us, particularly when she discovered my unfortunate habit of pulling leaves off bushes as I passed them. She cured me quickly of that habit by charging me one penny for each leaf that I pulled off. Grandma and Grandpa used to have Sunday lunches. These were gatherings of lots of cousins and my aunts and uncles. She was a great believer in the "Clean Plate Club."

We were both very much in love. I could not do enough for Harry or think often enough about him. There was never a day without flowers or some small present. I was completely spoiled in every possible way. For years, I never opened a window. I never poured a glass of water. Our house was a dream of beauty; 146 East End Avenue—the street was then cobblestone, every window had a flower box, and we looked across to Carl Schurz Park.

Harry had a promising job at Loeb, Rhoades, and fortunately for us, our families believed that if you brought your children up in the grand manner, you

**Sister during the early
years of her marriage.**

*should help them start their own married lives in the same style. My parents pro-
vided our beautiful house, which had been done entirely by Mrs. Brown of
McMillen—with Mother's help and suggestions, of course. Wedding presents
provided almost all of the furnishings. We had to buy one upholstered chair, at
Macy's, and I was appalled at having to spend forty dollars. (I still have that
chair in my apartment.) We had a couple who worked for us, and a laundress
twice a week, and we slept on linen sheets and big square pillowcases with mono-
grams so prominent that I often woke up and saw DMP stamped on my cheek.*

*For our first dinner party, our guest was Joe Alsop. Liver and onions had
been carefully planned, the candles were lit, and a second fire was burning
upstairs for after dinner. The telephone rang; he could not come. He had to write
an obituary for Mrs. Ruth Pratt. She died eleven years later.*

We had bought what we thought would be a very small dachshund that we could take everywhere, even when unwanted. His name was Otto. As I look back on him now, he was enormous and yards long.

When I was told that I was having a baby, the competition between the grandparents-to-be was keen. The Parish bassinet was starched up and out came the Parish christening dress with its yards of frills and pleats and lace. My parents produced the basket that had carried me to Dark Harbor twenty-one years before, along with silver rattles and bowls. Harry brought home fishing tackle and a baseball bat and was rewarded with a boy. Little Harry's first word was birdie, *which to us meant that it was time to move to the country. We found a small farmhouse in Far Hills, New Jersey—and the first stirrings of my career were about to begin.*

Opposite page: Sister, Harry, and the children in front of their house on Long Lane.

Chapter Five

Long Lane: 1930–1940

A few weeks later, I found a small room in Far Hills. I painted it myself,
brought in a few pieces of my own furniture, spread the samples about,
and then hung out a sign that said "Mrs. Henry Parish II—Interiors."

SISTER PARISH

OUR HOUSE WAS a thing of wonder. It was white, with yellow shutters, a picket
fence, and apple trees all around. Young, in love, and full of confidence, I wasn't
the least bit afraid of what I would put in the house or of what people might say
about my taste. When the Parishes offered to give us furniture from their own
town house, I chose, of all things, a suite of black ebony. The sofa and chairs
were covered in blue tapestry with pink flowers. There was a carpet to match, a
bit ragged, since it was the one the Parish children used to skate over. I then proceeded to do something no one had ever heard of: I painted the ebony white. I
soon discovered that Harry's mother would choke before allowing that the effect

was "interesting." But I knew what I was after, and I was delighted with the result. I then put white-striped paper on the walls, giving the room a bright, cheerful look that was hardly in keeping with the fashion of the times. I added two white sofas, a papier-mâché table with fringe, and two white-and-gold console tables with marble tops, which came from the apartment on quai d'Orsay. I then had another inspiration and used white mattress ticking for the curtains. Mrs. Parish thought they were sheets, and she wondered why I hadn't left the windows bare until the curtains arrived. The whole room was reflected in large mirrors, enhancing our pleasure and Mrs. Parish's shock.

Shortly after moving in, I was having another baby and we had to expand. We decided to build a master bedroom on the ground floor and connect it to the living room with a small greenhouse. The work was completed just when my daughter Apple was born. The greenhouse had an old polished brick floor. We furnished it with a huge sofa covered in yellow canvas and with dozens of soft, colorful pillows. Here was my first love—wicker. I added two white wicker chairs from my Morristown days. This is where we really lived, with the flowers, the pots of bulbs, and the trailing vines. (Thirty years later, my daughter Apple turned a greenhouse into the same kind of enchanted living room, and some of my happiest memories returned.)

Our bedroom was beyond the greenhouse, opening into it. It had a huge tray ceiling. I had our bedroom walls painted dead white, then decided to paint the floor as well, another daring innovation. I wanted it cherry red with white diamonds, and Harry spent much of the summer on hands and knees, making sure the diamonds came out right. The result was certainly the most unusual and striking bedroom that has ever been seen in New Jersey. Our bedroom had a fireplace with a mantel made from structural blocks of Steuben glass. The moldings were applied directly to the wall, which I painted cherry red. Over our bed, white silk taffeta bowed down like a crown. The first night we spent there, we kept the lights on because it was so beautiful.

I suppose all of this looked strange in the little farmhouse, and it certainly did puzzle people. But I knew it was beautiful and I could sense something beyond the usual hollow compliments from the people who came to visit us. I had accomplished something special. I knew it and they knew it. I had discovered a decorator's instinct that had been apparently been growing inside of me, waiting for the right time and the right place to express itself. It was the beginning of my career.

* * *

Apple, Little Harry, and D.B. with Sister and Harry.

MARI WATTS HITCHCOCK: It was a dream. Everything was perfect. Sister always had everything different from anyone else. Her house was always absolutely terrific. Her curtains were the best curtains. Sister had these really teeny love seats on each side of the fireplace that people could hardly sit on because they were so small. People kind of laughed at that, but it was very much like doing a painting—if you love something, then you put it in. She had two huge mirrors at either end of the room. I remember the rug was from the Parishes. Bright blue with roses. People would come and say, "I wish you would tell me what to do."

We were always going from one house to another with the children, all that kind of thing. Apple and D.B. were always dressed alike when they were on Long Lane. They always had the most beautiful costumes. They sat still and weren't allowed to run around like other children. It was very social when we were young. We played tennis. There were Christmas parties and birthday parties. Then the war came and we all disbanded.

Sister and Harry with D.B.

SUSAN: If Mayfields and her parents' house in Maine were Sister's inspiration, Long Lane was the house that she alone first created and loved dearly. At the small farmhouse, she first experimented with painting "brown furniture" (as she always called it) white and using casual cottons, bright linens, and mattress ticking, instead of the more formal, heavier materials of the day. She and Harry built a garden room that she filled with her favorite wicker and pots of flowers. She also experimented with painting floors in bright colors and using simple wallpapers. The white/off-white stripe she used in the living room became a favorite for many future living rooms. The effect was one of lightness, a kind of offhand glamour, housed in a country farmhouse. Some of her innovations were done, as she put it, to "make her mother-in-law choke," but the rest simply flowed out of her. She reveled in decorating her house and creating a stylish, cozy, yet imaginative home for her husband and young children. People tend to be good at what they do if they like it, and Sister clearly loved decorating. The effect she created must have contrasted dramatically with the staid, formal look of the thirties, and it did not go unnoticed.

Apple and D.B. sitting on
the miniature chairs that
were Sister's favorite.

It was a very happy time for Harry and her. Newly married, with three young children and a lively social life, they were very happy, I think. Her memories of this time before the war seemed to me to be the ones she held up as her happiest.

APPLE: Before the war, we lived on Long Lane in Far Hills in a little farmhouse my parents rented from Clarence Dillon. We had wonderful animals: Janie, the goat, who could pull a cart, plus the dachshunds Otto and Augie, the latter named for August Belmont. Later, I had rabbits and a yellow Lab nicknamed "YD," short for Yellow Devil.

D.B. and I were dressed alike until, it seemed, we were almost teenagers. In the summer, we wore pretty flowered dresses topped with white pinafores. In the fall, we wore handknit dresses with satin ribbon woven into the waists, or pleated, plaid skirts topped with Fair Isle sweaters. We wore beautiful knit English kneesocks and always very clean, shiny shoes. During the winter, we wore green wool coats, dark chocolate brown velvet bonnets with ostrich feathers and matching muffs, and, of course, brown velvet leggings. Mummy particularly admired Little Lord Fauntleroy and his velvet suits. I remember going to a coming-out party on Long Island, and Mum suggested I dress as Little Lord Fauntleroy. I believe she actually had her dressmaker make this suit for me, complete with a large, scratchy, ruched collar. It was not a very sexy costume for a seventeen-year-old girl.

Our nurse was named Miss Bremner; she was Scottish and extremely strict. We were kept upstairs in the playroom most of the time, even eating our meals there. Miss Bremner force-fed me spinach. I would hardly open my mouth, so she would force my mouth open and stuff the food in. I'd hold it in my mouth until she put us down for a nap.

Once I was in a school play, the *Princess and the Pea*. Mummy hired a moving van and she brought a canopy bed to our school. She put extra mat-tresses on it to make it high enough so that it would fit the story. I got up into the bed with a beautiful nightgown on. My mother was going to be so proud. After all, here was her daughter in this beautiful play and she was going to be wonderful. But I had gum in my mouth and I blew bubbles the entire time, throughout the whole play. "You ruined, ruined, ruined the whole thing," she said.

I remember my father as my friend. He was kind and gentle and would tell me if I had done a good job. He would employ the same fairness when telling me that I had not done so. He had a very clear sense of what was right and what was wrong. This trait he definitely inherited from his parents.

Our house had a stream running by it, in which Mummy and Daddy planted watercress. There was a large garden in front of the house—no veg-etables and no flowers, except for violets. It was very low-maintenance, although that wasn't a priority for Daddy, who loved to weed. Weeding was among his passions, and I always enjoyed doing this with him. Side by side we'd work, talking just a little. I remember Mummy saying to me in this same garden, "If you don't get that grumpy look off your face, it will stay there for the rest of your life."

Daddy was most attractive—very handsome, considerate, and polite, but always with a twinkle in his eye. He was a peaceful man, and I think he was most happy when he was in the country, at Far Hills, or Oldwick, New Jersey, or at Dark Harbor in Maine.

I never had the feeling that he liked his job in New York. I remember discussions at the dinner table when Mummy would say to him (very unkindly, I think), "Harry, don't discuss what you do at the office, because I'll never understand it and it really doesn't interest me, so just don't bother."

Dinner conversations were very general—about people, places, and so on. Politics were never mentioned. You were born a Republican and you died a Republican, and that was that. Mummy and Daddy always had friends in for cocktails on Long Lane. We were dressed up for such occasions and made to pass the crackers.

I remember the bedroom that they built; it had a red-and-white floor and the passageway to their bedroom had one of those huge Aitken sofas in it. In the evening, she would read to us there.

In the country, Daddy put up with D.B.'s and my passion—horses and dogs. He suffered terribly from asthma, but it didn't stop him from encouraging us to participate in horse shows and foxhunts. He asked simply that we

Apple, D.B., and Sister in the Garden Room.

change into unhorsey clothes before we entered the house. The dogs were a problem as well, but he loved them nevertheless.

FORRESTER SMITH (family friend): I knew Sister Parish, Mrs. Parish to me, from the time I was born until the day she died. She was scary as hell and seemed like a dragon with her razor-sharp tongue, imposing size, and biting wit. In Far Hills, where we all grew up, her son, Harry, and I played together constantly, and we took extreme pains never to tell her or even let her see what we did, because it was usually very naughty, and she knew just how to make my mother vent her fury on me. She liked my mother not only because she decorated our house in Far Hills, but also because my mother's family was Porcellian Club–oriented, and "those types" were the only people Sister felt were worth knowing. Because of their friendship, as well as their proximity to our place, I saw the Parishes quite frequently from infancy onward. Apple, three years younger than I, beat me in a pony show because she looked so cute sitting and bouncing in a basket on some fool donkey's back. I, who was doing brilliant Shetland pony equitation, was only a second-place (red ribbon) winner, for I had not been dolled up by Sister Parish and probably looked like a

Sister and Harry.

little hoodlum. I spent many days trying to best those Parishes, but I constantly failed, for they had Sister Parish on their side.

Sister did everything to the nines at her house in Far Hills, from its magnificent chintzes, to its flaming red upholstery, to its marbleized halls, to its sumptuous guest rooms, which made you want to stay for a year. She dazzled everyone in Far Hills, and Far Hills people were not easily dazzled. They were, as a group, far too rich and too jaded, but Sister was a step ahead, and a superstar to boot.

D. B. GILBERT: At Long Lane, I remember Janie the goat and the wooden rooster on the roof. That rooster is at the Summer House now. I remember Miss Bremner and my horse, ItsyBitsy. We went on one hunt that was very long—seven hours or something. I was written up in one of those little squibs in *Time* magazine as the youngest person to go hunting for that long.

FRANCES ELLEN PAUL (family friend): Sister invited me over to her house on Long Lane. I was so impressed when I went into this very bright bedroom that went right up to the eaves. She had all these pictures tied with little bows, and it was the first time I'd seen such a thing. First time anyone had. There were these enormous squares of lipstick red painted on the floor. Red and white. A beautiful bedroom, different than anything anyone had ever seen. I don't know where she got the idea or where it came from. That was the first of it, and then her friends came around because they thought it was so different and chic. Actually, her mother and father had great taste. I remember they had this gardener who would bring in these enormous flowers and put them on the piano. She grew up in a lovely environment of exquisite taste, so I guess she just took off from there.

JOAN DILLON DE MOUCHY: My first memory of Mrs. Parish is from around 1940. She lived with her family on Dunwalke, my grandfather's estate in New Jersey. Harry, Apple, and D.B. came often to play, swim, or ride. We all went to Dark Harbor during the summer, where we also lived side by side. I remember thinking that Mrs. Parish was different from Mummy because she always wore lipstick and had a "funny" voice. From that time until the day she died, I considered her an integral part of my world.

After the first compliments about our house in Far Hills, people came seeking advice. It never occurred to me that I wasn't qualified to give it. The living room at the Essex Hunt Club was looking shabby—could I do something about it? I decided to replace the stiff clublike, overly masculine chairs, which reminded me of the stuffiest New York men's clubs, with upholstered sofas and chairs. It was a risky thing, for this was primarily a men's club. I donated a large coffee table and improved the lighting. I had mirrors installed on either side of the mantel and across the top so that people could see themselves dancing in their pink coats and beautiful dresses. Again, the compliments were genuine.

My next attack on the world of decorating took place in Dark Harbor. My friend Phyllis Dillon and I were asked if we could redo the old ballroom that once had been part of the Dark Harbor Inn. It was a challenge we couldn't resist.

The ballroom had been a very special place when we were in our teens. It was always "leap year" when we had dances in the ballroom, for the boys considered us freaks of some kind. But if we were very aggressive, and struck with delirious luck, we might be asked out onto the porch at the side of the ballroom. There, usually under a foggy, drizzly sky, many a secret kiss took place—a secret that made the rounds of the island by dawn.

We began the job filled with childhood memories, but we were married then and it seemed that we had only pink and blue on our minds. The walls were painted pale pink, the rafters a bit deeper pink, and then a hundred chairs were painted blue. The tables we mixed—blue and pink. The best I ever heard about the room was that it looked like a very pretty bassinet.

Then one day, Senator Frelinghuysen, a neighbor and friend in Far Hills, told me of a new restaurant in the Somerville circle that desperately needed the help of a decorator. The place was called Howard Johnson's. His farm supplied the milk to the restaurant, and he offered to introduce me to the owner. I did what I could. I dressed the waitresses in aqua, did the walls in aqua, made the place mats in aqua. I guess I must have thought it was quite chic, but I haven't done a thing in aqua since. However, I still love Howard Johnson's.

I had never known a woman who worked. Certainly not a married woman—most definitely not a married woman with a child at home. It was impossible. I had decorated the Hunt Club for pleasure, and the Howard Johnson's for little more than free ice cream. But at that point, the crash had come, and I knew that our way of living had to change. Earning money, if not socially acceptable, was at least useful. Both my father's business and Harry's business were coming into very hard times.

* * *

Harry and his daughters.

SUSAN: Sister said that she went to work because Harry's business and her father's business had fallen on hard times—the hard times being the crash and the Depression. Harry's parents had the most money and were the hardest hit. They lost everything. My mother remembers them as very religious people, who accepted their change of circumstances as a fait accompli. Hermann Kinnicutt was also hard hit, but he did not accept it and eventually ended making a lot of it back. In 1933, when Harry told Sister that his salary at Loeb, Rhodes had been cut, she did not accept it. I will never know exactly what their circumstances were, as Sister rarely discussed money, but in a letter from Harry to Sister around that time, he refers to their escalating expenses, and that they did not have the income to sustain them. It was not difficult to detect the tension and worry creeping into his words. She was a young woman who had, in her own words, "never opened a window or poured a glass of water myself," and she decided to take her fate into her own hands. She had been accustomed to living a certain way, and she was going to do everything in her power to maintain it for herself and her children. Right after he told her about their change in circumstances, she opened her decorating business in a small shop in Far Hills and worked for the rest of her life. She was twenty-three years old.

APPLE: My first memory of Grandma and Grandpa Parish was in their very crowded apartment on Seventy-second Street in New York City during the 1940s. The world was recovering from the stock market crash and the Great Depression. Like many people at that time, they had lost everything.

Each room was crammed full of belongings—very large pieces of furniture, piles of magazines, newspapers, books, and clothing. There didn't seem to be any room left for people to move around in. They had moved from a much bigger house into this tiny apartment. It was all mysterious to me as a child—this "crash" business. Nobody ever explained it to us—going from a grand life to reduced circumstances. It was not something that you discussed with your children.

LETITIA BALDRIDGE (Jacqueline Kennedy's private secretary): It was probably, at times, humiliating for her, because in the thirties, during the Depression, the only ones who worked were those who had to: those who were considered poor, or those who'd lost their social status. So for her to proudly go to work in the thirties really showed a lot of guts. I think she was the first tremendously social decorator to make it in that world. She had a first-class pedigree and was never embarrassed to brandish it, which is fine. She knew what she had going for her. She knew it would be a very tough struggle for her to be considered a professional in her group.

JOAN DILLON DE MOUCHY: I never thought of her as "working." She decorated an apartment for me in Cambridge, Massachusetts, when I first got married. I always felt that she did it as a friend, as I suppose the bills were taken care of by the family. I first became aware that she was actually in business during my father's time as ambassador to France.

I was leaving to go live with them in Paris when Mummy developed jaundice and was relegated to her bed back in New York for a long spell. I wanted to give her something to make her sitting in bed more comfortable. After searching through many stores, I finally bought, for about thirty dollars, a rather ugly stuffed chair back with arms that one could use for sitting up in bed. It was hideous-looking, and I felt it had to be re-covered. The perfect solution was to pass by and ask for help from Mrs. Parish. I did so, and we chose a nice white upholstery material, which she took and got it re-covered. A few days later, I got a bill for $250, which, when added to my previous cost, made my present worth $280. My monthly allowance was less than that, so I was flabbergasted. My fault, and from then on I have always done my own decorating.

BUNNY WILLIAMS (former Parish-Hadley decorator): She wanted a lot for her children and grandchildren. That was her motivation, because she had come from money. She didn't know what it was like not to have it, and she didn't want anyone not to have it. Money was very, very important to her. If you have been brought up in a certain way and then all of a sudden someone tells you that you're not going to have this, then you're either going to kill yourself or fight for it.

FORRESTER SMITH: For some reason, it stuck in my mind that the Parishes had lost their money and that's why the children were going to public school. So every time I saw Mrs. Parish, I would look askance, because I had never seen a poor woman before. I was probably seven or eight, and I was asked to their house to have lunch with Harry and Apple. I was a very observant child. Now I remember everything, because I don't drink. That day, we had pheasant for lunch at the Parishes'. I figured they had run over the pheasant.

It was Christmas Eve and I knew something had happened and that Harry was worried. He tried to hold it back, but I knew. A week later, without telling Harry, I decided to go to work. Though I had no professional training, and no useful education, I knew in my heart that I was a decorator.

It never occurred to me to start anywhere but at the top, so my first move as a would-be professional decorator was to arrive unannounced at the office of the president of Stroheim in the Decorator's Building. Somehow, I talked my way directly into his office, and, fortunately, he was too polite to throw me out. He tried to convince me that decorating would never be a job for me, and with the market crashing down upon almost everyone with money, this was hardly the time to start a career. But I was too young and determined to listen to his arguments, and, after I'd told him my whole life's story, he gave me a charge card and begged me, for heaven's sake, to leave. I suddenly remembered the children, and I asked to use his phone to call long-distance to see how they were. I then asked his help in selecting samples from the showroom. To his credit, he showed no sign of losing his temper until I was leaving the building, arms laden with samples, and I had to ask his help again to get me through the revolving door that led to the street.

I had become a decorator, but I hadn't worked up the nerve to tell Harry. A few weeks later, I found a small room in Far Hills. I painted it myself, brought in a few pieces of my own furniture, spread the samples about, and then hung out a sign that said MRS. HENRY PARISH II—INTERIORS. *My shop was adjacent to a saddle maker, and was not very prominent, to say the least. When it was finished, I met Harry at the station in Far Hills. I asked him to drive slowly to see if he noticed anything new. We drove past the shop twice before he spotted the sign. When I took him inside, he slowly began to comprehend that this was my shop. When it dawned on him, there was a long silence, a slow shaking of the head, then, finally, a smile full of love and admiration. He had his doubts, but he approved.*

The first person to enter the shop with any serious intentions was Mrs. Andy Fowler, the daughter of a family friend. She was young, enthusiastic, and had a large country house that she wanted decorated. I really didn't know much more than she did, but she trusted me completely. I decided that they should have a dark green leather library and a white carpet with red roses. It was considered dashing. It was a very grand house for a very young couple, and they invested well over $100,000, which made it an auspicious beginning for me.

For some reason, I had complete confidence in what I was doing. The furniture arranging came naturally to me. It all seemed obvious. One of my principles from the beginning was that the room should look used, that every corner of it should be livable. I couldn't stand seeing wasted space. I knew what was necessary to make a room work, that there should be three groups so the room could be completely used. I had a feeling for the lighting, for which colors would work. I knew that the tables should be the same height so the lamps would be the same height. I did have to do some research on the valances, but that was all I got out of books. I made some mistakes, of course—you do in almost any house—but the final result was very interesting and notably different.

After that first job, I was established as a decorator. The word spread and, despite difficult times, commissions followed. I had not gone to school or served an apprenticeship or joined any professional decorating organizations. I had no credentials whatsoever, but I was a decorator. I had, of course, been extraordinarily lucky.

Opposite page: Sister, Harry, Apple, D.B., and friend at the VJ Day parade in Dark Harbor.

The War Years and Return to New York: 1941–1952

Harry was gone for two and a half years. His letters were sad, lonely, and terribly serious, and I prayed each night that it would be over soon.

SISTER PARISH

IT WAS A *perfect December Sunday in Far Hills. The fields were still green, and the air was so crisp and clear that the countryside seemed to stretch forever in all directions, with our little farmhouse the very center of the universe. I could see the various shades of gray in a post and rail fence a quarter of a mile from the house. That morning, the hunt went by so close to our house, I heard the hunting horn far in the distance, and the excited barking of the hounds. I stepped outside our back door as the hoofbeats came closer, in time to see the pink coats flying over a high wooden fence in a neighboring field. I waved, and some of the riders*

took a hand off their reins to wave back. They were having a glorious time, and for a moment I forgot my embarrassing falls at horse shows as a teenager and wished that I were riding with them. The children came to stand beside me as about thirty riders galloped and trotted after the hounds. I remember thinking that the children soon would be wearing riding derbies and shiny boots and be galloping by with the hunt. Young Harry was eleven, Apple was nine, and D.B. was seven, and they all enjoyed riding.

Their father was out in the fields, doing his favorite thing that morning—pheasant hunting with his closest friends. He returned about noon, holding three large cock pheasant by their ankles, upside down. He was terribly pleased with himself, but he tried to act nonchalant. He looked so happy, so full of energy, so young for his age. No one who saw him that day, in his loose hunting jacket, his face flushed from a morning in the fields, would have believed that he was forty-two. I gave him a kiss.

There was some kind of ball game he wanted to listen to that afternoon, so after lunch, we all went to the greenhouse, which was our favorite place in the world to be. Harry was listening to his game and I was puttering with the plants, when suddenly the radio seemed to go dead. For some reason, when that happens, even if you're not really listening, you pause in whatever you're doing and a feeling comes over you that something important is about to happen. I distinctly remember a quick feeling of dread when that radio went silent, and then a new voice of someone who seemed to be trying, unsuccessfully, to contain his horror.

"We interrupt this program to bring you a bulletin." The words that abruptly changed the lives of every American. "The president has just announced that Japanese warplanes have attacked Pearl Harbor. A state of war has been declared."

Harry and I looked at each other, stunned. I was trembling with fear, and I wanted to cry out, but I saw the children out of the corner of my eye. They seemed to be looking at us for reassurance. We listened to the news report in silence until it was over, and then the announcer asked us listeners to stand by for further bulletins. I went over to Harry and took his hand in mine and said, "Thank goodness you're too old." Unfortunately, my voice was filled with emotion and the words came out a little too loudly, a little too uncertainly. Harry seemed lost in thought, and when I looked at his face, I knew where his mind was. The children, understanding less than we at that moment, quickly asked if Daddy was going to be a soldier. The girls wanted to know if he would wear a uniform, and little Harry asked if he would carry a gun.

It was less than a week later when I said good-bye to Harry. The realization that he was gone hit me terribly hard. I tried to pretend that the war would be over in a year, but every news report from the Pacific seemed to be telling me, personally, to start being realistic. I spent the first nights alone crying into my pillow.

I moved the family to Mayfields, where we found a warm welcome from Mother and more comfort than a family deserves to enjoy in wartime. I was always on call, ready to hurry to the navy yard whenever Harry even guessed that he might be docking. I saved all my gas rations for those special trips.

The navy was so desperate for new naval officers that Harry wasn't even given a leave when his training was over. But when he called from his new station, the Jacksonville Naval Base, he had some good news. He had taken a house outside of the base—for how long, no one could tell.

I closed the house with sadness, and worry for the future, but grateful that we could all be together again for a little while at least. The children said good-bye to all their stuffed animals, which had been loved to shaggy rags. Our troop train to Florida was jam-packed with soldiers and sailors and military relatives with priority, such as our little family, but somehow room was found for Augie and Otto, our dachshunds, and the children's new kitten. Mother had a picnic made for our two-day journey. It included iced duck and eggs en gel, *which seemed hardly appropriate.*

Life was bearable in Jacksonville. There was a good public school nearby for the children, but life was too temporary, too fraught with rumors and anxiety, even to think about decorating our small rented house. Let's just say it was very American, before and after our stay. We had lived there for just over a year when word came that Harry's carrier, the San Jacinto, *would soon be ready for trial runs and he was to report to Pennsylvania. The news was a shock, even though I had thought about it constantly and had known it would be coming someday.*

When he left for the Pacific on a carrier, I took an apartment in New York, did Red Cross canteen work, and joined a firm called Budget Decorators. It was 1943. I was thirty-three years old.

Harry was gone for two and a half years. His letters were sad and lonely and terribly serious, and I prayed each night that it would be over soon. He told me that the only laugh he had in the Pacific was a time when he was under fire, and preparing for a typhoon to hit, and he received a package from me. It contained a pair of silk pajamas and some frogs' legs. I'm afraid that I pictured him lounging in a deck chair.

Most of his letters were about our future. He never wanted to commute again. He had definitely decided that Harry was to go to St. Paul's School, where three generations of Parishes had gone. Even in action in the Pacific, his thoughts were on the importance of family continuity.

APPLE: In Jacksonville, Mummy really took charge. There she coped with everything—cooking, shopping, and all the household chores. She always claimed that she liked to cook, but, fortunately, she always had the most marvelous cooks both in New York and in Maine. Good food was very important to her, but she gave me this advice when I was first married. "It doesn't make any difference how simple the meal is. What is important is how it's presented. Put it on a nice plate, with a pretty napkin, and you'll be all set."

While we were living in Florida, my grandmother Kinnicutt came down from New York by train to stay with us. There had been a gruesome train murder, in which a passenger had her head chopped off in a sleeping bunk. My grandmother simply put her feet where her head should be, and she arrived safe and sound. We thought her very brave.

My brother, Harry, found his first girlfriend, Bunky Reed, in our backyard circus, where she was the star acrobat. My poor sister, D.B., got a severe case of impetigo and had to have all her hair shaved off. We all called her "Tommy," even though she was still in her dress and pinafore.

SUSAN: Sister saved all of Harry's letters from the war. They are pages and pages long and describe life on the aircraft carrier and his longing for her and the children.

> My Dearest,
> ... everything continues on in its usual routine and makes you feel you never had any other kind of life; this one is real and the other existence of all that we loved is a dream. . . . I am so terribly proud of you, my sweet, and all that you are doing to keep things intact at home. . . . I love to try and plan in my mind the best possible vacation for us when I return. What shall we do? . . . God bless you, my dearest one, and keep you safe for me always—
> I love you and always will,
> Harry

Hallway in the Parishes' Seventy-ninth Street apartment.

Sister's bedroom in the Parishes' Seventy-ninth Street apartment.

Albert Hadley's apartment in New York around the time he met Sister.

The Summer House living room.

The living room at the Whitneys' house in Saratoga.

The Edgar Bronfman apartment in New York.

Sister's library at 920 Fifth Avenue.

Sister's living room at 920 Fifth Avenue.

The Parishes in Jacksonville, Florida, before Harry was sent to the Pacific.

Enough has been written about what it is like when a husband and father comes home from war. It is a wonderful time, in which you feel a sense of love and joy and relief greater than you know you could possibly ever feel again. You are together again. Your family has survived. Permanence has at last come back into your life. But, of course, it is a difficult time, as well. Time and war change people—that is inevitable, and nothing else should be expected. I found that Harry had aged noticeably when he returned. The picture in my mind had been the almost too young-looking man in his hunting jacket, bursting with energy. Two and a half years in the Pacific war zone had taken the glint out of his eyes, had turned the sides of his hair gray, had given him asthma, which was turning into emphysema, and had made him more serious than I had ever known him to be. But he was home, and he was Harry, and our reunion was glorious.

Harry was true to his word about not commuting, and, in 1944, we moved to New York for good. Our farmhouse in Far Hills was to be for weekends only. We took a lovely apartment on Sutton Place, and I was free again to do my favorite kind of decorating, making our home beautiful.

I poured all my feelings for warmth and security and "home" into our new living room. I had a high ceiling, long windows, and big French doors. I again bleached the floor, this time adding a rich stain in a herringbone pattern. Above each window, gilded poles with white melon finials held the swooping coral silk curtains that flowed to the floor, forming crumpled pools of silk.

I have a vivid memory of columns of sunlight streaming onto those lovely floors, of the walls looking like rich, dark soil, of endless sofas covered in chintz that made you think of beds of tulips and daffodils, of saffron yellow freesia and white narcissus sitting in old baskets, candles everywhere, and the luxury of the warm fire burning in the fireplace. I can smell the wax and the flowers and remember how I felt when the room was done—no one could dream of more.

APPLE: I think that the war changed Daddy immensely. He was on the aircraft carrier USS *San Jacinto*, which I believe was involved in many serious battles in the Pacific. He sent us photos of the Japanese kamikaze planes exploding right alongside his ship. I can't remember where or when his ship came to dock, but it may have been New York, because he took us all aboard. To a little girl, it was an awesome sight; it was enormous and scary, with huge guns. It gave us a mental picture of what his days and nights had been like. His letters were so sad, and it was apparent that he was counting the days and wondering when it would be over and he could come home.

As I remember it, life after the war settled down into a pattern of increased work for Mum, boarding school for Harry, D.B., and me, and Wall Street for Daddy. I know he was happy and relieved to be home. If he had vowed that Wall Street would never consume his life, then he was making good on that promise. He was at ease wherever his family was, and he reveled in civilian life again.

I worked hard for Budget Decorating during the war years; there were plenty of apartments in New York and houses on Long Island that needed help. It soon occurred to me that I was working too hard, that I was actually carrying the office. That's when I discovered that partnerships only work when they are just that, partnerships. If they ever become unequal, they should be dissolved. After about a year and a half, I resigned from Budget Decorating and took back the name Mrs. Henry Parish II Interiors. I moved into a small shop with wonderful potential at 22 East Sixty-ninth Street, where I was for the next thirty years.

I suppose that the rooms I decorated during those terrible years all looked pretty much alike. I still had limited knowledge, and of course it was a time of scarcity and austerity. However, I did know the words comfort and color. And I did know how to make a room work. That seems to have been appreciated by my clients, and they remembered when the war was over.

As I look back on that period, my favorite house belonged to the C. Champe Taliaferros. They asked me to do their house on Long Island, and I decided to be bold. It was the first time that I had tried bleaching the floors, and I'm afraid that my client was every bit as nervous as I was. When the workers began rubbing the bleach into the floor, she asked nerve-racking little questions. "It won't look blotchy, will it?... Are we going to lose the grain completely?... You don't suppose the wood is too soft for this, do you?" How relieved I was when we finally looked down at the result. We filled the room with old wood furniture. The curtains were honey-colored taffeta. I left them unlined, so they blew through the working shutters and made that rustling sound that only taffeta can make—like a beautiful ball gown. The chandelier was painted tole. It had crystal tassels and thirty candles. It was lovely to see and becoming to everyone. You would leave dinner thinking you had been in a small château somewhere in France. Off the big room was a part that we turned into a combined library and small dining room. I filled it with marvelous cool green pots of ferns. As an experiment, we pasted vinyl white wall covering on the floors. The pattern was large squares. It lasted for years and years, to the wonderment of all. I had taken a good many chances, but the experiments worked. It was very encouraging.

After the tragedy, chaos, uncertainty, and disruption of the war years, America only wanted to settle down again, get back to normal. People were refocusing their attention on their homes, I was by now fairly well established as a decorator, and so it was time to sprout my wings. I was suddenly terribly busy—far too busy to please Harry, who had successfully reestablished himself in the financial world, and so busy that my guilt over the children was becoming an obsession. I called them constantly, from whatever part of the world I happened to be in, to ask them how they were getting on. I had to learn to get used to their exasperated replies. "I'm terribly sorry, Mother," young Harry once told me over the long-distance wire, "but nothing terribly dramatic seems to have happened since your last call a half hour ago."

But the work was challenging. Two of the more interesting challenges were presented to me by the Thomas Emerys, who were friends of mine from New York. They commissioned me to take the furnishings from a very grand New York apartment and make them work in a farmhouse in Oyster Bay. When that was done, I was to transform a villa in Biarritz into a New York apartment.

In Oyster Bay, I had to marry two opposite worlds. Right on the water, it was a remodeled farmhouse with charm and character. The furniture they had inherited had been designed to fit one of the great high-ceilinged apartments of New York. When I first saw it, I felt sorry for it. It would never find happiness in a farmhouse. But I soon learned that even the unlikeliest of marriages can be made to work in decorating.

When we refinished the old floorboards, then polished them within an inch of their life, we found they were every bit as beautiful as the old parquet in the New York apartment. The materials were all changed from rich, elegant brocades to more simple cottons and flowered chintzes.

A large room had been added to the farmhouse at some early date, and to make the elegant, overscaled New York furniture feel at home here, we rechristened it "the ballroom." Thus the tapestries that the Emerys had inherited, the very finest, could be rehung happily. Once they were installed, the Louis IX and XVI commodes and armchairs came willingly into the room, seemingly unmindful of the fact that they had been created for a colder, more majestic setting. What pulled it all together was the pale pink-and-green Aubusson rug. Even the glittering candled chandelier didn't seem to mind the fact that it was hanging from less than half its accustomed height. I then added a concert grand piano. At night, Thomas Emery would sit at the piano with the candles lit and the fire sending shadows across the room, and you felt as though you were in a room tucked away at Versailles. The Emerys were enchanted, and soon they offered me their second challenge.

They owned a large French villa in Biarritz. Would I go there, have a look, and see if I could make it work in their new apartment in New York?

Biarritz is very cold in the winter, especially if you are staying, as I was, in a summer hotel. The winds were blustering, the sea was roaring continually, and I was alone, feeling like the doomed heroine of a very scary British movie. My mademoiselles *and school French did not help. I was fortunate that Mr. Emery had told his lawyer to meet me at the villa the next day, for otherwise I would have taken the first plane home.*

The villa was marble and was filled with treasures. I was overcome, and at a total loss as to where to begin. In every room, I found important furniture, magnificent chandeliers, graceful mirrors, the finest lacquer tables, great clocks ticking away to the second. The paneling and the mantels were all superb. I walked through the rooms with the plans for the New York apartment tucked under my arm, and my head filled with doubts that I could take all this to New York without a calamity.

I spent my days studying the furnishings, trying to figure out what would fit into the apartment. Inasmuch as I don't understand centimeters, cannot hold a measuring stick, and can't read a scale ruler, I was in a fix. I had somehow gotten away with it before, but this time I was caught. I could rely on my eye, the vivid imagination I was born with, and my heartfelt prayers that I wouldn't make too many outrageous mistakes.

I spent my nights shivering in my hotel room and poring over the plans for the apartment. Only the nightly overseas calls to Harry and the children kept me in touch with any semblance of reality.

In the end, I just picked whatever I liked myself and prayed it would fit.

I met the best packers and cabinetmakers in France. As I marched them through the villa, I would point to something and say in a very low voice, "Pack and ship." I would sweep my arm across paneled walls, floors, mantels, cabinets, and say, "Pack and ship." I'm sure they had no idea of the stark fear that lay behind my commands that day.

The months went by, and I did everything I could to forget Biarritz, to pretend that it had never happened. But the lawyer soon cabled, "Shipment arriving a month from today." For the next thirty days, my anxiety increased by the hour.

Board by board, panel by panel, crate upon crate, walls, doors, floors, arched windows, chairs, sofas, tables, lamps, clocks, priceless vases, all began arriving in huge porto vaults addressed to the Emerys' Fifth Avenue apartment. What now? I thought. I could only hope that the large, fat envelopes that I had handed the shippers upon leaving, and the anxious, pleading look I had given them, had made a difference.

It had. The French had done this monumental job as only they could do it. The packing was a work of art, and there were drawings enclosed for every detail. I began to breathe freely again as the workers reassembled Biarritz in New York. Each numbered board fit its intended mate. After many months, the work was done, and I found, to my astonishment, that my eye had not failed me.

The changes I made when the transition was complete were mostly cosmetic. A villa can be too somber for New York. I added warm chintzes, lots of pillows and flowers, and the largest paneled room, which had been of dark wood, I painted a pale yellow with white trim. The large, graceful mirrors shone across *the park as if they had been designed for that very reflection. The chandeliers glistened elegantly. The lacquer tables mounted with the finest ormolu fell into their new home as if never moved. The great clocks ticked away unhurt, and their chimes seemed to be thanking me. I knew that the proper thanks were due the Emerys for giving me my great experience, and for the big chance they had taken. I loved them for it.*

Opposite page: Inaugural invitation.

Chapter Seven

Jackie: 1953–1960

Soon letters went back and forth between Jackie and myself. I don't know
which one of us was the most naive about the undertaking ahead of us.

—SISTER PARISH

The Inaugural Committee
requests the honor of your presence
to attend and participate in the Inauguration of

John Fitzgerald Kennedy

as President of the United States of America
and

Lyndon Baines Johnson

as Vice President of the United States of America
on Friday, the twentieth of January
one thousand nine hundred and sixty-one
in the City of Washington

Edward H. Foley
Chairman

SUSAN: If Sister had tried to see into the future, I don't think she could have predicted the impact Jackie Kennedy would have on her career. They met sometime in the early fifties, possibly through their mutual friend Bunny Mellon, the wife of philanthropist Paul Mellon, and a close friend of both of theirs. Sister told me that Jackie had beautiful taste, a wicked sense of humor, and a vivid imagination, all qualities Sister valued in her friends. They worked together happily and successfully for more than ten years.

The beginnings of the rift that ended their friendship occurred at the end of Sister's work on the White House. I understand it was primarily a problem over money and Jackie's belief that not everything had to be paid for. Sister wrote that it was because someone had told Jackie that she had kicked Caroline. I wouldn't have put it past her, but that was not the root of the falling-out. Later, Sister would shrug off the questions with one of her glib remarks, like "Jackie got along much better with men than with women." Despite their differences, Sister was enormously proud of her work on the White House. No one who was touched by the magic of Jack and Jackie

Many of Jackie's letters were on this little White House stationery.

Kennedy during those few years of his presidency ever forgot it, and Sister was no exception.

I met Jackie at the Boston airport to make a short jump to Hyannis Port. It was early spring and she was young and gay and bursting with enthusiasm. Her husband was then a senator.

She had written to me that the cottage needed touching up—"Something gay, something fun." I had had several short letters from her describing the house, and I wish I had those letters now, as they were so full of personality and charm. Jackie had drawn little pictures of herself on top of a ladder, measuring for curtains. Next to the sketch, she would write, "I'm a little confused, but add two inches to be on the safe side." Then there would be a small sketch of a sofa, with a note: "The man said eight yards I think, but to be on the safe side make it ten yards. The exact size of a room could be nineteen feet by fifteen feet, but I'm not quite sure."

Hence the trip to Hyannis Port.

Their house in the famed compound was a typical, small Hyannis cottage with green shutters. The porch was pretty, with wicker furniture and a small terrace off of it. My first thought was that it desperately needed color and warmth.

"Let's call Mrs. Fishelson in Boston," I said to Jackie after a brief tour. "We'll have her fill baskets with ferns, tubs of multicolored foxglove, and we'll have her send some of her marvelous flowering begonias and gloxinia."

The living room, in spite of all the wrong measurements, did turn out to be gay and cozy. We used flower chintz, straw rugs, a hooked rug, new Staffordshire lamps, lots of different patterned pillows. With the flowers and the earthenware pots and the woven baskets, a knitted wool blanket to tuck under her chin, and a fire burning, Jackie now had a room that could be cheerful and cozy on those foggy Hyannis nights. She did seem pleased, for I have a telegram saying, "You did the trick and our trip was more than worthwhile. I feel happy. Love, Jackie."

Shortly after we had completed our small project in Hyannis Port, I received a call from Washington. Their house in Georgetown had just been finished. It had been done by her sister, Lee, and Jackie assured me that it was very pretty. She then ventured to tell me that it didn't have the charm she longed for, and no color.

Needless to say, I felt it a delicate situation. The job had been completed, and the other decorator involved was hardly a stranger. But Jackie was very persuasive, and the following week I arrived from New York with a large canvas bag filled with all the delicious things that Jackie had in mind. We had a glorious day in the Georgetown house, and we were overcome with our imaginings of what the enchanting outcome would be.

It did not take long, though, before I had a call from Jackie, who was virtually in tears. The senator had put his foot down. The house had been finished. A great deal of money had been spent. And that was that.

A few months went by, and then Jackie called again. Her voice was filled with her old enthusiasm. Her husband had decided that she could do the house over after all. She wanted to start right away, and though I was very busy, we began our dream again. Who could resist Jackie?

It was not an easy project for me, though the result was quite wonderful. Jackie was joyful about every aspect of the job, but she was pregnant and not feeling well. The work was done during the summer, and she was away most of the time. It was difficult getting her to make decisions, and certainly her husband had no inclination to make them for her.

And working in Georgetown during the summer was the very last thing I needed. Even then, Harry was begging me to stop working so that I could enjoy Maine and be with the children. And of course he was right. My heart was in Dark Harbor, and how guilty I felt every day that I couldn't be there.

But the firm couldn't very well be run without me, for I was the firm. Jackie's undertaking was just one of the many large jobs that had to be done. When I look back on those years, I am astounded at how much I tried to do with so little help. I had only two people working for me, Mrs. Green and Mrs. Adolph. Fortunately for me, they were both extraordinary. I couldn't possibly have accomplished everything I did without them. They taught me an important business lesson: It makes no difference how many people you have working for you, but it makes all the difference who is working for you. They were loyal, skillful, responsible, hardworking, and, until they had the good sense to retire, utterly indispensable. Thanks to them, we somehow got the Georgetown house completed by the end of the summer. Everything had been done over. The house vibrated with color. Jackie was thrilled. The senator seemed pleased as well, but he was too busy to enjoy it fully. He was running for president.

That November, I was lunching at a New York restaurant, when I was called to the telephone. It was Mrs. Green, and I could tell that she was bursting with some piece of news.

"I am not allowed to use any names," she said breathlessly, "but you have been asked to come to a big white house next month."

I did not take it in, and told her to be explicit.

"It has big white columns," she said. "In front."

I finally got it. Jackie's husband had just been elected president of the United States. Her next decorating job was about to begin. Mrs. Green wouldn't even let me ask questions about it over the telephone—she had been given strict instructions to keep the project absolutely secret. I didn't breathe a word to anyone when I went back to the table.

Soon letters went back and forth between Jackie and myself. I don't know which one of us was the most naïve about the undertaking ahead of us. I told her I would buy all the books I could find concerning the White House, and go to the public library to look up any blueprints that might be there. It was quite funny. I did spend hours in the library, and when I couldn't find what I wanted, I would get terribly upset and drive the librarians to distraction.

It never occurred to either Jackie or me that the First Lady-to-be might very simply call the White House and request any item that she might like to see. It wasn't until I had exhausted the library's research material, which I found quite skimpy, by the way, that Jackie and I finally came to our senses.

There was a slight problem of protocol involved in actually getting inside the White House, but Jackie was not easily deterred. By custom, outgoing presidents and their wives are not required to divulge any past plans or arrangements of the rooms or encourage the next occupants to come to the White House. But Jackie called Mrs. Eisenhower and asked, with the charm that only she could muster, for special permission to see the White House. Her baby had just been born and she wanted to make sure there was a nice place next to the master bedroom where little John could sleep. Of course, Mamie Eisenhower said she would be delighted to have Jackie over.

Jackie immediately called me with good news. I was to hurry to Washington, and we could start work as soon as we had been through the White House. She had one caution, however. She told me that I was to pretend that I was her secretary. I was to follow her around the White House and look as though I was taking shorthand, while observing every single detail of the rooms.

Naturally, I was thrilled at the opportunity, but on thinking it over, I decided that it was a rather strange way to start my undertaking at the White House. And it occurred to me that it could be embarrassing for both of us if someone I knew happened to spot me entering the White House grounds disguised as her secretary. I told her that she would just have to do without me.

Jackie went, of course. Since she had just had the baby, she appeared in a wheelchair. She was personally shown through the White House by Mrs. Eisenhower.

She didn't miss a thing. As soon as she left, she called me, and it was then I realized that Jackie did not have two big eyes—she had dozens. Every room was observed, down to the last detail. Jackie had never sounded so excited, for she had what she knew was a great challenge.

Now we had only to wait for the inauguration. Jackie went to Palm Beach to be with her family and her father-in-law, and I went to California to see my children and grandchildren.

I had only been there for a few days when I received a call from Bill Walton, who was one of the president's staff and a close friend of his as well. He told me that Jackie had decided that she and the president needed a nice house in Middleburg, Virginia, where they could go on weekends to escape the pressures of the White House.

He told me he was about to rent a country house for the Kennedys in Middleburg, although they had not seen it. I told him for goodness sake not to take any house until someone had seen it and that I would return home right away. By the time I returned east, however, he had already rented it for a year, completely furnished. So another considerable undertaking was at hand.

My assignment sounded quite simple at first. Since they would be renting the weekend house and it was already furnished, I had only to arrange to have some furniture moved from the Georgetown house to the Middleburg house and see that it fitted in with the existing furniture. There couldn't be any dramatic new decorating, I was assured. The owner had specifically stated that the house had to be returned exactly to its original condition when the Kennedys left. I was told that Jackie simply wanted me to make it "cozy."

When I returned from California, I went straight to Middleburg. The house was named Glen Ora. It was charming and comfortable, and I thought it was perfect for what Jackie wanted.

But Jackie, with her love of houses and her feeling for color and comfort, could not be content with things as they were. She would decide that new wallpaper was needed here, new curtains were needed there, and wouldn't this room be improved with lovely new rugs, and wouldn't that room be nicer with large, friendly chairs?

I kept reminding her that it had to be returned to its original condition. Her answer would be to suggest that we add an extra dressing room and bath— which we did.

THE WHITE HOUSE
WASHINGTON

Dear Sister —

I Think I have found some perfect things for Oval Room

A PAIR OF XVI CONSOLES I couldn't believe my eyes when I peeked through D'Alva window —

I told all the stores you would call them — so could you have these things sent down — & dont pay bills for a while — as you have to live with them a couple of weeks to see if they are ok

One of Jackie's letters to Sister.

And I'm sure that the original owner never considered what really happens to a house when a president moves in—even if it's only for weekends. Hundreds of workmen started rewiring the circuits, putting in special telephone lines and security systems. Heaven knows what it cost to put it all in, and I knew that it would cost even more to take it all out again. Soon Glen Ora had been completely transformed into Jackie's idea of a "cozy" home and into the headquarters for the president and commander in chief.

I went to Glen Ora for the last touches just after the inauguration. I had a White House car, which bravely carried me through the high banks of snow that remained after the inaugural blizzard. I had to admit that the house did look like Jackie. I fixed the flowers, left a bottle of champagne, and sent my love to Jackie and the president, who had never seen the house. It had all been a big risk, but I felt that they would both be happy there.

As I was closing the door to leave for Washington, suddenly the biggest helicopter I had ever seen dropped out of the sky. It was marked U.S. NAVY, and out stepped a dozen men, including Arthur Schlesinger, Jr., and most of the president's closest advisers.

As they approached the house, I heard myself saying, "You cannot enter this house. It isn't finished, and I won't allow a single soul to enter until it is."

A look of surprise mixed with anger came over their faces.

"Who the hell are you?" one of them asked, his eyes icy.

I told them my name was Sister Parish, and orders were orders. They were not to enter.

It ended happily, as they removed their shoes and agreed not to sit on anything. They even invited me back in their helicopter when their inspection was over. They asked me where I wanted to land, and for some inexplicable reason, I said, "The Pentagon." That sounded fine to them, and they called ahead to have a White House car meet me at the door of the plane.

APPLE: Having Mummy involved in the redecoration of the White House made the Kennedy years an exciting part of Joe's and my life in Washington. We had been living in Georgetown, as Joe was a clerk for Chief Justice Warren in 1960 and 1961.

Mummy brought Jackie to tea at our house after the election. The Secret Service were hanging around, and Jackie wasn't used to that at all.

Jackie was very helpful about getting our son, Charlie, into a local play group. When Caroline had a birthday party, Charlie was invited. I was obviously more excited than he was, and totally undone when he developed a terrible cold and high fever on the big day. I almost took him, but in the end, I decided that it wouldn't be too good an idea to infect the president-elect's daughter with some dread sickness. I did take Charlie by in his stroller. There were crowds of people outside the house, all agog, just like me.

When the Kennedys moved into the White House, Charlie was also a part of the play school, which was upstairs in the family quarters, in a big sunlit room. I remember one day taking him to the elevator, and, to my surprise, the elevator stopped to let the president on board. There we were, Charlie and my seven-months-pregnant self.

The only other time I went to the White House was to help fix the flowers for a state dinner. Mummy thought I would like to do this, and she was obviously right. First, Mr. West gave us a grand tour, including the kitchens. It was all so magical. The dining room was filled with buckets of flowers waiting to be arranged. Every flower you could ever dream of was at our disposal. Mummy and Jackie definitely had the same taste and ideas for decorating— beautiful tablecloths to the floor, marvelous china, and, of course, the flowers.

The first time I actually saw Jackie after the election was at my daughter's house in Washington. I particularly recall this meeting, as it was the first time she was accompanied by a Secret Service man. She told me that if this was the way her private life was going to be, it was appalling.

ELIZABETH "TIZZIE" KINNICUTT (Sister's niece): Sister did extraordinary things for me, but the biggest thing she did for me was to get me into the White House. Sister was my godmother as well as being my aunt, and there were times when I felt she really was my fairy godmother. She knew I had such a crush on Jackie Kennedy, and I think my father, Frankie, said to Sister just before he died, "Tizzie sure does love Jackie Kennedy, the way she looks at every photograph like she's the Queen Mother." He must have said to Aunt Sister, "If you could ever get Tizzie into the White House . . ." He was terribly impressed that she was decorating there. Mummy and Daddy were so amazed. That was the pinnacle. Here Daddy was working with Boston Irish Catholic juveniles, and he kidded with them a lot. For the times, what could have been more interesting?

This was in the spring of 1961, and it was springtime in Washington, so I was fourteen years old. I went down on the night train, and Apple met me, because she had a house in Georgetown then. Then she got me to the White House and I went in and met Jackie and Letitia Baldrige. First, Letitia took me around for a quick pass over through the public rooms. Then we went up in an elevator to the private living quarters. I remember this large sort of reception room with many rooms off it. The Lincoln bedroom was one of them. Then I saw Caroline's room, and I remember beautiful crisp white material. The thing I remember best was John-John's room, because he was in a cradle or bassinet, all very frilly and beautiful. Jackie took me over to a window that looked out onto one of the White House lawns. There was a nurse just standing in the background with us, all in white. I remember Jackie had on this simple short-sleeved blue dress, her signature. We just sat and talked a little bit. Most of it was just her being polite to this fourteen-year-old girl. It lasted twenty minutes, and then she ushered me down. I got myself back, and then it was just a school day. Everything had been stopped and rearranged for me to have a private audience at the White House.

Opposite page: Picture of the Yellow Oval Room.

Chapter Eight

The White House: 1960–1963

They had to have a family life up on that second floor. They had to put in a
kitchen and make the dining room livable and attractive. They couldn't have
the children go down to that family dining room on the main reception floor.

LETITIA BALDRIGE

SUSAN: Of course, when a newspaper article proclaimed KENNEDYS PICK NUN
TO DECORATE WHITE HOUSE, Sister's office was never the same. At that point,
she was alone, with only one assistant decorator and two additional staff people working for her at 22 East Sixty-ninth Street. All of a sudden, she was in
the spotlight, working for the most talked-about couple of our time.

From her point of view, she was there first and foremost to make the
White House a place where a young family could live. For Sister, everything
had to be "appropriate," so when she got her first look at the White House,
she was appalled. The White House, as it appeared during the Eisenhower

administration, did not look the way, nor was it run in the manner, a house of that stature was supposed to. The first problem was that the White House budget was minimal. For example, there was no money allocated for alcohol at state functions. There were so few funds allocated for fresh flowers that the ones Letitia Baldrige saw on a tour while the Eisenhowers were still in residence "wouldn't be fit for the cook's quarters," as she put it.

On top of the lack of basic necessities (the Eisenhowers were using an army cook, as well) such as good food and fresh flowers, many of the rooms were neglected and lackluster, furnished with department-store furniture and cheap hotel-style objects.

For Sister and Jackie, the first order of business was to make the private quarters cozy and attractive for Jackie's husband and small children.

LETITIA BALDRIGE: Jackie chose Mrs. Parish because she knew she was a woman of quality and taste, and that was very important to her. They'd already worked together before on the Kennedys' Georgetown house. Jackie felt comfortable with her. They were from the same social group. They knew the same people. That's always helpful, too. You can gossip while you work. Sister had a tremendous sense of what was proper and refined. Her voice was intimidatingly refined. She was concerned with making it a house where a young family could live with taste, which would remind them of what they'd had before, elegant and attractive and warm, warm, warm.

I'd been to the White House before several times, and I was always in awe of it. In my mind, the White House could not be wrong because it was the president's house. I just couldn't find fault with it. But then I realized it was all of our jobs to find fault with it, so we could make it better. That is when I realized all the faults that it did have.

I'd had a lot of experience by the time I went to the White House. I was trained in Paris by Evangeline Bruce and learned about foreign service, diplomacy, protocol, and entertaining. It was the best training I ever could have gotten. At the White House, I used all that I'd learned. As far as the running of the White House, the logistics of making people happy and trying to balance the family, and the friends who couldn't get to Jackie—that was really my job, to balance and juggle all of that. You had to pick up whatever you saw that needed to be done. You just did it. You didn't even ask questions. Everyone was on tiptoe the whole time. The house had been run like the military because the Eisenhowers and, before them, the Trumans were both military—and because of the war, there had been a military feeling.

SUSAN MARY ALSOP (family friend and author who was married to columnist Joseph Alsop): It was alarming. The first time we went there, the first thing we were shown by Jackie were the televisions marked HIS and HERS with large signs. It was odious and yet pathetic, because the Eisenhowers were terribly nice people. They just didn't know about houses. Jackie must have really needed someone like Sister, who was so practical.

My first trip to the Kennedys' new home began at five o'clock in the morning the day before the inauguration. The car had been loaded the night before with three large blue duffel bags, stuffed with swatches and samples marked "White House." Before I left, Harry argued that I shouldn't drive, that the weather report looked bad, that someone else could drive the samples to Washington. I simply waved good-bye as cheerfully as I could. I felt very responsible for the contents of those duffel bags, and I was determined to deliver them personally.

Mrs. Green, my secretary and office manager, was to drive with me as far as Baltimore, where she would be visiting her parents. I had to stop in Far Hills to leave Yummy, my beloved Pekingese, in the kennels. It was the first time that I had not taken him with me on a job, but when I thought of the confusion of the inauguration, and of Jackie's cat, I concluded that it might be better to go without him. Jackie's cat was bigger than Yummy, and more aggressive.

We had not gone more than half an hour after dropping off Yummy when the snow began to fall. Harry was right, I thought as the snow began to accumulate on the windshield and I found myself having to strain my eyes just to see the road ahead. It soon turned into the most perilous trip that anyone could have taken. I had no control over my car, nor did other people have of theirs. There was accident after accident every half mile. Poor Mrs. Green was in a panic as we slithered ahead in the left lane, passing hundreds of stalled cars. She had only to look at the white of my knuckles as I gripped the wheel to see that I was just as panicked as she was. We managed to get to Baltimore, and when I dropped her off at a service station, she begged me not to go on. But, by now, I had decided I was on a crucial mission, and I was determined to get through. The miles between Baltimore and Washington were a nightmare. I don't know how many times I either landed in a ditch or spun around, ending up facing backward. My main worry was not to turn upside down with everything in the car marked "White House."

When I finally reached the approaches to Washington, everything in the road had come to a standstill for miles. All I could think of was how much some of my friends in Maine would appreciate this sight—the nation's capital brought to its knees by one blizzard. Since no one was going anywhere, I abandoned my car briefly and dashed into a drugstore to call my daughter Apple. Her husband had just been made a clerk in the Supreme Court, and they were living in Washington at the time. It was then 10:30 and I was hungry, panic-stricken, and in tears. Two hours later, I saw my son-in-law walking toward me. The traffic hadn't moved an inch. There was nothing to do but leave the car locked at the curb. We could not carry "the White House" with us.

It never occurred to me to call Jackie for help—just as it had never occurred to me to ask her for a chauffeur to deliver her materials to Washington. Yet I knew how important my mission was to her, how anxious she was to pore over the wonderful things in my duffel bags. I had all the colors, the materials, the new blueprints to make her White House home livable—and I knew that as far as she was concerned, this was her first order of business as our new First Lady.

Apple gave me a bed and I managed to steady my nerves and even get a short, fitful sleep before setting out at four o'clock that morning to retrieve my car and its precious cargo. I enlisted the help of Sumner Wells, whom we had planned to stay with during the inauguration, and who had the rank I thought was needed to get my car out of the snow and into a safe, convenient garage. Even with his assistance, it took another two hours to get the car moving again.

Inauguration Day was bitterly cold, and the snow had made transportation to Washington very problematic. But somehow, Harry managed to fly in, and I was excited and deeply moved as we made our way to the ceremony. Jackie and the president had arranged wonderful seats for us, and I clearly remember how thrilled I felt as I realized that the senator would be president in just a few minutes. Some of our friends spotted us, and they looked in astonishment at the Parishes in such a choice spot. Anyone who knew us knew us as fervent Republicans!

I certainly wasn't feeling Republican or Democrat or anything but a proud American that day. My heart went out to those two beautiful young people. The cold was penetrating, but all any of us felt was exaltation.

Jackie and Douglas Dillon had arranged for us to have front-row seats in a balcony at the Treasury Building for the inaugural parade. As the parade went by, the excitement was intense. At last, I could see the president's car, with the president sitting high up on the backseat and Jackie sitting proudly beside him on the seat itself. Suddenly, she spotted me, and she blew a kiss, and her words to the bewildered president reached us clear as a bell. "That's Sister," she said, waving enthusiastically to me. I was feeling very special as I waved back.

Jackie had kindly sent us invitations to the inaugural balls and to some spe-

cial receptions preceding them, but there Harry drew the line. "Please," he said as generously as he could. "I will do almost anything for you, but please, I am a Republican. No balls." Instead, we had a delightful dinner at Apple's house, with Diana and Reed Vreeland.

SUSAN MARY ALSOP: I don't think Sister missed much not going to the balls. They were not a great feature. The weather was so bad, a lot of people lost their nerve and just didn't bother. There were lots of dinner parties that night. The president sneaked out of the ball and took Jackie back to the White House. She was tired, as she had had a baby not so long ago. Then he thought he could walk to Georgetown. Oh, it was so funny. He didn't realize that leaving the White House is a big thing in itself. He started out as if he were in his own house, and he was instantly hotly pursued, as you can well imagine. He started up Pennsylvania Avenue and the Secret Service grabbed him and said, "Where do you think you are going, sir?" And he said, "I am going to see my old friend, Mr. Joseph Alsop. He lives in Georgetown." So they said, "Jesus Christ," I imagine. They somehow or other got a car that would navigate, and they got to Joe's. It was very snowy. Joe had been receiving all evening, as people had been dropping by. He was quite tired when the doorbell rang. He thought, My God, I just can't answer it. But then he went, and there was this young man with snow in his hair; it was the president.

I had planned to be at the White House Monday morning at 8:30 to start work, but Jackie, obviously eager to get going, said I could come earlier if I wanted. I had hoped for a signed pass so I would have no trouble at the gates, but Jackie said not to worry—just to tell them I'd be coming often. I suspected that she hadn't gotten the hang of White House security yet. My car was in the garage, and because of the storm, finding transportation of any kind was a miracle. Somehow, Harry managed to get his hands on a pink sedan with no fenders, and dangling baby slippers and a jumping monkey hanging from the windshield. I got in, and he drove me right to the front steps of the White House, with no more than a slight rolling of the eyes from the guards.

I will never forget the strange feeling I had walking up those White House steps alone. I thought of my mother visiting President Cleveland, looking like "a piece of tissue paper." With no fuss, the door was opened, and the kindest face appeared, Mr. West, the head usher who had taken care of the needs of three presidents. He became a close friend of mine, and I think of him often.

* * *

LETITIA BALDRIGE: Luckily, J. B. West was an angel and a brilliant man who knew all the aspects of the house, as well as the dirty, dark aspects of the house. He was right there, and he was ever patient and understanding. He went through a terrible lot. He had to referee everybody's fights and never say no to the Kennedys.

Mr. West ushered me to the second floor, where the president and Jackie would be living until the private living quarters of the White House were redone. She was occupying the Queen's Room and he had the Lincoln Room opposite.

Jackie looked so young and touching. She was still feeling miserable after John's birth. We looked at each other, laughed, and said, "Now what do we do?" I assured her that I didn't have an idea in my head, so we laughed again. I realized that we couldn't spend the day laughing, so I finally decided that I should find my duffel bags, which had been delivered the day before, and start sorting things out.

I left the Queen's Room and walked to the living quarters, where the work was to be done. My duffel bags were standing in the middle of the living room, and there were aides at each door who looked like they had been assigned to watch me. I rapidly undid the bags and began sorting things into neat piles marked "Suggestions for the First Lady."

I had samples of materials, wallpaper, rugs, trim, and colors all neatly organized, with blueprints for the First Lady's bedroom, the sitting room, the family room, the president's room, the children's rooms, and so on. They suddenly looked so perfect for a small house on the Maine coast—so unsuitable for the mansion of the president. I had been told that the president wanted to stop by early to pick things for his room, and I suddenly looked up, to see the door to his room opening. I noticed the time on a clock that the Eisenhowers had left behind: 9:45. I watched him walk down the hall toward me, his head high. He had a broad smile as he said, "Is this my pile?"—like a boy making his first big decision. It occurred to me that this would probably be his first decision as president. I hoped he would make the right one.

It took him less than three minutes, and there was no hesitation. He chose a blue-and-white toile covered with angels. He said he had always loved angels, that that's what he wanted—and all over. He kissed Jackie good-bye, the elevator door opened, and off he went to face the real decisions of his life. His presence was so magnetic that it made one proud to be an American.

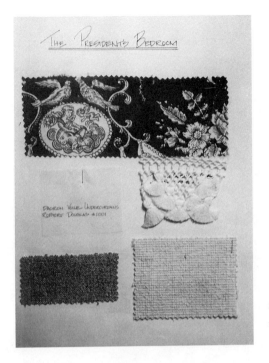

Scheme for President Kennedy's room with the angel toile that the president picked out.

Jackie knew exactly what she wanted in her bedroom. It was to be the same as the one in Georgetown, but blue. Her room was lovely, sunny, gay, and looked like her. She was worried about her closet space, and I jotted that down in my notebook. She had an idea that I loved.

"I want to have window seats that open," she said, "so the children can have a secret hiding place." I jotted it down.

Caroline's room was to have a pattern of small pink roses. For her floor, I had found a handmade multicolored rag rug made by Mrs. Gushee, who lived in the far reaches of Maine. It was perfect, and Jackie adored it. That decision turned out to be quite a boon to the rag-rug artisans of the world, for it launched the rag-rug craze that raged throughout the country.

The family room was somewhat of a problem, as it had one huge arched window. The Eisenhowers had given it a cold, stiff hotel look, and it was all there, including the TV sets. I did everything I could to take away that look. The problem of the arched window was solved with a soft, rather old-fashioned material. The furniture from Georgetown that had not gone to Glen Ora somehow fitted in nicely. The seating arrangement we worked out was comfortable, and the room worked for all. Fortunately, this was the most photographed family in the world, and I had no trouble finding wonderful family pictures to put everywhere.

Schemes for the children's rooms.

Everything, of course, had to be done tomorrow. Finding large stocks of available materials, and workrooms that were not booked, was not a simple problem. But because the client was special, and because the need to move quickly was very real, everyone tried hard, and I tried the hardest.

The budget could have been a problem, but this was Jackie. When I reminded her that the family rooms were on a White House budget, she would just wave her hand, give me her beaming smile, and say, "Hurry on!"

After our first morning of picking over fabrics, I suddenly glanced at the clock; it was 1:30. Jackie looked at me questioningly and asked, "What do you suppose we do about lunch?"

I mumbled something about calling Joe Alsop and seeing if he would take us to lunch. We didn't want to take the time to go out, and we were ready to forgo lunch altogether, when I suggested that we call that nice Mr. West and ask him. He laughed and said the entire White House staff had been waiting downstairs to see what Mrs. Kennedy would want. Her quick answer was soup and hamburgers that we could eat on trays in the room where we were working. She added that she'd rather not have anyone wait on us. The poor hovering men

looked sad not to help. Jackie also said, as Mr. West was leaving, "Do you sup-
pose we might have just a little wine?" Mr. West thought he could find one crock
that the Eisenhowers had left.

The lunch arrived almost immediately, but just as we had started, the pres-
ident suddenly popped in to see what was up. He greeted us with a cheery "Hi!"
He announced that he had just had a glass of Metrocal and was finished. Saying
that, he proceeded to clean our plates and then went off down the stairs with a
parting "I'll see you later." Jackie loved the wine, finished the crock, and then
wondered if she should fill it with water so that word would not get around that
she had taken to the bottle.

We worked a bit longer after lunch, until Jackie, on doctor's orders, had to
take a nap. While she was resting, I had a chance to wander around alone and
think what really could be done to make the White House more a home for them.
I knew that Jackie's dread was to have to live a formal, unfamily life.

As I toured the cold, badly laid-out family areas, it was apparent that if you
took Margaret Truman's music room and President Eisenhower's studio, along
with several smaller areas, you could have space for a nice new kitchen and a
wonderful upstairs dining room.

One of the first things I did was to convince Jackie that she should have an
upstairs family unit. There was no kitchen, no dining room. The previous first
families had had to go downstairs to the public areas of the White House to dine
or to go into the kitchen. So that morning, we had made the decision: Margaret
Truman's bedroom was to be a large, workable kitchen; President Eisenhower's
"painting room" would become the children's dining room; another room would
be for Caroline, and finally a room for John-John. Mrs. Kennedy's foremost
thought at all times was to have the children as close to her as possible.

I jotted down a few notes and took measurements my usual way—eyesight
and wild guesswork. When Jackie joined me again, she was full of enthusiasm
for the idea. Blueprints were to be started immediately.

Later, when Jackie went off to one of her functions, I had a chance to spend
a few hours downstairs. Clearly, it had been a long time since the rooms used for
state functions had been touched. They really were tattered, worn, and seemed
to have no rhyme or reason. I felt sad for the neglected rooms. It disturbed me
deeply to know that these badly designed, poorly maintained rooms belonged to
the United States. This was the White House. What did the kings and queens and
great statesmen of the world think when they came to our president's home? In

their eyes, this was America's palace. I shuddered when I thought what an impression these shabby, inconsequential rooms must make.

I left with my imagination working full force, and looking forward to a dream that someday might come true.

The next few weeks were devoted to our crash program with the Kennedys' living quarters. Jackie seemed terribly alone and lonely. The children were in Palm Beach, she missed them, and what she had to face was gigantic. She seemed not ready for it. I, too, was scared. Harry had gone, no Yummy, and my office in New York was being neglected.

Finally, we got all the orders in, and Mrs. Green and my assistant, Richard Nelson, came from New York to help. It was a miracle the way everyone rallied around to help. The fabric houses put through special orders, the workshops put people on overtime, and everyone involved seemed genuinely enthusiastic about getting the Kennedys into their new home. Gradually, sofas, chairs, and curtains started to arrive. The kitchen flew up, and the dining room was a miracle.

When the work was nearly done, our vision for these family rooms was becoming a warm, cheerful, comfortable reality. I then ventured to talk to Jackie in a serious way about my dream for the White House.

The following days were spent in planning, organizing, attic hunting, and exploring and working on many details. The different kinds of flowers and their arrangements for all the rooms were planned. Through David Finley, who was the chairman of a government Commission on Fine Arts, we determined which Washington parks we could draw on to have plants for White House use. I remember one desperate moment when it was discovered there were no ashtrays, so I went back to New York and bought Lowestoft reproductions for White House smokers. I discovered there was no linen except for official use. With Mr. West, I went through all the silver, china, and glass, afterward buying new sets. Even menus from years past were gone over carefully. And we searched from attic to cellar for furniture, draperies, anything that would be suitable for the new White House. We found a beautiful four-poster bed and also the bed that President Kennedy used.

On the second morning of that first week, Mrs. Kennedy and I invaded the president's office, switching furniture about, rehanging pictures, and surveying the office for improvements. The president was agreeable to everything, but he told us firmly that he must have his rocker and that it could not be removed. Mrs. Kennedy winked at me and said, "We will get it out somehow." As the whole world knows, the rocker remained. But the seat was re-covered in tweed that very *afternoon. The careful scrutiny of every room and the examining of every piece of furniture to determine if it should be replaced or re-covered continued throughout the week. Old curtains that had been stored away were taken out and appraised to see if they could be used again. Any piece of furniture we unearthed that did have historical interest was quickly put to use. Throughout all this, Mr. West was a fund of knowledge and unceasingly helpful. Nothing was too much in his desire to help us.*

During this initial period, Mrs. Kennedy was not feeling well, but she worked tirelessly. She was beginning to feel the enormous pressures of her position and its tremendous responsibilities. But with the arrival of the children from Florida, there was instant gaiety among the staff and throughout the White House. Caroline provided constant comic relief, running through the halls, hiding off corridors—and often naked!

After six weeks, President and Mrs. Kennedy's new upstairs quarters looked like a cozy, warm house with a comfortable family personality. Children's possessions were everywhere, and there was a definite glow about the house.

SUSAN MARY ALSOP: When we went to the White House, we never went into the state rooms if we were just going there to a cozy dinner. So we really felt that the upstairs, which Sister had decorated, was the place where they lived.

LETITIA BALDRIGE: They had to have a family life up on that second floor. They had to put in a kitchen and make the dining room livable and attractive. They couldn't have the children go down to that family dining room on the main reception floor. It would have been impossible. They had their friends dine there in the upstairs dining room, too, and never used the dining room on the first floor—which was called the family dining room—except for lunches on very limited occasions. Mostly, it was used as a dressing area for the waiters, a place to take off their coats, to get their trays filled, and to put their gloves on and take them off. It was a messy room, used for everything.

I've never seen anything happen so fast. Don't forget the National Park Service workmen worked and worked to have the top people who put in furniture stains and lacquers and all that. They had top people painting in the state dining room and doing the fancy stuff like tromp l'oeil. They didn't use regular craftsmen; they used super-craftsmen. They did it fast because it was the White House. The White House can do anything.

* * *

JOAN DILLON DE MOUCHY: President Kennedy called to invite me to dinner in the family quarters along with Tip O'Neill and Dave Powers. When I hedged about accepting, he immediately said, "But you must come and see Sister Parish's decorating. We have little cushions all over the place. I know that you are great friends, and I am sure that it will interest you to see what she has done."

So I went to the White House for dinner to see Mrs. Parish's decorating. There were lots of small pillows, and all rooms, including the Lincoln Bedroom, were done with great taste. I gasped only once, and that was when I saw the president's bathroom. It was covered with mirrors from floor to ceiling, and the ceiling itself was a mirror. The president roared with laughter and said, "Oh, no. Not Sister Parish. This magnificent bathroom was done by Eisenhower." Eventually, I became a friend of JFK, who often teased me about how he had gotten on my good side "thanks to Sister Parish."

I remember one small incident during those early, hectic weeks that is typical of the warmth one felt being with this young couple. They had a favorite cat, Tom-Kitten, who had been with them on N Street. The doctor decided, however, that the president was allergic to Tom-Kitten and that he had to be taken away. Mrs. Kennedy and I were standing alone in the ballroom when she turned and saw two men bringing Tom-Kitten's box down the stairs. She asked them to bring the box to her and open it. She then sat down on the ballroom floor, hugging Tom-Kitten over and over again. I asked her gently if I might have a car to drive me the airport. She replied, "If Tom-Kitten can have two men to take him away in a box, I don't see why you can't have one man to take you to the plane."

OATSIE CHARLES (family friend): Sister was an enormous help to Jackie with colors, thoughts, everything. God knows, that yellow Oval Room was one of the prettiest rooms I have ever seen. It was basically the upstairs sitting room, and with the fire going and all of the flowers and the candles lit, and the views of the Washington Monument, it was unbelievable beautiful. The second floor was divine. Sister chintzed it up and made it lovely.

KEITH IRVINE (decorator): Jackie was a very thoughtful person. She was very unusual and interesting. She could have done it all herself—decorating or whatever she was trying to do. She was so clever at seducing you with charming notes and little drawings. At one point after she had married Onassis, she was using both me and Billy Baldwin. They would call from the Olympic offices in the morning and say that Mrs. Onassis wanted such and such, and that it had to be there today, so it could be on the Olympic flight that night. I found out afterward that she was asking Billy Baldwin and me for all the same things, and whoever got it cheaper or got it there first got the sale. She was very clever, but she was also an admirable human being. The rooms Mrs. Parish did upstairs at the White House were fabulous. The yellow room was magic. It had an American purity about it, with this lovely lighthearted French injection. It was the combination of purity and a little French excitement, all done with a palette that was so sunshiny.

MARK HAMPTON (former Parish-Hadley decorator): I had some hilarious letters from Jackie, which are now in the White House archives. The usher said, "Oh, sure, read them. I know you are interested in them, and I know you know Jackie." She did write these adorable letters. She'd write to Mr. West, the head usher, who'd given the letters. She'd say, "Now, dear Mr. West, I'm off for Hyannis tomorrow. While I'm gone don't let Mrs. Engelhard or Mr. du Pont do anything crazy in the White House."

Then she'd send a letter from Palm Beach with a little tiny piece of material pinned to a piece of paper, and—it's so hilarious—she'd say, "This is Mrs. Wrightsman's shower curtain. Could we have curtains in this fabric in the breakfast room?"

If you look at the early photographs of the private quarters, you see them as Sister left them. That's really her work.

SUSAN: Sister and Jackie spent the entire budget allocated for the decoration of the White House on the private quarters during the first two weeks. They both felt that the rest of the house had to be tackled as well, and there was no money left. Sister told us many times to "start at the top," and it seemed that she and Jackie put this philosophy to work in concocting a plan to call on the most knowledgeable, intelligent, and, in Sister's words, "rich" friends of theirs to come together and solicit donations for the restoration of the state rooms. Thus the Fine Arts Committee was born and the historic restoration of the White House began. Mr. Henry du Pont, the preeminent historian and collector, was chosen as chairperson; Jackie was honorary chairperson. Sister was a member, along with many of her close friends, including Mrs. Charles Engelhard, Mrs. Douglas Dillon, Mr. John Loeb, Mrs. Paul Mellon. This committee's goal was to restore, not redecorate, and a premium was placed on historical integrity.

The group was bound together by scholarship, as well as by fund-raising ability, which resulted in bringing many valuable objects and the best of American furniture and paintings back to the White House. It soon became a matter of prestige to make a donation to the White House restoration.

When Mrs. Kennedy had seen all the rooms in the White House for the first time, she was in despair. We both came to the decision that the White House was to be done not only for their own personal comfort but, more important, for the whole country. Our imaginations ran wild, and the second morning in her bedroom, we discussed a master plan as to how the whole White House could be transformed into something of lasting value for all Americans.

She was sitting in her lovely four-poster bed, all eyes and ears, waiting to hear my plans. Why not form a special committee to redo the White House room by room—to return it, as nearly as possible, to its original state. We would need a small committee of the most intelligent, knowledgeable people we could find.

"They should also be rich," I added.

We got so excited, both of us, and we were filled with ideas, but we were really not quite sure how to start. I called David Finley, who was very close to the White House and knew its history intimately. He felt it was a brilliant idea, and he agreed to meet us in the morning in Jackie's room.

I worked hours that night, making a list of people for the committee. It was quite a list. Certainly everyone on it was intelligent, knowledgeable, and rich, and I thought they were all extremely well known. Jackie, being so much younger, hadn't heard of most of them—possibly because a lot happened to be Republicans. However, it didn't take her long to check them out, and she approved the majority of names. As time went on, she added great new people to the committee, and all rich.

Mr. Finley was thrilled, and he was the first to give a piece of furniture— a fine highboy from his own collection. We talked for hours, and the conversation might have gone on through the afternoon if Jackie's cat, Pusskin, hadn't jumped from the canopied bed onto Mr. Finley's lap. He was a small man and Pusskin was a large cat. Mr. Finley left hurriedly, looking startled.

That evening I felt a little more sure of myself. I went downstairs to the state rooms and asked Mr. West to have all the curtains drawn. He told me that as far as he knew, they had never been drawn. I had in mind a surprise for Jackie, and I worked that evening and most of the next day preparing it. I had fires made up in each room. I filled bowls with flowers, then put them where I thought a lit-

tle color and cheer were desperately needed. I had large tubs of trees brought in, and I placed them throughout the big, empty-looking halls.

The next evening, Jackie did not feel strong, but I begged her just to put her wrapper on and come downstairs for a little surprise. The look on her face said how enchanted she was as she took it all in. The fires were blazing, the candles were all lit, the flowers were showing off, and the trees were shining with health. She could see how easily the White House could be transformed from a cold, shabby museum into a warm, inviting, impressive home of the president. She gave me a shy little kiss and said, "Thank you. I can now see it all as it could be someday."

The importance of the committee cannot be overestimated, for it made the White House what it is today: a place that represents the hard work, great thought, and enormous generosity of many people. Although many of us were naïve at first, enthusiasm was unbridled. The first committee meeting was held in the Red Room, but despite our excitement and eagerness, there was no real direction for such a vast project.

Our energies and confusion on how to go about all this were focused into action when Mr. du Pont was made chairman of the committee. Soon after this and under his reorganization, the committee was well on its way to progress. A curator was installed in the White House, letters went out pleading for authentic, historic furniture, and every letter of response was answered. It was then that Mrs. Kennedy began to have a new feeling about her position and her work. She truly felt that the country was behind her in her great desire to create a White House that would always remain a prized and invaluable possession of the American people.

A meeting was soon called, and the group was very impressive and fascinating, both Republicans and Democrats. Jackie had called her lawyer in the middle of the night and told him to help present the plans. We announced that we hoped to retrieve the furniture that had once adorned the Red Room, Blue Room, state rooms, and dining room. It was really an extraordinary task that we laid out for those present, but the reaction of each and every person there was quick and enthusiastic. Some volunteered to be on the search committee. Some agreed to donate one piece, some two, and a few even pledged an entire room. This included chandeliers, paintings, portraits, rugs, furniture—all of great importance.

One part of the search would be quite delicate. We learned that as each president had left the White House, he had taken what he had wanted. President

Truman's items included the two mantels from the East Room! While our search proceeded, new laws went before Congress to make sure that no future occupants of the White House could dismantle all our work.

LETITIA BALDRIGE: Jackie had a remarkable mind. Remarkable. Before she came to the White House, she knew that she wanted historic preservation to be one of her great causes. She started a wave of historic preservation. She had tremendous expertise, taste, and the desire to make everything historically correct. The National Trust gained momentum and fame thanks to her.

The legislation that made the White House a museum—that legislation was Jackie's. She got a lot done behind the scenes with the Congress. She worked subtly, like a real female, calling up the congressmen with that little breathless voice of hers, quietly and without publicity. And, of course, they just voted to do what she wanted them to do. Before that legislation, anybody could take anything. The maids could take things if they wanted. It was unbelievable.

The members of the Fine Arts Committee were thrilled to be asked to serve. With such a glamorous First Lady, it was number one on everybody's hit parade. They were like little kids. All of this big, heavy-duty money. It was so exciting to be doing something with the White House and with this young Jacqueline Kennedy.

SUSAN: During the summer of 1961, Jackie put together a list of specific furniture, paintings, and objects that she and Mr. du Pont had targeted for purchase.

June 29, 1961

Dear Sister:

I know you have been waiting for suggestions of what is needed for the White House. At last we have a list.

All the furniture has been expertised by the Advisory Committee and approved by Mr. du Pont. The pieces are authentic and are beautiful examples of American craftsmanship of early nineteenth century. Some have excellent histories of ownership by American families, adding to their interest.

The furniture is listed by rooms so that if someone wishes to give more than one piece he can easily do so. I am also sending you Mr. du Pont's notes and suggested changes for the White House.

I do hope we will be able to find lots of generous people soon so that by early fall we will have something wonderful to show. When we have our first acquisitions installed, then we will have a meeting and announce our plans for the future.

Sincerely,

Jackie

P.S. Would you check with Janet Felton when you have found a contributor so as to avoid duplication?

August 15, 1961

Dear Sister:

I am sending this letter to everyone on our Committee today. Also, enclosed is a new list of things desperately needed for the White House to round out the things already acquired, so that some of the rooms will look unified by this winter.

It has turned out be impractical to ask people to donate pieces of their own furniture, except in rare cases where we know they have collected beautiful American things. We have also found that very few people want to give money without having a specific piece catalogued as their gift. Therefore, could you send to prospective donors a copy of this list? Any thing they choose to give will be registered in their names. Many of the things have not yet been found, but if they wish to give, for example, the appliqués for the Green Room, we will let them know when we find them.

It has been found to be more practical to have Mr. du Pont either find or approve all furniture; by keeping it under his surveillance we are assured of harmony in all the rooms. I fervently hope you will be able to raise the money to acquire some of these things by fall when we have our next meeting.

So many thanks.

Sincerely,

Jackie

SUSAN: Sister was proud of her role in the formation of the Fine Arts Committee. It included many of her good friends, who ultimately were responsible for funding the restoration of many of the rooms. Sister brought in Mr. and Mrs. John Loeb, who financed the restoration of the Oval Room. Jackie's letter to the Loebs demonstrates how the process worked.

July 7, 1961

Dear Mr. & Mrs. Loeb—

You cannot imagine how touched and appreciative I am that you want to help with our Oval Room—it is not a public room—so that makes you both so much more patriotic—to wish to help in a room which the thousands of tourists do not see (but they will in photographs).

It is my favorite room in the White House—the one where I think the heart of the White House is—where the President receives all the heads of state who visit him—where the honor guard is formed to march downstairs to "Hail to the Chief"—All the ceremony and all the private talks that really matter happen in that room—and it has the most beautiful proportions of any in the White House.

It has always been so ghastly and so neglected. Every future President would be so happy to have it a room he could be proud of. These are my thoughts on it—and you both must come and see it—and decide if you agree. (I hope you are coming to Mt. Vernon—maybe Tuesday or Wednesday you could come and look.)

I think it would be rather appropriate to have it Louis XVI which Presidents Madison and Jefferson all loved and had in the White House—

Now we have in it our Louis XVI bureau plat & 2 consoles and a lot of hideous stuffed chairs—As a gift we have been offered a beautiful plat XVI & a chair—so you don't have to worry about that—

These are the things I have been searching for for this room & have found—see what you think—a mantel—in a green & white marble with an eagle—of the period—a set of 1 canapé, 4 fauteuils plus 6 side chairs—then we would be all set—except for one thing—pictures—I do feel it should have some American pictures—they don't have to be fantastic—just something to hang which is American

& associated with our past—Perhaps the place of honor should be saved for Mrs. Lehman's Greuze of Franklin—it would be so appropriate to have it in this room which you do—

I keep praying some things will turn up which are associated with past Presidents—If they do later on—we can always sell what we have and get the right ones—but all my bright hopes are dimming—to find a suite of Thomas Jeffersons chairs—

Anyway—with a suite of furniture—a decent desk to replace ours (which we have)—a pair of consoles—a mantel & may be some pictures—this room would be a chef d'oeuvre—& every miserable future President—like the past ones I know of—& like ourselves—who stumble into the W. House & find it wanting in everything—would be so happy & proud to see something beautiful there—

You must come & see the room—Sister Parish can tell you a lot of my plans for it—I don't know how much you want to do—a tiny bit—or a lot—Anything you decide will be so terribly appreciated.

If we can't coincide between July 11–13—you can always go up and see the room anytime you want with Tish Baldrige and let me know your feelings—I will be at Hyannis Port all summer—

All my deepest thanks and I look forward so much to talking about it with you soon—

Sincerely,

Jacqueline Kennedy

SUSAN: For the White House restoration, Jackie relied heavily on the famous French decorator Stephane Boudin, who was responsible for the decoration of the state rooms. Loving all things French, and with the knowledge that Thomas Jefferson and James Monroe had filled the White House with French furniture, Jackie and Boudin (he was always known by his last name) transformed the state rooms with their mutual sense of history and style. Boudin was invaluable to Jackie, and his contributions reflected his European background and his experience working with great houses of the same size and scale as the White House. It appears that where Sister was responsible for securing the patron of the room, she, too, contributed to its decoration. This arrangement must have caused a certain degree of tension among Sister, Jackie, and Boudin.

June 30, 1961

Dear Sister,

I understand so well that if John Loeb should do the Oval Room he would like to do it with you. In that case, of course, I would not use the Boudin curtains which I have wanted all winter and are exactly what I would like, but we can find a perfectly wonderful one from Mr. du Pont's curtain book—in fact he suggested a design for the room long ago which is similar to what I have in mind.

So if John Loeb makes up his mind, the Oval Room will be you and him. I will, of course, never push him or ask you to, but if I don't hear from him by July fifteenth, I must go ahead and order the yellow curtains as planned. I will get someone to pay for them and just furnish the room piece meal. I am sure you will agree we cannot stay out next winter with flappy nylon glass curtains. We have had our period of grace this year as people knew we were moving in, but that room must have curtains and covered furniture by next fall. It would be so lovely if you could do it—I just hope things work out. If I should have to go ahead, you will understand it is because the President wishes to use the room as his formal drawing room and I cannot wait any longer to have it ready by fall.

Two gigantic things I must thank you for—Guertler's painting in the State Dining Room which will make all the difference in the world and the silk hangings and curtains for the Red Room.

I hope in a week or so to have documents and samples of material for an empire room and the moment I get them I will send them on to you so that the silk may be copied by whichever angel you have coerced into doing it. I hope to see you very soon. Do keep in touch with Janet as I will be up on the Cape.

Much love,

Jackie

January 14, 1963

Dearest Sister:

I was horrified to see the precious Benjamin Franklin was still here, and have ordered it sent back to you most carefully.

As for the Oval Room finances, I don't want John Loeb to go any higher than he has already decided; whatever we can't get out of his budget, gradually I can find and get out of Guide Book funds. This will never be mentioned, and it will always be referred to as the Loeb Room. I shouldn't think he would mind that as two White House chairs are in it now, a pair of White House candelabra on the mantel and, of course, some pictures.

I really think the Dalva consoles are too small; I just know that the next President will want some bigger tables there so he can put lots of pictures and everything on—so, I have told Mr. West to return these items to you. Maybe, we will have to build something. We can use my consoles for the time being; I am sure something will turn up.

Do keep looking for a sweet table for between the chairs and, when you find it, either send a picture or send it down.

If French & Co. takes the desk in exchange, fine. If not, don't you think Bensimon would take it back—they are old friends of mine, Stas', and have always been so nice.

We really only have two things left to look for: consoles, and table between the chairs. Let's just get whatever we think is perfect there, and when we go over John Loeb's budget, the Guide Book will pay for it.

Much Love,
Jackie

Dear Sister,

I was so sorry you were gone by the time I got back from Virginia. The Red Room looks so beautiful—oh, how I can't wait for the Oval Room—we will see it all finished when we come back from Christmas down South and that will be the best Christmas present in the whole wide world. Can we have little bronze busts of you and John Loeb on the consoles?

XO

Jackie

SUSAN: In 1962, at the end of Sister's work for the White House, a young decorator from Nashville, Tennessee, named Albert Hadley joined Sister's office. Eventually, Sister and Albert's partnership would become one of the most influential collaborations in the history of American interior design. It was the volume and complexity of the work for the White House that motivated Sister to hire Albert, and though he participated only at the end, he visited the White House several times as her representative.

ALBERT HADLEY (Sister's partner at Parish-Hadley): It was a very exciting time. Of course, going in with Sis that first time on the first day that I went, I really thought it would be a little different. We went in the basement door, used the back stairs, right by the guards, right by everything. There was nothing glamorous about it, but we were there. Sis knew all the back stairs.

I came in quite late, because I joined Sis in 1962 and that job was about over. I mean, everything had been done upstairs. The first time I went there, the yellow room was being done. The day we went was the day of the Bay of Pigs invasion. We arrived early in the morning and went by the Washington Monument, and all the flags were flying and the fountains were going. It was a very tense time, but we were there and the photographer was there taking pictures of the Loeb drawing room.

The next time I went, it was without Sis. Jane Engelhard arrived. I had never met her before. I had never met Mr. du Pont. They knew who I was and that I was there representing Sis, but they were agitated because Mrs. Kennedy wouldn't come down. They said she'd be down in about twenty minutes, then that she'd be down in another twenty minutes . . . half an hour . . . and they were pacing up and down the halls. They left the painter and me in this room while they paced. Finally, Mrs. Kennedy came in, breathless, and she spoke to Jane and Mr. du Pont and they were about to introduce her to me and she said, "So nice to see you again." I had never met her before but what do you say to the president's wife?

Well, anyway, I was surprised that she greeted me so warmly. I mean, she practically kissed me. Then they got into the discussion about what should go into a cabinet in the room. One of them wanted books and one of them wanted china, and Jackie said, "Come with me. I've got china upstairs." So she and I disappeared into an elevator, left the two of those kids sort of angling there, and we came back with the china that she wanted to put in the cabinet. Eventually, our curtain sketches were approved for the Oval Room and the room was finally finished and that was that.

SUSAN MARY ALSOP: I was lucky enough to be a member of the Fine Arts Committee with Harry du Pont, who was the chairman, and every now and then he would breeze down and lecture us on things, but Jackie was firm on what she liked. We were given a great many things. People were extremely kind to the Kennedys in the beginning. I remember someone gave us an awfully pretty little still life. It was a pretty little picture from the nineteenth century for the Red Room, and Jackie was delighted with it, as were we all. So we hung it. Mr. du Pont came the next day and took one look at the picture and said, "Ladies, surely you are aware that still lifes are only for dining rooms." I thought we would die. Jackie said, "Oh, Mr. du Pont, I am sorry. How stupid I am; take it away." And it was swiftly removed.

A few weeks later, I went to the White House for some social occasion with my husband, Joseph Alsop, and went into the Red Room by chance, and there was the picture. And in came Mr. du Pont by some extraordinary coincidence. So I said, "Hello, Mr. du Pont," and he said, "Susan Mary, how are you? Doesn't it all look wonderful?" He was really looking around, looking at everything, including the picture, and he said, "Really, Jackie is extraordinary. She is a genius. She has such natural taste."

Jackie always wanted to be near horses. They were building a house in the country. The president was very excited. I remember the last time I saw them; Joe and I had dinner with them alone. It happened to be a couple of nights before they were leaving for Dallas, a political trip. Jackie was so proud because the plans for the house were all ready. They were on the table for Joe and me to see, and I said it looked absolutely marvelous but that it looked too small. The president said, "My God, you're extravagant," as I remember. It was quite a lovely plan, and I don't know what happened to it. They seemed very happy.

SUSAN: Sister gave her all to the project, but it must have been sticky business coordinating the donations, keeping the donors happy, and pleasing Jackie, who at all times had political concerns to remember. The correspondence from Jackie to Sister regarding the donation of glass by Mr. Houghton reveals some of the undercurrents.

Dear Sister,

Thank you so much for your letter about the rug, but it is really impossible for The White House Committee to pay for it. As you know, our household budget couldn't include anything like that, and the whole proceeds of our guidebook for the first year will really go to paying back debts for furniture acquired, etc. So I think we will just have to leave the present rug, unless you can get the rug maker to give it. If it is imported, we better not do that, but if it is an American rug maker, perhaps he would be interested in making a gift to the White House and taking a tax deduction. If this seems feasible to you, do let me see a sample of the rug before you approach the rug maker.

About Mr. Houghton and the glass—before he goes any further you had better stop him. I would love to have Steuben glass, but in the beginning we did not have the money and I really didn't even think of it. Now I really love my West Virginia wine glasses all so very much—like Baccarat—and one millionth the price. As you know, West Virginia is the most unemployed area in the country and apparently our White House glasses did give two little towns a big boost, and I just couldn't take this away from them now. Also, I don't mind having plain glasses without a seal. It is almost a relief. Our flatware and china are all engraved.

That is so sweet of Mr. Houghton to think of that, but I just don't want to put a lot of people in West Virginia out of work now, especially as so many of them have just found jobs because of this glass. I am sure he will understand that, and the thing I would really love to have from him is the marvelous English furniture for the Queen's

Room, so you might try that tack. Do be sure to let him know that you had not consulted me when you thought of this. We had discussed glassware in the beginning, because I did not want him to think it is anything against Steuben glass which, of course, it isn't, and which I have myself in my own house.

Much love, and have a restful summer in Maine,

Jackie

LETITIA BALDRIGE: Jackie chose all the glass for the White House from West Virginia because of the poverty there. She really cared so much about things. She cared about every detail.

The project was immense. I spent days and days just contacting museums, sending letters and photographs to potential donors, and it seemed way beyond anything I could cope with. But my excitement was contagious, everyone's enthusiasm seemed to gather speed, and soon there was no stopping the idea.

I found myself counting silver and glass, and working with Jackie over plans for large state dinners, and ideas for less grand dinners, and even intimate but important dinners around small round tables. I ordered linen from Ireland over the telephone, and imagine what a shock it was to them to receive a call suddenly, and a large rush order from the White House.

There were endless tasks to help Jackie organize the White House for now, and prepare for its great renewal. Flower arrangements had to be designed; menus and wines had to be considered. Countless complicated details unfolded. I have never been so glad that I had training from home to help me along. I expected the work on the renewal to keep me busy, and it certainly did, but the new little assignments that always seemed to fall to me soon became exhausting. I wished so often that Jackie's mother would come to help, but she never did.

During all this, the press was driven to madness. They knew that a great deal was going on at the White House, but no official word had been issued by anyone. Rumors were everywhere, and they were printed as fact daily.

When I think back on my routine during those White House days, I become exhausted. I commuted to New York every other day so I could take care of things at the office and spend at least some time with Harry and Yummy. My hours were long and erratic, and because it was a snowy winter, the planes were never reliable. My only encouragement was knowing that everyone who was working for the Kennedys was working with all their heart, and it pleased me to be doing my small part.

The days and weeks went on, until a sad call came for me. I was en route to a warehouse, where past White House furniture had been stored, when Mr. West intercepted me. He told me that my oldest brother, Frankie, had just died of a heart attack and that a White House car was ready to take me wherever it was convenient.

I stayed in Boston for two days during the funeral, and Jackie called to say I should take some time off and not come back until I felt better. I did need the rest. I went to Ruth Field's plantation in South Carolina with Harry. We were in the middle of a croquet game when Thomas, her man, said I was wanted on the phone by a lady named Kennedy. We were immediately cut off. I asked the operator to please get me Mrs. Kennedy at the White House. She asked me to spell the name Kennedy, and when I had done it correctly, she wanted to know where the White House was. When I finally got through, I found that Jackie wanted me to return as soon as possible.

I could see why as soon as I got back to Washington. Changes were taking place every day, and the scale of the work to be done had become enormous. People were pouring in with ideas, immense sums of money were being raised, even more was being spent, and there were countless problems over who was to do what. In addition, hundreds of pieces of furniture, all of it important, had to be picked over, cataloged, decided upon.

During all this, I found Jackie very involved with Caroline and her schooling. I have never seen a mother fight for her children the way she did. Caroline was in a little kindergarten, and Jackie wasn't at all pleased with it. It happened that my grandson, Charlie Bartlett, was in the same kindergarten, and my daughter was as unhappy about the school as Jackie. The result was that Jackie moved Caroline's little class to the third floor of the White House, where President Eisenhower had had his recreation rooms. I, of course, was thrilled to have Charlie upstairs, and Jackie was glad that her child could have some privacy.

I had been warned that if you work closely with Jackie, over a long period of time, trouble, in some form or other, will eventually erupt. I didn't believe it would happen to me, but it did. One day I was reprimanded, for the first time, for ordering an upstairs carpet that had been made in France. I was told that it was vital that everything be made in the United States. I, of course, knew that was an overall goal, but something somehow seemed wrong. The carpet I had ordered was in keeping with our plans to return the White House to its original state. My plans had been initially approved. In addition, the White House had just accepted a magnificent present from John Loeb—the Oval Room was to be completely redone, at his expense, with much of it coming from France.

There was more to Jackie's reprimand than met the eye, and I could feel it when I was with her. Finally, I learned the source of our problem. She had been told that I had kicked Caroline, and she was convinced it was true.

At any rate, the relationship had become strained, and the work to be done too much to handle on a part-time basis, and so it was suggested that Mr. Harry du Pont take command. He did, and how great he was.

I went on working, and working hard, but not in the same way. Slowly but surely, the rooms were born.

Today I feel a sense of enormous pride whenever I think of the White House. Here was something not for me, not for the Kennedys, but for all Americans. I think of what I did in the White House as my contribution to my country, and how lucky I was to make that contribution!

Following page: Albert Hadley and Sister Parish after they had become partners.

Chapter Nine

Parish-Hadley: 1963–Onward

Parish-Hadley influenced a whole generation of decorators and many of the
top New York decorators went through the firm at some point in their careers.

HAROLD SIMMONS

SUSAN: Over the years, Sister came to hire many extremely talented young men and women, but it really all began in 1962 when she hired Albert. It seems clear that when Sister and Albert came together personally and professionally, something happened. I spent a day at the Condé Nast library tracing her published work, from the forties to the nineties, and in 1962, when she hooked up with Albert, it was as if something within her clicked. Her rooms came alive with color, texture, and paint, and yet all were tempered by his obvious academic approach. Their partnership gave them both a confidence, which can be seen very clearly in their rooms. It was as if the thirty years that she decorated on her own were all leading up to this fantastic point where she met Albert.

It happened in rather a natural way. My business was getting more than I could take care of, mainly because of my work for the White House. I mentioned it to a mutual friend, Mr. Van Day Truex. No sooner said than a young man named Albert Hadley called to ask if he could come and talk to me. I opened the door for him, and his story is that my first words were, "Will you zip me up and be my partner?"

He has stood by me and with me, never failing. Without him, many of my inspirations would never have happened. We have had hard times. We have had fun, and we have had torture, but all that goes under the word decorating.

ALBERT HADLEY: The first time I saw Sis, it was in the late fifties and I was with Eleanor Brown of McMillen, for whom I was then working. We were pulling together these table settings at Tiffany's. So there she was with all of her marvelous hair flowing, the camel-colored coat flying and Yummy in her arms, and she was directing this sort of tent thing. There was a bird screen in the background, and she had made a rug out of burlap. Here was all this chintz binding on burlap rugs under the tent thing, and there were pictures of dogs and pictures of her family. It was exactly the opposite of McMillen. So here was this marvelous woman, and I was introduced to Mrs. Parish.

I had never really known Mrs. Parish. I had passed her shop on Sixty-ninth Street, where it said MRS. HENRY PARISH II on this sort of baroque sign out front. I think she must have printed it herself. It was terrible. I used to go by in those days and see these little vignettes in the two small windows, but I had no idea who she was. So suddenly, I was introduced to this glamorous woman with a dog. Eleanor Brown was very cool to her.

The day came a few years later that I decided I would leave McMillen because I was young and I wanted to do more than Mrs. Brown wanted me to do.

One morning, Van Day Truex, of the Parsons School of Design, who was my close friend, called and said, "Do you know who Mrs. Parish is?" I said that yes, I'd met Mrs. Parish and I knew who she was. Van Truex said, "I sat next to her last night and she is going to have to give up her business unless she can find someone to take it over so she can finish the White House."

Then he went on to say, "She's waiting for you to call her." This was eight o'clock in the morning and I was in bed having coffee. I called her and we talked for a few minutes and she asked that I come to her apartment on Wednesday at five o'clock.

On Wednesday, I rang the bell and the door opened, and right away I was nipped on the ankle by this ghastly little dog. She asked, "Are you still standing?" She was in a marvelous black-and-pink dress. And, as the dog was biting me, I looked down, and she didn't have her shoes on. She turned to me and said, "Would you zip me up? Oh, Yummy, now don't bite this nice young man."

Then we went down this long hall into the drawing room, and she plopped herself on the big sofa and I sat down. Then Harry came in. And, of course, there was no introduction. She didn't even remember my name.

"This is my husband," she said. And so I introduced myself, and, well, he didn't know why I was there. He must have wondered where she found this guy. Anyway, Harry sat for a few minutes and then excused himself and went into his room.

The apartment was very glamorous. We talked a few minutes longer and she said, "I'd like a drink." Her bar, that big black lacquered thing, was just inside the door to the room. "I would like a bourbon," she said, but I was afraid to have a drink. I didn't drink that much in those days and I was afraid that I'd get drunk, but I made her a drink. She'd said bourbon. Well, I gave her something that looked like the palest tea you've ever seen, and she looked at me and said, "That's not a drink." So she got up and poured straight bourbon into a glass. I think I had a little straight bourbon in a glass. We talked and had a perfectly fine time.

It was decided that I was to start work on January 3. Early on the morning of January 2, the phone rang. "Good morning. This is Mrs. Parish. I was just thinking that since you're starting to work tomorrow, maybe we could get a little head start. I would love to show you the Bronfman apartment, which we will be working on."

SUSAN: The apartment that Sister took Albert to on that first day in 1963 belonged to the then-young Edgar Bronfman, who was married to Ann Loeb. Bronfman was just coming up in the world, and they had bought the old Webb apartment on Park Avenue. The redecoration of the Bronfman apartment would later be remembered as Sister and Albert's first project together.

Jack Coble, the society architect who was also Cole Porter's great friend, was working with Sister on the job.

Edgar Bronfman was the son of Sam Bronfman, founder of Distillers Corporation–Seagram Ltd., a Canadian firm. Edgar took over as president of the family's liquor firm following the death of his father in 1971. In 1974, the Bronfman family's wealth was estimated to be well over $400 million.

ALBERT HADLEY: We walked through, talking about plans. Then the young Bronfmans went off to Mexico and we got a wire from them: "Stop all work on the apartment. We've decided what we want is 'floating space.'" Those were the words they used.

Well, you can imagine Sis. She didn't know what "floating space" meant at all. I had been to school and I knew that this meant wide open, with few walls.

"But, Mrs. Parish," I said. "I think I understand what they mean exactly."

Anyway, they came back and they had seen a lot of floating space in Mexico and they wanted fireplaces with ledges so that people could sit down with pillows. Remember, this was 1963. Poor Jack Coble didn't know what had hit him. So the fun started. We knocked out walls and we changed the staircase, and we closed up windows and we opened up others. We did it with Edgar and the whole thing worked. Sis never really liked any of it. She would take Ann shopping for French furniture, and so this marvelous floating space was filled up with traditional furniture, which is really pretty good. It was one of the most exciting apartments we ever did together.

That was the first. That was the beginning of Sis seeing something that she had never seen before. From then on, there was no stopping us.

SUSAN: In 1963, Albert and Sister hired Mark Hampton. They remained life-long friends. With his fantastic eye for detail, he understood every nuance of her work.

MARK HAMPTON: There was a lot of tugging and pulling when they worked on the Bronfman triplex at 740 Park Avenue because Albert wanted it to reflect the sort of thirties atmosphere of the building, and that was not the sort of territory that Sister wanted to wade into. It turned out to be a marvelous combination of the two, because Albert and Jack Coble devised this design, this wonderful kind of Fred Astaire and Ginger Rogers background. It was a real New York penthouse for the thirties. Windows to the floor, all cleaned up and sleek, and marble floors and this sculptured staircase. Like a shell. All the furniture was covered in this beautiful sort of rough white silk damask. There was some old furniture, but just big, strong, cushy pieces of furniture. Very beautiful zebrawood library. Very stripey. Then it had this dining room with a dome, which was a nightmare because it created this acoustical problem. Awful acoustics, but a beautiful room. It went on and on and on, and there was no resolution to that room. Everything else was solved and done. I remember Mrs. Parish saying that all this money had come from liquor, so why didn't we paint it the color of whiskey? That was her story. And they did. They painted that wonderful glazed cognac color. It was beautiful. I'm sure she said that. It's a line, and she was always full of great lines.

The master bedroom was perched up on the roof, this penthouse bedroom. It wasn't very big, and there was no way to make it bigger. You just couldn't build on the roof. It wasn't allowed. It was all yellow, with this beautiful bed painted by York Kennedy. There was a commode between the windows. It had two windows facing south, and the commode bumped into the curtains. I remember that Albert said, "I can't stand this, but this is what Sister likes because it looks like they got it from some other house and brought it into this room." It was too big for the wall. She knew that; she liked that. The way that she liked to have a pair of chairs that weren't quite mates. They didn't cover them alike. It was very beautiful and very different. Completely outside the kind of look that you consider Mrs. Henry Parish II.

SUSAN: Shortly after Albert joined Sister, the firm of Mrs. Henry Parish II Interiors became Parish-Hadley, and together they brought in a series of young men and women who went on to become some of the most accomplished decorators of the twentieth century.

HAROLD SIMMONS (former Parish-Hadley decorator): Parish-Hadley influenced a whole generation of decorators, and many of the top New York decorators went through the firm at some point in their careers. They got their start there, really learned a lot, and went on to do all kinds of things. It was an enormously influential school. Mrs Parish's style was unique. She had her own way of doing things, and it was not always by the book. If you went to job sites, or shopping and on visits to workrooms with her, you couldn't help but absorb an awful lot. Albert, on the other hand, could teach his very disciplined and thought-out point of view.

ALBERT HADLEY: Soon after I started, we hired two young men. One's name was Bill Hodgins, and he was from Canada. The other one was Edward Lee Cave. The two men sat out front, and, of course, we were very formal. It was always Mr. Hadley, Mrs. Parish, Mr. Cave, and Mr. Hodgins. Eventually, the firm grew and other people came in.

In the beginning, accounting was down Madison Avenue in a separate place, half a block away. We were scattered in small separate offices all over and so we would have to go out of the office to get the samples. Clients would come, and I had to be the one to get up and walk out the front door, and people would wonder, Where has he gone? What is happening here? The decorators are all going out the front door.

Well, I had to go halfway up the block to Madison to get another chintz. It was absolutely comical. You don't like that chintz ? Sure, I'll get you another one, and out the front door I would go.

There were also these windows made from a silver material that appeared as a mirror on the street, but we could see through them. The other decorators and I would be sitting at our desks, looking out, and the people outside would be using the mirrored windows to primp in or to pull up their girdles. They didn't know we were watching. It was the best show in town. Eventually she moved into the large offices on 305 East Sixty-third Street.

When I first started with Sis, her big client was the White House, and, of course, the famous line then was, "Kennedys pick nun to decorate White House." This was the most publicity that she had gotten up to this point. Quite frankly, she really didn't like the idea that I knew all of these magazine people. That's how we complimented each other. She had all these clients, but she wasn't even running a proper business. Let's face it. It was all by word of mouth. There were not even estimates. It was very simple, but very good. She had the eye, but her business was not set up properly.

MARIO BUATTA (decorator): The rooms that I saw before Albert were kind of typical. Ladylike, with a little chintz, a little swag, yellow walls, green walls. There was nothing very exciting about them. With Albert, it was like a great marriage. He had this sense of architecture that she didn't care about. Albert's whole field was architecture, and the work they did together was truly incredible.

The firm shortly before Albert became a partner. Yummy is seated on pillow. Bill Hodgins is on the right.

BUNNY WILLIAMS: The only person I really wanted to work for was Mrs. Parish. So one day, I decided to walk up the street and see if there was an opening. They were on Sixty-ninth Street, and I got to know Mr. Emmitt, who ran the office at the time. They asked me if I could type and take shorthand. I couldn't type very well, but I said I could type thirty words per minute. For the first month I was there, I shared an office with David Easton, who had been hired at the same time. David and I sat in there by ourselves and talked about design and decorating and ate muffins, because nobody knew exactly what to do with us.

There were two tiny rooms. I mean, there was a little hallway, and two tiny rooms, a bathroom, and a closet. Mrs. Parish's office was right on the street, on the ground floor, and all her friends, like Mrs. Paley, could drop in. I stayed with Albert as his secretary and then I became the shopper. Finally, after about four years, they decided to give me the job as an assistant. I moved into a design position and worked directly with clients. There is no question that you couldn't have a better education. You can't buy that kind of education.

CAROLE CAVALUZZO (Parish-Hadley comptroller): In those days, I didn't know Mrs. Parish. I just heard about her. There was this shudder when her name came up. We knew that she ruled the roost and that everyone had to be there and do their thing when she wanted them to. First thing in the morning, the decorators would get that phone call and they had to know the schedule for the day. They were afraid of her.

ALBERT HADLEY: I usually made the decisions about whom we would hire. The only person Sister took note of was Mark Hampton. When he came in and I looked at his drawings, it struck me was that he had taken tables and chairs out of one room and put them in somebody else's house. They were composites, and all of them had a great style. The renderings he showed me were from his imagination. We talked for a while, and I thought he was very talented, but I didn't really have a job for him.

Sis, across the hall, heard him and wanted to talk with him because his voice reminded her of her brother Bayard. So the two of them, given Mark's personality, got along like a house afire. She took him under her wing in a way. They worked very closely together and she advised him not to be a decorator, but to go back to school and finish his education. She said, "You go get your education." So he left, but they kept in touch.

MARK HAMPTON: I went there because a friend of mine from college was a nephew of Hillary Knight, the man who, along with Kay Thompson, drew the character Eloise. He'd said, "When you're in New York looking for a job, you should look up my uncle Hillary because maybe he could help you get something." Because I drew, I thought I could get some sort of freelance work. So

Sister and Bunny Williams at the Parish-Hadley Christmas party, where dressing up was required.

I had my appointment with Hillary, who said, "I have a friend, Albert, who works for a very grand woman called Mrs. Henry Parish, and he hasn't been there long." Albert had been there for about a year.

This was in June 1963, so I made an appointment with Albert, then went in and saw him that day, narrowly avoiding being bitten by Yummy. Remember that little green dish of water by the door?

So I went in and chatted with Albert. Mrs. Parish was sitting so that she could see out but you couldn't see her sitting in the corner in her chair. No mention was made of her being there. That funny little black Humber they drove in those days was sitting out front, but I didn't have any way of knowing that was her car. Remember that funny little car? So weird, so Anglophile. It was a four-door Humber. A very staid English sedan. Very Mr. and Mrs. Henry Parish II to drive this strange English car. All black.

Albert said, "Mrs. Parish is here, as it turns out, and she would like to see you." So I went in, and she was just adorable. Sort of a defining moment. We chatted for a second and she said, "As it turns out I have an appointment. I really have to leave immediately, but I live at Thirty-nine East Seventy-ninth Street, and what are you doing at five o'clock?"

I said, "Well, I'm not really doing anything. I'm out here looking for a job."

She said, in that lovely girlish little high voice of hers, "Well, I'll be back around five, but I may be late. The keys to the apartment are in the drawer by the elevator, so just let yourself in and wait for me if I'm not there."

Which is a fairly bizarre and amazing story for a New York encounter. So I did get there at five o'clock, probably got there anxiously at three minutes of five, and she wasn't there. Eileen and Norma [her help] were out, so I let myself in, and, you know, I felt so creepy. I didn't know the person and had never been in the apartment, and I kind of tiptoed down that hall. All the rugs were gone because it was summertime. These wonderful brown-and-white slipcovers were on everything in the drawing room. It was just enchanting, and I sat there feeling like a thief.

She showed up in five or ten minutes, and that's when I started working for her. It was a great summer. It was marvelous. It was the summer they started working for the Whitneys.

Later, I came back to New York to buy an engagement ring because Duane and I had gotten engaged. So I called Mrs. Parish and asked if she was going to be around. She said yes, and invited me to lunch on Saturday. Her great friend Barbara Drum was going to be there. Lunch was your lovely, typical Saturday lunch soufflé and salad and a lot to drink. I said that I'd come to buy an engagement ring, and they both said, "ohhhh." Barbara said, "Oh, don't buy an engagement ring. It's the most awful thing in the world. I had a beautiful diamond ring and my second husband sold it to pay off a gambling debt. It just broke my heart. I wish I'd never seen that ring."

Sister said, "It's the dumbest thing on earth to give an engagement ring. I had a beautiful ring, but I sold it to buy a horse. Of course, I'd love to have that ring back."

I thought, This is typical of two people out of a movie. Amusing and funny, telling these amusing, cynical stories. I'll never forget that day. They were so adorable, and did you know that Mrs. Parish was younger that day then I am now? She looked the same. So dignified. So staid. Certainly she was on hold for twenty years, looking exactly the same.

ALBERT HADLEY: When Mark and Duane were getting married, we were invited, and we decided to go antiquing first before the wedding. I had a Sunbeam, this marvelous little convertible. We decided we would start out early, so we were having a fine time; the top was down and the whole thing. We went to the shops, and the wedding was at four o'clock. Well, we got almost to the wedding and Sis says, "Pull over." So we pulled over to the side of the road. It was wooded, so she got out of the car, took her little bag, went into the bushes, and changed from her sort of working-day costume. She came out all done up with a big hat, the whole thing. We got in the car, arrived at the wedding as if she had just stepped out of a bandbox. So Mark and Duane were married. Sis was always involved with them. He would send her those little drawings of his for Valentine's Day, birthdays, Christmas, or for any reason.

MARK HAMPTON: Duane and I were married late in the summer. Despite the fact that my father had just died, we decided to go ahead and have a wedding. Mrs. Parish and Albert drove together. She was wearing a pink summer dress and a funny white organza hat, kind of like a turban, and it tied back. It was one of those strange things that she used to wear sort of tossed in, with everything else being classic. Very chic, very strange.

Anyway, she said, "We got dressed in a ditch. We pulled over to the side of the road and got dressed." Knowing her as we did, there's some margin for exaggeration in that story, but the whole idea is just so hilarious. Albert said they did get dressed on the side of the road.

DAVID KLEINBERG (former Parish-Hadley decorator): When I was interviewed, I walked into this big room done over as a living room, with a conference table at one end with a faux painted top, and a big old mirror hanging over a sofa done in yellow. Mrs. Parish walked in wearing one of her classic knit ensembles and a string of pearls, pearl button earrings and low shoes with a stacked heel, and two dogs—whichever were alive in those days. They came in wobbling behind her, and one of them promptly peed on the carpet. Mrs. Parish looked at it, then looked at me and said, "Excuse me." I said, "If I can help . . ." We both walked out of the room and went and found some paper towels, and then we both stood there sort of blotting with our feet. That was basically the sum total of my interview. I had my drawings with me, but she didn't even look at them. She couldn't have cared less. I think she was interested in what kind of person I was—whether I wore a coat and tie and if I stood up when she came into the room.

SAMUEL BELL (former Parish-Hadley driver): What happened was, I was working for a company, Chauffeurs Unlimited, and I went to work for Parish-

Mark Hampton at Albert's
apartment.

Hadley on a temporary basis. They said I could work there after three months, but first I'd have to meet Mrs. Parish, and if Mrs. Parish liked me, then they'd hire me permanently.

I think our first trip was on Madison Avenue. She said, "Go over to Madison." I asked, "Where is Madison?" And she said, "You idiot. It's one block over." And I thought, Well, I don't know if I want to work for this woman. I had never driven in New York City. So I said, "You can direct me." She said, "Go one block and stop." Something like that. So after going there, with her directing me, we started fighting over which was the East Side and which was the West Side.

Eventually, she started easing up on me. I would ask the bookkeeper, "Can I get hired now? I've been working for the company for a while." She said, "I don't know; we are still going to have to see how Mrs. Parish likes you, because she hasn't even commented about you." I said, "Well, I will ask her, then." So I went upstairs to get her dog. She wanted everyone to love her dog, but I'm a person who loves people more than dogs. So Mrs. Parish said, "Samuel." And I said, "Yes?" And she said, "Would you take Nanny down to the car?" And I said, "Sure, no problem." So I was trying to take her, and she said, "Look, pick up the dog like a baby." And I turned and said, "This is not a baby. It's a dog."

There was dead silence. And she said, "Never mind." And then I went downstairs and waited for her. She came downstairs to the car and I was sitting in the front. She would normally sit in the back. She took the dog and threw it on my shoulder and said, "Watch my dog." I turned around and said to her, "I can watch it from the back."

I stood up to her, but in a nice manner, and she was steaming. Eventually, we drove two blocks and she stopped at somebody's house, a client's house, to deliver a letter or something like that. So I drove, and she said, "Turn right, you idiot. Turn left, you idiot." So I stopped the car and I turned around and said, "Here's the key. If you don't like the way I drive, that's okay, but don't call me an idiot. I'm a person. I go to the bathroom. I eat, just like everybody else, but don't call me an idiot. I am going to take this to the door, and when I come back, if you don't want me to drive, you drive yourself."

She apologized. She said, "I'm sorry. I'm just nervous. I didn't mean to call you an idiot. Let's go." So about six months into that, Carol said, "Mrs. Parish likes you a lot, so we are going to hire you on a permanent basis. But try to get a map of the roads and things."

She had a nice side. I found that out right away. That's why I stuck with her. She had this unusual smile, and you'd know she was kidding. She would say something in a mean fashion, and when she was sitting in the back, I could see her laughing. Then she started sitting in the front and we began talking. I would tell her about my religion, and she finally realized that my religion was most important to me. She would always tell her friends and clients how much she loved me. And I said, "If you love me, why are we fighting?" And the thing is, when I'd meet the clients, they'd treat me like I was so important to her. I would say to them, "I don't know you." And they would say, "But I know *you*." Apparently, she had these stories that she would bring up about me.

Yeah, she liked to fight. I only fought for things that I knew I had to stand up for, and she respected me for it. I think I was the only person she trusted totally going into her apartment. I would see her pushing Nanny on me. She liked playing games like that. Then about the tenth year of my being at Parish-Hadley, we started joking about people in the street. She totally rode in the front seat then.

MARCIE BRAGA (former Parish-Hadley decorator): Once I was at a cocktail party and Albert told me, "Did you know that you were the first woman hired by Parish-Hadley who wasn't a secretary?" And Albert said to me, "You came into that office. You were wearing a peach-colored suit, and I thought that you would look good around the office."

They were totally aesthetic people. Mrs. Parish was completely disinterested in my design portfolio. She was more concerned that I would look good around the office. If you were talented and you were good, then you would be promoted. To start with, it was how you looked.

Sister with the dogs on the way to the office.

BILL HODGINS (former Parish-Hadley decorator): I had graduated from Parsons School of Design. I worked for a guy who was a real killer, but you learned to do everything from him. I was already thirty, much older than most people. So after a year working for him, I decided that I wanted to work for someone whose work I liked. I picked out Billy Baldwin and Mrs. Parish, whom I always called "Madame." It turned out that Parish-Hadley needed a junior assistant. Albert interviewed me and made me do floor plans. I remember I drew these things he liked. I scratched away while we talked about other things. People whom Albert found and interviewed first, Madame usually never liked, even though they were hired. Quite often, if they were close to Albert, they were never close to her. She didn't like someone else being a good friend of Albert's. It wasn't that she didn't like the other person, really. It was just that she liked Albert.

The interview was in that silver room in his apartment. Remember that beautiful silver room he had? It was one of the most beautiful, quietly dazzling rooms ever. It was square with high ceilings, and the walls had silver foil paper on them, so it just glittered. I remember he had all linen furniture. Four very beautiful big, big chairs. You know, he was always into that plaster furniture. And then there were a few sort of emerald green glasses and objects in this room. And on the floor was wall-to-wall thick woven raffia—remember that? God, it was beautiful. The next time I met Madame, she was sitting there with her Jack Daniel's.

MARK HAMPTON: When I started working for her, she took me around to all the showrooms. It wasn't like it is now, with hundreds of showrooms. Crass. The fact is that it was a very cozy little group of showrooms. We knew everybody, and it was so different from the way it is now. She took me to every showroom that they used regularly, and she said, "Now, this is Mr. Hampton and he's coming to work for me. For us." That's a marvelous way to meet people. It's so correct, so old-fashioned. So polite. And all of those details of charming manners were so beguiling, and then out of the blue she could turn around and open her handbag and comb her hair at the dinner table.

On the one hand, she was so unconventional and said, "See if I can't." On the other hand, she had this marvelous, marvelous ability to, in a second, become this old-fashioned lady of such charm and great manners. And that's what made her so interesting to be around.

SUSAN: She cared enormously about the people who worked for her, particularly those who worked behind the scenes like Carole Cavaluzzo, who heads the accounting department. Carole told me that right before Sister died, she went to visit her. Sister held Carole's hand and said simply, "Thank you, Carole. Thank you."

CAROLE CAVALUZZO: Whenever she walked into the office, she would put her arm on my shoulder and say, "My friend." She was always caring and loyal, and I think she was like that toward everyone there.

I know that if there was any kind of illness, she made sure that whoever was ill was treated by the best doctor. She made us have flu shots every year. I know that she could crack the whip, but there was also such a soft side, a shy side. She would stand by Mr. Hadley at the Christmas parties and be so soft-spoken. At first, I was in awe of everything. I remember once when I came to the Christmas party and she asked, "What will you have to drink?" So I told her ginger and bourbon. She said, "*Ginger* and *bourbon?* Who drinks ginger with bourbon?"

She told me once that you never hire a housekeeper if she can't make a good soufflé. That was the test.

ALAN CAMPBELL (fabric designer who worked with Parish-Hadley for many years): I met Sister at a party in my building. My neighbor gave a dinner party and she was there. He'd hired the bartender from the Knickerbocker Club, who was always saying, "Do you want the other half of your drink?" He'd do it all night, until you were blind drunk on the floor.

I'd always heard about Sister because I shared a cottage out on Fire Island with people like Kevin McNamara, who worked at Parish-Hadley. They'd talk about her all of the time. Really, I just heard about this woman for ages before I ever laid eyes on her.

They were working for her, or with her in some way or another. They would go on and on for hours about her. Lots of it was not flattering. They'd be mad at her because she was always right and she would tell them what to do. And they were fascinated by her, obviously, because they wouldn't stop talking about her. It made me curious to meet her.

Anyway, she came to dinner that night, and there must have been twenty-five people there. They had little tables set up that had been brought in from the Knickerbocker Club or somewhere. I'd brought some coffee in to some pain-in-the-neck lady and she'd said, "I didn't want cream in my coffee," or "I don't want sugar." So I was standing there holding this coffee, and I wasn't the waiter, so I sort of looked irritated. My expression must have been pretty painful, and Sister said, "Oh, let me have that," with this beautiful smile. "Let me have that." I just fell in love with her immediately.

I started to do these batik things, and I gave one to Albert, who showed it to Sister. Then Albert asked me to bring some things over so they could see them. I went over there for dinner to Mrs. Parish's apartment on Seventy-ninth Street. So we had dinner and talked about it, and she said, "Well, you are going to make us some things."

I started doing these batik things, and Sister liked them and commissioned me to make some pillows. I made them, and they were published immediately. Then I started making things for Halston because he had heard about this.

They were sort of caftan dresses that Halston was making. He'd want me to do one for Mrs. Engelhard or Babe Paley. He'd say, "Use her honey colors." I didn't know what her honey colors were, so he'd tell me then and I'd print the batik material and he would make it into caftans.

Halston was very mannered, but he was funny and smart. He was a very big guy. Big, not tall. Nice-looking. Mrs. Parish didn't like him a bit.

ALBERT HADLEY: Alan was doing all of this in the bathtub because he was still with the Rockefeller brothers. We thought, Wouldn't it be fun if we had an exhibition? We did an American flag that was batiked and we had this little exhibition in the office, and *House & Garden* came by to see it. Sis introduced Alan to Halston, and soon all of the ladies, like Evie Gates and Babe Paley, were wearing caftans made out of Alan's fabrics. It didn't take long before Alan gave up his job with the Rockefellers and started his own business.

SAMUEL BELL: Mrs. Parish never lost her sharpness till the day she died. Never. Toward the end of her life, she appreciated how important life was and wanted to more or less accept and look for God, so to speak. I would go into her room and talk to her, and she was clearheaded. I would come back and say, "You know, Mrs. Parish, you are going to die soon."

She kept bouncing back. Her mind was still going well. She didn't put the dogs ahead of people for that time period. When she was sick, she realized that. I even told her one day, "Mrs. Parish, you have to treat people nicer." She said, "Why?" I said, "Because one day you'll realize that as much as you love Nanny and Ricky and all these other dogs, when you get sick, not one of them will get on the phone and call the doctor."

The most valuable thing she ever did for me was to show she really cared about me when she was dying. She must have told everybody about me, how much she cared about and loved Sammy, to the point of saying, "I love Sammy. Where's my Sammy?" All that sort of thing. When I got to Maine to pick up the housekeeper after Mrs. Parish had died, there were about twenty people waiting. They wanted to take pictures of me. I don't think a lot of them realized I was black. They were amazed that Mrs. Parish got along with this person. So they all wanted pictures and the whole thing. I guess that's a lasting memory that we did get on even after we fought. We were friends before then, but that just made a lasting impression.

SUSAN: Sister did not associate with too many people in the decorating world outside of her office. Mario Buatta was one of the few.

One of John Fowler's disciples is Mario Buatta. Mario's wonderful. He calls me up and says, "What have you done lately that I can copy?" I adore him because he's so fantastic at advertising himself and at that thing called licensing. I've been to three cocktail parties in my life that had to do with business, and I envy the decorators who go to three in an afternoon. The public thing—I'm just not made for it.

MARIO BUATTA: My first real brush with Sister was in London. I was staying at John Fowler's cottage. We used to have a lot of laughs. There would be people who worked for him and ladies who had houses in the country—Mrs. Oompty Boompt or whoever. We would kid around a lot. I would plant whoopee cushions around. There was this one time the rocket was going to the moon and everyone was watching it on TV. I was so bored that I decided to leave John's house and go in to London, but then I heard John on the phone saying, "Oh, Mrs. Parish. I have no one to give you lunch, but I can give you tea." So I thought, Hey, I'm not going to London. I'm going to stay here and see Mrs. Parish. I was about twenty-nine or thirty at that point. She arrived and really wanted to see John's new garden room, this addition he had put on. There were about six people there, and I turned to Mrs. Parish and asked, "How is the weather in New York?" She said, "Oh, were you just visiting there?" And I said, "No, I live there." Then John, who was in a nearby room and thought I was a friend of Sister's, screamed out, "That bloody fool. That big phony. I knew he was a faker."

You see, I used to write John these three-page letters, all typed up, about what was going on in New York and I used to sign the letters: "Bunny," "Betsey," "Billy," and "Sister." Bunny Mellon, whom I didn't know; Betsey Whitney, whom I didn't know; Billy Baldwin, whom I knew just enough to say hello to; and Sister Parish, whom I didn't know.

They were all clients or friends of John's, and it was just a joke. Sister had no idea what was happening, and later when she was back in New York, she told a friend, "I met this jerky guy in London—Mario Buchalalte or Buchellotti or something. He said he knew me and he was playing this game, but I didn't know what it was. I wish he'd told me, because then I'd have gone along with the game."

So that was the beginning of a series of things that happened over the years.

There was a dealer in London who used to work at Colefax & Fowler. She used to wear a babushka and was all painted up. She had more paint than anyone. She was sort of a difficult, unmarried English woman. She went on about how I should come over to her shop right away, as Mrs. Parish was arriving and was going to buy everything up. I said that I was very busy and that I would stop by on the way to the airport and look in the window. The shop was all windows, on a corner. So I got out this yellow piece of paper and listed twelve items and said I'd take this and that and so on, and I signed it, "Sister Parish" and slipped it under the door. The antiques were shipped to Parish-Hadley and Albert called and asked, "Is this one of your pranks?"

I ran into Sister a couple of days later in one of the workrooms and she said, "Well, I guess one of your jokes backfired." She had this way of looking at you like Lily Tomlin's Ernestine character. She had that quality about her of saying something funny and giving you a dirty look, but in the meantime, she really did get a big giggle out of it. She loved the attention.

SUSAN: In December of 1998, Albert hosted a special Parish-Hadley reunion Christmas party for everyone who had ever worked there. The party was at the new Parish-Hadley offices, the ones they had moved into after Sister died. After the party had been under way for an hour or so, everyone was asked to quiet down, as Albert had a few words to say. Looking as stylish as ever in the signature black turtleneck he always wore, he spoke with a voice filled with emotion.

As we listened to Albert, there was a sense, a feeling in the air, that the

Christmas spirit intensified, that we were witnessing a part of design history. There was Albert, who has always been a teacher, paying homage to the graduates and current employees of the firm that he and Sister built into what some consider to be the most influential decorating firm of the twentieth century. After toasting the past, which included a poignant salute to Mark Hampton, who had died that year, Albert spoke of the future. Both Sister and Albert were always looking toward the new, and his toast was in keeping with this. Sister and Albert shared a desire to be the best, to create the most beautiful, the most suitable, and, in some respects, the most daring rooms possible.

ALBERT HADLEY: The decorators who came to work for Parish-Hadley learned a lot about our basic point of view, and the philosophy that both Sis and I had. We knew that rooms are for people, and that you want to make them as attractive and comfortable as possible. That is what we hoped they would learn. I think anyone who was at Parish-Hadley with Sis came away with a lot of Sister's qualities. The good qualities of humanness and love. Sis loved the people she worked for, and she loved what she did; otherwise, she didn't do it. That came across.

As opposite as we were in many ways, we were totally on the same wavelength about what we were doing. We didn't always agree about the way we did it, but we agreed about the quality and honesty we wanted for each project.

Many people can learn to make a room appropriate, but they don't have that magic touch that she did. Some have come close, but no one has mastered it.

Following page: Mrs. Parish's dining room at 920 Fifth Avenue.

Chapter Ten

On Decorating

She taught me that it doesn't have to be perfect. That it doesn't have to match.
To follow your instincts.

LIBBY CAMERON

IT IS ONLY *my eye that has helped me. I am still hopeless with that thing called*
a scale ruler. I love color, but that comes very naturally to me. As in my dreams,
I am always in a garden, and in reality, it is where I am happiest.

I have heard I am supposed to represent the undecorated look. It is what I
like, but I am not sure that it is because I know no better.

I do not want you to think I do not like the "no color look" or "the pink and
green fascination" or even the "no clutter look." I enjoy them all, envy them,
admire them, but somehow I keep going back, I suppose, to the lovely old houses
of my mother and father.

From the beginning, I never followed trends. If I was aware of them, I didn't care, for I believed as I do now, that rooms should be timeless and very personal. I don't set out to achieve a particular style. And I certainly don't have a "look"—just a mishmash of everything that somehow, by instinct, usually turns out to be a warm, imaginative, "living" room.

If there is a theme to my work, it is the theme of my life—continuity. Things inherited from the past somehow always turn out to be the most interesting and beautiful things we can live with today.

I think it's so sad, seeing all those young people going up the elevators in the Decorator's Building, listening to them talk about the latest trends and styles and looks. I know that they'll never do anything the least bit attractive, that they're the reason there have to be so many hideous things on sale in the building. I'm appalled at what American taste really is today. I look in horror at the dreadful things that take up space in decorator magazines and in some of the good showrooms. The very worst is often the most expensive. The Palm Beach look, for instance—everything yellow and green, with dhurrie rugs and melon walls. Always two armchairs, two sofas, always a bridge group or a backgammon table, but not one ounce of imagination anywhere. Or the "modern" look. I see living rooms filled with furniture without backs, without arms, without sides—apparently, you are supposed to spend the rest of your life sitting with your feet dangling in front of you. There is also the industrial look, which belongs in factories, period. Right now, Art Deco is coming back, because they have nothing else to bring back. It is interesting, but again I am sure it will fall by the wayside. I have never developed a look or followed a trend because I knew that every person's life differs from every other, and everyone's needs are therefore different. The lessons I learned doing my own house and those I learned on my earliest commissions have been with me through my fifty years of decorating.

ALBERT HADLEY: With Sister, it was pure instinct. I remember one of the first jobs we installed was a job that she had been working on. It was Brooke Astor's Maine house in Northeast Harbor. We had the plans. Sister had obviously been there; she had it all schemed. I drove up from Dark Harbor to see the painter. I knew on paper exactly what the room was going to be. You know, the blue sofa was going to go here, the pink sofa was going to go here. Chairs, stools— everything was right on paper. The truck arrived to install all this, and there we both were. Pink sofas were flying one way and blue sofas were flying another. I was having a nervous breakdown. I thought, Who is this woman? She's gone crazy. This is not the plan. The end result was the most fabulous house. It didn't matter what had been planned. It was what happened when she got there and how she moved things and shoved them. And I mean, the sofas had been measured to fit exactly. They ended up overhanging the windows. They had no relation to anything. And of course that's the way she began. She'd walk in and she'd see a piece of furniture, and I'd be measuring, and she would say, "Oh, don't measure." And she made it fit. I can't do what she did. I have to know that things are going to fit where they're supposed to fit.

SUSAN: Billy Baldwin said the final judge in decorating is not the "logic of the mind, but the logic of the eye." At the Summer House in Maine, there are several rooms that have so much color in them that many people are taken aback. One guest room has a painted red floor, three of the walls are painted a different color red, and the fourth is papered with red-white-and-green wallpaper, which seems like it has always been slightly peeling. There are two canopy beds with an old flowered chintz on the canopies and stiff white cotton bedspreads. The rest of the furniture is very Maine—a bureau that was probably from the old Islesboro Inn, painted white, and a table, also painted white, with a set of ivory brushes with Sister's initials on them. The curtains are plain white muslin. The beds are high so that children have to climb up onto them, and the windows and door look out onto the porch. Looking in from the porch at night, the lamplight is soft and romantic as it bounces off the red glow of the walls. The adjoining bedroom's walls are painted a deep blue, and the rug is the famous multicolored striped wool first found by Sister and Albert in Ireland. In the blue bedroom, the canopy bed that Sister was born in is situated so that you can see out across the bay when you open your eyes in the morning. There is a chaise longue and a gigantic Aitkin sofa covered with two different chintzes. There are animal and flower objects and drawings everywhere.

Decorating of this kind cannot be achieved with "the logic of the mind," the elements are so baroque, so colorful, so mixed up. They have to flow naturally and instinctively from the maker's imagination. This was where Sister excelled.

HAROLD SIMMONS: She and Albert had a good influence on each other. Albert had an enormous sense of style, but he was very structured. Sister's style was a much looser way of decorating. She loosened him up; he gave her structure.

They did sometimes fight tooth and nail, but they worked well as a team, and the firm took off. In the sixties, when Albert joined the firm, they were doing work that no one else was doing. They used quilts and crafts, color and elaborate glazed walls, highly lacquered furniture, batiks, and painted floors done in patterns. They were one of the first to mix casual fabrics with serious furniture. Parish-Hadley rooms were not stylish stage sets; they were comfortable rooms.

ANNETTE DE LA RENTA (client): Sister admired all of Albert's structured architectural taste. She was proud of what Albert did, and of how he could bring off his minimalist look. Everyone who is sick of chintz goes back to that look now. Billy Baldwin and Albert promoted brown walls, white furniture, and bookcases, and many people have now ditched the chintz look and returned to just that.

ALICE ROGERS (client): In our house, there is a room she always referred to as the "card room" because we always used it in the evening for playing bridge or for the times when the children were playing games. That room had a fireplace and a wonderful mantel, but it needed something over it. Sister found these marvelous plates. So we were there at the house one afternoon and she said, "These should go there."

When she made an announcement like that, you didn't question it. You didn't question her, since it would make her unhappy because she knew she was right. So you sort of went with it, knowing that it was going to be all right, whether you were convinced of it at the moment or not.

There was a carpenter called Lyman Wardwell working there that day, so I said, "Sister, let's wait a minute. We've got to make sure these are spaced properly. I want to get a measuring tape." And she said, "Oh, don't be silly, Alice." Then she said, "Lyman, this one goes here; this one goes here. . . ."

She just did it, and when they were finished, they were right. No ruler. Just her eye. And her eye was so good. She couldn't be bothered to fuss with it. It just took too much time, and that was not her style. She and Lyman were quite a pair, if you remember Lyman.

DAVID KLEINBERG: When we decorated the de Kwiatkowski house in Greenwich, Alan Wozenberg was the architect. It was Mrs. Parish and myself and Alan, and he was taking us up to walk through the house. It wasn't under construction yet, as they were just starting. They had it staked out where the addition was going to go. So we went up to Greenwich, to the construction site, but the stone part of the original house and garage building was there, and we walked through it. Alan is very thoughtful as an architect. He is highly trained, has rationales and musings and historical precedents for every door trim and baseboard molding you've ever seen. Which is great. Mrs. Parish walked through and looked, and then she stood back and asked, "Where is the front door again?"

And Alan said, "It's going to be here."

She looked at him and said, "Well, you realize of course that the whole house is backward."

He said, "Excuse me?" thinking all the time that she was bonkers, that she didn't understand his whole two-hour tour. And she said, "If that's where their front door is going to be, then your parking is going to be there. I think that's where the garden should be. Who wants to go look out from the living room and see cars?"

Alan was completely thunderstruck. He looked at her and said, "Well, that's a thought." He called her back not very long afterward and said, "You're absolutely right."

He turned the house around. He flipped the whole entry. But it took her no time at all to realize the whole house was backward. It was things like that that made her so good. That she could see the big picture. She couldn't tell you why.

LIBBY CAMERON (former Parish-Hadley decorator): I think she always berated herself for not having a good education, but she just knew. She just was very intuitive and very sensitive to how people lived and how they should feel comfortable. So I think that, in a way, was part of her genius.

She taught me that it doesn't have to be perfect. That it doesn't all have to match. To really follow your instincts. I could never learn Albert's way because I'm not as precise as he is. I don't have the background in terms of education to really be able to pull up all these great houses. I've been to a lot of them—a lot of wonderful houses—but to be able to say what Chatsworth looks like—the dining room curtains or the drawing room curtains—that's just not in my memory bank. I don't study books the way Albert did, but I don't think that Mrs. Parish did, either. I think she saw something pretty and it stuck in her head as something she liked. And obviously, she was well traveled and went to some pretty nice houses, which in itself was an education.

SUSAN: Sister's rooms were obviously influenced by her many trips to England and her lifelong admiration for the so-called English country look, which her parents had brought into her childhood houses.

* * *

I sailed to England in 1948 with my old Foxcroft classmate Bunny Mellon to discuss a possible business tie-up with Colefax & Fowler. They sent me furnishings that I sold in New York, and I sent them things like tassels, which they had trouble producing in England after the war. But the arrangement was soon stopped because of currency restrictions.

By championing the so-called English country look—chintz, needlework, the most sumptuous upholstery—Colefax & Fowler became the most influential decorating firm in Britain. John Fowler was the motor. When I think of John, I think of impossibly detailed curtains with dressmaker furbelows, and of rooms that are romantic without being sentimental or bitsy, a look that is very difficult to achieve. The man himself was unassuming—as English as Billy Baldwin was American. Working in New York, Billy designed in a modern idiom without abandoning the past. He loved plain curtains, plaster lamps, straw, rattan, and bamboo. He and John liked luxury that didn't shout.

John's partner was my American friend Nancy Lancaster. When you were her guest at Ditchley Park, she could take you to any house you wanted to see.

Sister and Nancy Lancaster in England.

At Ditchley, the walls were hung with nineteenth-century damask that Nancy dared to bleach. And she approached the bathrooms as real rooms, filling them with furniture, an original idea at the time. At Haseley Court, where she later lived, Nancy sat at one end of the dining room in a Queen Anne wing chair, slip-covered in chintz and with pillows thrown in its hollows. Except for the man sitting opposite in a chair that was the twin to hers, all the other guests were given tufted William IV leather ones. I always found the contrast amusing.

SUSAN: Nancy Lancaster was the daughter of one of the famous Langhorne sisters from Virginia and also one of the great decorators of our time. She lived in England most of her adult life, where she was at one time married to Ronald Tree. Tree owned the famous house Ditchley Park, which Nancy completely remodeled using innovations that reflected her Virginia hospitality and the English charm of that fantastic house. Ronald's second wife, Marietta Tree, was also a friend of Sister's. Sister visited Ditchley after the War, at which time Ronald was married to Marietta.

Ditchley

Darling Harry,

I just hung up from talking to you. It is not very satisfying and really rather upsets me in the way that I feel guilty and wish you all were here with me. If only I could describe it better. In your most fantastic dreams you could not imagine such beauty. Michael brought me down. We were met at Oxford in a beautiful dark blue car. The countryside is just a mass of jonquils, bluebell blossoms, and lush green fields, walled gardens with fruit trees climbing up the walls, rosy-cheeked children, thousands of bicycles (no cars), horse and carts.

Ronnie and Marietta opened the door and in I walked to the most fantastically beautiful house that I have ever hoped to see. You feel Nancy Lancaster in every corner. Room after room of such pieces, the way they are placed, the needlework carpets, crystal chandeliers—all candles, china—Oh Lord, it's terrific. First is the great hall (where we had high tea), the china room (silk walls), the velvet room (velvet red walls), then the green and white writing room, then stucco room, then library (50 feet long), then Ronnie's desk room, then large dining room, then breakfast room. Each one is more perfect than the last. A good deal of the furniture was here from when it was built in 1700. The bedrooms are even better if possible. All four-poster beds with crowned tops. In my room now I had to get on a little stepladder (covered in white damask) to get up. The furniture is white lacquer with green jade! Each bath has a fireplace and such gems as needlework bath mats, beautiful consoles (as sinks), baskets of toilet paper with lavender bags—I could go on forever, but I have no power of description.

Dinner something—fresh asparagus, four glasses of one thing after another, just the boys and the D'Elangers—great fun and laughter—bed at one. I still have that boat rocking, but I had a good night. As I look down from my bed now in every direction vistas of trees. One vista is of chestnut trees (in full bloom), then elms, then beech. A boxwood garden with lime tree hedges—sheep are roaming the pastures and deer the park!

I have little paper left so I will go to London—the shop is wonderful. I am to have a business talk with Mr. Fowler tomorrow. Everyone is nice and kind. I can't remember if I told you that Nancy's (Lancaster) house is worth the entire trip.

I'm thrilled I came and I know I will get lots out of it—I only wish you could be here to see it. Next time we must do it together. No one talks of war here. Every other house in London is down with little building going on.

I must get dressed now. Bless you all.

Sister

KEITH IRVINE: Nancy Lancaster really invented the English country look. In an English house, there is no heat and there is little comfort. The houses are cold or underheated and the furniture is falling to bits. Springs are coming through the furniture, and they have lousy bathrooms. Nancy was the one who pulled up the standards because she always insisted on fabulous, comfortable furniture, beautiful antiques, and comfortable bathrooms. They had lamp shades and flowers, everything. Looking back over all those years, I think she was a bigger influence than John Fowler.

I find that many of my clients automatically talk about things for their house as a "good investment," something they can sell, rather than talking about what they can achieve for their own life. I find myself saying over and over again,

"Please do what you do well and don't think of it as just for now." I know that it pays in the end. Even if life does change, you will always remember what you did, and you will have glorious memories.

Expressing personal feelings and memories is the essence of decorating. I find that people who can abandon the old screened porch, hide the wicker without paint, or uproot the first rosebush they ever planted are lacking in feelings for what I call "home." Hundreds of roses can't make up for the pride you felt in that first bush. That is true of your room, your house, your first possession. The first thing I ever bought on my own was what is called a cobbler's bench. My pride in that purchase, my original love for that monstrosity, is still with me, and though I admit I tuck it away as much as possible, it is still right there in my study in Maine. It is a memory, a good feeling, not a cobbler's bench.

SUSAN: When you look at Sister's drawings, her focus on the objects is obvious. She told me that every house should have a collection, and I know that some of her happiest times were with Grandpa while hunting for things in antiques shops here and in England. In her papers I found a proposed article on how to decorate on a budget. This was right after the war and her first tip was on collecting. Sister began her first collection of Staffordshire figures with her father when she was a little girl in Far Hills. My mother has many of them now. Her collections were different in the city and in the country. In New York, she had an ivory collection on her desk, and in Maine, she had collections of just about everything she loved, porcelain fruits and vegetables, baskets, American flags, wicker, her mother's vases.

The habit of bringing home one's children a present from all of one's trips can be a great advantage in many ways for the future. The usual teddy bear, box of candy, or ruffled doll is not going to give the child taste, love of nice things, or any desire to create. Why not start with a Staffordshire figure for the mantelpiece (you will see that Christmas will bring another). A comfortable desk like a Chippendale dressing table gives them room for their long legs to stretch out, with drawers on each side for their correspondence. Such a desk gives dignity and importance to their work. You will find springing from that one piece a love to continue and make a room that will last.

LIBBY CAMERON: Usually when a house was being installed, she'd go on this mad shopping trip all over New York and cull all these things that she'd like, and she'd deliver them to that apartment the same time that the furniture was being delivered and then she'd set up. There would be the birdcages, the baskets. She'd go to Pier One and get trays, pretty blankets that Robin Goss made—you know, fuzzy blankets. Pillows. The one she liked—ribbony pillows—the more cottony woven ones. Dishes and plates that she'd put on tables. She would just choose things in shops that she liked personally and she'd put them in. Depending on the client, she varied in how much she would do. Some clients were opposed to it; others loved it. She loved animals—dogs, birds, dishes with creatures on them. She'd sneak in the little table that would go beside the chair. The basket that you could stick your notepaper in. She would bring all of that in.

She loved needlepoint pillows and then a whole lot of Victorian things, even though I don't think she was Victorian by any means. She had lots of bellpulls, those needlepoint strips that butlers used to pull to ring bells in the kitchen. I know she had a yellow one that had animals on it in her apartment in New York. She loved anything with color, texture, paint, interest and, I think, pattern. She loved cotton materials from Mexico and Guatemala, big Irish baskets, painted furniture, and she loved flowers. It was a big testament to her—always having fresh flowers around. She always did. And everything was always very neat.

She had her favorite ways of doing things. A single number of kick pleats, edges on pillows. The fact that she said that curtains always have to have edging on them; they can't just end. And the same thing—she hated stripes that just stopped on a corner, as opposed to having a piece of molding to finish them properly.

She had lots of tricks that she liked to use. Trimmings . . . she liked to mix it all up. She liked finding old pieces of fabric—not rags—that she could use along with something new. Put it in the center or use it as a border. She loved doing all that. Mixing it up. Which is what gives it character.

I think about that one little chair in her Victorian living room at Dark Harbor—a rocking chair that has quilting on front and something totally different on the back. That sort of sums her up. She was totally fearless about mixing it up.

JACQUELINE GONNET (magazine editor): I was the decorating editor at *House & Garden* for twenty-five years. I was responsible for all of the things that we did about Sister. Sister could throw a scarf over something or put on one of her favorite tablecloths and make it look right. She loved crazy objects and all kind of crafts. Sister put people in business, got women sewing. She certainly put that look on the map. She used wonderfully happy colors. I would say that was one of the differences between Albert and Sister. One of the reasons they did so well together. Albert had this very different palette from Sister's.

Sister taught by example. People learned by looking. She would send somebody into the market and say she wanted such and such. Originally, Parish-Hadley had none of their own fabrics or their own furniture. All that had grown through the years.

She did a lot of antiquing, and I think she knew antiques extremely well. To see her go to one of the big antique shows with her clients was extraordinary. She knew exactly what she was looking for. She went through the show at the Seventh Regiment Armory in New York with a fine-tooth comb. Not just antiques . . . but everything Americana. For instance, wicker, which is not an antique, but is an American art form. I remember once up in Maine, being in the backyard with her when a truck went by filled with wicker. She said, "We've got to get out. Run, quick, and get in the car and follow that truck, because I've got to find out where it came from and where it's going!"

BUNNY WILLIAMS: In a way, her rooms were all about the great objects. When she died, look what they sold for because they were beautiful.

Some of them were very good and some were not so good, but the objects she chose had an intrinsic kind of warmth and style to them. That's what makes decorating magic. It's not about mixing a material and matching it up with the other thing. That'll kill decorating faster than anything. It's what's interesting.

She wasn't a furniture collector herself, but she knew good furniture because she'd inherited some. If she wanted a beautiful big pair of gilded sconces, when she found them, they'd be fantastic.

MARCIE BRAGA: In a quietly grand manner, her rooms were built around comfort first, a quality where, as you sat there, nothing jumped out at you. These rooms were completely unpretentious. She was brilliant at that. You never went into a room and said, "God, these people want to look rich."

Her rooms—you didn't even notice that there was a Degas horse except after a while, until you put it together and realized the quality of the objects.

She was the person who taught me about silhouettes in a room. If you looked around, she had animals on her candlesticks, the shaped birds; her

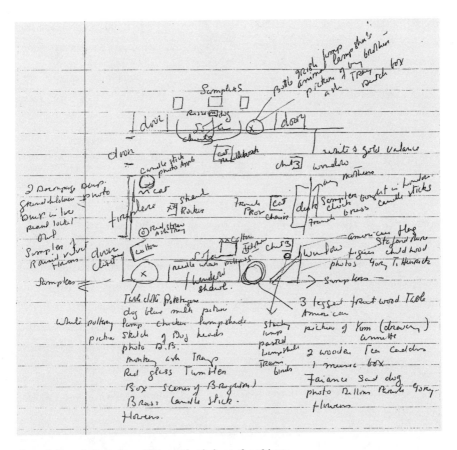

One of Sister's floorplans. The emphasis is on the objects.

tables were just beautiful, and you really had to look at them to see what you were looking at, as opposed to a pair of candlesticks, a few books, and an ashtray. She never had a simple table like that. She had real treasures, though. She had an incredible eye for them.

CARL-PETER BRAESTRUP (Sister's cousin): The scale of her houses in Maine—it always seemed that the ceilings were low and the furniture was low. When I, as someone who is over six feet tall, sat, I always felt that my feet were up around my nose and I might break everything I touched. I went to a couple of cocktail parties with Susan, Sister's granddaughter, and Susan's husband, Doug, and there would be other men there. All of us looked ridiculous—just huge—compared to everything else in the apartment. It was all sort of scaled to her. I remember a formal living room in her New York apartment and there was this little park bench in that room. I can remember thinking, Why is there this park bench? I guess that was what was interesting about her work. She would put a simple, inexpensive item in a very formal room.

MRS. CHARLES PERCY (client): She used needlepoint rugs, antique gold furniture, and painted furniture. She loved flowers and always said Ann Getty in San Francisco knew instinctively how to arrange them in huge masses. She believed everything should be kept up. Always paint a little so that things look fresh. She was always looking for the unusual, and if she saw something in a window in London she would buy it and send it to me.

MARY JANE POOL (magazine editor): Her rooms were put together with an artist's eye, so that from every angle they were just filled with interesting things and wonderful colors. She put together little vignettes that appealed to her. I always loved what the photographer Horst said once. He said he would watch where the owner sat, and he would go and sit there because it was always the best view in the room. Sister's rooms were never boring. They welcomed you. They didn't put you off. And they varied so. It wasn't always the "Sister Parish look." Each room was individual, and children and dogs were welcome there.

RICHARD MANDER (oversaw construction and custom furniture at Parish-Hadley): Sister was a good, smart businessperson. She didn't get hung up on what might have been or could have been or may have been. Let's go on and let's get to the next one, and that's an art and a testimony to basically courage and being smart and being self-assured. And knowing that virtually anything that she did, she would do well because she was good. You know, she didn't have this big self-doubt that an awful lot of decorators have, which is a crippling thing. Once the customer senses that insecurity, they come back in your face and make you redo it. Then it's a disaster. Those are some of the real reasons I think that Sister was a genius.

The elms and maples around the house started with a tinge of yellow traveling to golden yellows, then flaming reds and rust. Again, I was always aware of color that continued to follow me all of these days. When I say that colors do not fit together, my partner, Albert, answers that there are no colors that don't get along. Take, for example, a bunch of mixed flowers that he was holding in his hand. No two like colors, do you see, and yet they all work together.

* * *

BUNNY WILLIAMS: I can't think that she ever missed with color. She had an extraordinary eye for color, and sometimes I would think, This is a little stronger than I might like, but that's what she wanted. She was never afraid of it. She always, somehow, even when she was working with a stronger color, managed to find the old fabrics and the old piece of needlework to take the edge off the brashness of it. And that is something that most people don't get right. I mean, once they start with a strong color palette, they never stop, and so you walk in these rooms and they are an absolute nightmare. And yet she knew how to balance the clarity of an enhanced color with some old piece of fabric to suggest that there was a sense of patina. In that last apartment that she had on Fifth Avenue—I mean that very strong dining room with the chintz walls and the orange sitting room—it was pretty intense. And yet there were old pieces of needlework, and somehow you never felt that it was screaming *color*.

MARK HAMPTON: I think the immediate impression that her apartments made was a bit of excess—not excessiveness. Just cushy and soft and delicious, and beautiful things everywhere. Whimsical touches of color cropping up everywhere. Mrs. Parish was a brilliant colorist and had a marvelous way of injecting color into rooms where the materials of the room itself didn't have color. She always had tremendous flowers. All the things in the Seventy-ninth Street house she had—before she made it all dark brown and put those wonderful flame-colored curtains up—were cream with beautiful green, sort of French, what you think of as Madame de Pompadour green. And that antique Aubusson. And it was an Aubusson with a pile. It was a very beautiful carpet. It had to go out every single summer to be majorly repaired. But the whole room was off-white, with that green lettucey-cabbagey faience that she loved. She always had those leaf plates on the dining table and that Leeds ware, that Pierce Leeds ware. Always those delicate Battersea candlesticks. I remember one evening idly counting the number of candles burning in the living room. There were fourteen, plus the lamps. But the other thing, apart from the beauty, was the oddity of the objects. Those three-legged tables with funny little chairs. There was a terrific sense of lightness. She wasn't keen on brown furniture. I mean, most things were beautifully painted and kept up. There was a Frenchness about it that didn't have that "elderly lady" quality that a room filled with French things and crammed with objects so easily can have.

MARIO BUATTA: She had the tea cart to take things away that she didn't approve of. That's one thing I've never copied. I've never copied the cart thing. They used to say I copied her, and I would tease her about this and call her up and ask, "Anything new I can learn? Anything new I can copy?" She loved it.

I've always been a very, very neat person. My father always used to say, "Never leave the room without doing what you have to do. If it's a scrap basket that has to be emptied, do it now, not later." Having been brought up the way I was, with every glass sparkling and every dish put away, I know no other way. I don't think I've ever gone from one room to another in my little apartment without doing two things at once.

MARK HAMPTON: Her houses were the result of great housekeeping. In New York, remember those shiny floors down that long hall? And the brasses were brilliantly shiny. The windows were always clean and the curtains were always fluffed out. She must have been a tyrant for the parlor maids. We know she was.

DAVID KLEINBERG: Good housekeeping was the most important thing for her. She cared about nothing more. It used to make her so sad if we went back someplace and she thought it wasn't well maintained. She hated that. She didn't care if things were worn out as long as they were clean. She didn't like things to look messy, all disheveled, disarranged. She cared about the hospitality of a house a lot. It was interesting to me that she was this famous decorator and at the end of the day she didn't care about whether the room was blue or green, but, rather, how the room felt. She liked some things better than others. I don't think I ever saw her pick up a chintz with a black or brown background. She liked certain colors of pink rather than other colors of pink. She hated beige—just because, I think, Albert liked the color. She called it "kicky." She'd say, "That's a terrible kicky color." She didn't like fabrics that were too shiny, because she thought they were slimy. She didn't like things that looked skimpy, like skimpy curtains. She thought curtains should look full and delicious. She could put a four-poster bed with bed-hangings in any room she went into.

But really, at the end of the day, I think she cared most about housekeeping. If there were fingerprints on the door trim, that would drive her crazy. The quality of the food in the house and the bed linens mattered to her—

what the tray looked like if someone brought you tea. She could accept big flaws, but it was the little things that just showed how people lived.

APPLE: The linen closets in Maine are beautiful. Each shelf is edged in a pink-and-white scalloped paper and there are lists of each piece of linen drawn up by the island laundress (and Mummy's friend), Mrs. Hale. They're carefully thumbtacked to each shelf. Each desk always had a multitude of sharpened pencils, rolls of stamps, and boxes of the house stationery. Next to each phone were the same masses of pencils and little white pads with DON'T FORGET at the top, where she was always writing endless notes. And, believe me, she did not forget. The flower room in Maine has shelves and shelves of vases that were my grandmother's, along with those that Mummy found. Everything was always in perfect order.

D. B. GILBERT: When I think of Mummy's houses, I think of coziness and comfort and just feeling totally happy. They are happy houses. They make you feel good. They make you feel that this is where you want to be and you are happy to have people see how cozy you can be.

Both of my parents loved flowers, and this undoubtedly had a strong influence on my life and work. My father specialized in raising spray orchids, and he became as enthusiastic and scholarly about horticulture as he was about furniture. Thanks to my parents' care, and Angelo's hard work, our greenhouses and flower gardens were always well tended, the earth moist and freshly turned, the cuttings spaced in precise rows in the greenhouse, and instant death to any weed that poked its head above the ground. The smell of the box gardens brings such memories back to me. I can picture all of our family sitting on the terrace, talking about who wore what to the party, and the smell of the boxwood would be so intrusive that someone would invariably interrupt to say, "I think it smells even lovelier today." It would turn our minds, and our conversation. I grew up with enormous pots of geraniums and chrysanthemums that banked the house, and vases of roses everywhere. I often spent hours with Mother arranging the roses and the sprays of fresh-cut flowers. One of the specialties were our bowls of potpourri. Mother and I would dry the flowers until they were crisp, add lavender and orrisroot, and arrange them loosely in bowls.

I still have all of my mother's vases, and each one holds memories as well as flowers. I feel a tenderness toward the little cracks in the china, or a handle that's been glued back on, because I can remember when it happened long ago.

Today, I beg each of my clients to keep vases or pots of flowers, however small, in each room. Somehow, it makes the rooms so much more alive. It becomes a pleasant part of daily life to make sure the plants have water, a dead blossom is cut, a brown leaf removed.

I have had some of my plant trees for years and years; they've been with me so long, they're part of my life. Into the little greenhouse they go in the autumn in Dark Harbor, in winter and spring, and in May, back they go to the exact spot on the porch for the summer. I think of my love of flowers, my need for flowers, as a precious inheritance.

APPLE: I think of Mummy sitting on the porch and fiddling around in the garden and saying, "All I want to do is stop working and get my hands dirty in the garden. I just want to get all muddy and dirty." I never saw her actually work in the garden. She'd say, "Steve [or Wallace], move that pot," and they would spend hours, particularly at the beginning of summer, moving the pot two or three inches. And then a brilliant idea. "I'm going to have only one or two types of flowers." Of course, the white garden was in memory of her mother. For the new garden, she had elaborate plans made by a landscape architect from Boston. Actually, this person helped with the white garden also, sprucing it up. The woman unfortunately got some lilies for the white garden that turned out to be yellow. And that was a terrible thing. And she actually suggested for the new lattice garden that soil be brought in from the mainland. Mummy did not want that. She would ask, "What was wrong with the island dirt?" She was always so practical.

She always talked about the food from the "gahden." "Have some beets. They're from the gahden." And the garden cost millions of dollars every year to plant. It was so beautiful. The new vegetable garden was one of the prettiest she'd designed; it had a snake fence. She was very, very proud of that garden. She'd walk down there with the dogs and go look at the gahden.

SUSAN: She certainly felt a house was incomplete or second-rate without flowers. She did not mean forced hothouse arrangements—she would die rather than use the phrase "flower arrangements"—but bulbs, primroses in clay pots, orchids, flowers from her cutting gardens, huge tubs of bay leaves from the fields in Maine. She would tell guests that the vegetables were from the "gahden," which gave them a sacred status. The apartment in New York was also always filled with flowers. Flowers have always given me a feeling of luxury and comfort, a sense that everything is going to be okay somehow, that there is security.

Once when Sister was in the hospital, she became furious with me because I didn't know the names of all the flowers that had been sent to her. She thought it was a deficiency in my education. I shot back at her, "Well, you don't know all the presidents."

MARK HAMPTON: To go there for lunch or dinner was to see all these flowers and vases. I went there for lunch one day and she had these vases that were all sort of urn-shaped, but different, and all filled with three different shades of pink carnations in the green-and-white room. With these big, long stems all sort of dripping over, they were beautiful. I loved how they looked, and nobody liked carnations. Still nobody likes carnations, but I loved them. Carnations in the finest rooms. The only spot of color in the room other than the green and white was this beautiful paprika-colored silk velvet on that sofa between the columns of the cockatoos. There was always this repeated love of anything botanical.

Mrs. Parish said, "I was given this Japanese wallpaper. A very valuable wallpaper. I asked Mr. Crowninshield to look at it because he knew a lot about Oriental things." He said, "Oh, its Japanese. A confused style, I would say." She loved telling these things. Anything that made fun of herself. Which was so attractive, I thought.

I loved those panels, a paper bag brown, and those white chrysanthemums and that mirror-polished floor, and then there was always that lacquer cabinet that had the drinks on top of it. But this love of anything botanical—for a New York apartment, this gave an incredible garden atmosphere.

JACQUELINE GONNET: Sister knew where to put flowers in the room and what colors to use. Her things were always very natural. She helped to innovate the "just went out and picked" look.

I had a lot of fun with her. Mostly, I remember elegance and comfort when I think of Sister. With all of the elegance, you could always find something that the owners had, some very intimate things that humanized the rooms. Her attention to detail on the curtains and on the tables and, of course, the colors and the flowers. She had a wonderful eye. *House & Garden* always used wonderful flowers. The famous photographer Horst had a way about photographing them, and Sister understood that very well. We did a lot of assignments with Horst, and she loved to work with him. They got along very well. He was so charming and elegant, very elegant.

I remember Horst was a good sport, because we went to Maine one time on a little puddle-jumper and were left off in a field. There was no one to meet us, not a soul around, and this was before the days of portable phones. When Sister finally came to meet us, she was in a great big truck. We had just been standing around waiting. We took a walk to a local farmhouse and called up. She said, "Oh, you're right. You're due here today. I'll be right over to get you."

MARK HAMPTON: Before I came to New York, I had worked as a student in London for David Hicks. Which is the only thing on my résumé that looked like it had to do with decorating, that day I talked to Albert in 1963.

We went to stay with David and Pammy Hicks in this incredibly beautiful house they had in Oxfordshire for many years, and then they sold it and got one of their cottages. Pammy was the daughter of Lord Mountbatten, who was Viceroy of India and, of course, very close to the royal family. David and Mrs. Lancaster didn't like each other. She didn't get his point at all. At that moment, he was a great rival because he was becoming so famous as a decorator and also doing these beautiful rooms, in the days before he became all so purple and red. Crazy. Sister said, "Now if you're going to be staying with Mr. Hicks, then it's just a few miles from Mrs. Lancaster, and you should call her. I'll let her know that you're going to be there."

Well, she did indeed give me Nancy Lancaster's number. I chickened out because I knew that David and Nancy Lancaster were not great friends and I thought it would look too pushy, and I'm pushy enough as it is. To go stay with David and Pammy and get on the horn and call Nancy Lancaster would never have done. So I never called her. The minute we got back—at some point very soon after—we had drinks with Mrs. Parish, and she said, "How stupid, you never called Nancy Lancaster." So she followed through on things in a remarkable way.

Sister did love furniture. There were these famous red lacquered chairs. David and Pammy had owned them, but they now belong to someone here in New York. They were made by a great cabinetmaker. They were Queen Anne chairs with a back shaped like a shell . . . the most marvelous chairs. They had been bought in the thirties by the Mountbattens, Pammy's parents, for their big modern flat at the top of Brook House in London. Their decorator was an American woman named Nell Causton, who had been married to this very rich man whose fortune had sort of slipped during the Depression, as so many did. Sister went over once with Mrs. Lancaster to see David's house. Like him or not, Nancy Lancaster wanted to see this house. He was thrilled to show them the whole house, and he took them upstairs to where these twelve chairs were lined up against the paneling of this beautiful T-shaped hall. You couldn't use them as dining chairs because they were too expensive and fragile. The minute Sister got upstairs, she looked in and said, "Oh, Nell Causton's old dining room chairs." She hadn't seen these chairs since the thirties, and this was the sixties. And she always pretended not to remember anything. She had it all up here. Remember how I used to say to her, "Well, what was it like?" and she'd say, "Who could remember?"

It would be so fascinating in life if you could just see something through someone else's eyes for just a minute.

As a child, I discovered the happy feelings that familiar things can bring—an old apple tree, a favorite garden, the smell of a fresh-clipped hedge, simply knowing that when you round the corner, nothing will be changed, nothing will be gone. I try to instill that lucky part of my life in each house that I do. Some think a decorator should change a house. I try to give permanence to a house, to bring out the experiences, the memories, the feelings that make it a home.

SUSAN: Sister never used the word *design*. If she did, she would shudder as she said it. Any reference to someone connected to Parish-Hadley was referred to in connection with the "office." Work was the office. She would also never speak of anything in terms of decorating or, egads, "design principles." What she would speak of was the importance of family, and this was obviously what inspired her work, as well. If she had a decorating philosophy, this was it.

Sister began to develop the so-called American country style in the thirties, when she decorated her first house in New Jersey using simple mattress ticking, wicker, painted floors, and painted furniture. All of these things seem familiar to us now, even hackneyed, but when she brought them to a wider audience in the sixties, the look was considered revolutionary. When *House & Garden* first published photographs of the Summer House, her house in Maine, in 1965, the design world was wowed. Here was the Americana everyone knew from their grandmother's house, made sophisticated and new. With Albert's help, Parish-Hadley elevated the American country look by mixing it in some of the of the most sophisticated rooms in the world. The sixties were also the perfect era to champion American and ethnic folk art, which emanated from simple craftsmen who handed down their crafts from generation to generation. Sister and Albert both had a nose for finding these people, and eventually they were working with folk artists from all over the world.

Recently, a decorating book listed the "innovations" of our firm, Parish-Hadley. My partner, Albert Hadley, and I were delighted when patchwork quilts, four-poster beds, painted floors, knit throws, rag rugs, painted valances, and handwoven bedspreads were listed among our innovations. The list sounds old-fashioned, but we were pleased, because in decorating, innovation is often the ability to reach into the past and bring back what is good, what is useful, and what is lasting.

Both Albert and I, I think, were born with imagination, and that has helped us go a long way. Certainly we did not invent quilts, and I wish now that we had never revived them. Painted floors—another revival that has swept the country. Four-poster beds—certainly nothing new, but it seems now one can't live without a canopy. Highly glazed walls now are imperative. Last but not least, that old battered basket that makes your life.

ALBERT HADLEY: One day, Diana Vreeland called us and said there was a man in her office whom we should meet right away. He was from Alabama, and he was the head of the Freedom Quilting Bee.

So we talked to him, and we felt working with him could be a terrific idea. Sis did not like his colors or fabrics, so Jim Wagnon from our office went down to Alabama. He took bolts of fabrics that we chose, and they interpreted all their traditional patterns with our colors and fabrics. We had material made, yards and yards of each pattern in brilliant colors.

The first thing we did was upholster a big sofa at the Paleys' country house in a quilt material. It was bright yellow and orange. Then, when we were moving Senator Charles Percy and his wife from Chicago to Washington, we had curtains made for their dining room in a quilt material. Years later, when Sharon Percy married Jay Rockefeller, who was then the governor of West Virginia, Sharon remembered these curtains and thought of working with the people of West Virginia, doing the same kind of things with quilts. It was a successful venture, and that was the beginning of the public's exposure to reinterpreting old patterns in a new way.

You see, this was in the sixties, and Sis had the most wild sort of sense of color and pattern. From then on, we were on the cutting edge. There is no question about it. I don't think anyone was doing anything like what we were at that time.

MARY JANE POOL: When I think of Sister, I think of change. I think of color; I think of crafts. She was never bogged down by tradition or by getting stuck in a period. She just always went forward; she never stood still. I think it's because she understood all periods of furniture and she loved the best of them, the most interesting and the most colorful. Wherever she went, she found wonderful things made by craftspeople. She loved those things that showed the work of the hand.

Her use of crafts was the beginning of an awareness for many people. Of course, there were collectors of Americana. But I think she introduced it to a wider audience through the magazines. She didn't only do the collector's pieces; she did the contemporary pieces that you could buy, such as quilts. She wasn't just a collector of old things, but she really recognized and encouraged the craftsmen of her time. Alan Campbell's materials are a great example.

SUSAN: In the orange room at the Summer House, there is a huge standing bureau filled with Sister's material scraps. She loved to decoupage and she would hoard all of these swatches and prints for cutting out. The houses in Maine are filled with lamp shades that have been decoupaged, as well as screens and mirrors that also have been covered in material or paper designs. She also loved to pinprick the lamp shades around the decoupage print and then paint a design on the background. Sister was always working either on her needlepoint or decoupage of some kind. Her rooms were filled with the work of her own hands or that of others.

A local carpenter in Maine, Lyman Wardwell, sculpted dogs out of wood that she was crazy about. They filled her houses. She was always the first at the Baptist church's fair, scooping up the handmade pot holders, mittens, and quilts that the Maine island ladies had been working on all winter.

APPLE: The rag rugs in Mum's house in Dark Harbor, and the ones that she had made for Caroline Kennedy's bedroom in the White House, were all made by the same talented woman, Helen Gushee, from Appleton, Maine. The rugs were all pastels: pale prints mixed with the palest solids: light blues, yellows, pinks, and lime greens. They are as wonderful today as they were when they were first made in the sixties.

Later, when Helen was in her eighties, she would make place mats for my shop in Boston. They were of the same colors and patterns as the rag rugs, and they sold like hotcakes. One time, I called to order more and I asked Helen how many she could send. She replied, "Well, that all depends on how big a box my son brings to me. If it's a very small box, there might only be four. If it's a larger box, there might be a dozen or two."

There were many people like Helen Gushee whom Mum encouraged and supported.

ALBERT HADLEY: We were introducing all of the handmade things and combining the simple and the primitive with the sophistication of good furniture and lacquer, which Sis had a good eye for.

We were using things that people had seen but had never used for decoration. For example, Guatemalan cotton, which we used a lot of. I was doing a room for the Kips Bay Show House, and I wanted to use a real zebra rug, but you couldn't use them, so I said, "Why don't we get the woman in Maine to make big hooked zebra rugs?" So they did make them for years. The charm was the combination of the homemade next to the more glamorous or the more sophisticated. Just the way that Sis would put some wooden dog that was made by some man in Maine on the most marvelous lacquer table. We'd do anything if we thought it looked good.

JACQUELINE GONNET: You know she always loved and used crafts before everyone else did. She was certainly a forerunner in that. Martha Stewart, Mary Emmerling . . . she was way ahead of them. But it was always with a great deal of sophistication; it was never a down-home look.

APPLE: Mum was not only interested in quilting, weaving, and decoupage; she also wanted to know how to do it herself.

She hired Robin Goss to help her get started with weaving, and she had a loom in the barn for years. Mum was an avid decouper. She was a scissors and glue person, but she was unable to paint the backgrounds, so she always had someone in the office do that for her. Her collages were totally whimsical— anything that caught her eye. She used ribbons, wallpaper borders, clippings from newspapers, and swatches from the office. She would mix rabbits with ribbons, priceless botanical prints with some little doily from the hardware store. There was no end to her imagination for combining different things. In fact, her collages looked rather like some of the rooms she created—a mish-mash of color, texture, and whimsy.

SUSAN: Sister and Albert traveled extensively in search of handmade rugs, baskets, and local crafts.

ALBERT HADLEY: Sis said, "Let's go to Ireland. You know they make a lot of baskets in Ireland." So we went.

Sybil Connelly, our hostess and the great Irish fabric designer, said, "The only place to get baskets is on the West Coast." It was a beautiful drive and the driver was marvelous. It took quite a long time, but we didn't see baskets. We had a nice lunch at a pub. Sis went into the bathroom and came out dragging an old piece of carpet she'd found outside the door of the ladies' room. It had multicolored stripes, and it was so dirty, you couldn't see the colors. Nobody could remember where it had come from. Somehow, she found a line to it and started ordering carpet, and we used it in a number of places, including her houses in Maine. Our first order was for Jock Whitney for use at Greentree.

JESSICA PARISH (Sister's granddaughter): I remember Sister came out here to California. She had a fair number of clients out here. She was going to speak. I think she had just finished decorating the Getty house. She spoke at the Herps Theater, which probably holds two thousand people. I remember getting the day off from school because I was going to listen to my grandmother speak, and thinking, Who are all these people and why are they here? There was a line out the door and there were people trying to get tickets, but it was sold out. I think it was my first realization that she was this incredibly well-respected and famous person in her field.

I can remember sitting in the audience, thinking that I still didn't understand what decorating was. Because I've always lived in beautiful houses, it was just my assumption that all houses were beautiful. I do remember the slide show, and I can remember her standing up on this large stage in a big auditorium and speaking into a microphone in her little voice. I can remember being very nervous. It was very endearing. She talked about family and the importance of including family pieces in your home and having your home be a place for family to come. That was her message.

Mr. Hopkins, ladies and gentlemen:
I would like to thank all of you for asking me here today. As I have
never spoken in public all these years, I find it a terrifying experience.
I must tell you that my summer has been—without a doubt—the worst.
No sleep, just worry.

I decided my only hope was to spend a large part of my days reading this speech in the pulpit at our little church off the coast of Maine. The church where I have gone all my life with friends and, often, the dogs. I suddenly felt speechless when I climbed the steps to the pulpit—glasses on, speech in hand and a clock.

I tried first to think this was an everyday event. In fact, what could be easier? Well, it turned out that was not so. No voice would come. My heart was pounding as I looked at the empty church. Luckily, I suddenly thought of my granddaughter, who would go with me to see the auditorium and to advise me how I should look. Her suggestion was that I should be concealed by potted plants. I did forget to tell you my granddaughter is here today, and I'm not even sure that she is not behind the palm tree, encouraging me to go on.

With that in mind, I felt a little better and my voice did come. Alas, it must have been a frightened voice, as BumbleBee and HoneyBee, my two pet Pekes, who were sitting in the front pew, let out a howl.

The sun was shining through the windows, with the pine trees freshly covered with summer dew, and so, once more with hope, I tried. . . .

You are all wonderful to still be sitting here, so now I will show you some slides. The slides are of rooms and houses from all over the world. They stretch from South Africa, South America, Russia, England, France, and now onto San Francisco. They represent a patchwork of every type and kind of house and environment. Some small, some large, some thick, and some thin. Each house was done with care and love. Our clients have helped us fulfill our dreams. Our dream is to have made them happy.

Opposite page: Sister having breakfast in bed, which was a daily routine.

Chapter Eleven

A Day at the Office

Every job we did was sought after to be photographed and was
honored as being genius.

RICHARD MANDER

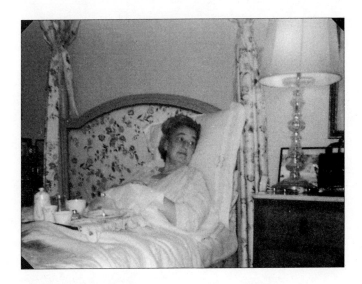

I AM MRS. ASTOR between 7:15 and 8:15. Breakfast in bed, the papers, the deli-
cious feel of soft sheets, all the possessions that I love, pictures of children,
grandchildren, dogs, sunny and rainy days in Maine. Books, magazines, papers
piled high at the foot of my bed to be read and looked over. Lots of pictures of
greenhouses, gardens, follies, pools, banks of hyacinths, articles on hemlocks,
fall planting, descriptions of furniture, pictures, porcelains, magazines to be kept
with descriptions of gardens, menus and houses from all parts of the world—
each idea to be used someday.

I'm still Mrs. Astor—I average waking at least three people each morning.
Some try for politeness, some are cool, and some hang up. I'm always sure of

Albert Hadley. He vaguely tries to answer my first question, "What is your day?" I can tell he is dripping wet or sipping a lukewarm cup of coffee. Conversation always ends by my saying, "See you in twenty minutes." I suddenly realize that Mrs. Astor is slipping away and my loved hour is spent.

Yummy is waiting at the door. Celestia is waiting for the "doom" news if we are in or out for dinner. "We'll have anything, but have it good tonight." I say not to forget the electric lightbulbs, to order candles, wash windows—perhaps get a better furniture wax (a tactful way of saying that no wax had ever been used). My last night dress hangs tidily on the back of the door—should I mention pressing? No.

It is 8:35, the car is waiting. My first stop is the office, to hear the good and bad news for the hours ahead. Painter has not called. Floor men unavoidably have the flu. Plumbers on strike. Workroom closed because of snow. Electrician cannot remember what we said yesterday, wants to be sure. Second painter calls, can't place color samples—was it red or apricot? Not sure he is in the right house. Call the telephone company, remove dead plants, no pencils sharpened. No one in yet. Time to call the grandchildren (it is the moment they are choking food down and struggling to get off to school). Another quick call. "I'm sorry, Madam is still asleep." I think it just can't be possible. I'm in a rage already.

My engagement book is open. The outside of this book says "A Line a Day" in bold gold letters—somehow they are confused. It has every fifteen minutes marked, and every one I see is filled. It is thought possible that I can be on Twenty-ninth Street to decide details of an entire house at 8:45 and then, in a leisurely way, I'm to get to Ninety-first Street at 9:00 to convince a client that her bed is not a "mistake" and that I know she will grow to love it.

Receptionist working at 9:00. Please bring schemes for 9:30 appointment. Some confusion: Which 9:30 appointment? Blueprint mislaid, accusations hurled around as to who last had them. Schemes had all but been ordered, and I suddenly remembered Mrs. H. had called to say her husband did not care for blue. Her daughter changed from rosebuds to a "horse print." Library to be put off for a little while; my living room plans shattered, as Oriental must be used— fifteen minutes to adjust. Long-distance call: "Could you change appointment to tomorrow instead of Wednesday?" Wednesday is so far away that nothing was planned anyway. Urgent call: Could we find reproduction Renoir paintings for servants' dining room—must be hung this afternoon—cook allergic to empty walls and very testy. Three minutes left before Mrs. H. arrives—Oriental-rug room still a blank. Albert Hadley saves the day—finds a ten-year-old sample.

Perfection. Tearing out of the room, he calls in haste, "Will be back from Washington before lunch. Don't forget, we have that new modern house that must be 'unique' at three-fifteen." One last scream from the moving car: "It is to look like sea foam, only yellow." Nine-thirty client arrives full of vigor, to tell me everything changed again. Blue is on. They can't find the Oriental, so forget it. The horses, however, are still a necessity. Looking out my door, I see my secretary wildly beckoning me to come. With distress, she tells me a mantelpiece has been lost. What should the mantelpiece man do now that he has reached Palm Beach to install it? Tell him that mantel left London eight months ago and should arrive any moment. Now, back to the horses—with pride, I drape the large sample with various types of hunters and ponies doing almost everything. I notice my client looking stony-faced. "I told you, they have to be jumping." How could I have forgotten such a serious thing? The blue, unfortunately, is not the blue they had in Maine—didn't I remember it should match the towels and the set of books on the left side of bed? Horrors, how could I have forgotten? An interruption from Mr. Hadley, calling from the airport. "Sorry to bother you. Could you help me out? I meant to get six baskets, different shapes, with exotic plants before eleven for Mrs. X. On your way, could you stop and look at a Venetian mirror for Mrs. B.? I don't think it is perfect, but I promised it for twelve. (I just heard a whisper from my secretary that the truck was broken.)

Now, out of the corner of my eye, I see the six decorators watching me in order to have a word. One is holding a birdcage, the other a battered rocking chair—I think that with five hundred dollars' worth of repair, paint, and recaning, it might be possible. Another—a bundle of samples ranging from needlework to potato sacking. Another lugging a fur rug sample that looks like it has a bad disease. The last one seems to have a bassinet. (I vaguely wonder, Whose baby?) Eleven o'clock is coming on, but Mrs. H. is sitting solidly in her chair, gazing at the horses, wondering if I could possibly make them jump. It is finally decided that I will call her the first thing in the morning. (I know I will be in North Carolina in the morning, but I have to get on to the exotic plants.) A call from Mrs. C., wanting to tell me her room does not look like a crushed tomato, as I had promised. A call to the painter to hold on, that I will get him a tomato and we will "mix" together.

Twelve-thirty—maybe a bit of lunch might bring some strength back. In any case, Yummy, having been driven all morning, has not had too much chance of entering my beautiful house or apartment and he is now hungry. He does not care for the wholesale district—in fact, he won't get out of the car.

Driving up to 770 or 960 is another matter. He looks forward to feeling the marble floors and enjoys the highly polished parquets. He has an eye for lacquer, no question about it. It becomes his dignity and his heritage. I must tell you now that he has a slight failing: When he is not calm, he savagely takes a little nip. I always hope that I can explain it by saying, "He is sorry for what he has done, but, you see, he was in China at that moment and did not want to be disturbed." Not all clients take to him, and he is pretty unpleasant unless they at least show great interest. He rules the office with his majestic ways and perfect taste.

News is a little better at the office. Albert Hadley has called the office from Washington to say all is well—the van has arrived, nothing seriously broken; curtains touch the floor; sofa is in proportion; furniture has taken on a look of charm and great importance. If we can just get a chandelier, a hall lantern, two bedside tables, eight lamps, a needlepoint rug, a pair of unique and interesting chairs, candlesticks for dining room, a Chippendale clock, scrap basket for every room, bibelots with great quality—all before Friday—he feels quite sure that everything will work and be charming in many ways.

Later, on arrival at the workroom, I find eight sofas, six upholstered chairs, wrapped and marked for living room, library, hall, master bedroom, guest rooms—one, two, and three. I trust that they are perfect. The curtains and valances are hanging, waiting to be packed. I begin to wonder, Is the fringe deep enough? Is the tape set back far enough? Could the valance stand more bells? My eye goes to the curtains for the master bedroom. I can't help smiling, they are so beautiful. The bed stands alone, and, even against the dreary workroom walls with bare lightbulbs, it demands a look of wonder. The canopy is a dome, made like the most beautiful parasol; the pale green fluted posts justify holding this miracle of white muslin bound in grosgrain ribbons, with magic workmanship. The folds meet the center like a star, each point standing alone. One wonders, Who could help but sleep? The bedspread of white roses on chintz is like a cool summer garden, lined with light flannel to give it a quilt look. The tiny bows that keep it together are bound in pale green. The headboard is quilted, each rose standing out, showing perfect design. The dust ruffle, like the canopy, is white, full, and frothy, and just right to pull it all together. I would not have picked guest room two, but Albert Hadley would say, "Yes, it has a real look, very interesting." I'm sure that if he were with me, his eagle eye would catch a stitch that would make just that special difference. I am pleased and will tell him all before the 3:30.

* * *

RICHARD MANDER: Talking about Parish-Hadley during its height: It was fabulous; everyone was so busy. Every day presented a new set of challenges. If you had the money, and you had the taste and the artists, then how were you not going to come up with a great job? We were working with all this incredible art. I hung Gauguins. I hung Grant Woods and Modiglianis and Leonardo da Vincis, and handled the faucets from Caligula's tub, the dancing monkey from the steps of Versailles, the self-portraits of Rembrandt and Picasso. These were paintings that weren't even seen in museums.

Working for a decorator is like working for a star. I looked at my job as making the star look incredibly bright and shiny. Sister was the star, and what we did was to make Sister's star shine brightly.

LIBBY CAMERON: Mrs. Parish would usually meet with the client and they'd establish that they wanted to work together. There'd be a contract. The drafting department would probably do a floor plan in twenty-four to forty-eight hours. If she wanted it, then she wanted it right away. They'd give her a blank floor plan. They'd trace the house and then Mrs. Parish would draw in the furniture, which was hysterical, because her sofas were the size of a grain of rice and her chairs were the size of peas. She had no sense of proportion in her drawing at all. She'd draw this little chair and then she'd draw what looked like a little half-moon. I think oftentimes she had to compensate for the furniture by using a lot of pattern and color, because I think that's what carried her rooms off sometimes—for people who didn't have big collections. But if you look at some of the older houses she did, everything was sort of muted, because there she had great paintings.

Then they'd go back to the drafting department, and, on the jobs that I worked on with her, I'd have to redraw it based on my meeting with her—to interpret and get it going. We'd have the client meetings and then she would say, "Let's do the house." Then I'd go shopping and collect a bunch of materials, and we'd look in the sample room and also get the rugs. She wouldn't talk about it in terms of structure; there was nothing intellectual about it. She'd say, "She'd look very pretty in a pink room." So the bedroom would be pink. She'd work it that way, and then she would say, "I've always wanted to do an apple green dining room." So she'd put in what she wanted to have. She would convince the clients, and I think that, given her presence and her reputation, people would listen to her. She was looking at the house from the point of view of what she'd like to see in it and in relationship to what she

Sister and Bunny
Williams at the office.

thought the people were like. And then you would go forward. Sometimes a client would say, "Red? Red in that room? I don't know about red." And then she'd get quiet and she would say, "Well, we'll work on it again." Then they'd come back within a week or so, and she'd get red in that room somehow. She was very stubborn. And then as you were working on it more, she'd introduce more, like all the trimmings on the curtains and the borders and the painted floor pattern. She would do all that behind the scenes and then ask the client, sort of toward the end, if that was okay. But she'd just do it.

JOSEPH SALZBERGER (Weidl Painting Company): We started working for Mrs. Parish in the mid-sixties. Parish-Hadley was like a school for most decorators who are quite successful today. We did all kinds of glazing, antiquing and lacquering finishes, all the techniques. All of Mrs. Parish's colors were mixed on the job site. She would usually have a piece of material or a piece of wallpaper. When she met with us, she would say, "This is it. I want something between this and that." We worked for her so long, we knew what colors she was looking for right away. Lacquering is a complicated finish, and Parish-Hadley used it a lot. It is complicated because the lacquer is a hand-rubbed finish. It's a method of paint where you put it on and keep lacquering it over and over again. Once a base coat is established, you can put on eight or ten coats after that. It's time-consuming, so a good-size living room can be in the twenty-thousand-dollar range. Depends on what condition you get it in.

As far as working with her, she'd say, "Well, look, this job has to be finished in two weeks or in a month, you understand?" They were beautiful years. No question about it. There was nobody better, in my opinion. We picked up a good reputation through her, too.

JOHN ALBERTELLI (Weidl Painting Company): Mrs. Parish never knew what a color deck was. All her colors were custom-mixed on the job site. Mrs. Parish had her own style. She used very rich colors. We used a lot of deep red lacquers, and some aubergine. She was very positive about her color. When she would go on a job, you knew things were going to get finished on such and such a date and you said, "Yes, it's going to be finished." Case closed, and with her there was no such thing as "Can't be done." She was not always easy, but she was fair.

She chose the colors when the client was there. When we mixed the paint and put it on the wall, she said if she liked it, and she said to the client, "Do you like it?" And the client said, "Yes." That's was it, good-bye. She was very definite.

She had such an easy time with people, too. The people she worked for were her peers, people who she had grown up with. It was much easier for her than for most of the decorators nowadays. The same people she'd be choosing colors with, she'd be having dinner with that night. It was much more comfortable for her. She had a different type of client. There was a lot of class. Today, some of the people have huge egos. They say, "I'm not sure that I want that particular color." She would never accept that. Never. Ever.

JOHN ROSSELLI (antiques dealer): Sister had this sense of entitlement. When she wanted something at my shop, she subtly let me know she wanted it. It was my obligation to give it to her. She would shop here and spend a lot of money; then she would see some object and make it known, just like Queen Mary, that she wanted me to give it to her as a gift. She made that plain, saying, "Oh, I would love to have that for myself." So it would go into her car with the chauffeur.

Ever since Beau, my life has, in many ways, revolved around dogs. After Beau, there was Otto, the huge brown dachshund. Then came YD, the yellow Labrador that entered our lives when Apple was born. Next came Yummy, who became famous all over the world and was the true lord of the firm of Parish-Hadley for thirteen years. He attended every client meeting, visited every house and apartment and firm we decorated, and, possibly because his fur matched the burnt sugar upholstery of the company car, always made clear his privileged position, even after biting a client's fingers. Perhaps my dogs have not influenced my decorating, but certainly no one has ever hired me without hiring my dogs, as well.

SUSAN: All of her Pekingese could be mean and bite, but Yummy was really vicious at times. I was terrified of him as a child and knew never to go near him when he was having dinner, which was always chicken and rice.

BILL HODGINS: One day, there was this loud, awful noise, and there was Albert; Yummy had a hold of his pants and Albert was trying to get the dog off. Albert was so controlled and good, and he tried to smile, but Edward Cave and I just looked at each other. That was actually the first time I got to know Cave. Because, after seeing that, we went for lunch, and he had a double martini. He just wolfed it down.

SAMUEL BELL: I remember that one day I was driving across the Triborough Bridge. I knew how she loved animals. So I was driving and there was this older dog crossing the street, and she said, "Don't hit the dog." Got all emotional. There was a pigeon in the street and I stopped. She almost went through the windshield. She said, "Why are you stopping?" I said, "There's a pigeon." She said, "Don't worry about the pigeon."

SUSAN: Jack and Alice Rogers were clients and friends of Sister's for many years. She decorated their houses in Maine and Palm Beach, and later an enormous boat they had built for them in Japan.

ALICE ROGERS: When meeting with her at the office on Sixty-third Street, the appointment was always a little earlier than you wanted it to be. I always loved going there because it was like an apartment and you immediately saw Sister's signature.

It was comfortable and cozy. There were always wonderful magazines and books around. You never had to wait for her. When you would go in, there was always someone to receive you very graciously and cordially.

The wait wouldn't last very long because she would get up from her office and come out and greet you. Then you would walk back into her office, and it felt as though you were in her house. The dogs were always there on their perches, whatever that might be. They would sort of stare at you, blink their eyes, and run their tongues around their noses, and that was the only recognition that you got from them. Sometimes Sister would pick them up and hold them on her lap, stroke them and play with them while she was talking to you.

You felt so warmly greeted and welcomed. Her office was like a bedroom, almost, it was so feminine. When you came in, she would tell you where to sit, which you would do, and then you would get started immediately. The meetings never lasted very long. In the past, I've worked with other people in a similar business. It was just endless hours of indecision. They'd say, "Well, what do you think?" or "I'm not sure." Inability to come to a decision. Not with Sister. She knew what she thought you should do before you got there.

She would bring in every material, swatches for things, and then, too, she would have someone bring in a piece of furniture. She would pick up the phone or call out to the receptionist in the hall and say to bring her such and such chair. She always had a name for everything. Sometimes things were named for clients, and, of course, you know about the "Paley chair." So a chair would be brought in, and it was obvious that she'd had something to do with its design.

She'd say, "Now, I think we ought to use this. Why don't you sit in it and see if it needs changing a little bit to fit you and make it more comfortable."

Then she'd say, "And I think we should do this in a certain room and a certain place, and this is the fabric I think you should put on it." Sometimes she'd give you a choice, but not always. You had to learn to speak up, because if you didn't speak up, it would be done and there wouldn't be too much of your input. I was intimidated by her, but it didn't take me long to realize that I really could speak up and that she appreciated it. She liked input from clients, but she was not going to stall around and wait for them. Unless she thought they were really off base. Then she would tell them that.

Shopping with her was wonderful. She had incredible levels of energy. Not only was she up before the birds in the morning but she would just run all day. Even as she got older, she always wanted to get out and go. Sometimes we would go in that car that the firm had—with Samuel, her driver. They had a station wagon or sometimes just a small sedan with four doors. Nothing special about it. Sometimes she'd get in that and go, and other times she'd just go out and hail a taxi.

BERNIE KARR (owner of Hyde Park Antiques): Mrs. Parish and Albert were good clients of mine. They shopped at Hyde Park frequently. They were bright enough to realize they could not do everything themselves. They did assign competent decorators working for the firm. Mrs. Parish was more on a supervisory level or dealing with the major clients, like the Whitneys.

I'd been in business for thirty-five years at this point. I get into a lot of trouble because I say things people don't want to hear. I call it the way it is. She had sophisticated taste, beyond most decorators. Most decorators buy things on a decorative basis. She was a quantum jump beyond that, in that she had solid knowledge of antiques as well as a sense of the decorative. She was such a commanding presence, and she was so well regarded in the world of decorative arts. No client would ever consider passing on anything she recommended. They had no choice. She was not a lady to say no to. When she came in with a client, I knew several things would be placed. I don't remember anyone ever saying, "No, I don't like it." It just didn't happen. Courteous, polite, not a rude bone in her body. She was very decisive, a professional who would look at the price tag last. If she didn't respond to the item, the price would be irrelevant. The opposite is the person who doesn't even look at the item. They look at the price tag.

She respected the people she worked with—like antique dealers and painters and the whole gamut of the trade. The truckers she used, the movers. Everyone regarded her well because she was a lady.

Parish-Hadley had the best clients in the United States. Mostly, she would come around and preshop for them. When she came in with clients, she knew exactly what she was going to suggest, where the item was going to be placed. She never came in with a client on a random sweep.

SUSAN: Sister was smart about money. She loved to say that she had no education. She was emphatic that her ability was based on her instincts. What was also true was that not only did she have good instincts about houses, she also had good instincts about money. A year after I shifted to a part-time work schedule, the head of my law firm decided he could no longer afford for me to do this and that he needed a full-time associate in my position. Because I had two small children and was committed to part-time work at that time, I was essentially out of a job. I was devastated. I called Sister and went to see her for advice. It was right before Christmas and, as I sat down to pour out my tale of woe, the first thing she said was, "Well, I hope they guaranteed you your Christmas bonus." The thought hadn't yet occurred to me. She went on: "If you have to cry to get it, then go ahead and cry." In her rarefied world, she was street-smart.

HAROLD SIMMONS: We first worked on the Getty house in San Francisco and then on their apartment in New York City. They were both huge jobs. Ann Getty was wonderful because she had an enormous interest in furniture and beautiful things. She was self-taught, and she bought books and books and really educated herself. She was interested in collecting fabulous things. We heard there was a sale coming up of Nancy Lancaster's things at Christie's in London. She was a friend of Mrs. Parish and so Mrs. Parish got Ann interested. All of a sudden, on the spur of the moment, a trip was planned. She told me she and Mrs. Getty were going to London and I was to go, too. She asked Ann what flight she was on—a TWA flight out of New York—so she told Ann we would get on the same flight. She called Continental Travel, which Gory owned, and said to get us two tickets on that flight. They called back and said, "There are no first-class tickets—they are all taken." She had a fit. She said, "This is terrible, this is impossible. I cannot fly over on the plane with Mrs. Getty in the front of the plane and us in the back. I don't care what you have to do. Get those tickets." She made such a scene and phone calls flew back and forth, and finally something broke and we got those two seats. She called Ann and said, "We are all set. It's all straightened out and we have two seats in first class." Ann said, "But I'm traveling economy." So she hung up in panic, there was another flurry of phone calls, and we traded in our first-class tickets for economy. So there we were in the back of the plane, with the three of us squeezed into a triple-seat arrangement. Ann chose the window seat, I was in the aisle, and Mrs. Parish was in the middle. You can imagine how she hated this. She was just seething the whole way over, and of course she couldn't say a thing.

DAVID KLEINBERG: We traveled and were the most unlikely pair. I remember those lunches in the car, where she would have Pilar [her cook] make peanut butter sandwiches and hard-boiled eggs. She would hand me those as I was driving, which always made me nervous, because Mrs. Parish hated the way everyone drove but herself. So she'd hand me bits of peanut butter sandwiches and then a hard-boiled egg that she would have peeled herself, so there were bits of shell on it. And then you'd be choking in the car and you'd sort of say, "By any chance is there anything to drink?" She'd rummage around in that little cooler and say, *"Oh, that woman!"* She was always complaining about Pilar. So we'd get where we were going and you'd leap out of the car, gasping for water, with crumbs and little bits of shell clinging to you.

Oh, we traveled together. We went to London. Those were actually my favorite times, sitting down with her on trips at cocktail time. It would get to be 5:00 or 5:15 and you'd be mixing the vodka and Clamato juice for her. And you would sit and gossip or talk or catch up. She could be the most human person.

Before I started out at Parish-Hadley, I went on a road trip with her to go see the house that Tom and Olive Watson, who had been old clients, were moving to. Tom had taken over IBM, following his father, and was making a huge success of it. They were moving into a new house on the water. The office called me and said that they knew I wasn't starting until such and such a date but could I meet Mrs. Parish? She was going to see a house and she wanted me to accompany her. I had to take the day off from my job, which I still had. She said to meet her at 8:30. I got there at 8:20 and she was already standing in the lobby.

Pilar said, "Well, you don't look so hot." I thought, God, there's my future. I'm doomed. I got in the car and we drove off to Greenwich. We were to meet Mrs. Watson at the old house and then go to see the new house. En route, Mrs. Parish described the house that the Watsons had been living in, and from the front door to everything throughout the house, it was exactly as she had described: colors, what was on what, what she liked and what she didn't. Her memory of houses was amazing.

SUSAN: Visiting the Parish-Hadley offices always made me feel as if I were stepping into a fantasy world where everything was based on comfort, beauty, and efficiency. There was nothing officelike about it. The front hall at the Sixty-third Street office, which they moved into in 1986, had that silver tea paper on the walls and the floor had their signature zebra rug. Beautiful books and objects as well as Albert's renderings lined the hallway. Parish-Hadley's stock furniture and objects were there, along with a smattering of unbeliev-ably beautiful antiques and objects being held for client approval. Sometimes the extravagance and beauty of the objects would simply bowl me over. The sample room at the end of the office was meticulously kept. Here walls of bookshelves held swatches of lush, expensive materials that were orga-nized neatly in color-coordinated stacks. Albert's office was more sparse and painted a brilliant red. His famous bulletin board—a beautiful collage of photographs, pictures, swatches, and quotes—reflected his eclectic taste. You could study the bulletin board for an hour and not absorb all of it.

I used to meet Sister there for lunch, and it was as serene as a ladies' lunch at the Colony Club. First we would chat in her office, which was feminine and light and looked like a bedroom. We would then proceed to the dining room, which doubled as a conference room. Each time, we ate the same thing: soup to start, a split avocado filled with shrimp salad, French bread and Brie, and sometimes Jell-O and a cookie for dessert. Gladys, one of Sister's favorite people in the office, served us in her blue uniform.

Though outwardly everything seemed quiet and muted, there was a whirlwind of activity around us as smartly dressed decorators buzzed in and out between appointments. The design studio in the back housed a full staff of architects working on various house models and renderings. Albert and Sister were both perfectionists and the office always felt sleek and shiny to me, not a wrinkle or blemish in sight. One felt that Parish-Hadley was a place where things got done. Here clients' lives were organized and made more beautiful, stylish, and efficient.

Sister would survey these employees with the most scathing of stares. It seemed to me that she was examining every particle of their beings, the way that children do when they meet another child. She had her favorites and, like a child, she was unabashed in her likes and dislikes. If she felt that someone was disloyal to her or to the firm, she was simply terrible to that person, either forgetting his or her name or asking him or her to hold the dogs at a particularly inopportune moment. She could be a tyrant, and sometimes it pained me to witness her degrading certain people. On the other hand, she was absolutely loyal to those whom she liked. She knew everything about their families, and she tried to include them in situations that would benefit them. She ran hot and cold and made no bones about it.

JOHN ROSSELLI: Sister could be the you-know-what of the Western world when she wanted to be. Anybody with great talent is not easy. Nor should they be. Talent can be a very condemning thing, because you're never really happy with what you have. Sister was very competitive in many ways. I'll never forget one evening. She said, "John, Mario [Buatta] is coming, so please come by for a drink." So I did go by for a drink, and when we were sitting there, all of a sudden Mario waltzed in and they began talking. Then there was the most knock-down-drag-out fight between Mario and Sister. It was because Sister accused Mario of being practically a whore. Mario was in his heyday, with his chintz and his sheets. Sister was saying, "Mario, how could you compromise your profession?" and so on. Mario stood up and said, "Sister, you know what the problem is? You're jealous!" She sat there for a minute, took a swig of her bourbon, and said, "Maybe I am. But still, I don't see why or how you could do it." Mario is, in his own way, extremely talented. He is also certainly the legacy of Sister.

BUNNY WILLIAMS: I also don't think I've ever really known, in my whole life, a person who was two people. Completely Jekyll and Hyde. She could be the most charming, the funniest, warmest, and delightful company of anybody you've ever met. On the other hand, something would go off in her brain that could turn her into the biggest ogre and she would be really humiliatingly mean. There were these rages; I mean, it was like what you would see in a two-year-old child. I would see her sit in the office with her hands in a fist, in a rage, just like the child who didn't get her candy. But you didn't throw it in and say, "Oh, the hell with this," because there was this other side that was totally engaging and inspirational and a whole lot of things. But I don't think I've ever met somebody who was that extreme from day to day.

She never spent any time on self-examination. The rest of us at some point in our lives may stand up and say, "Why did I do that?" I don't think there was one minute to the day that she died that she would ever have allowed that.

I think that was very much a generational thing, and I think that it cost her a tremendous amount of anxiety, and certainly her insomnia and anger were due to the frustration. You know, she may have thought, I haven't done this, or I should've done this, and so it came out in anger or control or whatever.

SAMUEL BELL: If she liked the decorators, she treated them like gold. She respected them and she would work with them. But if it was somebody she didn't like, they would kind of tremble and she would needle them. A lot depended on how they treated her, whether they had respect for her. Now, Mr. Hadley may have still liked them, but she didn't care. She was going to find a way to force them out. She could taste loyalty in a second.

I don't think she ever did this with any other driver she had, but she would invite me to go inside her house, just moving the furniture or something. She said, "Come in and help." She would invite me to go places and set

Parish-Hadley office outing, 1985.

up. She would say, "Samuel will be helping us on this." Yes, I went into major places and helped. She would want everyone to know that I was part of the crew. She understood and she wanted me to be there.

SUSAN: Sister never retired. She was of the generation who were taught to use "discipline" and "soldier on," whatever the circumstances. She never gave herself a break, and, as a result, she didn't sleep well. She was a chronic worrier. Despite having a very strong character, she had a vulnerable side few people saw. She was also working extremely hard in her sixties and seventies, when Parish-Hadley really hit its stride. When she became older, her health problems, such as her bad back and insomnia, became worse, but she never slowed down. She was completely driven, but also sensitive and emotional, as I believe most true artists are. This is not always an easy way to live.

I know that I was a supersensitive child, as I now am as an adult. Tears flow in me at the smallest incident. I have ached all my life, thinking I have done wrong or could have done better. Because of discipline, I keep it hidden in me, and my aching heart takes place alone.

I have never slept well, and I know it's because I am so unsure inside that every detail becomes a mountain of questions. Outwardly, I will cry if I see the American flag flying, or an automobile plate with New Jersey on it (when in Europe), and I am longing to be back in my own room. I cry so hard about my own funeral that it causes me to pull up on the road side to collect myself, and to try to decide if I had died popular and wish I could be there, or, worse, if I had died unpopular and no one came to my funeral.

That is true also of my children, my husband, and any animal. When we were first married, it was always Harry who would have a tragic end. I would picture myself in trailing black veils, a locket of his hair on a chain, and little Harry dressed as Little Lord Fauntleroy. We wandered from hotel to hotel, each with a lobby filled with fashionable people. All would stop to say, "You know that is Sister Parish, whose husband died a tragic death!" I would cry and cry into my pillow, or at almost any given spot.

Remember, I always had a lurid imagination, but usually under that word control, *I held it inside. I still cry unashamed when the movie* Lassie *comes on. When I did badly riding or hunting, and would fall off, I would never feel bad for myself, but I would cry for my horse, whom I felt I had let down. A sick child or a sick dog on the street stays in my memory, and then that memory in my imagination brings large tears all night. I think of how lucky I am, and then I make myself "slip it."*

PETER GATES: The way that I got involved in her business is that she essentially decided that she wanted to sell out. I was very fond of Albert Hadley and what struck me about them was how joined at the hip they were. She could do no wrong. He would back her in whatever she wanted. The idea of selling out and moving on was in the front part of her mind. While some structural steps were taken in the business along this line, she never really wanted to lay down the tools, as tired and sick as she became.

She loved to work, and I think that if she had stopped working completely and lived in her apartment and went around visiting Mrs. Engelhard or Betsey Whitney and others, and went to Dark Harbor without any work, that she'd have withered and died. Albert fully understood this, so I never thought there would be a time when she would retire.

Sister had a passionate personality. She functioned on many levels. The intellectual level, which was sharp. Superb. What drove her daily, minute by minute, was her emotional self. Very inductive. Her mind worked very fast and she didn't know how it worked. When she reached a conclusion, it was all or nothing.

ALBERT HADLEY: The only disagreements we had were about the performances of the employees. She expected so much of everybody, and in her mind, some people didn't have the right shoes or the right pants and thus didn't measure up. With her, it was you either have it or you don't. Our personal relationship never wavered, but in the business end, we fought like cats and dogs. The telephone calls I got late at night, you could not believe. There is no point discussing them because that was all about business and, in her view, the terrible things we all had done, the terrible people in the office, and who those people were and how one could stand all of them.

It was a very personal relationship or connection. I was involved with her family, with Harry and the children. I was involved in her life almost from the beginning.

BUNNY WILLIAMS: Being between Mrs. Parish and Albert wasn't always easy, yet the genius of the company was the two of them together. To be the person going out to get the cotton samples and being a part of this tugging and exchanging of ideas and thoughts was just amazing. I think that left on their own, they were not as good as the sum of the two.

Sister and Albert in Albert's barn in Maine.

DIANTHA NYPE (public relations director of decorator show houses): I worked for twenty-five years for the show houses for the Kips Bay Boys and Girls Club. Parish-Hadley did a great number of them. Mrs. Parish was involved in all of the rooms, but I remember one in particular. It was an upstairs sitting room in a very grand house, and she agreed that she would do it for Parish-Hadley. Of course, Mr. Hadley was going to be involved, as well. Because I was doing public relations, naturally I was roving all around the house. I would see one vignette here and another there, and it was fascinating. I remember a wonderful gros point rug, possibly Portuguese, with big red roses on a black background, that had just arrived for Mrs. Parish. Then a lot of nondescript furniture appeared, and I could not understand exactly what was going to happen, because there were some very nice antiques, but there was also some upholstered furniture, and I couldn't see any rhyme or reason to any of it. Suddenly, a man appeared with red-and-white slipcovers, and then everything began to make sense. I saw Mrs. Parish with her hat and gloves and purse, walking very calmly up the stairs, headed toward the room she was doing. Behind her was that wonderful man, Samuel, her chauffeur, who worked for Parish-Hadley for many years. He followed her, carrying large wicker picnic baskets, and they went into the room and closed the door. About a half hour later, Sister came down the stairs, leaving the door open, and I could see that magic had happened in there. Everything was out of the picnic baskets, all the bibelots and everything you could want in a room, and these things had been placed around the room, until it had come magically to life. It had become an absolutely glorious room, and I thought, Well, it is very nice when you have a master magician.

BILL HODGINS: I remember seeing Sister's hands and how she would pick things up and look at them. "It's just an idea," I would say. If she agreed, she would say, "That'll do." That would be her highest praise. After work, Sister and Albert would sit down around six o'clock at the Westbury Hotel and have a Jack Daniel's. I didn't drink, so it would get better and better for me as they had their Jack Daniel's. We would talk about jobs, about how this one was to be simplified and how that one was to be done. She was a fascinating woman. She was subtle, very coochy-coo in the nicest kind of way.

BOB ISRAEL (antiques dealer): She had tremendous enthusiasm and she loved painted furniture. I'll never forget one time when she was in a great deal of back pain, and we took her upstairs in the elevator to show her something that had just arrived. We had received a wonderful William and Mary chest painted in sort of a delftlike manner. In a matter of minutes, her face changed. It just lit up like the Fourth of July when she saw this chest. In her excitement, she looked like a little girl.

Another thing that I remember that impressed me was that she had a real concentration, a focus, when she was with a client. You could never talk to her about another client. One time, I mentioned showing her something for someone other than the person she was with. She said, "I'm with . . ." She would only focus her energy on the client she was with.

RICHARD MANDER: Sister didn't cheat. A lot of people in the industry do. They go out and buy a piece of furniture for a thousand dollars and sell it for three thousand and put their commission on that. Sister went out and bought it for a thousand dollars, fixed it up for fair price, and put her commission on that. She was fair. They were very aboveboard. That was mostly from the way that Sister believed life should be run. It was an absolute marvel that she could operate in a cutthroat industry in this way. Her genius was not as a decorator. That was not her ultimate strength. It was being a terrific friend to her clients. She saw her job as being supportive and making sure her client was not being abused and making sure that she got a great job done. Some do not envision inviting their decorator to their parties, but with Sister, that was different.

She had her work in perspective and she realized that if a nine-inch molding met with a twelve-inch molding, and you were living in a $25 million house, the molding just didn't mean bunk. One of the things that gave her her great sense of humor was understanding that and having it all in perspective and not getting hung up on these little tiny, trivial, ridiculous things.

ROBERT JACKSON (painter and trompe l'oeil artist): I was at the Summer House several times painting floors, walls, everything. The colors were infectious. Once you saw what she already had—the chintz, quilts, antique fabrics—you had to compete with those colors. She wanted to use a full palette. Once you have done one painted floor, you see the possibilities for others. I think I did a different design for every step at the Red House. She was open to anything painted—an eighteenth-century table or a simple box. It all appealed to her. She also knew that you can achieve a lot of control with paint. On a job, she was always very supportive. She enjoyed the process, and she was absolutely clear about what she wanted.

Sister and young decorators at Parish-Hadley during a magazine photo session.

Once, we were working on a floor at the Watsons' house in Greenwich. It was white, symmetrical, and my assistant and I were on our knees, working it out, when she came in. She said, "Why aren't you painting?" I said, "Well, we have to work on the design first, and it's going to be cheated a little bit in the corners over here and there." And Mrs. Parish said, "Oh, I understand completely. Cheat is my middle name." She was a lot of fun to work with.

D. B. GILBERT: The best times I can think of when I was older were those times when I was met at the airport by her and Samuel and they would take me and show me all the apartments she was working on. That, to me, was the most fun. She took me from one apartment to another. I remember the Bronfman's, his wife was a Loeb, and basically it was totally unlike her, but terrific. That was the first apartment that she worked on with Albert. Very modern. From there we went to Mrs. Whitney's apartment or wherever she was working on. She would never say much. She'd just show me.

KK AUCHINCLOSS (family friend): She was like a lioness with her cub, and her cub was her business, in that instance. She had an extraordinary interest and therefore it sparked her energy. Ambition. Not only ambition but maintenance of what she had. I mean intimidating anybody who would interfere with her. But what the outside world saw of her was her charm and her humor. She really had immense charm and humor and she could turn it on at the drop of a hat. Which is a great gift, you know. She went after what she thought would be a good thing for the firm, and then in her hierarchy of priorities, if it was good for the firm, it was also good for her daughters, and it was good for Harry, and then for her daughters' children. But, of course, her children and everything came into this. She was rather like that by nature. She adored her children; she adored her grandchildren.

She was compelled to do better all the time, to keep going and to make sure it was better than anybody else's, because she had that motivation or ambition.

APPLE: I only remember that when I was growing up, my mother worked, unlike all my friends' mothers, who simply took care of their households. That would have bored her. Obviously, I don't remember the Far Hills shop, but I do remember her working in New York and how, over the years, we saw less and less of her. She never talked about business even if she was prodded to.

Christmastime was usually a very hard time for her. She was so tired, and the last thing she wanted to do was make an effort to have a Merry, Merry Christmas, buying and wrapping presents. She usually had someone from the office do it.

I actually think Mum did a remarkable job. She wasn't a hands-on mother—she didn't dream of her children coming home from school to the smell of freshly baked brownies. If we did, someone else would have had to have been in the kitchen to accomplish it.

When the White House job came along, I think she realized that she couldn't do it alone. Having Albert as her partner was, as everyone has said, "a marriage made in heaven." When we got older, were married, and had children, I think her aim was to help us financially in any way she could. She was driven in this. One part of her wanted to retire, but the other part wanted to keep going to earn as much as she could for both herself and her family. In my eyes, it was a conflict. Nothing her children ever said to her about this had any effect on her. Her life was hers, and only hers, to control. It made it hard on us, but that's the way she wanted it. Both she and Albert were so modest about their accomplishments, but I'm sure they knew in their hearts what wonders they had created.

Opposite page: Portrait of Sister painted by Aaron Schickler.

Chapter Twelve

At Home

*She was straight out of an Edith Wharton story. She would have been the dom-
inant character in any of her stories, the catalyst that got everything started.*

KENNETH JAY LANE

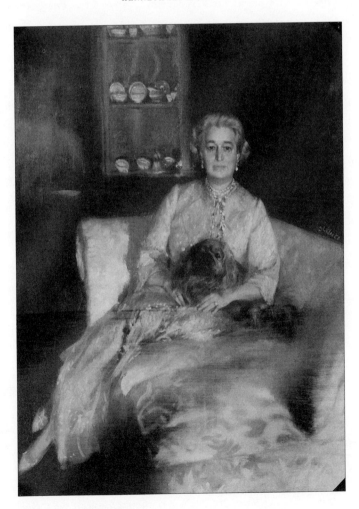

WHEN THE DOCTOR'S advice for Harry had been that he should spend as much time as possible in Maine, where the air was clean and fresh, I knew that our apartment would have to be sold and that I would have to find a smaller one.

After looking for months with an agent to see what was available, getting more mournful with every apartment I saw, a remarkable thing happened. I was walking home on Fifth Avenue when I saw that at 960 the door of a maisonette on the corner of Seventy-seventh Street was ajar. I could look in just enough to see that the ceilings were high, the entrance hall was marble, the cornice was of great quality, and that the living room was square—my favorite shape for a room. I knew that I had to have this apartment even if I had to murder the tenant.

The doorman of the building told me that he couldn't divulge whom this dream belonged to. My agent had never heard of it, so it couldn't be for sale. But I wouldn't drop the matter. I hung out in front of the building every afternoon until I caught the owner, a lovely lady, walking in the front door. I accosted her, saying, "Is this your apartment? Is it for sale?" She looked at me as if I were demented. I was.

Well, she did let me in. I realized that the apartment was small and that it lacked a room for me. That didn't hinder me. I was determined that something should happen. It did happen. I was told that at a price, it could be for sale. That settled it for me, so I set out to find a way to make another room. I realized that by sealing the door to the street, I could make a tiny bedroom, five feet nine by nine feet, where the entrance hall had been. Once I'd worked that out, we made the owner an offer that she accepted. The apartment was ours.

I made a room for myself as I'd planned. Harry's room was moved exactly as it had been on Seventy-ninth Street. We didn't move a single picture from its position on the desk. It was a wonderful room. Sadly, Harry was only to spend three nights at 960 Fifth Avenue.

We moved in just before Christmas. Then we went to Dark Harbor, where Harry stayed. For the next four years, I commuted, spending ten days in Maine and a week in the office. When Harry died, I moved into his room. Except for the four-poster bed with its beautiful painted canopy, that room has never changed.

The furniture in the living room has never changed, but otherwise I've made two huge attempts at being different. The idea, both times, was to make a room that would need no fussing and little upkeep. It was to be—for me—a modern room.

The doors were raised to nine feet to give the room some more grandeur. The walls were covered with plum-colored vinyl that could be easily washed. The good herringbone wood floors were bleached and polished. The windows were hung with simple mauve curtains, their color taken from a shell on our beach in Dark Harbor. The lamps were white plaster. There were no ornaments except the essentials. It was an almost empty, very pure room.

Well, it wasn't me. I felt out of place in it and never truly comfortable. I kept sneaking back into Harry's room, with its old blue-and-white chintz, where I'd curl up on his sofa under his wonderful tattered old quilt. This was my idea of home. No more white plaster!

Before the room became the way it is today, I made one more attempt at being modern, with Albert's help and exasperation. He told me that I needed something racy, something jazzy. He told me to buy a few modern pictures, mirror the walls, cover the ceiling with silver tea paper, and to change the curtains. Of course, I do everything he tells me. I had to go away for a week on a job, so I told the staff to change the curtains while I was away. When I came back, I walked into the room and nearly fainted dead away. The curtains were flaming magenta! I felt that Albert had made me into Mae West—on my stage. "Take those hideous things down at once!" I said. "By morning!"

Well, morning came and no one came to take the curtains down. They stayed for a year. Secretly, they gave me enormous pleasure and fun. But I think my friends were rather embarrassed by them. They admitted that the curtains had something and that they made the room into a conversation piece.

Finally, the day came when I decided I had to be by myself and live my own way in my own room. I banished the plum-colored vinyl walls and replaced them with a French moiré wallpaper with blue-and-white stripes and a thin gold line. The floor was covered with an English Axminster rug and the furniture was one of my favorite old chintzes. The curtains became pale blue silk. Finally, I brought back every bibelot I've ever owned.

One last change was accidental, but I love it. One night, mysteriously, the silver tea paper ceiling turned gold. Don't ask me why—but these days, not everything silver turns to gold!

SUSAN: Her last two apartments, at 960 and then 920 Fifth Avenue, were the ones I knew best. Arriving at her apartment, I never failed to feel the workaday world fall away as I walked through the door. The curtains were drawn because she lived on the ground floor, and the only sound once inside was the hum of her maids, Noel and Christina, puttering around the kitchen. Sister was at her command post in the library, with its coral-colored walls and the

Sister in her living room at 960 Fifth Avenue. The caftan and faux jewels were standard evening wear.

huge Chinese murals. The door to the garden would usually be open, as she liked the cold air. As I took off my coat, I would hear the familiar "Hoo-hoo," signaling where she was. Usually, she would be in her favorite high-backed chair, with her phone and the *Social Register* at hand. If it was early, she would still be working and would wave me on, telling me to take a bath and have a cup of tea, which Noel would provide.

After both of our baths, we would meet back in the library for a drink. At this point, Noel would be in and out of the library, clucking over something— the dogs, the ice bucket, whether the windows should be open or closed. She and Sister carried on a never-ending dialogue in "kitchen French," which ran from morning until night. Every night "on the dot of six," Sister had a vodka with ice and a dash of Clamato, which gave it a pinkish tint. When she felt well, she invited people over for drinks and dinner, which many times would be served on trays in the library. Before whoever was coming arrived, we would watch the news.

If I was going out for the evening, she would say, "Pet, go in my bathroom and get . . ."—usually a piece of jewelry or a scarf to jazz up my appearance. The little bauble always gave me a lift, bestowing her incredible confidence on me for the evening. I felt taken care of and cosseted, as my mother and her cousins had told me that Mrs. Kinnicutt made them feel at Mayfields.

JESSICA PARISH: We could bring our friends to my grandmother's, but you never knew what the result would be. When I was in college, I had a boyfriend whose nickname was "Pancho." His real name was Frank, but he was called Pancho because Francisco is the Spanish name for Frank, and Pancho is the diminutive of Francisco. Sister met Pancho and immediately decided that she wasn't sure about him. So she refused to call him Pancho; instead, she called him "Bronco." He has now forever gone down in history as Bronco.

JUDY COWEN (client): The first time I ever saw her apartment, it was like being in Europe. I was so amazed at all of the beautiful things she had, and amazed at how passionate she was about them. But it was also no big deal to her, as this was the way she lived and had always lived. This was just part of her. I remember her bathroom was like a little drawing room. It was so elegant, but comfortable, with beautiful wallpaper and the little chaise, and nothing like a bathroom at all. Neither of us slept well, and she and I used to talk about sheets. She said that sheets are only good when they are very, very old and so soft that you could slip on them. I thought she was right about that.

MARCIE BRAGA: She wanted to be at home. She was so much more comfortable there and at her friends' houses. Her friends' houses were the most beautiful houses in the world. People had chefs in those days. Occasionally, we would go out to lunch. When I was working with her, her lunching spot was the Westbury. It was old-fashioned, old-world, and very much like a hotel. But it wasn't a public thing. When David and I got married, one of the waitresses gave me a gold pineapple toothpick. That thing just doesn't happen in New York anymore. Also, the Madison Room on Madison Avenue, which was like the old Women's Exchange.

APPLE: Mummy and Daddy had dinner parties in New York and at Dark Harbor. Daddy was the perfect host for the eclectic groups that Mummy put together. Their Christmas party in New York was a mixed bag of people—some who had nowhere to go for Christmas and others who could have gone anywhere they pleased. For these parties, D.B. remembers that round tables were spread throughout the Seventy-ninth Street apartment and everything sparkled. Mummy would always give the same toast; "To all my friends, thank you for coming. Can you believe it? All these people for dinner and only one sink." I remember people singing and whistling with Daddy. It was always very jolly.

ALBERT HADLEY: There was a marvelous party she had when she had just moved into the new apartment. She asked for my help. She wouldn't pay to have the wall painted in glazes—too expensive—so she put up this eggplant-colored vinyl. We did those pale pink curtains and she had a lot of Alan Campbell materials and that big modern picture over the sofa. She had plaster lamps. She had her first cocktail party in this new modern apartment and she invited some of her "modern" friends, including Mr. Halston and several others, plus her Dark Harbor friends. She mixed it all up. There were two or three groups sitting all around, so she moved from one group to another. When she got bored with the Dark Harbor group, she moved over to the other sofa, where Halston was sitting. She sat in the middle of the sofa and she looked him up and down. Then she looked directly at Halston and said, "How do you decide to dress like that?" He was, of course, in a black turtleneck, black pants, everything in black, and he said, "*Sister*, I always imagine how Babe would dress if she were a man."

Andy Warhol was there about the same time. He stood there silently. He didn't speak; he would just stand around and observe.

Gory and Sister in Maine.

SUSAN: Andy Warhol came to a few parties and basically lurched around, saying nothing. At one of these parties, he spent the entire evening in Sister's bathroom. He told Mum it was his favorite room. He couldn't get over the reverse paintings that covered one wall. Eventually, he wasn't asked back because he was, in Sister's words, "no fun," which was her worst insult.

MARCIE BRAGA: I don't know how it came about, but at one point she had bright shocking-pink curtains. She said to me, "Marcie, will you do something about them?" I found a cream-colored wallpaper with a little stripe of gold and a little stripe of blue, which I showed her. She loved it and she was going to use plain blue linen curtains with it. She went up to Maine before we made the changes. We went over the things we were going to remove from the apartment, and one of them was this pair of blue Chinese jars. She told me to sell them to a Mrs. so-and-so for lamps. So I went to the apartment with my secretary, and, for some reason I put my hand into the jar and came out with a wad of hundred-dollar bills, a big fat wad, thousands of dollars. Three to five thousand dollars. That was a lot of money then. I really didn't want to take it home and carry it in my pocket. I couldn't think what to do, and I couldn't get in touch with Mrs. Parish. There's a beautiful big clock that you see in all the photos, and I saw that there was a back on the clock that would come off. I stuffed all the money in the clock, left it there, and went home. I spoke to Mrs. Parish later that day and told her, "I hid the stuff." And she asked, "What stuff?" I replied, "The stuff, you know, the stuff, the money!" She asked, "What money?" I told her, "The money in the jar." She asked again, "What money in the jar?" And I practically shouted, "The hundred-dollar bills that you had stuffed into the jar." And then she said, "Oh, was there money in the jar?"

Did you ever see her wallet in the clock? She laughed about it and told me that, from then on, that's where she hid her money.

MARIO BUATTA: Once we were at Albert's house in the country in Southport, where I'd stopped by for lunch. The three of us—Albert, Sister, and I—were out on the back porch, which is very close to the train. Whenever the train went by, I would look at Sister and mouth words, though no sound was coming out of my mouth. Sister caught on immediately, and she did this with me whenever the train went by. Albert would stare at us and say, "What did you two just say? I didn't hear any of it." Sister loved playing these games.

She used to enjoy telling her friends how expensive I was. She would say, "How can anyone afford him?"

OATSIE CHARLES: The last time I saw her was when Betsey Whitney, she, and I had dinner together on trays at Sister's apartment. Three old dames sitting there. It was absolutely marvelous, one of the great evenings of my life. No one was more entertaining than Sister, or more outrageous. Whatever the real content of a story was, she could make it great because she was a storyteller. Sister's voice was marvelous; I always loved her voice. It struck you immediately, and certainly added color—if a voice can add color. I adored her.

SUSAN: Sister liked strong women, and one of her favorites was her close friend Slim Keith, who was right up her alley. They had met when Slim rented the Red House in Maine for the summer. Sister had known her for about ten years, which meant she was a "new friend." It was a joke between them that they called each other by their real names, Dorothy May and Nancy. They would talk about everything from the latest Christie's sale to the best corned beef hash recipe, with a strong dose of hard-core gossip mixed in. Their affection toward each other was obvious, as was the competitive and stubborn streak that ran through both of their personalities. Sister would make one of her exaggerated comments and Slim would be right there challenging her with "Now, *Dorothy May*, you *know* that's not entirely true." Slim was a world-class conversationalist, and I ate up every word she uttered about Ernest Hemingway, Truman Capote, and the Hollywood set she had grown up with. She was smart, and she was kind. Doug and I knew that an evening with Dorothy May and Nancy was about as good as you could get.

SAMUEL BELL: It was always tradition where she shopped for her food. She would shop at Paradise Market on Eighty-third Street and Grace's Market on Third Avenue. She would say that it was the best place to get this or that. They would rip her off, but that was her store. Leonard's, the fish store next door, was just as expensive. I'm sure that wasn't the best place to get all those things, but she became locked in with tradition and people she liked.

She did most of her Christmas shopping for rich people in bazaar stores, like Woolworth's. Sometimes she would give stuffed bears to some of the housekeepers who had children or grandchildren. She would also take some of the gifts she received, rewrap them, and send them to some client. I think the joke was once that some client sent her a gift and she sent it back, not realizing that the person had sent it to her.

MARK HAMPTON: She once said—it was one of her great quotations—"I've never even been to a cocktail party." She used to have these wonderful cocktail parties. The food was delicious. Who was that Spanish or Portuguese cook? What was she called? Pilar.

Do you remember those egg-salad croquettes? The food was celestial. The food was always divine. Then there was Molly Corbin, the elderly Irishwoman. She had worked for Sister's mother and then she worked for Sister. Duane and I saw her at Sister's again and again. One night, we were at a friend's, and there was Molly. It was always the same things: ham wrapped around a pickle with some Philadelphia cream cheese, sliced on the diagonal, and cheese puffs and little sandwiches. Very good. Then Pilar came on the scene and everything changed.

So I boldly said to Molly, "What a treat to see you here . . . and what a surprise." She said, "Oh no, Mr. Hampton. I work for a lot of people. I'd love to come to you." So we then used her for as long as she could still work. She told this story about how hard on the maids Sister was. Sister had this way of just cramming a lot of things into her schedule but never seeming to be in a rush. She never blustered into a room. She was never out of breath. She just worked it all out. Once, she'd obviously been with some grand client until 6:15 and she had people coming for drinks at 6:30. She walked in, and Molly and the girls had just put out the hors d'oeuvres, so I guess by now it was 6:20. And there was this thing on the table—hard-boiled eggs with a little crisscross of pimento, exactly what Sister would hate. She stood there—one of the dining rooms had a bare floor on Seventy-ninth Street—picking all the pimento strips off and dropping them on the floor.

She had a way of hitting on a method of getting people to do things her way. And because she spoke in that tiny voice, everybody who wanted to hear, which was most anybody who knew her, would quiet down. She could silence a room by whispering these stories. They were brilliant. She had this great, forceful personality. I think that kind of strong, assertive personality is irreplaceable.

With all the new people whom Sister injected into her life—Andy Warhol, Halston—the fundamentals were always people she'd known all of her life. The women she'd gone to school with, the people from Far Hills, and people like Billy Baldwin or Van Day Truex, who were old, old decorating friends but who were older by ten or twelve years, and who, like Sister, knew everybody but, unlike Sister, hadn't been part of that world.

And she had all of those new friends; she picked up friends all the time. People who interested her. She had her old Foxcroft life, which spilled into her Far Hills life, her Maine life, Harry's Wall Street life, her professional life. It's all very complicated. And she was still this incredible family person. Susan's little closet dollhouse was of as much interest to her as Mrs. Whitney's new commode.

MICHAEL KINNICUTT: I was fascinated by her. I was her brother's son, so it was not a complete surprise to me. I think I always liked to test her. I was frightened, but at the same time I was fascinated, and I did enjoy engaging her. She was a very wily conversationalist. She always held back much more than she gave out, but what she gave out was tantalizing, and it was always sort of drew you in. I think she also enjoyed talking to me because I provided basic insight into her brother and what was going on in his life. She was very good at getting the type of information she wanted. Even as a youngster, I was aware that we were doing more than just chatting.

SUSAN: Sister had fixed ideas about how one was to behave socially. It was a plus to be from a family she knew, but very wrong to talk about the "right" people. One night in New York, we had some friends for supper at her apartment. One of the young men spent a lot of time name-dropping, hoping to impress her. When he left, she said, "He has known too many people too fast." He did not come back.

CARL-PETER BRAESTRUP: You'd have to move thousands of things to clean, but they were so beautiful. They were almost like performance art; there was so much to look at. You would walk into these rooms and almost couldn't get an overall impression. Everywhere you looked, there was something to meet the eye. In other words, there was no corner of the room that she hadn't anticipated you looking at, and she'd put something there to sort of reward you for making the quest. At all of these cocktails parties at the houses in both New York and Maine, I didn't always have anything to say to anyone, so it was actually nice for me to have a little eye candy, to be able to look at things.

Aunt Sister and my grandmother, her cousin Ibby, never forgot a thing. Once I went with Susan to Aunt Sister's apartment; it was in the summer, before she'd gone up to Maine. It was ninety degrees outside and I was wearing shorts. It was daytime when we stopped by to see her. She didn't say anything while I was there—but I heard more about the fact that I wore shorts from more people than you can possibly imagine. I must have heard about it a million times. I heard about it from my mother, who had heard about it from my grandmother. I heard about it directly from my grandmother. I think Aunt Apple actually mentioned it. I asked Susan if it was a big deal and she said, "You don't wear shorts in New York and go to somebody's apartment."

In Sister's world, people had uniforms. There was something you knew to wear in a certain context. I didn't know what these rules were. I certainly didn't know it was inappropriate to wear shorts. Aunt Irene mentioned it to someone else. It wasn't as if they were hot pants. They were just khaki shorts.

MARK HAMPTON: She was an incredible flirt and enjoyed skating close to thin ice. I remember the things she said about the most well-known people. They

(left) Sister and grandson Charlie Bartlett. (right) Sister and grandson Harry Bartlett at a family wedding. Sister was famous for the hats she wore to weddings.

were rarely flattering. I asked her what Adlai Stevenson was like, and her comment was, "Oh, that Adlai Stevenson was so touchy, touchy. Touching everyone all the time." It was not the answer I had expected.

SUSAN: For Mum's fiftieth birthday, my brothers, Charlie, Harry, and I gave her a small dinner party at her apartment in Boston. When it came time for toasts, Sister, who always spoke, brought out a minuscule ivory box, which looked vaguely familiar. She toasted Mum and then presented her with the box, which she said was very special. She said it had been in the family for generations, and then went on for some time about how this box had a connection with my mother. Accepting it gracefully, my mother turned it over, to see MADE IN CHINA $29.50 stamped on the bottom. Mum then realized that she had bought this box herself and that it was in the guest room where Sister was staying.

SAMUEL BELL: She would always make sure that her family was treated like gold, but Mrs. Bartlett and Mrs. Gilbert always feared her. I always wanted to say, "Why are you afraid of her? Don't you know her the way I know her?" I knew she must have had a good disposition, because Apple and D.B. are the nicest people on the map. Mrs. Parish would have me take them to different places. They would have their own schedule, but she would say, "Take them to this place" or "Take them there." Apple and D.B. would get halfway and say, "Let us off here, but don't tell Mum you dropped us off here." She had some schedule for them, and they hated it. Then when I would get back, she asked me, "Did you drop them all these places?" I would say, "I dropped them at some of the places." I didn't want to lie, because she could see through a lie.

SUSAN: Her method of ignoring someone was to focus all of her attention on something else, like the dogs. I saw her do it to people who some would consider very important, but who she felt were acting boorish. She wanted everyone to compliment the dogs, but most of the time they were so mean you were taking your life in your hands attempting contact.

DOUG CRATER (Susan's husband): I first met Sister Parish, Mrs. Parish to me, in the late seventies. I remember walking down Madison Avenue on a Sunday night with Susan, when the weather was getting unbelievably cold, and we happened to be right near her apartment at Seventy-seventh and Fifth. We walked in on one of her typical Sunday-night gatherings of old friends (those whom she had known all her life). There in the living room was her brother Gory, her sister-in-law Irene Kinnicutt, and what would become the usual group, all of whom, with a rare exception, had summer houses in Dark Harbor. I remember Gory Kinnicutt pontificating about the St. Mark's scores and asking us whether or not they had won their recent hockey game.

The same group would assemble every Sunday night in the fall, winter, and spring. When we lived in the city, we would usually join them for drinks and, after they had left, for dinner with Mrs. Parish. Her usual was straight vodka colored with Clamato juice. She used to say that she never took a drink before 6:00 P.M. and the best way to go was to have two powerful ones and then stop. I guess vodka was a switch from the days when she drank bourbon, which was her drink of choice because, as she said, "It is the color of mahogany." She would hold court, relaying stories of weekends spent in Far Hills, New Jersey, or with the Whitneys on Long Island. She told us of her lunch at her friend Mrs. Engelhard's house with Imelda Marcos and Doris Duke. While showing Imelda Marcos around the house, she eventually stopped at Mrs. Engelhard's shoe closet, where she asked Mrs. Marcos if she liked Mrs. Engelhard's shoes. That was when Imelda Marcos was getting all that negative press about her personal expenses, including a ridiculously large shoe collection, so it was a typically wry question for Mrs. Parish to ask.

There was the time she had been at Mrs. Whitney's for the weekend and found herself pinned to her bed by an extremely heavy breakfast tray. According to Mrs. Parish, "Everyone in the house had forgotten about me," and the buzzer to call someone was not within reach. "I spent the whole day in bed before anyone discovered me," she told us. She liked to be amused and believed it was one's obligation to say something interesting.

Mrs. Parish would say things like "I crave morphine; it is simply delicious." It was something that she had once experienced during a hospital visit. At her last costume party in Maine, she wore an orange mop on her head, a Groucho Marx nose, and an eyeglass getup, and sat quietly with a friend, the minister's small daughter, on her lap, watching the contestants. She really did look incredibly freakish, and I am sure that she knew it, but she couldn't have cared less.

She really took care of Susan, probably because they, as many family members have said, were a lot alike—artistic, mercurial, independent, and curious.

Driving with her was always interesting. Once on the way back to the city from Long Island, she missed the turn onto the Grand Central Parkway and instead found herself continuing on the Long Island Expressway, passing that huge cemetery in Queens with the zillion gravestones and sarcophagi. I'll never forget her suggestion that we pull over and die right there on the spot. Not a bad idea at that moment. She then backed the car up on the Long Island Expressway as six lanes of traffic careened past us toward the Midtown Tunnel. She always prided herself on her driving ability.

ALAN CAMPBELL: She was sort of an outlaw in a way. She was very strict about people doing the proper thing, following the rules and regulations, but if they were inconvenient for her, she just didn't do it and never batted an eye. We were driving down the highway once after going to see Albert up in the country, on our way back to the city. I got onto the New York Thruway, headed the wrong way. She said, "Alan, we are going the wrong way." I told her, "Well, we'll just have to get off and get on again." She barked, "No, no, just turn around." I replied, "We can't turn around." It was a four-lane highway. She said, "Just turn around." And so we went bumpity-bump over the center of the thing, with signs saying NO TURNS—and I headed back.

I would stop by after work or on my way somewhere and sit down and have a drink with her. She'd want to hear what you'd done. Then she would tell you stories.

She made magic. She really did. She had wonderful little parties, where you'd see all kinds of people. She was also sort of slightly off balance. She did not like everything to go smoothly. If there wasn't something wrong, she'd make it wrong.

Sister and her maid Pilar, who was Spanish and had a very quick temper, had these terrible exchanges. Sister would tell you the awful things that Pilar had said. She would say, "She calls me Mrs. Garbage."

MRS. LEWIS PRESTON (family friend): Mrs. Parish gave showers for both of my daughters, Pansy and Electra, when they were being married. She made her living room feel ageless. It was old-fashioned and warm, but also modern. There were different generations there—a lot of Foxcroft people, a lot of the old school, and she served the kind of old-fashioned food that we understood. We had peanut butter and bacon sandwiches or cinnamon toast. It was the best of the old world blended with the new. Anyone from twelve to ninety would have been perfectly at home. There was nothing stiff about it.

MARK HAMPTON: She got it all done and you could never figure out when in her life she had time. She was so wrapped up in these houses that we knew about, but you never saw her doing them. That comfort was so important and also that insouciance of how you would live in a room. Do you remember how she always put her shoe under her? She sat with her leg under her. Black shoe, white silk sofa. It didn't matter.

Once at a Christmas party—really a buffet supper—at the apartment on Seventy-ninth Street, all the people who worked for her were standing around nervously, not having a very good time. And they were sort of stiff and didn't want to sit in one of those Louis XV chairs. Well, I was having a ball.

I always remember one night sitting on that sofa at the end of the room. This was after the room was brown, with flame-colored curtains. Mrs. Mellon Bruce was there, wearing a purple brocade suit and tons of rubies—and I mean *tons*—and she just sat there like an inanimate object, with everybody waiting on her. These strange grandees would arrive. And you'd think, My God, what are *they* doing here? She mixed people up. Anyone she asked would come. Andy Warhol or Mrs. Mellon Bruce—they all showed up.

**Sister horsing around at Van
Day Truex's house in France.**

I was sitting there—and do you remember that little red rectangular
table? It always had a cabbage rose and a Battersea candlestick and a box. It
always had about as much as you could get on it. And Barbara Drum, the great
troublemaker, was lighting a cigarette. I had a match, because I smoke,
though I wouldn't have smoked in that drawing room. I lunged forward to
light Barbara's cigarette, and when I did, I knocked a candle over. It being
Christmastime, the candle was red and had been burning for two hours by
then. It got on the white damask sofa, caught on the curtains. I don't know
how, but it just did this sort of wheel, this cartwheel of hot red wax. Sister was
planted down in the corner, where she usually sat—by the screen that hid the
door. She said, "Oh, forget about it."

Anyone else would have been running to the kitchen looking for the
maid, the Renuzit, anything. She was so casual and irreverent about those
rooms she lived in. And that, of course, is what signaled the great comfort.
That was the vibe she sent out: that you live in a room. Sit down and put your
feet up in the chair if you want to and have a good time.

LIBBY CAMERON: She would get that look in her eye. You knew it was coming . . . some trouble, stirring things up. I remember her once making soup for
me out of Velveeta cheese. It was one Sunday night. We'd been somewhere
together, some little show thing. And when we came back, she said, "Oh,
you'll have to stay for soup." Pilar had gone somewhere, so Mrs. Parish made

this soup. She'd pulled out this block of Velveeta and sort of threw it in the pot and put in some broth, and it was actually quite good.

She hated restaurants. Too noisy. She took me to Jo Jo once—I can't remember why we went. I think she wanted to try the calves' brains there, and Slim Keith had told her they were very good. I remember her complaining that there was all that tile floor and it was so tiny. I mean, it's a nice restaurant, but I remember going out and her grabbing me and saying, "Oh, I thought I was going to die in there." She hated the food, but then later, she was telling people how good it was.

ALICE ROGERS: At one fancy dinner party in Dark Harbor in the summer, Sister came dressed in a beautiful flowing caftan. She had on her pearls and she looked so pretty. She was sitting there, and all of a sudden, when she moved her feet, I saw this zippered thing fall out from under the bottom of her skirt.

I said, "Sister, what is that?" And she said, "Oh, that's my nightgown." I asked, "Sister, why do you have on your nightgown?" And she said, "Oh, I always do that if I can camouflage it. I have on the caftan and I have my nightgown underneath so that the minute I get home, all I have to do is just drop my caftan to the floor and crawl into bed."

ALCE ROBERTSON (year-round resident of Islesboro): I was staying with Mrs. Parish in the Red House once in Dark Harbor. It was winter, around Christmastime. She had just been asked to decorate in England for the Duchess of York. She had the letter from Buckingham Palace that her office had framed for her. They'd put it under glass. She never did do that job, because the British people thought they had enough decorators over there to pick from.

She was going out to dinner, probably up to Apple's, because they were at the Brown House and it was cold out. She had on a long dinner gown, and underneath she had on her long underwear. Well, out the door she went, with the long underwear hanging down under this dinner dress, so you could see it.

I said, "Well, you sure look some fetching."

And Mrs. Parish said, "From Islesboro, Maine, to Buckingham Palace," and ran out the door.

GLENN BERNBAUM (owner of Mortimer's): The monumental story about Sister Parish was that she was at Mortimer's, looking around the room, when

Apple, Sister, D.B., and Susan in the library at 920 Fifth Avenue.

she said to me, "Who *are* all of these people?" I had a lunch for Sister here at Christmastime with Maisie Houghton and I decided that the thing that Sister would like best would be what she had eaten at the Women's Exchange. We did everything—fish cakes, martinis, everything they used to serve at the Women's Exchange. It really was funny. I think it started with asparagus vinaigrette, then something with sauce mousseline. We had a full meal, including coconut cake.

I went to her apartment for dinner, and it was the most high-cholesterol meal that I had ever seen. It started with asparagus with hollandaise, creamed spinach with chopped egg on top, the way they used to do it. When I was a child, that was the type of food I had. Then you would have whipped cream on the dessert or heavy cream or crème fraîche.

I remember once I was at an antiques show with Sister and Slim Keith— I have pictures of that—and Slim was in a wheelchair, and Sister was so jealous of that wheelchair.

ALBERT HADLEY: You knew you would have a good time if you were going to her apartment. You never knew what was going to happen. It was more her than the house. The house was secondary to the evening.

Dear Sister
  I still can't find my
crochetting needle, so you'd
better find me another one.
  Meanwhile, have a very
Happy Birthday & let us
see you very soon - please.

          Lots of love,
          Duane & Mark

Tuesday

Watercolors painted by
Mark Hampton for
Sister on her birthday.

ABOVE Scheme boards for the Oval Room presented to President and Mrs. Kennedy.

OPPOSITE PAGE TOP Caroline Kennedy's bedroom.

OPPOSITE PAGE BOTTOM Jacqueline Kennedy's bedroom.

TOP Bedroom at the Summer House with the multicolored rug that Sister and Albert found in Ireland.

BOTTOM Mrs. John Hay Whitney's bedroom at the Whitneys' horse farm in Saratoga, New York.

Sister's living room (top) and sitting room (bottom) at 960 Fifth Avenue.

TOP Mrs. Whitney's bathroom at Greentree.

BOTTOM The billiard room at Greentree.

ABOVE The living room at Kiluna Farm, the Paleys' late-nineteenth-century white clapboard house on Long Island.

BOTTOM The front hall at Parish-Hadley.

The living room of the Paleys' Fifth Avenue Apartment.

KENNETH JAY LANE (jewelry designer): I had a marvelous time with Sister. She had fascinating dinners with people whom I wouldn't necessarily have imagined were her cup of tea, you know. People whom she would know, but not know that well—for instance, the Schlesingers. One night, just Alexandra, Arthur, Sister, and I had dinner, and we had the best time. You know what I mean. Serious men. I was delighted that I was one of the chosen ones.

ALBERT HADLEY: She was a man's woman. Let's face it. With her women friends, and with her old friends, she liked to pretend to hate them. She would say the most horrible things and then pick up the phone and ask them over for a drink.

SUSAN: She had some very close women friends, but she preferred the company of men. Mum and I would be at her apartment, sitting in the library, and she would be in the worst mood, sagging, as if she had been alive for one thousand years. A man would come in and, miraculously, she would be twenty years old again. Tom Watson, Charlie Engelhard, Jock Whitney—she loved the powerful men. She was a first-rate flirt.

JAMIE HOUGHTON (married to Maisie Houghton, Sister's niece): She loved my father. She decided early on that men were all right. Of course, she thought my father was also rich, and rich men were better than poor men. No question. She tried to bug my father about being cheap, too. She used to say, "Why don't you just redo the whole house?" My father had a twinkle in his eye and he sparred with her. I think they got along fine.

KENNETH JAY LANE: I remember once we were going to Annette de la Renta's and Sister was driving us up. We were taking a friend with us, a friend of the Engelhards'. A wonderful man. On the way to Sister's, I was telling him a little bit about the von Bülow case. Claus lived in her building. I used to say that Sister was the concierge at 960 Fifth Avenue, as her apartment was on the first floor. We arrived at the building; Sister was already in her car, practically with her foot on the gas. And I said, "Sister, darling, you've had a little excitement in this building this summer, haven't you?" Because that was the summer that Claus was indicted. She said, "Oh, I came in the side door the other day and who did I see but Claus. I didn't know what to say. So I looked at him and I said, 'Have you had a nice summer?'" She said he just collapsed. She thought it was funny, too. She never laughed at her own jokes, but she'd smirk.

BUNNY WILLIAMS: At Mrs. Parish's, the food always looked homemade. You sensed it in seconds. Mrs. Parish knew how to entertain because she had been raised that way. Most people today have to learn it. Because they don't know how to entertain, they call the caterer and say, "I'm having people for drinks and I need you to come over." If Mrs. Parish wanted people for drinks, she could start it at 9:00 in the morning and have twenty-five people for drinks that night. It allowed her to be completely spontaneous. At her apartment, you could fix yourself a drink. There didn't have to be five people in uniform doing that for you. It wasn't a big production.

Now, people think, Oh well, I have to have a bartender fix the drinks. And I always say, "You know, we are just going to put the drinks tray out." Then they ask, "Why? They don't want to see the bar."

Our exposure today is to hotels, not to grand houses that are run like the Whitneys'. Nobody sees that anymore. There is a vocabulary that is going out of our society completely. When you went to Mrs. Parish's, there was always a housekeeper or someone who had greeted you before and knew you. There was a sense of being relaxed and welcomed.

She was funny. Terribly funny. She could hurt you. I mean if you overheard her. I know Mr. Pierpont used to say, "Well, I don't care what she says about me as long as she says something, because she is so funny." But often the things weren't so nice about people she knew.

SUSAN: She was interested in everything. For example, one night at dinner, she became fascinated by the topic of safe sex. She asked, and so we started to talk. The grandchildren would tell her about condoms. She would have that little-girl voice and she would ask, "Are they called con-domes?" And she would really want to know. Things had to be couched in a certain way. But after we talked about "con-domes," she went into the Dark Harbor Shop in Maine, and when she saw the balloons at the counter for the children's birthday party, she asked the proprietor there, Billy Warren, "Now Billy, are those your con-domes for sale?" She just sort of took life and wanted to know. Whether it was the newest garden furniture or "con-domes," she wanted to know.

I remember one of her Sunday-evening cocktail parties, just when crack cocaine was coming into vogue, and we were talking about it. Sister always said things in that dry, irreverent way, her face giving away nothing. We were talking about it and she said, "I hear it's like having a thousand orgasms." Total deadpan delivery.

Sister with her close friends, Barbara Drum (left) and Mari Watts Hitchcock.

I remember her humor. She was someone who got the message, who got the same joke, who could pick up on little subtleties, ironies, absurdities, pretensions. She got it. We were on the same wavelength. Well, there aren't any personalities like Sister anymore. You know, people are always asking who's going to take over for the ladies who were great personalities. Not many. Not the same way. Not with one foot in another era, which is post–World War II, and sometimes post–World War I. Remember the Roaring Twenties and all of that. We had a lot of mutual friends. We used to go up to Betsey Whitney's together fairly often and have lunch, the three of us; it was great fun. After, when we were going back to New York, Sister would say, "There must have been trouble in the kitchen."

BROOKE ASTOR (client and New York philanthropist): Sister was a lot of fun. Well, sometimes she didn't like people. Her husband was really very attractive and they gave wonderful parties, especially at Christmastime. Somebody played the piano and we used to sing. Sister sang, and Harry used to sing very well. I used to sing. Imagine, I have no voice at all now. I used to sing and then I'd whistle the song, and then go back to singing it again. In those days, we played games all the time. We had a lot of fun. Nobody does that anymore. We had teams and we'd act out these charades. If you said that to someone today, they'd have a stroke.

I think that Sister's last apartment was very nice. It had the little garden, and that's where she had the dogs. She loved them just the way I do. I have dachshunds. They're called Boysey and Girlsey.

I think New York was much easier in those days. Of course, society in New York, or so-called society, was quite different. Today, everyone is supposed to be everyone else's equal. We're much more equal now. I mean, you don't go and see the same people again and again like you used to.

I can tell you more about Sister. She could be nasty, too, but she was a character. Sister was an extraordinary woman because she had wonderful taste. She was brought up as a lady, which in those days meant that you led a very closed life. She went around and saw all sorts of people because she was interested in people. She opened up and she had a way of doing things. Now people have decorators and they don't even bother to talk to them.

Opposite page: Sister and Albert in England.

Chapter Thirteen

Clients

For Sister, it was the intrigue of the people. It was getting to know them and
running their lives. She would talk to them on the telephone every day
and she told them exactly what she thought. And they simply would do
anything she said. They were hypnotized by her. If they weren't
hypnotized by her, forget it. I am not exaggerating. That was it.

ALBERT HADLEY

SUSAN: Sister had two kinds of clients: those she knew socially and those who came to Parish-Hadley cold, without any connections. Sometimes there was a difference in her friendships with them, but she cared totally and absolutely for both. When she liked or approved of people, she connected with them on a very personal level. With that connection came tremendous support and attention.

RICHARD MANDER: She brought in the great clients, and her ultimate strength was being a friend to them. Also, her friends had Modiglianis,

Rodins, and Renoirs, which really helped. They also had ten-foot ceilings with fourteen-inch cornices. Now, as Sister was brilliant and had friends who were willing to let her be creative in these spaces, and had collections of really wonderful bits to choose from, plus having access to the world to fill in the spots, this gave her a wonderful ability to make the most incredible places. She did make the rich look right. There was even an article about her in *Women's Wear Daily* called "Making the Rich Look Right."

PETER GATES: It was good business, because if you went to Sister Parish, you knew exactly what you were going to get. What you were getting was class, old-style class. In the old days, people wanted it because it made them comfortable.

She was, from the few situations I observed her in, brilliant at getting paid. Every now and then, she drifted into doing work for people who were notorious for not paying or paying slowly, but she collected. She collected mostly because they could not afford to make an enemy of her. Because they couldn't afford not to have her as their decorator.

She was a ruthless competitor, and she didn't tolerate bullshit from anybody. Anybody. Whether it was a valued client or not. She expected people to play straight, and she was quite ruthless about it. And she managed to do that without seeming to turn them against her when they were her clients. She did just dominate them. They would tremble if they dared to make a suggestion.

SUSAN: Because Sister often found herself acting in the role of psychiatrist to some of her clients, she was cautious about whom she agreed to work for. Her relationship with clients was often personal and so she chose them carefully. I would hear her lecturing many of them about everything from which schools were appropriate for their children to where they should buy a summer house. Not everyone who sought her help in decorating became a client of Parish-Hadley. Having enough money to afford the firm was, of course, paramount, but it was certainly not the only factor. There was a girl I knew vaguely who married a very successful Wall Street type, and in her role as "trophy wife," she wanted Sister and Albert to fix up their new apartment. During the initial meeting, Sister did not take to the tycoon husband, and thus they were turned away. It was not a matter of snobbery, but one of "connection," to use Sister's word.

Sister's selection process also included her finely tuned instincts about whether or not people were good credit risks. Nonpayment was only occasionally a problem for the firm because she was well connected enough to make the situation embarrassing for the client. New York, despite its size, is a very small town, and Sister was not someone to whom you wanted to owe money. The firm's accountant, Carole Cavaluzzo, told me that if there was a problem, she would tell Sister, who would send them a handwritten note, and the bill would usually be paid.

GLENN BERNBAUM: I met Sister when I had an apartment in the Fifties. I was starting from scratch and I wanted somebody to help me. I thought of Albert, so I called him; he had just started there. He had to get Sister to approve me as a client before they would do it. So I said, "Albert, have Mrs. Parish come to lunch," and I was approved.

Half the trick of decorating is being sensitive to your clients—feeling them out, understanding what they really want, worming out their problems, making them feel safe with you. That's where tact comes in. You have to have the courage to say what you think, without downing them. You've got to inspire them to be responsive to you and your ideas. It's very difficult, because, from the beginning, you're involved in personalities, and whether you get along with them or not is really up to you. That's the secret of the beginning of the job and the end of the job, and often you have a very sinking feeling that it's all for naught.

The process usually begins when we meet the clients in the office. "First of all," they will say, "you have to see what we have." They will then produce some wretched blueprint of their new apartment, or some photographs of a house they've just bought, and talk about it as though they'd been there all their lives. You know, "This is where the children play. We have tea out there," that kind of thing. So it's up to you to say, "Oh, well, I see perfectly how lovely it all is, but is it that you want to change that look? Maybe you ought to sit on the other side of the house—and make a terrace down there." You just have to talk along. You have to give your body and soul to them. Hopefully, they catch on immediately and they feel comfortable with you. That's the best thing that can happen.

JUDY COWEN: She was such a presence. When she spoke, you sat up and listened. I remember when she came to our house in the country. The first time she came, I had chicken for her dogs, and I think she drove, which was very scary. She looked at the house and said she would be back. She came back with the office driver, and a large sort of Santa Claus bag filled with the most beau-

tiful things. She started pushing things around and hanging pictures and placing the beautiful things around the room. It was like magic, what she did. I
always felt so good after I'd been with her.

*Nowadays, you have to establish whether you are getting them out of the kitchen
or into the kitchen. This usually has nothing to do with money. A great many
people these days don't think it's right or chic to live in the grand way they used
to live. It's an approach to life that is certainly in the air and is very catching.
People's houses are often just too big for what they want, and you have to rethink
their house, make it function without a big staff, and with at least an honest effort
at fuel conservation. It's as hard for some people to cut back as it is to go forward.*

    *At the outset, you try to discover something of a client's true personality.
You'll have lots of hints right away. If they talk about their treasured two-inch-
square Picasso lithograph, signed, you know about their illusions of self-
grandeur and you can be quite certain that they will always have to have a
"deal." If they've inherited everything, always lived a certain way, don't care to
discuss new approaches, they are a closed book and it's pointless to go on. If
they're concerned about "rules," and quote a magazine article declaring it's
mauve this year, there is no hope. If they say they want the "thickest shag you
can get," you know that they think shag says money, and you will loathe working with them.*

PETER GATES: One day, one of her more arriviste clients had an opportunity
to buy a table, one of two tables. He needed a table and he chose the one that
was five times more expensive, and it was the wrong table, and she was very
offended. She said, "This is the table you want." He said, "No, this is the table
I want. I want to pay a million. I want to make a statement." Her life was not
about making statements.

*I like to work with people who know their minds, but whose minds are open. You
can tell right away if they have any taste, or if there is hope that some might be
developed. If people are alive and alert, they can't help but grow. Young people
are usually the best clients. They are willing to go to museums, expose themselves to the best design—if they care. The young are very open-eyed. It has
nothing to do with money or possessions, but with caring.*

    *Lifestyle, personality, taste, hidden desires—you have to analyze all these
things before you can start designing in the correct way. We begin at the begin-*

ning, and a great deal is established at the first meeting, the whole design direc-
tion—casual, sophisticated, sleek, cluttered, more elaborate or softer, moving
ahead or cutting back. You can tell almost at once whether you can work togeth-
er, if you can cope with it, if it's worth it, if you can make the house one they
can live in comfortably—and when you've both decided you can, it may be only
a matter of days before you both realize there's been a terrible mistake.

For the next procedure is to go to their house or to the house they're going to
live in. In the car, one tries to imagine what one has to face, and one's imagina-
tion is already working as to what one is going to see, or what one knows one is
not going to see.

You know immediately when you walk into a house whether it's well kept,
whether they have a staff or no staff, whether the flowers are alive or dead (or
whether they have any flowers at all), and, really, how much they care. You get
a general quick picture, and this impression tells a big story right away. When
we are summoned to view a house by total strangers, Albert always accompanies
me. If it is hopeless, I become terribly fragile and say, "Please take me home,
Albert. I'm not feeling well."

We find out how they live. Is someone serving dinner every night? Do they
put their feet up when they read? Do they need the dining room, or can it be com-
bined? Is there furniture, or will we start fresh? How will this room be used?
That room? How do they entertain? Do they entertain?

DAVID KLEINBERG: She was always trying to change people's household staff. She was like a one-woman employment agency. Once, she had a client who was somebody "at sea" when she met him. He really needed someone to whip his life together. Sister said, "Your life is a mess. Your children are running amok. There are holes in your sheets. You should be ashamed of yourself." She went out and hired him a household secretary. Sister basically found her, hired her, and sent her to him. That woman ran his house for years.

People don't live the way she did growing up. Those people who do live that way almost always overextend. Not financially, but instead of doing with a housekeeper, a cook, and a yardman, they'll have four people standing around in these little uniforms. She hated that. She just thought that was so awful. She loved that these houses looked good, and that you never got a glass of iced tea that wasn't served on a little silver tray or without a nicely pressed napkin, but she hated that there were four people who sort of handed it off to one another. That was ostentatious.

BILL HODGINS: Sister was able to control people without anybody feeling they had been controlled.

MARY JANE POOL: Enid Haupt said she was so pleased because Sister Parish had recommended or suggested she use the same chintz that Sister herself had used. It was a personal thing. We published Enid's apartment several times, and, I must say, it was a charming room.

MARIO BUATTA: A lot of people were afraid of Sister. She loved making trouble. She loved gossip, making mountains out of little tiny hills. She would make every day bigger than life. She loved to be wicked. You would see that little twinkle in her eye and you knew she was up to the devil.

She treated her clients a certain way because, at her age, who needed people to come in and argue about what was right and what was wrong? Here was a woman who had traveled all over the world, knew everybody, knew everything about living the way one ought to live if one has the money to do it with. She knew what to have.

If you decide to go on, you must go on with tact and courage. You've got to convince the clients that they're safe with you, that you're not going to throw out everything, not going to down them. It's important to convey a certain amount of encouragement as to what they have and what you hope to be able to progress with—that their house is going to be what they've hoped for. Yet you have to say what you think, point out what you can and cannot do something about.

Frankly, I'd rather start with something of the person's character and then work around it. Of course, that depends on the person's character. The lucky person has a lovely desk or something to begin with. Sometimes you have to search quite hard for that something.

JACQUELINE GONNET: It was the personality of the owner and the personality of Sister that came through. Because, with all of the elegant things, you could always find some very intimate things that belonged to the owners and that humanized the interiors a lot. There was always an attention to the details, which added so much.

There was a house outside of Boston. An unknown couple called me up and asked if I would come. She sounded very nice over the telephone, and so I stopped there on my way to Maine. When I walked in, well, everything in the house was unattractive, including the house itself—ugly. It all looked like it came out of a catalog. There wasn't a thread about which you would possibly say, "Isn't that lovely." I was composing a polite letter in my mind, when in the corner of one room I saw a small bathmat-like thing woven in many colors, like a rag rug. I thought, If she likes that rag rug, maybe there's some hope. And I said to her that it was a pretty one, and she may have said, "Well, that's the look I really would like to have," but without my being able to know what she was even talking about. But she knew she liked it, so there was that glimmer of hope. I would have written that polite letter, about our tastes not matching, about not being able to help them in enough ways, and just gotten out of it but for that glimmer.

When we went to work on that house, we put in painted furniture, rag rugs, quilts, everything that she wanted but didn't know how to express, or put together. And I don't know a happier client. Now she and her husband are expanding. They own another house in Maine; their taste is developing, and you could never change it now. In fact, it's reached a point where they probably know more than I do about crafts. That's what they really like.

Sometimes, when you can't find even a glimmer of hope, a good way to proceed is to ask if they have any photographs of things they like. And they'll rummage through a drawer and produce pictures they've clipped from old magazines—often of things that look totally unlike anything they own. They've hoarded these pictures over the years and put them in a folder, and all of a sudden they give you this clue and you realize that you are on the same wavelength.

You sometimes have to peek into a person's secret life to get a job going properly. I am teased for my interest in closets, but you can tell more from the inside of a closet—you can tell the whole character of a person. It's a secret life. Like one client—she's a little mouse of a woman who wears a little khaki skirt above her knees and flat-heeled sneaker-type shoes and a Brooks Brothers shirt, and that's it, day in and day out. Always immaculate, but always exactly the same. I never saw her wear anything else. They bought this enormous house, and for some reason or other, I opened the closet door and there were these beautiful negligees, nightgowns, beautiful evening dresses, slippers to match, everything to perfection—everything. But never a stitch ever worn. That gave me the clue as to how she secretly wanted to live. We turned her house into a very dressy, beautiful, grand house—and it's just like her clothes. They eat in the kitchen, sleep in maids' rooms, won't let anyone sit on anything, and never have a soul inside the house. They walk in and look at it, and that's it. But she seems perfectly happy.

When your client has a very large house, there is always the question about how formal and impressive they really want it to be. Again, you look for clues. I was asked to look at one of the most beautiful houses in Far Hills some time ago, and it was immediately obvious that it could become one of the grandest places in the country. But I knew the family had lots of children and lots of animals, and loved them far more dearly than priceless furnishings. I was trying to decide between sheer comfort and sheer elegance, when the front door flew open and one of the daughters rode her horse through the hall, up the grand staircase, turned gracefully, and trotted down and out the way she had come. Family ruled our design.

There are times when I am not sure about my first impressions of a house, and when that happens, I try to be candid about it. The other day, I made a two-hour tour of a very large house that had to be completely redone, and I didn't say a word. Finally, I said, "This is either the worst thing I've ever seen or the best, and I'll just have to go away and think about it." I went away, and two weeks later I called up and said, "Let's go."

Involving the husband doesn't always work to my advantage, however. One day a few years ago when a woman brought her husband to the first meeting, I knew it wasn't going to work. They wanted different things and neither could represent the other. They were interviewing me, rather than me them. Soon the man moved into the corner, absolutely bored. I saw him pluck at a slipcover, and then he came out with "This lady makes slipcovers that don't fit. Is that why we're in this place?" He obviously did not approve of the English style of slip-cover. You could tell that his wife was ready to shoot him. Later, she came back and said, "We have had a fight and he has won." They hired another decorator.

There have been times when I have gone into a prospective client's house and admired their taste, just loved everything in there immediately. But I think you are far more likely to love the person than the house. And you can love them for many reasons. You can love them because they are begging you to help, you can love them because of a personality that you take to immediately, you can love them because they have given you a fascinating challenge, and you can love them because here is an interesting person that you would like to help.

But however the job begins, however you feel about your new client, once you start, you are immediately involved in the most personal relationship in the world outside the marital bed or the psychiatrist's couch. You are not just rearranging furniture, you know; you are rearranging lives. That's why I take such an enormous personal interest in everyone I work for. There will be times when they could easily kill you, and when you could just as easily kill them. There will be moments of terror, fury, intense frustration, and God help you if the truck arrives late or the curtains are too short. If things happen to be going well, before you know it, you'll find yourself totally responsible for getting their children into dancing school, and finding them a cook. But there will also be moments of joy and love, and in spite of everything, many of my clients are now my dearest friends.

MARIO BUATTA: She would say over and over about certain houses and clients, "It's going to kill me." She had an eye that was amazing. She was also a very hard worker. She could not relate to many kinds of people, or to what some people were all about. Unfortunately, in our business, people used to want to hire Mrs. Parish or Mark Hampton if they had just come into some money. Sometimes these people wanted only to hire a decorator who was well connected, as Mark Hampton was, in the hopes of being invited to his parties and meeting his friends. Oftentimes, firms do a lot of that, as well. There is always the new girl in town who used to work for an airline and has just married the guy from Wall Street. She hires a decorator and has parties, to which she invites all of their friends, and the next thing you know, they are attracting people like flies. Now, because of their decorator, they are socially on that team; they are in "the group." So the decorator can play a great social role in getting the client into whatever circle of friends they want to get into.

Sister did some of that, but there were many people whom she wouldn't invite into her circle.

SAMUEL BELL: If she didn't like the client, then she would play games with them. That client would get Nanny in his or her lap no matter how dirty Nanny was. If she didn't like them as a client, Nanny or Ricky was her sword to get at them.

Looking at it from my standpoint, if they had a lot of money, she treated them graciously. But then if they had an attitude about their money, she didn't care about them. She said, "You're going to respect me." And she demanded that. Money was not the most important thing. It was about how they respected her, too. You could have a personality and no money, and she would care about you and like you, but if you had a lot of money and a bad personality, she would just treat you badly. But that's just from my observation and from sitting in the car watching. These clients and friends of hers learned that I was not a chauffeur. I would never get out and open the door except for Mrs. Parish, and then I got out of doing that because I got her conditioned to the fact that the handle was there and she could open it just as easily as I could. This one client, a good friend of hers, got in the car. Apparently, she always had people open the door for her. We were going to the theater, so I stopped, and all of a sudden I hear this thing in the back saying, "How do you open this————door?" Well, Mrs. Parish said, "Just use the handle." Then the lady said, "Can't someone come around and open it for me?" And Mrs. Parish said, "Samuel doesn't open the door for anybody."

There's a difference between old money and new money. Old money to me means people who have it, and have always had it, and they are generous with it. They don't care about money as much because they have it. New money—they want to keep up with the old money social life, but they have an attitude about it. They more or less say, "I have money. You are my slave." They have a superior attitude, and she could see right through that. They looked at her as just a decorator, instead of a friend. Mrs. Parish tried to be friends with the clients, and if you were her friend, that way she could get her point across easier. If they came across like that, then she took their money and put them in the background. She would take their money and she would work with them, but she would turn them over to people she didn't like at the office. That is what I observed.

I have mentioned the importance of tact when first visiting a client's house, but I confess that it is not always a strong point of mine. I tend to be candid. On another occasion, it was the opposite, however. I had been invited to Estée Lauder's New York house—a beautiful house that I had visited many times when it had been owned by a family friend. I was touring the house with one of my assistants, thinking we were alone, when I declared in what I thought was a whisper, "Oh, what I could do with this house." With that, our hostess appeared at my elbow, touched my cheek, and said, "Oh, what I could do with that face." She did not become a client, but she did send me, the very next day, a kit containing all of her best cosmetics.

OATSIE CHARLES: I met Sister because I had that house in Washington and I was struggling with it. Lily Guest came to me one day and said, "Stop all of this nonsense and call up Sister Parish." I did, so Mrs. Parish arrived, and we adored each other instantly and became very good friends. We always enjoyed one another. Sister just had the eye. You cannot acquire that unless you're born with it. It's just that simple.

Husbands are always interesting. You may find yourself on the same wavelength with the woman at the start of a job, but you still have to sell your ideas to the man, who, more often than not, couldn't be less interested. At first, you have to draw him in. You find out if he's interested in sailing, and you find some interesting boat pictures that can go in the library. If he has a gun collection, you search for a place for it. That all of a sudden wins him over. We did the largest, most elaborate job in San Francisco for the Gettys and Mr. Getty's sole interest was the piano. We paid a great deal of attention to the acoustics in the music room, and everything else just fell into place beautifully. If you do that, you can have two people on your side, instead of one. When all of a sudden a man begins to sense his environment, it can be quite exciting. He becomes eager to keep going, and so appreciative when people come in and say, "Oh, how beautiful." It can be terribly unfair if he is unaware of what he is going to be presented with. The wife has an enormous tendency, because she wants it so badly, to not quite come out with the truth. There are many, many cases where the truth is not known at all. But I think it is always better, for everyone, if the husband is deeply involved in everything, right from the start.

Often the husband agrees to do just one room, but if you've won him over, and it turns out to be exciting, you're just going on and doing more and more— and you've won.

JOAN TILNEY (client): When I married Robin Tilney, I moved into his house, and he was determined not to change anything. He felt it was perfectly acceptable. He and his former wife had spent thirty years in that house and had had lovely times, and nothing needed to be changed, as far as he was concerned.

When Sister came out to Far Hills to visit the Engelhards, she used to come here first to wash her dogs so they would go to the Engelhards' all clean. Once when Sister was here, I said, "Sister, you've got to try to persuade him." So Sister said, "Robin, this new lovely wife of yours needs some help with the house. She needs to have things spruced up. How long has it been since you changed the covering on that couch? How long has it been since you painted that room?"

He said, "I don't think it's ever been painted. When my wife and I moved into this house, we just moved our furniture in." Sister was very tactful and very thoughtful of some things and she was able to persuade Robin. And Robin melted, absolutely melted.

We had discussions over certain things that had to stay, a painting and so on, and Sister would say, "Joanie, he has to have certain things." And I would say, "But Sister, don't you think that crummy table in our bedroom that the television sits on can go?"

And Sister would say, "Joanie, don't worry about it. Let him have it. He has had it all his life. He had it as a young boy. This is a thing he needs. Just put some shoe polish over it." So I did that, and it's still there.

BARBARA ALLEN DE KWIATKOWSKI (client): No one really wanted Calumet, the stud farm we bought in Kentucky. It had been on the market for a long time. The day before the auction, someone told my husband, Henryk, about it. We were in Bermuda and it was up for auction the next day. The auction was in Kentucky. I knew something was up because Henryk shot out of bed that morning at five o'clock. By the time I was on my way to lunch, I found out that he had bought it, because it was all over the news.

My husband named a racehorse after Sister, and it did very well. Then the horse had a foal and we named her something really fabulous. Sister used to call and say, "Does she need anything? Can I bring her any cashmere blankets or filet mignon?"

Sister was a battle-ax. She was very crusty, and she was old enough to do exactly what she wanted to do and get away with murder. The first time I ever worked with her was on our house in Greenwich. We went shopping in London together and had a wonderful time. She'd go into a store and say to my husband and me, "What do you like in this room?" She loved the little ceramic things the most. I'd say, "Well, I like this, and I like that." I would then pick up the plate and it would say "Reserved for Mrs. Parish." I felt I had passed the test.

KK AUCHINCLOSS: Her clients knew better, you see. They did. They had a very good idea of what they wanted. It was not only that they wanted to be comfortable, but they wanted their eyes to fall on beauty for beauty's sake. Not to impress anyone else.

MRS. CHARLES PERCY (client): I am always grateful that Sister entered my life and changed it so much for the better. Her influence on me has been profound and continues with each passing year. As a person, she was very unusual and beautiful in all her daily acts. She was a real inspiration to me. I think of her often. She also was witty and knew all the news. She was quite a gossip. She always knew the latest gossip—who was with whom. I saw Olive Watson's Maine house and called her to help me. I loved their brown-flowered chintz. I had previously used Billy Baldwin. She wanted me to pick out pictures from magazines. She and Albert came out to our house in Illinois. Billy Baldwin had black-and-white silk tassels hanging from some yellow silk curtains and she said they had to go. She said, "Just cut them off." She also told us to paint the wood-paneled walls in another room coral. I was horrified, but by adding pillows made from antique quilts and a zebra rug, it was transformed, and I never looked back.

When our daughter was murdered, Sister had her entire bedroom changed when we were away. She made it into a sitting room. She also came to sit by me after my mother died of a heart attack on the night before our daughter's marriage. For me, her signatures were the pearl necklace she always wore, her knit suits, and her dogs, which always went with her to the office.

We usually try, at that first meeting, to get some sense of who the clients are, how they live, and what they want.

We review family statistics. How many children do they have? Do the children live at home? Do they get along with the children? Do the children have their friends over?

ALICE ROGERS: When we first met Sister, we had this tiny baby. When we met her again, we had two tiny babies and two little boys who were toddlers. I think that her own family and the families of people whom she felt close to were the most important things in her life. I feel that so strongly because she paid so much attention to our children. She always remembered the children. Always. Whenever we would see her for the first time in the summer, she would come with little presents for the children. We had one daughter, and all the rest were boys, and she loved our daughter. To this day, our Callie is very feminine, and I think a lot of that is because of Sister. From the day Callie was born, Sister sort of encouraged this, and Callie's room was very pink and very feminine.

Sister loved miniature things. She loved little animals, too. Sister would bring the children little things that weren't necessarily valuable, but they were special. She would bring a pretty autumn leaf over for one of the children or she'd bring a special stone or something like that that she knew one of the boys would be interested in. She would particularly remember Callie with a pretty flower. And in doing rooms for Callie, she seemed to take such joy in making it just right for the child.

At the first meeting, of course, we also establish what kind of budget the client has in mind. Occasionally, this stops all discussion in its tracks, but this is rare. Fortunately, most people who come to our office know that we insist on quality, and they have a reasonably good idea what that means in terms of money.

Sometimes, when I get to the client's house, I see immediately that their budget is much too small to do what they have in mind. My advice, always, is to do less but do it well. Just buy a couple of things, but be sure what you do buy is basically good, and otherwise forget about it until next year. We avoid buying junk under any circumstances. The things that we put into a room are always the best no matter what the budget is. The sofas for a big budget and for a small budget are always the same; we don't compromise on that. And that's true with young people just starting out or with old people pinching pennies. That's a very strong point.

MAISIE HOUGHTON: She loved our little house on the water because it was so practical. I'll never forget when she came over for dinner and looked at the plans—very casually—because, as you know, she didn't like architectural plans. She had had several vodkas, and after dinner I said to her, "Come on, Aunt Sister. Give us a few ideas." She said, "Bedroom isn't big enough. Porch is too small." We did those two things, thank God.

When we were young and started to have a life in New York, she came to the little apartment we rented on Fifty-sixth Street and Second Avenue. I told her, "This is just a rented apartment, so let's go to Conran's." It was literally across the street, and so I said we'd buy everything there and just make it fun and crazy. She definitely corrected me. She said, "No. You have a certain position in New York and you cannot live as though you have Conran's furniture." She was very much the arbiter of the way things should be, and I wanted her approval. I remember Jamie asking her when she first came to Corning, "How much do you think all of this is going to cost?" She said, "Some things will cost five thousand dollars and some things will cost five cents."

EDWARD LEE CAVE (realtor and former Parish-Hadley decorator): I really do think that the whole point of Mrs. Parish was that it was beautiful. Of course it was a wonderful mixture, which no one else can do, of an English chair and a French chair and a Chinese vase. The thing to me is that she really understood how people with taste and a certain amount of affluence, of course, can live attractively, comfortably, and appropriately. Everything about her, the houses she did, didn't scream, I'm rich. They didn't scream, I'm chairman of the board. They said, Come in, sit down, have a lemonade, make the phone call, and look out the window. Isn't it a pretty day?

RICHARD MANDER: We had a house and it belonged to these people whom I would call very wealthy, and yet not necessarily people who had always had money, but they still had this illusion about wealth and how everything in life should be perfect. Sister truly understood that life shouldn't be perfect and doesn't have to be perfect. Life is very boring when it's perfect, because it's just not real. I mean, come on. Wake up. So we were doing this place and there was this old wing added to the other side, fluffed to hell. The clients looked at Sister during a walk-through and said, "But Sister, on the old wall there is a twelve-inch baseboard and it joins with a new baseboard that is only nine inches high. Why don't they match?" She sort of lowered her eyes and said, "Well, it adds character"—really meaning "class," a word she would never use. Well, what were they going to say? "I don't think so," or "I am terribly sorry, but I don't have any?"

APPLE: One day, Mummy announced that she might be coming to Boston more often, as she had new clients who lived there. I asked who the clients were and she said, "It's Mr. and Mrs. Rabb and they own a grocery store called Stop and Pee, or something like that." Obviously, she was confused, not ever having been into a supermarket, never mind one called Stop and Shop.

BUNNY WILLIAMS: She was resentful of other people who were not working as hard as she was. She used to complain, "They don't get up until noon." There was a real dichotomy between her and the ladies who lunch or her friends who were getting their hair done and going to jewelry shops while she had to work.

BILL HODGINS: We never called them "the client" or "them," as almost all decorators do. Mrs. Parish didn't love everyone, but it was always very personal. It was about whether it was appropriate for Mr. and Mrs. so-and-so. *Appropriate* was the big word. She was the one who always said, "It has to be appropriate," and she meant it.

Opposite page: Sister, in her favorite red costume wig, with Betsey Whitney.

Chapter Fourteen

The Jock Whitneys

My God, I remember Greentree. Mrs. Parish took me to the Whitneys'
because she knew I had never seen anything like it. Up the driveway we went,
for miles and miles, and finally pulled up at the house.

BILL HODGINS

NEW YORK TIMES OBITUARY, FEBRUARY 13, 1982

SPORTSMAN, INVESTOR, PUBLISHER, philanthropist, political mover and
ambassador, he hated to lose at anything, from polo to racing to golf to bridge
to investing. Jock Whitney—the nickname dates from childhood—delighted
in savoring the deluxe things in life, and he enjoyed great wealth; estimates
early in 1982 put his fortune through inheritance and his own efforts at more
than $200 million.

Mr. Whitney was a solidly built man who stood 6 feet, 1 inch. His ruddy
face was generally set in seriousness, an appearance accentuated by his eye-

glasses. He was an amiable companion nonetheless, but with a limited fund of small talk. His friendships included horse trainers and jockeys, professional men and men of public affairs, artists and fellow millionaires.

Mr. Whitney made his Manhattan home in a duplex on Beekman Place in recent years, closing a town house on East 63rd Street while subway construction was going on underneath.

He also maintained a 500-acre estate and mansion, Greentree, in Manhasset; a spacious summer house on Fishers Island, off New London, Connecticut; a 12-room place at Saratoga Springs, N.Y., for occupancy during the August race meeting there; a 15-room hideaway in the heart of 19,000 acres of bird country and cornfields at Greenwood, Georgia; a modest golf cottage at Augusta, Georgia; and a flat in London.

What really dazzled visitors to the 63rd Street town house was Mr. Whitney's art display. More than 55 items from his collection, among the finest in private hands, dotted the walls. These included two Rembrandts, two Michelangelos, three Picassos and a number of works by Vuillard, Monet, Cézanne, Degas, Manet, Toulouse-Lautrec, Renoir, Pissarro and Braque. In addition, there was a sizable collection of Matisses, Mr. Whitney's favorite modern artist, whose pictures traveled with him from house to house.

He married twice. His first wife was the former Mary Elizabeth Altemus. They were divorced in 1940.

In March 1942, he married Betsey Cushing Roosevelt, the former wife of James Roosevelt, the eldest son of President Franklin D. Roosevelt.

One day I was sitting at the office, looking over a list of unpaid bills, the bookkeeper glaring at me as if it was my fault. I prayed that the phone would ring and that the call would be important enough to let me wave the bookkeeper away. The phone did ring, and it was Betsey Whitney, who had a large New York town house. I waved, and the bookkeeper left me with an accusing look.

Betsey told me that her house was finished except for the fourth floor. She said that this was to be "a very special place for a very special husband." I agreed to meet her at the house the next day.

It was a special place. There was a large room with doors at each end, ceiling to floor, that led to two terraces. The room also had concealed doors on either side, one leading to a bathroom, the other leading to a small kitchen. It was like a large self-contained studio apartment sitting on top of a big house. It was a pri-

vate, protected place, sunny and cheerful, and the trees on the terrace gave it a sumptuous look.

The room did have a slightly modern look, but Betsey was not modern. I knew that it would be a challenge to balance her very good but quite conservative taste with what I felt were the design demands of this room. At first, things did not go at all well. She seemed more distressed with every suggestion I made. She had a dream—"a very special place for a very special husband"—and I was not fulfilling it. I left the house after my third try just sunk, feeling that it was all my fault.

I walked around the block, contemplating an early retirement, when my eye happened to light on a vanload of old shutters that was just then being delivered to a store. I stood transfixed, believing in my heart that I had hit it. The shutters were old and had a soft honey color. I walked into the store and immediately bought half of the shipment on the spot.

I carried as many of them as I could back to the office, then called Betsey right away.

"I think I have a find," I said, almost pleading.

Her voice was dull, unenthusiastic, but, out of politeness, she said that she'd let me bring them to her.

Two hours later, we were both filled with excitement and she couldn't wait to get the room started and finished. She could see immediately that those old shutters would make everything work.

By a miracle, the shutters fit perfectly. They matched the big doors, and no curtains were needed. Betsey had a blue-and-white geometric dhurrie rug, and I designed much of the room around it. I found a beautiful long oak table to be used as a desk, and one of the finest Gothic bookcases—very narrow, with the old glass untouched, and high spiral cornices. I covered two large sofas in blue-and-white linen, the design of blocks. I added needlework pillows, oak tables, and a Gothic book table with old velvet inlaid on the top. Flanking the beautiful beige-and-white Italian marble were two bookshelves with cupboards below. I had these painted a soft mustard color. There was also a French Provincial bridge table, made of fruitwood, and four comfortable oak chairs. I covered the chairs with an old checked material in various shades of blue. The lighting was perfect. It came from the rafters and was completely hidden. Next to the fireplace, I put two off-white linen upholstered chairs with large pull-up stools. Each chair had one of our beautiful knitted throws lying across the bottom, to pull close under your chin for dozing. I covered all the walls in coarse linen, painted off-white. A Braque hung over the mantel, and on the walls, Rousseau and Toulouse-Lautrec. It was, indeed, "a very special place for a very special husband." Here you could nap, read, or write in complete luxury, with no one even to know where you were in this big, massive city. The room was loved and used in many ways—as an office, a place to play bridge, for special meals, and, best of all, as a place to hide. I always loved Betsey for giving me the second, third, and, finally, that successful fourth chance to make it what it was for the most charming man I have ever known.

MARK HAMPTON: In the house on Sixty-third Street, the town house, they had a modern room built on the roof. They were going to have sliding glass doors on the south wall, facing the street. The north wall faced the garden, which was quite nice, very nice. Mr. Whitney owned the houses opposite, so the whole thing was arranged quite tidily. It was very big and one of the few town houses, if not the only, that was built after World War II. On the top was this modern glass room. It had been made contemporary. Mr. Whitney was a big force at the Museum of Modern Art, and I think Philip Johnson had been involved in that room. It had very bare white walls and Barcelona chairs and a big Moroccan rug. The Whitneys didn't like it, and obviously they wouldn't. It had been an experiment, a folly; but then it was a failure. So they came around to Sister, who had never worked for them before.

Sister looked at the room and had this idea. They had drawn up a very elaborate trellis and beautiful rendering of a trellis room, which would be an obvious solution of how to use this space. It had terraces on either side of it and plants and things. Two beautiful magnolia trees in pots, and tubs on one side. They didn't think they wanted the trellis room.

This is typical Mrs. Parish. I don't know where she found it, but she discovered an old shutter that had been primed twice and had lost all of its paint. It might have been painted white, but the paint had all flaked off. There were just traces of white on this old pine—the kind of finish we love but can never achieve. She bought the shutter, showed it to the Whitneys, and said, "Now, this is sort of how I'd like your room to look." Well, they immediately got the point of all of these bleached, sort of flaky white shutters really covering these ugly glass walls, but left open so you got plenty of light. It meant something about them that they knew what she meant by that shutter.

So she did this charming room with a huge Tibetan rug the color of old Levi's. And a lot of whites, off-whites, some yellow, some blue. And in it they had a Picasso, a collection of Matisses, Toulouse-Lautrecs, and maybe some late School of Paris pictures. The walls were sort of crusty white on a heavy canvas linen that they'd put on top of the paint and then painted. It was just this wonderful cozy room. They had a lot of early furniture in it. Louis XIII tables and sort of Flemish tables. Earlier things, so that it was strong and immensely cozy, and it was a huge success. That was her first job for them, and from then on, it's all history.

My guess is that Mr. Whitney got involved with the decorating. I don't mean sitting and looking at swatches, but he had such wonderful ideas about things. I was looking at that catalog of paintings of theirs. The collection was just brilliant.

EDWARD LEE CAVE: When I first went to work for Mrs. Parish, she had just finished Jock and Betsey Whitney's house on Sixty-third Street. The top room was extraordinary. It was glorious, with those two pavilions outside facing north on the terrace. The pictures were unbelievable. In the living room, there was an enormous Chinese lacquer screen next to a van Gogh—no, I'm sorry, a Gauguin—and the contrast of the pattern on the lacquer screen and this wonderful picture—it was a killer. I've never seen anything so exciting.

BUNNY WILLIAMS: Jock Whitney was an incredibly attractive man. He was bright and refined and good looking. He was who he was. It was the combination of the power, the energy, and this extraordinary ability to know how to live. Mr. Whitney set the tone. It didn't occur to him that other people didn't live like that. Today, I don't see that as much, because the rich and powerful today are missing what he had. He was the real thing. With the houses, it wasn't only the grandeur and the pictures; it was the way it was run. Going to Greentree was going someplace that when you opened the door, you knew you had stepped into something different. It was polished. There were flowers everywhere. The smells were good. There was somebody there asking, "May I take your coat?" or "Let me get you a drink." There is so much grandness today, but no sense of humanity.

ARCHIBALD GILLES (former president of the John Hay Whitney Foundation): I think Jock himself had lots of style and lots of taste, which I attribute to his mother, whom he would refer to as having been a literary, intelligent woman.

He spoke more about her than he did about his father. My recollection is that he started to collect Impressionist paintings right after World War II. He was in Europe with the air force and was actually captured by the Germans.

I got the impression that there was quite a competitive atmosphere among Whitney, Paley, and David and Nelson Rockefeller in terms of who was collecting which paintings. They all had different taste. I would have to say that Jock's collection was by far the most dramatic and strong. He had the strongest taste of all of them.

Jock was involved with the Museum of Modern Art early in the 1930s. I think he had a great eye. He collected the paintings. I didn't get the impression that Mrs. Whitney was as interested in paintings as Jock was, except from a decorative point of view.

BILL HODGINS: We did, among other things, the Whitney's big house on Fishers Island. They had a big sort of contemporary house there. We had to float the furniture over on barges. We did have fun doing that job. Albert and Sister guided me along. Madame bought a beautiful mirror to reflect the ocean.

Albert and I have done all the rooms in the Whitneys' house in Manhasset, Greentree, but our most frantic undertaking was preparing for the arrival of Princess Margaret and Lord Snowden. Betsey called me one day to have lunch and discuss "a problem." The problem turned out to be the royal visit. The couple would be arriving in September for four days, the house wasn't at all ready for them, and it was now May. Could I do it?

My first instinct was that it couldn't be too difficult a job. If any house could handle a royal visit, it was Greentree. It was certainly large enough to take care of any princess and her entourage. Greentree had started as a tiny farmhouse about 150 years ago and had just grown and grown and grown.

There were the details as to who would go where—the royal couple, ladies-in-waiting, valets, maid, security people—but the house had a guest wing of ten rooms that I thought would be perfect with a little touching up.

A few days later, Betsey took Albert and me on a tour of the guest wing and I rapidly changed my mind about the job ahead. The wing hadn't been used for years, and as we walked from room to room, Betsey kept repeating, "This can't be," and I kept agreeing with her. We started out by making lists of things to be

*done, and as the lists become more and more formidable, Albert and I retreat-
ed to the shop to draw up formal architectural specifications of what had to be
done.*

*The truth is, the entire guest wing was a labyrinth of dreariness. Yet it was
a fascinating place with enormous potential. All the rooms ran along a hallway
that must have been a hundred feet long and ten feet wide. It was like a museum
gallery—and it was a gallery of sorts. There were old bicycles placed almost
like pieces of sculpture, curio cabinets running over with things, lots of chairs of
every size, shape, and description scattered down the hall. On the walls were
things like Jock's oars from the days when he had rowed for Yale, polo sticks that
had belonged to his grandfather, thousands of wonderful family photographs,
pictures of various Whitneys with various kings and queens.*

*It was all very interesting, but utterly disorganized. The only light that fil-
tered through was a rather gray, gloomy light that managed to find its way
through a skylight that was overgrown with branches. The walls had been covered a hundred years ago in burlap, and the trim was all the same color.*

*Though the rooms themselves hadn't been touched for years, and desperate-
ly needed some loving care, they were big and lush in their tattered, old-
fashioned way. And there were the most wonderful old white tile bathrooms, of
marvelous proportion, with big fixtures, six-by-six-foot tubs, basin tubs in white
porcelain and highly polished chrome, and old-fashioned lights and mirrors.
They were big and each one had a full-sized window that looked out over the
trees and gardens.*

*Our first task was to make order out of chaos. Soon we were back shuffling
furniture, going from room to room, taking things from all over the wing, and
from other parts of the house, trying things here, there, and everywhere, moving
things back and forth, until we got them worked out.*

*The key problem was devising a plan to make the space work for Princess
Margaret and Lord Snowden. We decided to put Lord Snowden in the first room.
Next came his bathroom, and beyond that was a room that we wanted as a sitting room. That, in turn, should have opened into his wife's bedroom. They would
then have their own apartment, with complete privacy. But in order to get from
the sitting room to the princess's bedroom, you had to go out into the hall. This
wouldn't do. There was a closet next to the fireplace in the princess's room, and
we broke through the wall to give us a passage from her room to the sitting room.
The only difficult part was making the passage without destroying any of the*

nineteenth-century French wallpaper with its magnificent American scene, the lovely Zuber paper that made us choose this room for the princess.

Once that was accomplished, our plan for the rest of the wing was easy. We assigned two more rooms for the princess—one for her clothes, the other for pressing and odd jobs that might have to be done. The other rooms went to her ladies-in-waiting. There was ample space elsewhere in the house for the maids, valets, and security people.

The long gallery was completely transformed. The trim was painted off-white, the burlap was painted a soft yellow, the skylight was cleared, and new lighting was added, and it went from dreariness to cheerfulness. The clutter was removed and the important family mementos were put back on the walls but rearranged to make sense.

We had a bit of a to-do over the princess's sleeping arrangement. Betsey and I decided to put twin beds in her room. Albert insisted that it wasn't proper for a princess to sleep in a twin bed. He was adamant.

We gave her one lovely bed with a soft off-white headboard that was upholstered in a beautiful old quilt. We found the most beautiful spread to put on the bed. It was quilted and had garlands of flowers, scenes of children, animals, houses, lakes, and church steeples. Bill Hodgins was one of our decorators then, and when the bed had been moved into the room, we were found lying on it together. We were trying to decide if it was firm enough.

We decided that it would be appropriate to make the princess's room more or less Regency in feeling, and we had no trouble finding enough things scattered about the house that had been made during the reign of Prince George in the early 1800s. There were some white-and-gold American Regency chairs that we sort of spotted around the room, and a big comfortable chair near the fireplace, and a wonderful old Regency dressing table for the window side. It had a beautiful black lacquer mirror stand, with a little drawer, and an attractively shaped mirror above it. On the dressing table was the thinnest, finest, sheerest embroidered mull. The curtains were the same material. They were held back by big American Regency brass tiebacks, and the valance, which Albert found, was a softly shaped Empire one, embossed gold. It was a classic drapery. The curtains were caught up again with big brass buttons that went into the wall and then draped from there.

We had worked out a color scheme for the entire wing so that the colors would balance from room to room. We decided on yellow for Princess Margaret's room. Albert wanted yellow because he said it went with the blues and soft greens in the next room. I wanted it because it went with a beautiful yel-low throw on one of the tables. Of course, the truth is, we have no rigid principles for selecting our colors. We pick a color because we think it will look pretty, and Albert and I almost invariably agree. The yellow looked wonderful.

No detail was overlooked. The finest linens and blanket covers were found, new down went into the pillows, the needlework rugs were repaired and refreshed, new backing was put on all the needlework pillows, the Kleenex was done up in ribbons, and we made sure the vases were perfect and the fresh flow-ers were arranged to suit the coloring of the room. We couldn't find the lamps we wanted in the house, so Albert bought some marvelous big candlesticks that we had wired, and then we had soft, pleated silk shades put on them.

Lord Snowden's room featured a high mahogany four-poster bed, hung with a beautiful red damask: it had been Jock Whitney's bed when he was young. The curtains were of the same old red damask. We left the burlap on the walls but painted it a soft white, almost a putty color. Again there were needlework rugs, and bits of old chintz, and there was a corner fireplace, with its andirons shining like gold.

We decided to paint their sitting room a very strong yellow and fill it with all sorts of tufted Victorian furniture. We used lots of black lacquer and papier-mâché, and a few fancy pieces like gilded rope stools and an Empire sofa that was upholstered in a striped chintz with flowers in it. When we were designing the curtains, a pink-and-cream-striped taffeta, we found one of the few things that we did buy for the room, pressed tin Victorian valances that had garlands of roses. We thought that the garlands of roses were appropriate for Princess Margaret Rose.

BILL HODGINS: My God. I remember Greentree. Mrs. Parish took me to the Whitneys' because she knew I had never seen anything like that. Up the drive-way we went, for miles and miles, and finally pulled up at the house. We went in to look at this big drawing room, sort of a huge, eight-sided Victorian room. And the paintings—God, they were something.

Madame pulls out of her bag this sample of chintz with birds on it, and even then it was a hundred dollars a yard. And I said, "Oh boy." That is what we used all around the room, with pea green coloring. The Whitneys had the most incredible collection of sofas, chairs, pillows, tables, lamps, and things. We did make one new coffee table, and they took a lot of things out.

Jock Whitney was an attractive guy. Big. Very big guy. When Princess

Margaret was married to Lord Snowden, they spent four days at the Whitney house on Long Island. There were guest rooms in the wing off the pool. The pool was white and had white tile—an indoor pool, with all these arches in it. We made these big upholstered things covered in that rose chintz. There was all this almost medieval-looking furniture, Spanish and Italian stuff, and we sorted it out, the three of us. This was all done for their arrival. Albert, Mrs. Parish, and I moved things around. I remember I was in one of the bedrooms and Albert walked by, holding up a table, and at the other end came Mrs. Parish, shuffling along, carrying the other end. They didn't want it around anymore, so it had to go.

MARCIE BRAGA: I think we were buying old rugs and new, old furniture. We would go out to Greentree with our red sample bags, because in those days, everything we took had to be in a red canvas bag. I think they were from T. Anthony. The Parish-Hadley bags were giant duffel bags, red, with black leather.

I remember once we went there and Mrs. Whitney was sick and couldn't come downstairs for lunch, so it was just Mr. Whitney and Mrs. Parish and me. He was elegant and gracious, really incredibly polite. We had lobster as our first course, tongue as our second course, and some amazing pastry. And there were footmen—could there have been three footmen? It was extraordinary. We ate in the little dining room, not the big room, but the one that faces the garden.

And then I remember it was time to show everything to Mr. Whitney, and a whole new group of people showed up, with uniforms different from the ones the staff inside the house wore. They helped us take in all our bags and unroll this giant rug we had brought to show them. We'd shown everything to Mrs. Whitney before, so I think he was just okaying everything.

Finally, we had everything packed up to leave. We were in the office station wagon. Mrs. Parish had driven out. She was a terror in the car and she was always driving herself somewhere. We got in the car and found we had a flat tire. That was not a problem because there was the most beautiful garage on the grounds. There were all these beautiful cars inside; most of them were old and almost all were dark green. There was a whole group of men with different uniforms, and they were so happy to see us because they didn't have much to do.

BRIAN MURPHY (Parish-Hadley decorator): Greentree. Not a leaf out of place. I helped Mrs. Parish in the late eighties when we did some small things for Greentree. Later, I helped her redecorate the plantation, Greenwood, which she and Albert had done before in the sixties. Once a week, we would go out to Mrs. Whitney's for lunch and to show schemes and fabric and furniture. We would be picked up in Mrs. Whitney's special green Mercedes, and it would inevitably be an awful, miserable day on the Long Island Expressway. And then the gates would part at Greentree and the sun would come shining through. You'd see these Thoroughbred horses romping, and Mrs. Parish would say, without fail, "Not a leaf on the ground."

We would have these incredibly lavish lunches. No one eats like that anymore. You would start out with soft-shell crabs swimming in butter. Then you would have chateaubriand en croûte. Then came some incredible dessert that was brought out on a silver tray—some type of custard with whipped cream on it. That kind of thing would make you lapse into a coma after you left. It was just deadly.

In the beginning, Mrs. Whitney used to let Mrs. Parish bring Ricky, and then for some reason, Ricky was banished. It made her so mad. At any chance she got, she would kick, really kick, one of Mrs. Whitney's dogs. They were Pekingese, too. They were almost a different kind of animal, like stuffed animals, all combed and fluffy. Ricky was always smelly. You'd pet that dog and you'd just want to go and wash your hands. When we went to Greenwood, which was in Georgia, Mrs. Parish was so mad because Mrs. Whitney wouldn't let her bring the dogs. Every time the telephone rang, Mrs. Parish would say, "It's Ricky." It got to be a point of such annoyance that Mrs. Whitney finally said, "Since when does Ricky dial a phone?"

Greenwood is one of the great plantations in the South, and it has always been used by the Whitney family for grouse, dove, and duck shooting. It is one of the most romantic houses that I have ever been in. Outside, it is like something from Gone with the Wind. *The house stands majestic and alone, with four large Doric columns holding up the most lovely veranda. The house is surrounded by huge magnolia trees with the shiniest leaves and largest white blossoms that I have ever seen. The magnolia is the emblem of the plantation, and an enormous open magnolia blossom is carved into the pediment that rises high over the second-floor veranda. Holly trees, wisteria, and jasmine cling to the gables of the roof.*

You enter through the main garden onto a porch that must be forty feet long and ten feet wide. On the porch are the most extraordinary pieces of old wicker furniture, which have been there forever. You then go through big double doors with oval plate glass that give into a wide hall with a spiral staircase at the end.

Here is where the Gone with the Wind *look ends. Most southern plantations are like old Long Island. Lace curtains, boring, stiff Victorian furniture covered in velvet or damask. You can't find a piece of comfortable upholstered furniture in a* Gone with the Wind *house. But in Greenwood, there were big downy sofas and floppy oversized chairs, and it had a comfortable look. It had a quality and ambience that southern houses never seem to achieve, and it was because the Whitneys had also lived in Europe, had traveled everywhere, and were used to entertaining some of the most important people in the world. They had sophisticated taste, and the house said it clearly.*

Albert and I were summoned because years of use had worn the house threadbare and it needed attention to bring it back to life. Every single room had to be freshened and rearranged. Houses do speak, they do have personality, and their own special quality, and our job was to bring out the personality of Greenwood, to make a bigger and better statement, to gay it up a bit with fresh colors and fabrics and materials. But also to maintain its essential character.

Our first effort was simply to rearrange the furniture, every stick of it. The house had a great sense of style, but it didn't have a great sense of order. Some of the rooms needed rearranging. We started with the front porch and moved through every room in the house. It became quite hilarious. A table upstairs would come down, a chair downstairs would go up, a bedroom lamp would become a hall lamp, and a hall lamp would become a living room lamp. Everything was juggled around. I would stare at a corner and sense that something else would look better over there than that table. Albert would poke around and say, "Let's try this one," and we would carry it through the hall and into the room and put it down. And it wouldn't work, so back it would go. This went on for weeks and weeks. Albert and I did most of the lugging and hauling ourselves. There was a household of servants, but they thought we had gone mad. Even Betsey got caught up in the spirit. I don't think she had ever bent over before in her life, but when she came down to see how we were doing, she was soon tugging and hauling things along, carrying rugs from room to room and moving sofas.

Eventually, everything fit and everything worked. There was no need to add new furniture anywhere. Everything that was there was part of the house and was appropriate and made its point. There were lots of wonderful old family pieces, and it was just a matter of making them look their best and work their best. I remember a long table between the doors that led to the master bedrooms.

It was piled with books and magazines and centered by a white Carrara marble bust of Thomas Jefferson. An old farm hat had been thrown onto his head and left there, and so he looked rather ridiculous sitting there. That was typically Greenwood.

There was certainly no need to scour the countryside for pictures and rugs. The house contained one of the world's finest collection of old prints. They were in the front hall, they went up the stairs, and they appeared in almost every bedroom. It also contained the largest collection of Early American hooked rugs. They were in various sizes and various patterns and scattered like a gigantic patchwork quilt all over. They were laid at random down the hall, and turned up again in bedrooms, sitting rooms, almost everywhere you walked.

Only once did we feel we needed something that didn't already exist in the house. There was one spot at the end of a sitting room where there was a group of chairs and a table, but something was missing. Nothing in the house seemed quite right for that spot. Betsey asked what we thought was needed there, and I immediately announced that we had to have "a character chair." Thus began the search through all the shops of New York for our character chair. We finally found a strange, idiotic thing that looked absolutely wacky but somehow seemed made for the house. It was a classic Victorian piece, very low, with great scrolled arms, heavily turned legs, a tufted back, and a tufted seat. It was quite small, and we left it in its original color, black and gold and red decorations. It was perfect.

The house did need new curtains and the sofas and chairs needed new chintz, and though we added lots of fresh color, all the fabrics and materials were totally appropriate to the house. Because the furniture was old, almost everything needed new down and stuffing. The most notable exception was Jock's mattress. It was old as anything in the house, horsehair was coming out of it, but he refused to have it changed. It was his, and he liked it just the way it was, no matter how much horsehair was sticking out.

When we were finished, Greenwood had an English country house look, comfortable and grand and luxurious. The master bedroom downstairs has all-white furniture. The headboards are cane, with garlands of carved flowers. A glorious big chaise is covered with white fluted pillows and a soft pink-and-white mohair throw. The chintz curtains have pink roses scattered with wildflowers. Throughout the room there are bowls and bowls of fat red roses from the garden. Two wicker bedside tables hold lamps of twisted glass with pinpricked lamp shades. The rugs are some of the finest hooked rugs I have ever seen. There are beautiful Staffordshire figures on the mantel, and the fire burns the first thing in

the morning and the last thing in the evening, casting soft shadows and the won-
derful smell of burning pine.

I doubt if there is a more opulent, or more livable, living room anywhere in
the South. There is a large Brussels carpet, needlework rugs, lots of needlework
pillows on the high and low tufted sofas, and a wing chair covered in an old quilt
of many colors. We covered the bridge chairs with black horsehair with a dia-
mond pattern. It is a high-ceilinged room, with a very fine carved cornice.
Hanging from the cornice are off-white cotton curtains, very full to the floor,
with a vine twining through the stripes. The rooms glows with red, the color that
runs, in various shades, throughout the house. And it is always alive with fresh
flowers just cut from the gardens. My memories of Greenwood are always
touched with the soft smell of jasmine, magnolias, and roses.

BILL HODGINS: Greenwood was divine. It was a glorious nineteenth-century southern house. It had a big pediment on top, way up high, and carved in it was an enormous magnolia. It had all kinds of farmhouses and fields. There was a little house for Jock's fishing crowd when they came down. They didn't even go inside the house, which was one of those big wide-halled places, with a staircase going up. There was a big drawing room and sitting room, and a little woman named Mrs. Hanley was the housekeeper.

When I went down, I was really more like a seventeen-year-old than a thirty-year-old. I'm Canadian, and I didn't know there were parts of the United States where you couldn't drink—where you couldn't go to a cocktail lounge—but down there you couldn't. They rolled up this little town at six o'clock.

Albert told me about this. Mrs. Hanley showed me around, and she couldn't believe I was this creature twice her height. Then she asked, "What do you drink?" She thought I would just be embarrassed to ask. She said, "Come on. We'll go downstairs and get you a bottle to put in your room." There was a whole cellar filled with bottles.

One day, I was there at Greenwood with Mrs. Parish, and I thought this was the first time I was really going to make Sister see it my way. There was a sitting room with a chair that faced the sofa. I adjusted it so that it was straight. I came back and the chair was at an angle, so I straightened it out again. I went away and came back in, and it was at an angle again. Every time she went by, she would put it that way. So I finally came back, and she was standing with her hand on her hip. She asked, "Do you really think it should be that way?" I said, "Yes, I do."

She would always turn things a little on the cockeye. She was very sure of what was right. When you tell somebody, "That's a wonderful lamp and a beautiful shade; it looks perfect there," then they feel better about it, whether it is true or not. She was never like the rest of us. We'd say, "Oh, that's wonderful," while she would say, "That's fine." That was enough. You knew that you'd gotten about as good as you could get.

BRIAN MURPHY: Greenwood was on something like forty thousand acres in southern Georgia. If you didn't fly on Mrs. Whitney's jet, then you'd fly to Tallahassee and drive for an hour. Stanford White called it the finest example of Greek Revival in America. White himself had designed an addition for it at the beginning of this century. You'd go through these big iron gates, by big trees with Spanish moss dripping off them. It had these large columns. What made it unique and charming was that in the pediment was a giant carved magnolia tree. There was also a guest house, really a hunting lodge. They shot quail mostly, and pheasants. There were dog kennels, as well. You would hear barking all night long.

The house had been built by some Whitney general and had remained in the family for 150 years. Presidents had stayed there, and in the lodge there was this giant stuffed turkey that Eisenhower had shot.

There was a lot of great history and furniture. Albert and Mrs. Parish had worked on it in the sixties, and then in the eighties, when Mrs. Whitney decided to completely redo it, I was involved with the redecoration.

I went down to Georgia with Mrs. Parish to put the finishing touches on Greenwood, after we had redone it in the eighties, and it really was magnificent. Mrs. Parish and I were there for two nights. The first night during cocktails, the staff came around and drew all the curtains throughout the whole house. Nobody does that anymore. They would have a cocktail and watch the news. I was working for Connie Chung at the time when she was anchoring the news. The two of them were crazy about Connie Chung. They would ask, "Can we meet her?" The second night we were there, we had this incredibly lavish dinner. The dining room had been painted a tangerine color. It was a beautiful room, with several tables, and there was a big Italian chandelier made of iron flowers that had probably two dozen candles in it. The dinner was all illuminated by candlelight. Mrs. Whitney told Mrs. Parish, "Oh, you've made the house more beautiful than I've ever imagined, and it's just a dream come true."

Mrs. Whitney was wearing diamonds and emeralds—bracelets, necklaces, and earrings. I remember saying to her, "Oh, you look wonderful in green," or something along those lines. After dinner, I went back to the guest house, where I was staying, and then, an hour later, an alarm went off. We heard it coming from the big house, across the road from us. We ran over there, and half the house was in flames. It was the back half, by the kitchen. Flames in every window. Unbelievable. We ran around to the front of the house just as the two nurses were helping Mrs. Parish and Mrs. Whitney down the front porch steps; then they put both women into a station wagon and drove them over to the lodge. They didn't want them to see anything. The firemen later said that if the women had been in the house for five more minutes, they would have died of smoke inhalation. Then this huge fireball came down the staircase and blew out all the windows. The whole house was on fire then. One of the Whitney men and I were grabbing all the old wicker furniture off the porch. Because the house was so remote, it took a good forty-five minutes for the fire department to arrive. They scrambled around trying to find the hydrants, which were hidden in the hedges. It was like something from *Gone With the Wind*. All those beautiful curtains that we had just made were going up in flames. It was absolutely surreal. I remember the magnolia falling in flames. Then there was nothing left.

They got a plane in so they could get Mrs. Whitney out of there, because they didn't want her to see the place the next morning.

BARBARA ALLEN DE KWIATKOWSKI: Do you remember the fire at Mrs. Whitney's Greenwood plantation? They had just finished redecorating it and there was a celebration because it had been renovated. Mrs. Parish was there with Mrs. Whitney, and luckily, they got out alive. It was so scary for Mrs. Parish, because she couldn't see well at that time. We were in the Bahamas at our house there and we got a call at midnight. It was Sister, and she said, "Henryk, I am at Greenwood. I am at the Whitneys' plantation and it has just burned to the ground. I am standing in front of the house with Mrs. Whitney and we are in our nightgowns. Now, I know that you are in the aircraft industry, and we need a plane right away."

SUSAN: Sister was terrified of fire. She'd been in another fire, an electrical fire at her apartment at 920 Fifth Avenue. The Whitney fire marked the beginning of her decline. It does seem like the most sinister thing, and how fast it happened. To be caught up in what she had always so feared really left her permanently shaken. She told me the butler knocked on her door and said, "Madam, the house is on fire," and then he left her to go help someone else. She didn't have her glasses and was just completely terrified. Somehow, she made it down the stairs and got out.

ARCHIBALD GILLES: Jock had a good eye and he was appreciative of taste, but that was something he grew up with. I don't think he was an active force in any way in terms of shaping any of those residences. I think that was all Betsey. She made all of the fundamental decisions about what rooms were decorated and Jock saw it more as a continuation from his childhood. Those places were changeless. I think the Betsey-Sister relationship must have been incredible; I mean enormous. The amount of work that went on in those places was tremendous. Jock got credit for being Jock and for the things he did in his life professionally, and he gets credit for his eye for paintings, but the driving force with the houses was Betsey and her relationship with Sister and Albert.

BILL HODGINS: She and Betsey Whitney did have fun together. Betsey was always part of it. You know, she didn't want to figure out how the curtains were made, but Mrs. Parish would show her the things and they would move them back and forth and settle on it. And then we would do it. It was very much a nice collaboration.

LINDA GILLES: Betsey so loved working on the houses. I always got the impression that she loved working with Sister and buying things and changing things right up until the end of her life.

Following page: The Charles Engelhard apartment in London's Grosvenor House.

Chapter Fifteen

The Charles Engelhards

Sister had an enormous capacity for friendship and an old school sense of loyalty. When I asked Kenny Lane what made her so good, he said, "She had dream clients and dream houses." Some of them, like the Engelhards, were not only her clients but also her dearest friends.

SUSAN CRATER

NEW YORK TIMES OBITUARY, MARCH 3, 1971

BY PLACING HIS trust in gold, along with platinum and diamonds, Charles William Engelhard in twenty years ran an inheritance of $20 million into an industrial fortune of more than $250 million and became a power in the international financial and business community.

His success in the turf, his principal avocation, rivaled that in business. Here and abroad his horses won scores of races (he had 14 stakes winners in the United States in the last 10 years) with an investment of $20 million in racing and breeding stock. Nijinsky II, one of his horses, won eleven races in succession, including the English Triple Crown.

Because of his gold dealings, Mr. Engelhard was sometimes indentified as the basis for "Goldfinger," a spy thriller written by his friend Ian Fleming in the nineteen-forties.

Books and books and books could be written about Charlie in the world of minerals and metals and high finance. I never knew him in that world. What I remember about him is his charm.

He was a character. He never failed to be either enchanting or unforgivable, torturing you one minute and then delighting you the next. He always won you back. He had a greater appetite for life than anyone I've ever known. He only liked jokes. Some people who didn't know him mistook his vitality for vulgarity, but it was so much a part of his character that it wasn't remotely vulgar. His laughter is what I remember most about him and what I miss the most. I loved him, and over the years, the Engelhards have become almost family to me.

I first knew Charlie when he was a little boy. His family lived next to mine when we lived at Mayfields. I say "next to mine," although they were a mile and a half away. They lived at what we called "the top of the hill," in Bernardsville, and we lived at the "bottom of the hill," in Far Hills. Bernardsville was fifteen hundred feet above sea level and Far Hills was a thousand feet lower. And Charles, as his family called him, wasn't allowed to go below fifteen hundred feet except to visit our house—because of the air.

The Engelhards were German. Everyone knew them, but not to speak to— we were going through World War I, you see. Then my great-aunt and -uncle built a little chapel in Bernardsville and the Engelhards gave the money for half of it. They sat on one side in the first pew and we always sat in the pew behind them. We knew them from church. My mother was very fond of Mrs. Engelhard—what little she knew of her. She and her husband were both wonderful, old-fashioned people. They both wore high-buttoned shoes and couldn't possibly say the word damn. He'd sit in the club car, going to Newark on business, wearing a homburg, hidden behind a newspaper, speaking to no one ... greatly respected.

Charlie was seven years younger than I, so we weren't great friends—there was always that gap. But he was my brother Bayard's best friend until the terrible day at St. Mark's School when Bayard suddenly collapsed and died while he was playing baseball. Then Charlie and I more or less lost track of each other. I didn't see him again until years later, when he'd become engaged to Jane and I was invited to a party to meet her.

By this time, Charlie had become famous in business. He was a rare type— Bill Paley's another—who inherited one fortune and made it into another, much greater fortune. Jane turned out to be an extraordinary creature in her own right. She'd been brought up in France, married at an early age, and had her first child, Annette, before she was eighteen. After her first husband died, she'd taken over as the head of a company in New York, which is where she met Charlie.

Soon after they married, they lived in a small farmhouse and then bought a large Georgian house on top of Bernardsville Mountain, in Far Hills, near where Charlie's parents' house had been. McMillen did it over for them, but something went wrong. Charlie was tremendously sentimental, and seeing me again had brought back many memories of our childhood. He and Jane decided that I should enter the picture.

ANNETTE DE LA RENTA: The Engelhards were originally from Germany. They had been industrialists in a precious-metal refinery business in Germany. They built for themselves a Rhine-like castle, the most hideous Rhinish structure you have seen in your whole life, on top of Bernardsville Mountain. Daddy's father was frightening, but I liked him because he had six white horses. He used to let me ride them with him. He was the first person I ever knew who had diabetes. I used to be given a silver dollar to sit with him. Mrs. Engelhard lived on until she was ninety something. She lived on forever. She never lost her German accent, sort of a Henry Kissinger accent. They had Daddy when they were near fifty years old, or some age that was really medically impossible.

They had lost a lot of children, so when they had Daddy, this precious child, he could do no wrong, as far as his mother was concerned, but as far as his severe and dramatic father was concerned, he could do very little that was right.

He and Evan Pyne would go and lose all the samples of platinum and gold that they were supposed to be selling people.

When Daddy married Mummy, they lived at 1107 Fifth Avenue, and then they bought Cragwood in Far Hills, New Jersey. That is where my sisters and I were brought up. I don't think they wanted to tell the elder Engelhards for a long time, because Mr. Engelhard would have thought it was incredibly opulent for his son to have moved into a house as big as his. He wouldn't have liked that. But they had a very good time. In Sister's day, Cragwood was filled with chintz and flowers, as well as people and help and dogs. There were five children living in the house, so it was a lively place.

He wanted a new second apartment in London to celebrate when Nijinski II won the English Triple Crown. No other horse has ever won the English Triple Crown to this day.

Both Mrs. Parish and my father were life-enhancing, life-loving, bigger-than-life people. They got along, but I imagine that they could fight together, too, if they ever got into it. They both had the same sense of humor—totally irreverent and sarcastic. Saying whatever came out. They were both wonderful.

My most vivid memory of my first visit to the house is of Annette, who was ten years old at the time. She was a wild little girl. Apparently, she wanted to make an impression about something, so she rode her horse right into the house and right up the red-carpeted staircase—swearing so hard the whole time that a truck driver's hair would have stood on end. Imagine: Of all of Jane's five fascinating daughters, Annette is the one I've come to know and love best, and I can tell you that, today, the word darn *never crosses her lips.*

ANNETTE DE LA RENTA: When I met Mrs. Parish for the first time, I was on a horse. I think I was eleven or twelve. I brought my horse into the house, and the butler, who was called Arthur Clarke, was screaming at me that my mother was on her way from New York and would be there any minute and to get the horse and myself out of the house. Mrs. Parish said that she'd never heard such foul language coming out of any child in her entire life. She was sitting in the living room. That's how I first met Sister.

On Samuel's and my twenty-fifth wedding anniversary, Sister got up and told everyone in the restaurant the story about the bad language, and I think she used the word *shit.* She used it out loud for the first time, because she never, ever used profanity. And then the whole way home—we took her home in our car—she said, "Please don't tell Betsey Whitney I used a four-letter word." Then she added, "My God, everyone here is going to tell Betsey."

The house, which was called Cragwood, was beautiful to start with. There was an enormous living room with long windows overlooking a lake and Far Hills, miles away. Box gardens sloped down to a swimming pool, and there wasn't another house in sight. The size, smell, and beauty of it all was really beyond imagining.

The "big" room is now one of the finest rooms I know. We added an old parquet floor that creaks and shines with years of use and wax. On it, we laid the most beautiful Bessarabian rug with multicolored flowers on a dark ground. The curtains were a corncob silk. We covered most of the upholstered furniture with off-white silk and cotton damask. Painted fruitwood Louis XV chairs have seats of old leather. A twelve-fold lacquer screen, twelve feet high, stands in one corner. To balance the screen at the other end of the room, we placed a seventeenth-century Louis XIV cabinet. It was almost like a huge French armoire except that it had a superb-quality lacquer panel set in. Jane had bought it in Paris. It had a bonnet top, and on the platform of the bonnet, Jane placed a seventeenth-century Chinese lion, one of the treasures that Charlie and I found on our London shopping spree. The highlight of the room is the ravishing collection of French Impressionist paintings, which show brilliantly against the off-white glazed walls.

It's now a room where royalty could be—and has been—entertained. So have presidents of the United States. Most of the time, however, it has been filled with children and animals—all completely at home. Jane is a fantastic mother. Both a friend and adviser to each daughter. I think they are never out of her mind, no matter what gigantic project she is working on. There were always children everywhere, each with dogs, one more enchanting than the next. There were also always dogs sprawled on every sofa. "Leave them be," Charlie used to say. "It's good business for Sister."

NANCY PYNE (family friend): There were always fascinating people there. I remember when the Duke and Duchess of Windsor would come. She once arrived wearing pink hot pants, with those terrible stick legs of hers. She would bring people over to sit with the duke. Bring them right over there to sit with him for a few minutes.

At Easter, Jane would have hunts on the lawn for eggs. I spotted this huge emerald ring the size of an egg and I thought, My God. It turned out that it belonged to the duchess and she'd been searching for it all weekend. She would bring fifteen suitcases for the weekend. One time, she forgot one bag out of the fifteen and the chauffeur had to go back to New York to get it.

Sister was always at Charlie and Jane Engelhard's for the weekend. She and Johnny and Charlie had grown up together. Then there would be people like Mike Tyson, who was there with his wife, Robin Givens. He was charming, with that gold tooth. He ate nothing but a huge plate of salad because he was training for a fight with Spinks. After dinner, Jane told me to take him to the pool house to show him what Mrs. Parish had done. I took him around, and John, the Engelhards' butler, came. There were twenty-one in service at the Engelhards', all dying to see Mr. Tyson and all wanting his autograph. I said, "Come on now, Mr. Tyson. Come and see the staff." We went out to the kitchen. The staff was all in the kitchen, eating this fabulous food—a great plate of blintzes and caviar. Mr. Tyson said, "I'm starved." Well, Mr. Tyson sat down and started to eat the blintzes and caviar. He ate the whole thing.

I left him and went back to the living room. Jane asked me, "What did you do with Mr. Tyson?" I couldn't tell her what he was doing, so I said that he was signing autographs in the kitchen.

ALBERT HADLEY: Every spring, the Engelhards would always have what they called a "royal weekend" at Cragwood and invite the Duke and Duchess of Windsor.

I met the duchess at that show that we did for Sotheby's. Sis had me do this simply marvelous, yet perfectly simple cachepot. I brought it back and put some flowers in it for the show. The duchess came around. She was the honorary chairwoman. She looked at this cachepot and commented on it. The next day, we had a call from her secretary, who wanted to know where they could get one of these cachepots. I said, "Does the duchess really want it?" Because Sis was sitting there, she said, "She wants you to give it to her." So anyway, we sent it to her. They were leaving, so we sent it to the ship.

A couple of years later, at one of the royal weekends at Cragwood, I saw her again. It was the idea that you could invite the duke and duchess anywhere and they would go. But anyway, it was big-time stuff. We all went down, and we were staying with Harriet Wells. So we arrived and went into the drawing room. Finally, the duke and duchess came to the receiving line. We had cocktails and dinner, then went down to the pool house, where there was music and dancing. The duke was a marvelous dancer; he loved to dance. The duchess didn't like to dance, so she was sitting, and I ended up sitting next to her at one point. She loved talking about decoration and all of that. We were having a very good time, and suddenly she turned to me and said, "Do

you know that one of my favorite things is that cachepot that you sent me?"
She remembered it. After all that time. She had that kind of mind and she
was so pretty. No photograph I've ever seen of her looked the way she actually
looked. She had such vitality and sparkle and beautiful skin. She did have
great style, much greater than his.

*Not long after I finished Cragwood, Charlie came to me with a new project. He
asked me if I'd help with a house he'd bought in South Africa, outside of
Johannesburg—making it seem like the easiest of jobs. "Just look around
Johannesburg and see how everyone lives," he said. "I don't want to start wrong,
so you can decide on the look. Everything can be bought in the United States. You
can install it from here six months later. Name your price for going. I'm sure it
won't take you more than ten days."*

*Well, that's not what happened. Harry must have known. He'd been dead set
against me going, but he gave in at the last moment. And I'm not the sort of person who had a burning desire to go to Johannesburg—then, after all, it was a
new city, only about fifty years old. But it was the challenge I responded to. Little
did I realize how much of a challenge it was going to be.*

*This was before jet travel. The trip took thirty-two hours. And somehow, the
Engelhard office had made a mistake. I was put in tourist class and had to sit
there the entire trip. As the plane droned on over mountains and rivers and rivers
and mountains, all I could think was, All this over a slipcover.*

*I was met late at night by a company man and taken to a hotel. I'll never
forget my room: a large bowl of fruit, a gangster bouquet of flowers, and a
big fat letter from Charlie. "I hope this won't be a blow to you," the letter began,
"but I've had a few new ideas." He wanted me to add a library. He wanted
me to add a ballroom—or a "stoop," as they called them in South Africa. He
wanted me to do over the kitchen wing and the servants' quarters. If I had any
time left over, he wanted me to find a landscape architect to do over the driveway and to make some special gardens. And he wanted it all done from London, rather than from New York. "P.S.," he wrote, "I'll see you for dinner here in
four days. Arrange your trip home so that we can meet in London the Sunday
after that."*

I was stunned.

*The company car met me at 7:30 the next morning to take me off into the
unknown. A nice young man, Charlie's architect, took me to see the house, Court
House. It was a good Dutch copy, about fifteen years old—a nice suburban*

house, no more. It was in a neighborhood where all the swells of Johannesburg lived, where all the other houses were exactly like it—suburban. I never saw a country club, but I assume there was one. And Charlie wanted to live like everyone else—so he'd said. So the architect and I went to see the house belonging to Harry Oppenheimer, Sr., Charlie's partner's father. The old man's house was what you'd call a "mansion." Well, Charlie could live that way. But I felt he wanted something a little different—a little better.

The architect and I plotted and schemed at my hotel well into the night— for the next three days. I was there for pure work—and was it work! I've never worked so hard. But on the fourth day, I said, "Am I ever going to see a zebra or a giraffe?" And that day, I went out and saw Charlie's forestry project, which was just getting started. He'd planted little pine trees a foot tall . . . on land that stretched as far as from New York to Boston—squared! Imagine! Well, it was a different world. And Charlie produced his whole empire from it.

The manager of the forest, I remember, had just become a father, and Charlie, my grandson, had been born within two days of his son. As I looked at that baby, I wept again and thought, What am I doing here?

That night, I was to meet Charlie at a dinner given by his great new friends, the Barlows. Black-tie—8:30. Charlie was to be the guest of honor. I arrived. All the other guests had arrived except Charlie, and at once, I sensed that something was wrong. I walked down into the living room and twenty-six faces stared at me coldly. I couldn't imagine what I'd done wrong, so I stayed very quiet and didn't even have a drink. Finally, dinner was announced. Still no Charlie. Luckily, I found myself on the right of my host, the nicest man I've ever met. Eventually, I pulled myself together and asked him why I was so unwelcome. Very gently, he explained that they already had a famous decorator, Mr. L., right there in Johannesburg, and that no one could understand why I had to come so far when they already had him. Well, I got the point. I decided that the moment Charlie arrived, I'd take him aside and explain the situation to him—even if it meant taking him by the scruff of the neck.

Well, finally, he did arrive. It seems that this was the day he'd bought his first racehorse, that his horse had just won a big race, and that Charlie had gout. He was undone with pride and gout! I didn't care what he had. I took him into the library and said, "Charlie, you're making a fool of yourself and a fool of me."

"Sister," he said, "don't worry. Just hire the other decorator. He can take care of this end when you're in London. It's very simple. I'll see you at Claridges on Sunday and we can do some shopping. We'll have a spree."

"It's impossible!" I said. "You know that all the shops in London close so that they can take their dogs to the country and all that...."

"Oh, you can fix it somehow."

"But it's impossible...."

"Good night, Sister."

And then he was gone.

I left Johannesburg the next morning, having had a long talk with the famous decorator, Mr. L., who couldn't have been nicer. I arranged for the shops in London to stay open over the weekend, and I carried the most exact blueprints the architect had been able to make up on such short notice. At least I was in the air. Then we were grounded. I could look at a map and tell you where it was. It wasn't a desert, but it was still a desert town. At first, we'd been forced down because we got into a sandstorm and that was near death, but the plane took off again. Then we wound up in this town for repair work, and we were there for two days. I just sat there on a bench—for two days! Without sleep—with nothing! All the time thinking with panic about Harry and the children at home and Charlie arriving in London and all the shops that had so nicely stayed open during the famous English weekend.... I was so naïve. It never occurred to me that this town might have anything to do with America. "Why didn't you go to the embassy?" Ronnie Tree asked me later when I told him about this. "They're the most charming people ... charming."

Well, I got to Claridges—desperate that I'd missed Charlie. They told me that he'd decided to stay another day in Paris and would see me the next day at six. Again, I arranged to have all the shops stay open late.

The next day, I had a car to make the rounds of my favorite shops. My spirits lifted when I saw one piece after another—each more beautiful than the last. I picked everything that morning—all the key pieces. It never occurred to me that they might be different from what the other people in Johannesburg had. I just had a glorious inner feeling that everything was so beautiful that nothing could go wrong. I was totally exhausted—and totally exhilarated.

Late that afternoon, Charlie finally arrived. Our first stop was to see a break-front I'd picked for the library—one of the best breakfronts I've ever seen. "That's what I want, Sister, that kind of a thing," he said. "I want that and that and that and that. Now let's have some fun. I want to see some silver and a few paintings."

I hadn't even touched on that, but I soon realized that Charlie had a wonderful eye. He took me on a tour of his own. On Bond Street, he picked out within a few minutes two of my favorite Vuillards. Then we went to look at some extraordinary silver. I found out that Charlie knew every hallmark on every piece, so the silver for Court House was very well taken care of. We had dinner together. "Now Sister," he said, leaving me, "I'm off to New York tomorrow. I'll leave the rest to you."

And then he was gone.

I'd been put up to something, but that's when I think I'm at my best. I think the next week in London was the most fun I've ever had. With blueprints in hand, I bought everything down to bibelots and ashtrays. I bought beds, sofas, and upholstered chairs; carpets, rugs, curtains, and upholstery material for every room; bed linen, table linen, glass, and two sets of Lowestoft china for twenty; mirrors, mantels, trays, breakfast sets, brooms . . . everything! It was all like a dream. Then, at night, I'd mark each piece on the blueprint. Each piece had a number corresponding to the room where it would go and the place in the room where it belonged. Every table had an exact spot where it was to be placed, and for each table, there was a precise vase, lamp, and bibelot that belonged on top. Ashtray number six was numbered for table number six, breakfast tray number three for room number three, and so on. I plotted and planned until even every broom was in place.

Somehow, I got home on the day I'd promised I'd be home. The shipment left for Johannesburg and everything was installed exactly as I'd instructed. I went back to Johannesburg six months later, but only for pleasure. It turned out that not one thing was missing, and I was proud that nothing had been moved. Court House was a happy place, and it gave so many people a good time. People would come and stay from all over the world, and the hospitality was always warm and charmingly done. Court House was closed several years ago, but it had done its duty. Many of the pieces are now scattered around at other different Engelhard houses, and I can still spot every piece.

ANNETTE DE LA RENTA: The South African house was Queen Anne in style. It was white. I remember double-hung windows that obviously went to the ground, and then you walked into a garden. It was at the end of colonial rule when my parents had Court House. It was beautiful and wonderfully run. All the men were dressed in white, with sashes to delineate their position in the hierarchy of the household. Green ribbons with red denoted higher rank than just green, or maybe it was the other way around. I don't remember. Now people are all dressed in khaki jackets.

The garden was perfectly beautiful and there were all these women who spent the day on the lawn picking weeds by hand. They'd be there in their hats, with their children singing songs. Big vast circles of them, and they would just move inches at a time.

Sister had bought beautiful English furniture. Samuel and I were asked if we wanted any furniture at the time, but I was then very into twentieth-century furniture. So I thought, Who would want that? Luckily, Samuel was smart enough to say that, yes, he wanted the library. That beautiful English bookcase that was in the library. The house was filled with extremely beautiful things.

My last job for Charlie was in London. By this time, he'd become deeply involved in racing. He knew it. He'd learned it—by reading, just as he'd learned about silver. He was the sort of person who once he'd gotten started on something couldn't stop until he'd learned everything. I was told by a great trainer that Charlie knew more about the bloodlines of horses than any man alive. And when those racehorses finished the races, he was there.

*I knew all this. But Charlie didn't explain to me why he wanted me to take his apartment in Grosvenor House in London, connect it to a second apartment—and have it ready in two months. "That's not the way the English work,"
I said. "It's impossible!"*

Charlie was lying on a sofa at the time, eating cherries. His reply was to throw a pit at me, hitting me directly in the eye. Charlie didn't know the word impossible. *He let me know that without even replying. Once again, I couldn't refuse him. Again, I took the challenge.*

It was an enormous job, requiring a lot of architectural work, and I never could have done it without the help of Betty Hanley on the London end. Walls were torn down, bathrooms were added, and all the latest equipment was installed. Then I made the first trip there for another fantastic spree. I made three more trips to say, "Hurry, hurry," before I realized what the rush was about. Charlie had a horse running in the Derby and he needed a suitable place to celebrate, because he was going to win.

Soon I heard the foreman saying things like "Urry up, it's got to be done for the bloody Derby!" I realized that that was the kind of deadline the workmen could appreciate. They became fascinated by the job and, somehow, it all came together. The dining room, which was very small, was all mirrored. With its Russian chandelier, it looked like a palace. In the living room, the walls were glazed a Chinese yellow I'd taken from a piece of porcelain I gave to the painter—highly, highly glazed. No one had ever seen walls like that before. They gave the illusion of continual sunlight on those dreary London days. It turned out to be one of the jobs I loved the most.

Well, the job was finished—the day of the Derby. And, that day, Charlie's horse won.

Near the end of Charlie's life, the Engelhards took a house in Dark Harbor. Dark Harbor didn't know what to make of them at first, "new people," you know, but soon everyone grew to love them as much as I did. They had movies for the kids, every kind of boat, and they donated big silver cups to the dog show, making it very grand. They were a terrific addition to the island.

ALBERT HADLEY: The only time I really saw Charlie was in London when we did the apartment there. He kept us waiting for a long time to get into the apartment. And, when we did get in, he was still in the bathtub and we had to go into his bedroom. Sister gave him hell. That was one of the best apartments we ever did.

BILL HODGINS: I worked on the Engelhard apartment in London. I walked around and looked in the antique shop windows at night, because I was really busy during the day. I would take pictures of furniture and zip them back to Mrs. Parish. She would call and say, "You get that black Queen Anne console." She said, "Get that, and get that, and get that," and, of course, I was thrilled to be buying this grand, grand furniture. It was very exciting for someone who had only been working for two years.

Jane and Charlie always spent their winters in Boca Grande, on Florida's West Coast, and after Charlie's death, Jane carried on the tradition of wonderful Engelhard hospitality in one of the most enchanting oceanside houses that I have ever known.

By Florida's standards, Boca Grande is an old town. It is one of the country's simpler, better established winter communities. The same hundred or so families have been coming for years and years, with the populations swelling with children and grandchildren during the Christmas and spring school vacations. People stay in the Inn, or in the cottages, or in the comfortable houses along the Gulf that were built long ago, when almost everyone arrived here by train. The pink stucco railroad station, now empty, is a Boca Grande landmark, along with Fugates, the one store where everyone buys toothpaste, shoes, dresses, shell pails, bathing suits, fishing tackle, and hair nets. The post office, and Evelyn's, the hairdresser next door, pretty much complete the town.

There is a lot of golf, tennis, and swimming, of course, but the big sport in Boca Grande—especially after storms—is shelling. When one huge squall was tapering off, Mr. du Pont, who adored his shells, was found naked in the surf with his valet getting the best pick. When a resident finds a secret shelling place, he or she will most likely die with that knowledge, unable to reveal it even to next of kin.

The Engelhards' house is a hidden, self-contained complex, right on the beach, with a large main house and a network of cottages, patios, boat houses, swimming pool, Jacuzzi, gardens, terraces, and a pool house that is also a movie theater. The main house hangs over the Gulf. The planting is so cleverly done that, as you walk along the beach, you are unaware of this secret place.

My decorating challenge was to enhance the natural beauty and tranquillity that was already here. The main house is simple, open, and beautifully made, with big sliding glass doors everywhere, and sand-colored stone floors. We used no curtains so there would always be an unobstructed view of the ever-changing Gulf. There are two dining rooms, connected, one large, the other smaller. The walls of both are off-white, rich and calming. The smaller dining room is octagonal, and here we designed a marbleized table with a crisscross border.

Before dinner, drinks are served in the inside terrace, where you can watch the sun go down over the Gulf. This room is so beautifully understated that you could call it the no-color room. In it are comfortable sofas, soft chairs, lush tropical flowers and trees; marvelous music filling the room through hidden speakers. Occasionally a terrifying storm will come up—the wind howling, the sea raging—but in this calm room you always feel safe watching the storm.

The inside terrace opens into the living room, connected by the same stone floor. Again, a profusion of flowers and large trees standing in the corners expresses the beauty of Boca Grande. Here we used a light, cheerful chintz, an element continued into the dining room, a bright Chinese lacquer desk, and four sofas in white cotton, heaped with pillows of off-white and coral, woven like ribbons that we had made in England. Everything says luxury, and everyone has a table nearby for reading, looking at albums, or to place their frosty mixed drink. There is a beautiful large mirror on the wall facing the ocean, and whenever you glance through the mirror, you feel as though you could reach out and touch the sand and shells on the beach.

Lunch is either a luxurious picnic on the boat or a special meal beside the protected pool. Here you sit in your bath wrapper, a drink of parsley and fruit juices in your hand, chatting with bright, interesting people, and seriously wondering if you are in heaven. Promptly at 4:30 each afternoon, tea is served, with delicious cakes, in the large, open front hall.

After tea and conversation, everyone slowly wanders away to their separate cottages for naps. Each cottage consists of a single or double room; each has its own enclosed porch. No two are alike, but they all convey a sense of comfort and luxury. We designed most of the materials in our shop—all cotton, pattern-on-pattern, bursting with color. The floors are either painted or stenciled. Trompe l'oeil designs cover the tables, mirrors, and walls, near-perfect illusions of animals, birds, latticework, or a panel of books. Some rooms have French soft-colored fruitwood bureaus and chairs. Everything has a country look, and there is not one piece without a special charm. The bedspreads are quilts, some old, some new, and a feeling of freshness and sunshine is everywhere. No one could possibly leave this beautiful, hidden place without feeling inspired and renewed.

ANNETTE DE LA RENTA: The Boca Grande house was a hideous house. Hideous. But it had whimsy. It was filled with good food, good help, comfortable chintz rooms. It had a lot of sparkle.

We would be out on the boat for hours and hours, and if we all have skin cancer today, it is because of that boat. The captain's name was Coleman. He made delicious bacon; the boat would be pitching and rocking and he would make the best bacon you had ever tasted. We did a lot of bird-watching and fishing.

BUNNY WILLIAMS: I was asked to go down to Boca Grande to help freshen things up. I was about twenty-five years old. Mrs. Parish said, "Go. You'll have a great time." I was to arrive on Thursday, work Thursday and Friday, and then stay for the weekend with the other guests. Anyway, I went. That Thursday night, Mrs. Engelhard said, "We'll have dinner. Just us." After the other guests had come, I was told, "Don't dress for dinner, but Mrs. Engelhard would like to see you over in her sitting room around five-thirty so that you can talk about what you're going to do and she can have a visit before everybody arrives." I thought, They said, "Don't dress for dinner." So I put on a long cotton skirt and a silk shirt or something, which was not the dressiest thing I had brought. So I went and sat in her sitting room, waiting for her, because her bedroom was off by itself. I was nervous about this whole thing. Mrs. Engelhard was just extraordinary. She had that strong, very exotic voice, a result of European upbringing. When the door opened, there was this giant of a person there with this hair—it was like a lion's mane—that extraordinary hair, which was always perfectly coifed, about five inches high all around. She was in black crepe pajamas that had tight pants, and the whole top was black crepe made into a long fringe. It was stitched down, but loosened up in places. She had on a ruby and diamond necklace—the rubies were huge—and she had a bracelet and earrings and maybe a pin to match. I was so dazzled! I thought to myself that this was not Kenny Lane. I had some junk Kenny Lane, and this was definitely not Kenny Lane. She was so funny. She said, "Isn't this stuff ridiculous? I have no place to wear it. Charlie gives it to me all the time. It's in a box, so I have to wear it down here." In one second, she made me so comfortable. Here was this apparition of jewels, the likes of which I have never seen.

And she was so smart. She had this extraordinary gift of drawing you out and making you feel comfortable and feel like chatting. Mike Mansfield was coming for the weekend, and other politicians, and Mr. Engelhard, and President Johnson. Some of the most powerful people in the world.

BILL HODGINS: At one of the Christmas parties, I remember looking up, and in came Charlie Engelhard. Sister had given him red-and-white candy-striped boxer shorts. He had them on, even though it was black-tie. She gave everyone a present. When he got out of the way, there was Jane Engelhard. I can still see her. She had a black dress with big sleeves, and no jewelry at all except a pair of earrings that I swear were gigantic. Solid diamonds. She was damn good-looking. She just stood at the doorway for a minute.

APPLE: I will never forget after my first collage exhibition in Boston, Mrs. Engelhard wrote me a wonderful letter encouraging me to keep on painting, because she thought I had real talent. Her sweet letter meant so much to me. She was always taking the time and making the effort to do such kind things.

SUSAN: As Sister composed her thoughts on the Engelhards, she made three notations before she began: "atmosphere of love, children, and animals"; "friends from all over the world"; "kindness, generosity—the most loving family." In these simple notes, she summed up her feelings for them best.

Opposite page: Tom Watson, Olive Watson, and Sister in Maine.

Chapter Sixteen

The Thomas Watsons

Tom was at the controls. When I climbed aboard, awkwardly and nervously,
he said nothing, and neither did I. He looked competent enough, fiddling with
the dials, but I couldn't help wondering when the president of IBM had
found the time to learn to fly.

SISTER PARISH

NEW YORK TIMES OBITUARY, JANUARY 1, 1994

THOMAS WATSON, JR. led IBM and America into the computer age prompting Fortune magazine to call him "the greatest capitalist who ever lived." He became an ardent advocate of nuclear arms reduction and served from 1979 to 1981 as the U.S. Ambassador to the Soviet Union during the Carter administration. A child of privilege, private schools and wealth, Mr. Watson was an indifferent student, who once confessed that he spent his years at Brown University mostly "flying airplanes and fooling around," though he graduated in 1937. But it was in business, especially after a five-year stint in the Army Air Corps in World War II, that Mr. Watson's energy, intelligence and shrewd instincts became apparent.

Decorating is hardly considered a hazardous occupation, but I have found that there can be nervous moments, especially when you are decorating an island summer home during the winter months.

The Watsons called me one day years ago to say that they had bought a house and barn on North Haven—one of the islands I can see from my front porch in Dark Harbor. They wanted their house to be ready by the following spring, which meant coping with a desolate winter's work, with the owners, and final decision makers, far away.

I went over to the island to meet them and to figure out where each child, five girls and a boy, could have a room. It was the most charming old Maine house, placed in a large field surrounded by pine trees and dense forest. It looked out to sea, toward the small islands just off the beaches and the Camden Hills in the far distance, which looked like towering mountains rising from the deep blue water.

The house was typically Maine, with lots of small rooms, one leading to another, fireplaces everywhere, all with simple mantels, paneling over doors and staircases and around each part of the room; windows still with the old glass; wide honey-colored floorboards; and low ceilings to keep the warmth in the house during the bitter winter months. The house was in poor condition after years of neglect, and so Tom had a real problem as to who could manage such a large undertaking in such a short time. After tactful talks with the great and charming local carpenters, it was obvious that it would be quicker to have boat-loads of men come from the mainland each day. I already feared for the men in those fishing boats, crossing the sometimes-perilous sea at ten below zero to arrive at 7:00 in the morning.

I convinced Tom and Olive that it would be best to have the curtains made, the sofas covered, and the chairs done right in Dark Harbor by Harry Mills, who has taken care of all of us for years. There was a great deal to be done, and it was quite a challenge for him.

October came, and plans were made and changed and made again from all sides. The air was getting nippy, but it was still beautiful. December was soon upon us, and it was time for me to take a trip to North Haven to see the improve-ments. I chartered a boat, the only one left in the harbor in December, and off I went to meet Olive, who was coming from New York on the Watsons' plane.

The plane couldn't land on the island, so she, too, had the boat to cope with. She decided to go with the workmen, leaving at 6:00 in the morning. The day started calm and clear, with only the gulls overhead making the usual noise while diving for fish in the freezing waters.

At that point, the house was almost open to the skies, with the new roof half-finished and most of the windows out to be repaired. To me, it looked hopeless—how would it ever be ready by spring? Olive and I worked hard, and made the usual changes, until suddenly, at one o'clock, the wind came up without notice. Soon the trees were bending this way and that, and the sea was raging, with huge whitecaps that looked terrifying against the blackness of the ocean. I suggested, timidly at first, that we should get off the island—and now. Olive hesitated, but she called Tom in New York to say that she was asking the men to take her off the island—it was getting windy. His reply was that the men were supposed to work until three. She hung up.

I got in my boat and asked the captain if he thought we would make it. He nodded but looked grim. Olive noticed the same expression on the faces of the workmen. We waved good-bye, and she headed for her shore; I headed for mine. I kept looking back, and the last thing I saw was her boat disappearing under a colossal wave. Al, the skipper of my boat, looked desperate for her, and the question was, Did we dare turn back? He shook his head. It was too late now—we had better fight for ourselves. We were frozen almost stiff and were green with fright, but we somehow made it to Dark Harbor. I rushed to the nearest phone and called the Coast Guard. I asked for news of a small craft that had left North Haven during the storm. I sank to the floor with relief when they told me that they had been following news of the boat on a ship-to-shore radio, that things were getting safer, and that they would be landing within the half hour.

Overcome with relief, I called Tom in New York to tell him that Olive was safe. There was a brief silence; then he said, "But the men missed two hours of work!"

I spent several days in Dark Harbor working with Harry Mills on the many, many details of the house. The walls were to be papered, some with matching little printed chintz. We wanted each curtain in that meandering house to be different, and so we invented different borders, different material, piping, rousing—never matching.

Large sofas and upholstered chairs were made in our New York workrooms to correspond with the different rooms in the house. The dining room had a long pine table and benches to take care of fourteen children and parents, or whoever showed up. For the smaller parlor, we used Victorian furniture, and for the windows, dotted swiss curtains looped up and tied back, a tassel fringe bobbing away with the summer breeze, ushering in whiffs of newly cut hay. This charming room might have been furnished 150 years ago and never changed. Olive loved that room. It was hers—and so like her. We stenciled the floor and put a hooked rug in front of the charming curved fireplace. All the woodwork in the house had the same wonderful look, made by some sea captain on his leave home from journeys to the Far East.

March came, and I had a call from Tom saying that he was flying up to take a look for himself and asking me to join him. His secretary made a second call to say that Mr. Tom would send an IBM car at four o'clock in the morning to take us to the airport where the planes were stationed. I dared ask if they really meant four o'clock in the morning, and I was assured that they did. I arrived at the airport, still in a daze, saw a large jet with a red carpet, and stepped right aboard. Suddenly, I realized that people were wildly beckoning me to get off—I was on the wrong plane.

I was horrified when they led me to the contraption that was supposed to take me to Maine. It was at the end of the line of impressive company planes, and it looked like a mosquito. Tom was at the controls. When I climbed aboard, awkwardly and nervously, he said nothing, and neither did I. He looked competent enough, fiddling with the dials, but I couldn't help wondering when the president of IBM had found the time to learn to fly. It was not until we had taxied into position, struggled down the runway, climbed, too slowly, into the sky, and turned toward Maine that he finally acknowledged my presence with a smile.

"You're probably wondering if I can fly this thing," he said cheerfully.

I was, and the shakes remain with me today. After what seemed an eternity, we finally approached the islands, and he asked if I would like to dip down over my house in Dark Harbor. I assured him, rather loudly, that I wanted to get no closer than I was at the moment.

Fortunately, the seas were calm when we journeyed to the island by boat, and the house was coming along, as they say. The house was ready on time in June, and to this day, they thank me. All this took place twelve years ago, and as I sit here now in Dark Harbor, writing these notes, the telephone has just rung. It was Olive, asking me if I would consider doing the state dining room in Moscow. Tom had just been asked to be ambassador. An uncanny coincidence? Telepathy? Maybe just another example of one of the nicest parts about decorating—one satisfying job often does lead to another. I don't think Moscow will be nearly as terrifying.

* * *

SUSAN: Sister loved the Watsons. She loved that Maine was important to them, too, and she was like a little girl about her flying adventures with them. They used to land their helicopter in the field by the vegetable garden and pick her up. She never yelled, ever, but when any kind of plane flew over the porch in Maine, she would give her version of a shout, looking up at the skies—"Hoo-hoo. Hello, Tom. Hello, Olive"—while waving madly. In later years, the plane was usually John Travolta's, but she didn't care. To her, any small plane or helicopter belonged to the Watsons.

OLIVE WATSON: Tom bought the house in Maine in 1962. It was an old farmhouse and a disaster. An old, old farmhouse, and just the thing that Sister loved the best. We had been going to Fishers Island. It had the great Hay Harbor Club, lots of children, lots of parties, but my husband never liked it. He had gone to Maine as a child, so one day he came home and said, "Olive, I've had enough of this. We're going to Maine this summer. I've bought a place on North Haven."

He took me to see it. It had been built in 1880 or sometime around then. It hadn't been lived in for twenty-five years. It was huge, and people had been camping in it. I've forgotten how many bedrooms it had. I think there were seventeen. I was continually losing my way, but Sister kept saying, "Oh, this is wonderful. This is wonderful." Tom said, "Oh, this is wonderful." There were 350 acres and it was miles from town.

Sister said, "Don't worry. It's just September. I'll fix the whole thing up." We didn't have any furniture. Just a couple of things, but not much. Sister knew where to send the few little things that were in it to be fixed. She knew little old ladies who could stitch up the curtains. All Maine people. She hired somebody from Camden to come over and live in the house and work all winter. Then she took a room in a warehouse in New York, and we did just the basics like the couches and chairs. We'd send everything there as we'd find it. Then we moved up in June, and it was wonderful. All finished. I don't know how she accomplished it. We went up a couple of times during the winter. We went across the bay, and there were lobster boats, with the water coming over them. It was scary, but to be with Sister was always good fun. We'd take a picnic and spend the day up there.

ALBERT HADLEY: When Sister saw the plane we were to fly in, she said, "Oh my God. Don't go," but we climbed aboard. The two of us were sitting in the backseat; Olive was next to Tom. We took off. Olive was giving us coffee and doughnuts and Tom was pointing out all the scenery and talking about how beautiful it was. Then, when we got to the island and to their house, Tom landed in a cornfield, and that was the beginning of our day.

We had a perfectly wonderful day until we got in this boat. It was a cold, windy day, and of course I was more terrified of the boat than I was of the plane ride. I knew that if the plane went down, we would be killed—that would be it. If I fell in the water, it would be a slow death.

OLIVE WATSON: Sister loved the helicopter. It was a long flight from Westchester up to North Haven, so Tom would leave it in Maine. It was wonderful because we could fly over to see Sister. We'd just land in a field or anyplace else. It was a great thing to go picnicking in. I think one time in the fall we went with Sister up to Stowe, Vermont, where we have a ski house. We all got in the helicopter and flew along, looking at the sites and the leaves. Then suddenly, Tom or Sister would say, "Let's go eat there." So we'd land in a field and go in and have some lunch. Of course, people would think we were from Mars.

One of my favorite stories about Sister is that on one hot July day when we had just done the second alteration on the house in Greenwich, she called me to say that she'd be out. But no luncheon, she said. She was in a big hurry. I thought, What am I going to do? It's a hot day. The air conditioning isn't working. Sister has got to have something to eat. But what? what? what?

And then I went out to the old barn that we have here; it was cold, because it is stone, built in the 1880s. I spotted an old Rolls-Royce in the corner, a town car that my husband had bought years ago. I thought, "Oh, that's where we are going to have lunch."

So I went to the Homestead, a restaurant in Greenwich, and ordered a wonderful luncheon, this cold salmon. I had two little folding tables, and I put them in the back of the car. I got out some little Porthault cloths. The architect was there, too, and he sat up front in the chauffeur's seat. He had some kind of little table, or maybe a tray on his lap. And I had two little fans, two tiny fans. We had our conference there. Sister loved that. We took her picture and she had it for a long time. When I went to Maine, she had it there on her desk.

ALBERT HADLEY: Well, I have to tell you the story about our trip to Russia with the Watsons. I had a friend, Elaine, who was in the fashion world, and she said to me, "Albert, if you are going to Russia, you really have to have a fur coat. It's very cold." And I said, "I'm not ever going to wear a fur coat. Don't be silly." Then she sent two or three up one night for me to try on, but I returned them all because I thought there was no way I would wear one. On the way to the office that morning, I was wearing a little brown wool coat, which everyone said would be warm enough. Andrew, our Polish driver, told me, "Mr. Hadley, you know, I think I may have told you wrong. If you can still get that fur coat, I think you'd better, because I've known people to freeze to death in Russia." I thought he was just being mean, but I called and learned that I could still have the coat, so I sent him after it. When I met Sister at the airport, I wasn't even wearing it. I was just pushing it aside. She had to see it and she said she liked it.

When we finally got to Russia, Olive was in the car waiting for us, and she gave a big screech of laughter when she saw me in the fur coat. She said, "Tom wanted a fur coat, but I didn't let him have it."

That, of course, did it. I couldn't possibly be comfortable wearing it then.

We went to the embassy and had a few perfectly wonderful days rearranging furniture and doing everything. The residence was a beautiful house leased by our government, but it had been very neglected.

We'd go out someplace every night. One evening, we were invited to a party for one of the Watsons' friends, who was in politics. I went out with no coat but wore all the long underwear I could manage. We always went in a limousine, but I was afraid that the limousine would be stolen and then I would really freeze to death. I would rush from the car to the indoors. One night, we went to a restaurant and there was a young group there, an extremely animated crowd. Lots of music and dancing. The young Russian kids were on one side of the room and we were on the other. The dance floor happened to be on our side.

You know how Sister liked a little vodka. The vodka was in little glasses and they would come by and refill her glass. It wasn't long before she decided that she and Olive would dance. Neither Tom nor I would dance with them. I was as looped as they were. Soon Olive and Sis got up on the dance floor and danced together. Then they started a conga line. The music got louder and louder and faster and faster, and soon they were not on our side anymore, but on the Russian side. They were all dressed up with Kenny Lane pearls and the whole business.

We were there during Red Army Week in November. The day of the

Sister and Albert in Russia.

great army parade, Olive and Tom had to go and be in the stands, so Sis and I were invited to the home of one of their friends, who lived on the main parade route. We had lunch there, and it was all very scary, watching these big ominous tanks roll by.

We went out one night to a circus, which the Russians are famous for. We went to this marvelous round pavilion that was all glass. There were walkways around the perimeter and you went inside to find the circus. When we went in, the entire floor was covered with a marvelously bright-colored satin, and as people gathered, the music played and the band struck up. This satin cloth went *zoom*, right up into the ceiling, and the show started.

After intermission, it was time for the animals to come out. A little bear came out and, in unison, Sis and the Watsons screamed, "Albert." For then on, and to this day, Olive Watson has called me "Mr. Bear."

Then, of course, coming home, we had to go through the procedure of leaving the country. As we went through the check-out station, again it was very scary. There were steel bars that came down so that only one person could go through at a time. We got to our seats, the engines started, and we got off the ground. I said, "Oh my God. Thank heaven we're out."

OLIVE WATSON: I didn't feel nervous in the Soviet Union because they wouldn't have dared to hurt us. Every time that I'd go out walking, I would always turn around quickly and see people, but I'd think, They're just taking care of me. Another thing that was intriguing to me was that when I would take my dogs walking, the people would love it. They'd come over and try to scoop my dogs up in their arms. People would come up to Tom on the streets because he never wore a hat, which really upset them. They would grab their hats and point to his head. So finally, just to save himself, he started wearing a fur hat like they did.

The embassy was like one of those big old town houses in New York. We had a lovely garden with beautiful roses, and a high fence all around it. It had been built by some very wealthy man in the early 1900s, and then the Americans bought it and made it the embassy.

The Russians and the Americans weren't very friendly at that time, so the way we entertained ourselves and the rest of the diplomatic community was to give lots of parties. I remember that at our first dinner party there was this great long table, and we must have had thirty people for dinner. I had a rather weird seat as the wife of the American ambassador, and then I was told that you were seated according to how many years you'd been in Moscow, and not by protocol. Eventually, after many people moved away and I had been there a year and a half, I got moved up. The staff was mostly Italian, and the major-domo had black-market connections in Moscow, so we had everything. We had salads and things that no one could get. Our food was always delicious. Tom kept saying to this man, "Now, if you get into trouble, I'm not going to have anything to do with it."

We shared a lot of adventures with Sister. She was wonderful in Moscow. Oh, we'd have a wonderful time. You couldn't help but love her.

Opposite page: The combined living room–dining room
at the Paleys' house in Southampton.

Chapter Seventeen

The William Paleys

They were absolutely extraordinary, but you have to take them separately.
God knows she was beautiful. Great style, great taste. She was an artist. She
was far more intellectual than Bill and he was a very smart guy.

ALBERT HADLEY

NEW YORK TIMES OBITUARY, OCTOBER 27, 1990

A 20TH CENTURY visionary with the ambitions of a 19th Century robber baron, Mr. Paley cultivated CBS from a handful of struggling radio stations in 1928 into the most powerful communications company in the world.

Handsome, tall and ever rakish, Mr. Paley had a lifelong passion for the company of beautiful and accomplished women. He wed two of the most dazzling. His 1932 marriage to Dorothy Hart Hearst ended in divorce in 1947. Later that year, he married Barbara Cushing Mortimer, known as Babe. She came from a prominent Boston family, seemed to glide effortlessly through social circles and was described by some as the most beautiful woman in the world.

NEW YORK TIMES OBITUARY, JULY 7, 1978

Mrs. Paley's sense of elegance set a standard for style-conscious women for three decades. Her approval lent an immediate cachet to almost anything in the world of fashion, beauty and decor, and her appearance at a public event was a signal for the kind of attention accorded such woman as the Duchess of Windsor and Jacqueline Onassis.

Mrs. Paley, a gracious woman with a ready and warm smile, achieved her greatest recognition in the 1960's, before fashion became widely influenced by youth and a more-casual "anything goes" approach.

In that decade, Babe Paley was to many the ultimate symbol of taste and perfectionist chic, the inspiration for mannequins that lined the windows of Lord & Taylor and for countless sketches, photographs and articles in magazines and newspapers throughout the country. Her appearance in pants gave them a stamp of acceptability; when her hair became threaded with gray, she made no attempt to hide it, and scores of silver-toned heads began to emerge from hiding.

RICHARD MANDER: I walked into the Paleys' apartment on the first day, and I was looking at this $60 million painting, *Boy Leading a Horse,* from Picasso's Blue period. Right there in the front hall. On the right, there were five Rodin sculptures in this incredible foyer. We were there that day to hang Mr. Paley's art for his dressing room because Sister had just redone it. His master bedroom opened into the room he called his "oxygen room." He would breathe pure oxygen and it would make everything click.

Sister and I were sitting there with Mr. Paley, and it all got fairly presumptuous. There were fifty or more old master paintings, eighteenth-century paintings that had just been brought up from his art vault, and we were choosing twelve to hang in his new dressing room. They were looking at these things that should have been in a museum and saying, "Oh, *hideous.* I couldn't stand to look at that. I couldn't bear it." These were the most beautiful paintings you have ever seen in your life—I mean, masterpieces. They were saying, "Turn that one away. I can't bear it," and "Oh yes, that one is charming," and "Oh yes, this is lovely," and "What do you think?" We probably spent four or five hours just going through all of these paintings, all stacked up in the foyer, scaling them on the wall. Then Sister and Mrs. Paley left, and by the end of the day, I finished what I do.

BUNNY WILLIAMS: I had been at Parish-Hadley for about two weeks when I was asked to take some samples to the Paleys'. I rang the doorbell and the butler opened the door. There behind him was the Picasso painting of the boy and the pony. I had studied this in art history. This was my first realization that people really had this kind of art collection. I was standing there thinking, This is not a poster, and the butler, who was very sweet, asked, "Oh, would you like to come in and see the pictures?" So I went into this extraordinary apartment. There was this big entrance hall where they had wonderful books. On these two big book tables, deep, with lamps in the middle, were stacks of every magazine that you would want to read: *Time, Newsweek, Fortune, Architectural Digest*, art magazines and design magazines. And not just one issue—all twelve issues—in these neat stacks. I'm sure that it was Babe's idea. She was, after all, a woman who spent her life running a house and knowing how to do it. Babe Paley spent her whole life being beautiful and making sure that everything was perfect.

She used a lot of decorators, including McMillen, Billy Baldwin, Mrs. Parish and Albert. She would do different things with different people. She was always working on something in the apartment. There were Gauguin paintings in the living room, a French-paneled room with taxicab yellow walls. I've never seen anything so beautiful in my life. She had these big lacquered screens on either side of this huge Gauguin painting. Everything was in brown satin. It was elegant and grand, and yet very comfortable.

APPLE: Mummy lent the Summer House to the Paleys, something she rarely did. She put an enormous effort into it, making sure everything was perfect—the flowers, the food, everything.

She left the house before their arrival and went to the Town House (one of Sister's other Maine houses), feeling everything was "perfection." Shortly after their arrival, Mr. Paley's butler called to ask where Mr. Paley's shower was. Mummy said, "Why, there is no shower, only bathtubs, like in most Maine island houses." The butler told her in no uncertain terms that Mr. Paley had to have a shower.

Mummy hung up the phone, went in search of a showerhead attachment, and returned to the Summer House. She took a garden hose that was outside the house, ran it through the bathroom window, and attached the showerhead to it. She then put some kind of iron garden chair in the bathtub with the hose, and that was the end of it. She never heard another word about Mr. Paley's shower.

SUSAN: Sister had a black-and-white photograph of Babe Paley in her office, displayed prominently on her desk. It immediately caught your eye as you entered the room. In the photograph, Babe was sitting on the lawn, beautifully dressed in Capri pants, a simple cotton shirt, and a wonderful straw hat. Her silent image lent an air of glamour to the room, something Sister clearly intended.

MARCIE BRAGA: I remember being intimidated by Mr. Paley. After Mrs. Paley died, I helped Mr. Paley redo her bedroom. I also worked on his bedroom, which was then in the back of the apartment. I remember he had three televisions in a case, one on top of the other. We were meeting in the library in his Fifth Avenue residence. I remember his cuff links. He had the CBS logo—the eye—done in black and white.

BILL HODGINS: Mrs. Parish always had this wonderful Christmas party for just clients and friends. I remember Babe Paley was there. I had never seen a woman who looked like her before. She had a beautiful, beautiful face and an incredibly perfect sort of shape and skin and big, big eyes. Also, she carried herself distinctively: She never moved quickly. I remember that she was sitting on the sofa. I didn't see her come in, but I saw her and thought she was stunning.

ALBERT HADLEY: They were absolutely extraordinary, but you have to take them separately. God knows, she was beautiful. Great style, great taste. She was an artist. She was far more intellectual than Bill, and he was a very smart guy.

They were both involved in the decorating. I always felt that Babe had great instincts and knew what she liked. She also had an open mind. She asked for advice only so that she could benefit from the result. Bill asked for advice, but he had more definite taste and more definite preferences. He was extremely impressionable. Whatever yacht he was on would be the springboard for his next move, and yet he loved the whole process. I used to go to his office late in the afternoon, at 4:30 or 5:00 P.M., and we'd simply move furniture around. He would keep the moving men there so we could work.

Babe liked the process as well, but she really liked the perfection. She wanted to get it right; she wanted to get it to please Bill and make everything perfect for him. Babe obviously had a great sense of her own being and her own style. She was the presence. I used to see Babe, because we liked to talk; we liked to play house and get it all right. But Sis adored being there when Bill was there. You know, the spark. They would carry on, and you know he flirted and she flirted back. That was the fun of it. They giggled and laughed.

Following page: The living room at Coolidge Point.

Coolidge Point

From the house, it seemed that there were acres and acres of manicured
lawns going down to the sea. The Point was wide and you were struck
by this vast expanse of water.

APPLE BARTLETT

SUSAN: Clients who became dear friends of Sister's were Catherine Coolidge and her husband, Thomas Jefferson Coolidge, or "Jeff," as he was called by his friends. Mr. Coolidge, who came from an old Boston family, served as undersecretary of the treasury under President Franklin D. Roosevelt and was a banker and industrialist for many years. A Bostonian to the core, Mr. Coolidge needed Sister's prompting in order to make the improvements that she and Mrs. Coolidge envisioned.

Many years ago I was visiting a friend in Boston, when I was told to hurry and get ready, that we were having dinner with the Thomas Jefferson Coolidges. I was completely charmed by Catherine and Jeff, and eventually a long, wonderful friendship developed, but that night I hardly thought that I'd made new friends.

Their house in Brookline was large, impressive, and as Bostonian as a house can get. At dinner, Catherine, in her endearing way, asked me, "Do you really like this room? I find something lacking."

She looked at me closely as my eyes searched the room, looking for something nice to talk about.

For some reason, I completely forgot my manners. "I'm afraid everything is the matter," I blurted out.

"Oh," Catherine said, surprised.

I was in it now, so I decided I'd better try to be specific. "In the first place, the curtains are so skimpy, they can't be drawn."

"I'm afraid we tried to save on material," she confessed.

"In the second place," I went on, "why don't you light the candles in those fantastic appliqués?"

"It's too expensive," she said, as only someone from Boston, living in a house filled with treasures, could say.

I realized that I was being rude, but what could I do? Here I was, in a house where Gilbert Stuarts hung in room after room, a house bursting with important antiques. Here we were, in the dining room, eating off of Thomas Jefferson's Lowestoft service. Yet my honest assessment was that I had rarely been in a house so lacking in comfort, gaiety, or charm; in a house at such odds with the people who lived there. I held my tongue after my initial frankness, but I never expected to see the Coolidges again. I came away thinking of English brown—it was the only impression the house had left me with.

To my surprise, Catherine called me about a year later, asking if I would come to Boston and look at a model that had been made by their architect, Page Cross? They were planning to move to Coolidge Point in Manchester, where Jeff's family had a real palace looking out to sea toward Boston, but as I hung up, English brown again popped into my head.

"What do you think of the model?" Jeff asked shortly after we had greeted each other. I promise I looked all over the room, searching for something resembling a model, and I never found it until it was placed in my hands. I did not know whether to laugh or cry. It looked like Uncle Tom's cabin without the outhouse.

"We want something small and practical," Jeff said. "Something we can run ourselves."

I looked at the model again, dismayed. I understood their intentions. They were tearing down the palace and replacing it with a nice comfortable house set farther back from the ocean. They would live in this house instead of in Brookline.

Fortunately, Jeff began to laugh before I could issue any comment. Even Jeff, who was the most careful of Bostonians, could not see his lavish Catherine or himself squeezed into the space indicated by the model in his hands. The ice was broken and we laughed until we cried. Jeff had allowed only his most conservative Boston instincts to rule when he had issued instructions to the architect—with no thought to Catherine's love of entertaining, his own need for a dignified, comfortable study, or a place to put the five portraits of the presidents by Gilbert Stuart, or even a proper place to sit and enjoy the magnificent surroundings and to watch the sunset on the ocean.

Page was called immediately, and, to his relief, was given vastly different instructions about the sort of house the Coolidges wanted. In the end, it was as long as a city block, and when Jeff looked up from the final set of blueprints, he turned to Catherine and said with a smile, "Pretty nice ranch house I'm building you, what?"

Indeed it was. A cheerful, unpretentious house in the most perfect setting imaginable. It is a considerable drive, through fields and marshes, from the main road to the new house. As you approach the house, you see the love and care that have gone into the grounds and the gardens. Not a single branch of a hedge has not been snipped. It is a low, modern house, but dignified modern. The gardens are simple and practical, but still formal. The swimming pool beside the house has Roman fountains. Lush green fields stretch from the terrace to the edge of the ocean, where the old palace stood. In its place today stand two enormous *amphora, which have become a nautical landmark known as "the Coolidge Pots."*

When Catherine and I set about planning the interior, she had gathered portfolios of pictures that she had collected—from Italian villas to French châteaus. To my vast relief, there was nothing brown. Jeff gave in to her on almost every point. We did use some of the English brown, but I had it all painted. Jeff was nervous, but I kept muttering things like "It won't lose it's value. It's just water paint and you can wash it off anytime."

The result is a really magnificent house—gay, light, and room after room of color. The living room is a wonder to all. The floor is designed in scallops of off-white and brown, with the outline of each scallop being incised. Then one of the truly great housepainters, Louis Perry, painstakingly and lovingly applied layer upon layer of paint. A huge bay window, which Catherine justifiably called "the bay window to end all bay windows," opens the room to fields and ocean, and to floods of light. At night, the handmade shutters are closed, giving the room a new, although still majestic, look. All 175 shutters are handmade, and every one is closed every evening and opened every morning.

On the floor, where a seven-foot margin was left to show the scalloping, is the finest Ooshak rug, made in the nineteenth century. It is all light colors: pale yellow, tangerine, light blue, and a light sand color. The walls are a glazed, faint yellow, with streaks of the undercoat showing through.

From the ceiling hangs a Venetian chandelier with a seven-foot spread, tiers of candles, teardrops of amber and blue. The furniture is covered in pale corals, corn colors, and touches of stinging green. A nine-foot armoire, painted off-white, is at the far end of the room, and two beautiful Chinese Chippendale mirrors hang over a pair of gilded consoles. One the far wall, there is a cheerful modern Italian painting given to Catherine by her children. Fine lacquer pieces are throughout the room, and a mixture of French and English furniture.

The room is always filled with bowls and tubs of the most exotic, delicious flowers. There is a change of flowers throughout the house once a week. Catherine has complete faith in her famous gardener, Bruno. He has an eye for color, and each room always seems more wonderful than it did the week before. The Coolidge greenhouse stands as one of the most famous today, which makes me even more chagrined as I recall my unwitting early attempt to help Catherine with the flowers. Not knowing of Bruno's skill, I once asked Catherine to have Antonio, one of my favorite florists, come up from New York to teach her how to do bowls of mixed flowers. He did come, was put up at the Ritz, and arrived with twenty large boxes of flowers. Upon entering the hall, he threw up his hands in horror. "Why am I here? I have never seen such beauty!" Bruno sulked only briefly, and Catherine agreed that I never should have mentioned such an adventure.

The entrance is quite remarkable. It is round, with a slightly domed ceiling—partly because Catherine claims that she loves circles (her gardens are also round) and partly because Page Cross wisely decided that it was the best shape of room in which to hang the famous five presidents by Gilbert Stuart. Catherine decided early that she didn't want the portraits in the dining room. "I really don't want those old men staring at me while I'm eating," she said firmly. The problem I had was to keep the hall from looking like the entrance to the National Gallery. The solution was to give it a pale sand color. The floor is unpolished marble, tinted pink. The design of the marble was created especially for the round hall, and it works remarkably well. As you enter, you face a marble mantel, raised from the floor. And of course you stop and slowly walk around the little room to admire the five portraits—reproductions now, for practical reasons, but still magnificent. I was especially proud to do this room, for the portraits had once belonged to my ancestors, the Gibbs family. When Thomas Jefferson Coolidge, Sr., bought the paintings from my ancestors, he sent a note to his wife saying that he had purchased "some nice portraits, but the price was outrageous—nearly three thousand dollars!" I groan inwardly whenever I look at them.

The library, designed by Page Cross, is of bleached wood. The most beautiful of bookshelves, ceiling to floor, are filled with the rarest books, plus Jefferson glasses, family heirlooms, locks of hair, family pictures, and all sorts of personal things standing between the books. It has a large bay window, with two columns standing on each end. At the back of the room, facing you as you enter, is a magnificent partners desk. Catherine often sits behind the desk, glorying in her letters of praise and thanks for her marvelous hospitality.

But the place where you are most likely to find her is in the Trellis Room, among the banks of rare orchids and beautiful jasmine trees. The room is a large, cheerful part of the home, but it almost seems a part of the fields and the sea, as well. It is never the same, but always a treat. Simple bamboo furniture on straw rugs with pale pink as the base and a red Italian chandelier give the room an extra little zip. "It's jazzy," Catherine said when she first saw it finished. "But I like it." I find that warm praise from a Bostonian.

There are so many things about this house worth mentioning—the painted four-poster bed in the master bedroom, the special dining room table that we had made in our workrooms in New York; almost everywhere you look there is something remarkable. The only criticism I ever heard about the house came from Harry du Pont, when he first entered the hall.

"This room is too small for these portraits," he said quite definitely.

Catherine didn't miss a beat. "Any room is too small for five presidents," she replied.

I only wish that Jeff could have lived to see the house finished. He died two weeks before they were to move into their Uncle Tom's cabin, but I know that he is pleased that his Catherine has been so happy and proud of Coolidge Point.

LIBBY CAMERON: My grandmother Dolly Hooker and Catherine Coolidge were sisters and they were from Pittsburgh. There were six brothers, as well. Their maiden name was Kuhn. Catherine and Dolly loved to sing and dance, and they came to New York and, as the story goes, they were asked to be part of the *Ziegfeld Follies*. My grandmother at that point had already fallen in love with my grandfather, and Catherine had gone to Boston and met Jeff Coolidge, whom she married. Catherine was very beautiful, and I think my grandmother was the little sister who was always trying to keep up. They were very close, as they were about eighteen months apart, and they remained close all of their lives. We used to spend about three weeks with them on Coolidge Point every summer on our way up to Maine, and when my family lived in Cambridge, we spent weekends out there with Aunty Catherine.

Coolidge Point was owned by the Coolidges, but there were other houses there, too. Dr. Thorn, their family doctor, had a farmhouse there. Lindsey Coolidge, one of Aunty Catherine's sons, and her daughter, Kitty Coolidge, all had houses. And the Bigelows had a house, too.

Originally, there was a huge brick house that took up half of the point. Aunty Catherine and Uncle Jeffy ripped it down and built this beautiful one-level house that Page Cross designed. It was beautifully detailed, contemporary without being starkly modern. You walked in and there was a round room, not a proper rotunda, but a round entrance hall and you could go either right to the living room and sunroom and the whole living area. Going to the left, you'd enter this beautiful dining room that looked out over the point. The round entrance was built for Uncle Jeffy's paintings, once the original Gilbert Stuarts, but later they were replaced with copies when they gave the paintings to the National Gallery. The copies hung in the rotunda.

They had these great big urns that stood on the edge of this beautiful piece of land. There was a wonderful alley that ran along the harbor and Kettle Cove. It was beautiful and very wide. I remember going there as a little girl. Aunty Catherine had two white inflatable swans floating in the pool for us. We'd walk through the alley of trees and greenhouses. There was always coconut cake in the pantry and ginger ale in the little icebox below the counter. Angelina worked in the kitchen and there was a houseman and sweet Bruno, their gardener, who would teach me all about plants.

The Coolidges were an old Boston family. Uncle Jeffy was related to Thomas Jefferson on his mother's side. I think he was Uncle Jeffy's great-grandfather. Aunty Catherine was very chic and had a wonderful laugh. She wore lovely clothes and her hair was perfect, flipped softly to the side. She was a very kind woman. I often went to stay with her when I was in boarding school, and she would have me down with all of my friends for the weekend.

APPLE: From the house, it seemed that there were acres and acres of manicured lawns going down to the sea. The point was wide and you were struck by this vast expanse of water. You could park on either side of the house on terra-cotta-colored pea stones.

In the dining room, there was an apricot-colored marble dining room table. I remember she had gold silverware and the food was delicious. I had tongue with a delicious mustard sauce for the first time. I was forced to eat it to be polite, and I found out how wonderful it is.

The house was always filled with beautiful flowers that were all grown there. The Coolidge house was on the garden tour, and Bruno was very much a part of it. He had one greenhouse just for orchids, just as Grandpa Kinnicutt had done, and I remember he gave me orchids for my greenhouse. At Christmas, there were banks of apricot-colored poinsettias in the round front hall. I have never seen that color since.

Mrs. Coolidge was a real lady and had a down-to-earth sense of humor, exactly the kind of woman Mummy loved. She loved her dogs, which were some kind of Norfolk terrier. She and Mummy had a lot in common, as they both loved their dogs, good food, and beautiful things.

Opposite page: Sister's letter to the Duchess of York with regard to the budget for Sunninghill Park.

-►►-───────────────────────────────-◄◄-

Chapter Nineteen

The Duke and Duchess of York

She was exactly like the girls you had gone to school with. Really, she could
have been on your lacrosse team. She didn't know yet what she was in for.

DAVID KLEINBERG

PARISH·HADLEY
ASSOCIATES
INC.
305 EAST 63ᴿᴰ STREET · NEW YORK, N.Y. 10021
(212) 888-7979

April 25, 1988

H. R. H. The Duchess of York
Buckingham Palace
London, SW1, 1AA

Dear Madam:

We have reviewed our plans for the furnishing of Sunninghill
Park in order to prepare an estimated budget for your consid-
eration. In doing so we find ourselves faced with many
questions and alternatives that can only be answered by you.

We know you have many exciting ideas, and a definite point of
view about the house. These need to be shared together to
determine how best to fulfill your wishes. Since we have not
yet had an opportunity to discuss with you in detail the
furnishing and decoration, we hope during our meeting on the
23rd of May we will be able to concentrate on these issues.
We will then be able to provide you with a realistic and fair
budget.

We feel sure that you will agree that this is a necessary pre-
requisite to establishint a working program for the decoration
of Sunninghill Park.

Yours sincerely,

Sister Parish

Mrs. Henry Parish II

love from Ricky and Nanny!

DAVID KLEINBERG: It all started because Sarah Ferguson, the Duchess of York, was in Greenwich for some benefit, polo or what have you, and she ended up at the de Kwiatkowskis' house in Greenwich, which we had done. She said, "Andrew and I are doing up this house and I'd love it to look like this." Henryck said, "You should call Mrs. Parish." She called and said, "Hi. This is Fergie." Mrs. Parish didn't know who she was. She could have been Kermit the Frog, for all she knew. Mrs. Parish thought this was nonsensical, but at the same time she was intrigued by the idea. This was a girl who had married the son of the queen of England.

They had an architect and they hadn't started yet, and so we asked if she could send us the plans. She came to the office with her security people and her lady-in-waiting. She stopped and talked to everyone and yet she was sort of royal. She behaved very properly, shook everyone's hand, and introduced herself. She was the press darling. She was young, fresh, and adorable.

Mrs. Parish and Albert and I had a meeting in the conference room. We sat around and the security people sat in the front room. We'd been cleaning for days, putting things away. The whole office was just abuzz. Sarah said it was all her idea: She wanted to do her new house up like a newlywed. She wanted to deal with it herself. She said the architect had been hired by the queen and asked if we could help her. We said, "Of course."

We were never sent a contract. It was all very informal and not the way we usually did things. We all kept thinking, This is interesting and exciting, but it's never going to happen. Somehow, word got out that the Duchess of York had been to see us and that we were going to work on the house, so newspapers and people in London started to call us. The *Observer* did a magazine article about the office, and we thought this was wonderful press, if nothing else, but in the back of our minds, we all thought this was never going to come to fruition.

She said she had gotten the worst things for wedding gifts; she did have an album of the things they got, and they were terrible. They were on a very strict budget and the queen was giving them the house, but the budget for the decoration was very small.

We just kept thinking that this young woman didn't know anything. There would be things in storage and of course there would be money. Mrs. Parish and Albert and I went to London and did some shopping for other people.

We went to meet with them and to see the house they had rented at

Windsor Park. We were driven out, and the atmosphere was a funny combination of relaxed and over-the-top. Basically, they were a young couple living in a rented house. It was a perfectly nice large-scale suburban house, but it was right on the road, behind the garden wall. Nothing special, and they had rented it furnished. They had a few pieces of their own, but the house had no personality, and gave no clue as to what they were like. She came bounding down in a skirt and sweater and sneakers. Andrew was actually very nice, and they were still very happy at this point. They were both quite chubby. He was very jolly and not intellectually challenging. They weren't stupid, but they weren't sophisticated. They had no idea how to go about building and decorating a house. Fergie's only concern was this huge dressing room, because she was very into her wardrobe. So she had this dressing room and a spiral staircase that went to additional closets, but there was only one bathroom and a nursery.

We had come with revised plans, and we told them, "You can't share a bathroom, and you have no place for the staff to sit." Earlier, Sister had told them in a phone conversation, "Yes, there are problems with these plans. You have too few bathrooms, and you don't have enough room in this nursery; there's no playroom, and you've got the nurse sleeping four miles away from the children's room."

It was all ridiculous. They had said could we make some suggestions about the plans. Albert, Harold, and I had basically erased the original plans. We showed them our plans during lunch, but we never got the feeling they understood. At the same time, it wasn't *their* money, so we were really talking to the wrong people. Then the suggestion was made that we should meet with the architect.

They said we could, but they didn't really see what was wrong with the first set of plans. It was not as if all of a sudden it became clear. They were just in over their heads.

They weren't aesthetic people. Well, none of them are. That's a Windsor trait.

We went to London to do a show house and then went up to Edinburgh to meet with their architect. He was a sort of scholarly man of a certain age who was stuck in the sixties design mode, and he just wouldn't get off the mark. So we had dinner and talked and he told us about the house he'd done for the Rothschilds, which the queen had seen and liked. He was a very nice man, but we could tell that this was not going to be a warm and fuzzy meeting. Then we went to his office to show our drawings. We walked through our changes with the architect and two people on his staff. And it was one of those meetings where everyone talked to everyone else in the most civilized way. Albert and I got back on the plane to London, and Albert turned to me and said, "Those plans will never be referred to again."

And they weren't. Then the press got out of hand, and there was this backlash about Americans doing this work and how inappropriate it was. Albert, Mrs. Parish, and I were asked to return to London one more time to see the royal couple. We were invited to a meeting at Buckingham Palace and we stayed at Claridges or the Connaught. I remember Mrs. Parish was getting dressed and cursing out whoever had packed for her. Of course, she never really cursed anyone out, but she was very angry because someone had packed her dresses without the belts. She unpacked everything wrapped in yards of tissue paper, but the belt wasn't there. I remember going through the suitcase with Mrs. Parish, who was furious because her hatband was missing. Here she was, going to Buckingham Palace, and she had only one pair of shoes. She said, "I told her to put those beige shoes in! She does this deliberately!"

She had a beige silk dress that buttoned down the front, but since the belt was nowhere to be found, she came up with something else to wear. It was spring, and she had a summer hat with her. I can't tell you why. She wanted to change the band on the hat, because she had a safari band on it. When we couldn't find the hatband, she ended up wearing this straw hat—which she had sat on—with a leopard band. She wore it to Buckingham Palace. Just plopped it on her head and went. She was upset for a minute, but then it went right by her. She could stay angry for the longest time, but things that she didn't want to stay angry about were like clouds passing in a quick sky. There would be a huge storm, and then it would be gone. All the years I knew her, I never knew what was going to last or what to expect.

We drove off to Buckingham Palace. We went through a private entrance to a private apartment and then down a hall. We were looking out the window. Now we were on the other side of the gate and we could look down and see the crowd and the guards. It was amazing. Up an old elevator, and on to the meeting with Andrew and Fergie. Basically, as it turned out, we were there to be fired. That's what the sum total of the meeting was. "Thank you," they said, "for all your input, but it's become increasingly difficult for us to continue and we need to do this in a more scaled-down way."

They said they needed to use English decorators. Mind you, we had never charged them for airfare or for our time. They hired Nina Campbell to do the house, and she later said it was not a good project. It was very difficult because basically there wasn't any money. They practically had to get things donated, and no one was interested in donating things because it wasn't an official residence; it was a private house. Nina had to use these terrible leftovers, just a mishmash of things. You never saw a photograph of the house because it was so undistinguished. Nina took me out to see it at one point when it was under construction, and it really was unattractive. It was a two-story house, but it had this one long room like a brick barracks. It was not very pretty and, again, it was right on the road, behind a brick garden wall.

By the time the house was finished, they were already splitting up. During the course of this—and it was a fair amount of time, probably six or eight months—the press had changed their mind about Fergie. They'd decided she was capricious, selfish, foolish, and vulgar. Everything they had previously thought was charming was now not so charming. She was gallivanting around and acting silly. We had one of our meetings at the Plaza Athenée, where she was staying. We thought, Well, she's changed a lot from that sweet girl who first came to our office.

When Albert and I met with her at the hotel, she was kind, if a little bossier—not with us, but with the staff. A little brusque and not so sweet, and we thought, Oh, this is not good. None of it boded well.

ALBERT HADLEY: They had little interest, I would say. The queen had chosen their architect, as she had stayed in a house that he had designed, but she didn't know anything, either. They didn't know how houses run, because everything had always been run for them. That's the difference. The duchess came to our office with her mother and, I think, a lady-in-waiting. Her mother was very good-looking, a horsewoman. Sister was sitting there with her head hanging, because she didn't know who they were, and she didn't get any of it. The duchess kept saying, "Oh. It's the *New York* style." She was bright, charming, vivacious—everything you would want. She couldn't have been better. We got into the budget, the costs, and everything was going well.

When we went to London on our last trip for them, we got the cold shoulder somewhat from our friends. We had an appointment to go to the palace. We didn't have to be there until eleven o'clock, but, of course, with Sis, that meant you had to be ready at nine o'clock. Sister came out in a hat that she had either sat on or slept in the night before—I mean all night. It was so crinkled, and she was carrying a parcel that was sort of wrapped, but not well. We got to the palace and then we were kept waiting in this very dreary room. Then we walked down this long hall, which was at the back of the palace. It looked out on the gardens, and it looked like a warehouse. There was furniture in the hall, and other things. We finally got to their apartment, and there were masses of things stored in the hallways. We went in, and Fergie came out first, all lively and attractive. Suddenly, Andrew came out, dripping wet; he had just come out of the shower. We sat at a very long table and Sis presented this wrinkled gift for the baby, who hadn't yet been born. Well, they had just told us in no uncertain terms that they had so many presents, they didn't know what to do with them. All the things in the halls were their wedding presents, which they hadn't been able to unpack.

Then we got the cheerful news that the queen had said no—great apologies—and as we left, they walked out with us to the door. Fergie's last words to us were, "Don't worry, Mrs. Parish, someday you will do a house for us."

LIBBY CAMERON: I don't think Sarah Ferguson had any particular taste at all, but she was willing to learn. I think that was something Mrs. Parish liked in clients—the ability to listen. Mrs. Parish did like Fergie. She was bubbly and fun. And I think having her as a client gave Mrs. Parish a sense of power. It was far beyond what anyone else was doing in terms of glamour and importance, and Mrs. Parish was very competitive. She liked to know that she got jobs over someone else. It's a very competitive industry.

The Duke and Duchess of York were on the queen's dole, essentially. They built this house. Hideous. It looked like something out of Texas. Southfork—that's what it looked like. A low sort of splashy thing. A big ranch house with no warmth or character whatsoever. It was designed by an English architect, and millions of dollars were spent on security. That's where the money was eaten up. So when it came to decorating, Fergie kept saying that she had no money.

SUSAN: After Fergie's first visit to the office, Sister really liked her—mainly because she played with Sister's dogs and was very enthusiastic. She was also very natural, which always impressed Sister. After Sister met with them in England, I felt she was beginning to wonder about the project. She said that she had told Andrew that there were far too few bathrooms in the new house and he had replied, "Oh, you Americans and your bathrooms." With total conviction, she shot back, "My bathroom is *very* important to me." And she meant it. Press was important to her, too, but she had no time for haggling over bills and trying to work on what she viewed as an inappropriate house with no bathrooms.

ALBERT HADLEY: So Nina Campbell got the job. They were given whatever was budgeted for them by the queen. They would have been perfectly happily married if they had been left alone. They would have gone on doing whatever they wanted to do.

Following page: Sister and Harry.

Chapter Twenty

Family

The differences between the two of them were extreme and yet he adored her.
They were civil and respectful of each other until the day he died. They
certainly had their ups and downs, and it was very complicated,
but they were devoted to each other.

BUNNY WILLIAMS

APPLE: When Daddy's emphysema became so bad that he couldn't live in New York anymore, he moved to Dark Harbor year-round. He loved it all—taking adult education classes at Islesboro High School or having dinner with his friends—but he missed Mummy tremendously. At that time, she was working so hard and felt guilty about not being with him more often. He was so proud of her and wouldn't ask her to give up her work.

When the time came to leave Seventy-ninth Street, I knew that it wasn't just the size of our apartment that was changing, but also our life. We'd been everywhere that might help Harry's health. He'd been to every doctor and tried every cure for this terrible disease, emphysema. Nothing made him comfortable, but his fight was stronger than ever. After every session with the doctors, he never failed to say that they had finally caught it. I'd believe it, too, because of his faith, but deep down I knew that we were fighting a losing battle.

One day, I could tell he had made a huge decision. I could also tell that it was final and he wanted me to take it in the way he was presenting it. In a calm voice, he began by saying, "Sister, this apartment, which we both adore and which we thought would be for always . . ."

I can see him now, sitting in his blue-and-white chair in front of the long French doors with the sun pouring in, landing on my father's beautiful Queen Anne desk, which gleamed from years of polishing. Even the brass handles on it looked like gold. Leaning against the cubbyholes on the desk were pictures of Harry's paternal grandfather, Henry Parish, and a picture of his mother and father holding hands. So much love had been poured into that room. The fire was always burning and flowers and bulbs on tables burst with color, giving the room a fresh smell that made you feel you were in a garden. Sitting there, Harry went on to say, "As heartbreaking as it is, I think we should sell the apartment as soon as possible and find a small apartment with just enough room for me to be with you when I get better." The doctor's advice had been that he should spend as much time as possible in Maine, which was our real home and where the air was clean and fresh, but he wouldn't let me think of leaving my work life. "Now my Sister," he added with his beguiling smile, "you have to work."

For the next four years, I commuted, spending ten days in Maine and a week in the office. When Harry died, I moved into his room. Except for the four-poster bed with its beautiful painted canopy, that room has never changed.

SUSAN: Most women did not work the way Sister did in her day, and she did not have the type of marriage that other people had. My grandparents came to lead lives that were fairly separate, but despite that, or maybe because of it, they were devoted to each other. They were committed to the institution of marriage, to the family of Mr. and Mrs. Henry Parish II, to the houses they created together, and to their friendship.

Harry had emphysema and asthma, two very debilitating illnesses. He was allergic to dogs and horses, but the Parishes always had both. He moved to Dark Harbor permanently in the 1970s. He simply couldn't take the air in New York any longer, so he settled into the Town House, the house where we

Harry holding his son, Harry III.

used to stay in the summer. The Town House is a real farmhouse, with low ceilings, lots of fireplaces, a cozy upstairs with a long hallway, and a treacherous back staircase. It was painted a brighter yellow than the Summer House and had a matching yellow barn for our ponies.

I think that, having developed a real affection for the island people, he was happiest there. Sister was working hard and came to the island only for weekends, holidays, and the summer months. She was happiest working, and he was happiest with the simple life he found there. There are pictures of the Town House piled high with snow, drifts banking its sides, and Sister and Harry bundled up in their Abercrombie & Fitch winter outfits, smiling broadly. At Christmas, the fires were stoked and cocktails started early. The skies darken at around four in Maine in the winter, so I believe things got going very early. I have a picture of them together in the living room with its pale blue walls, the fire roaring, and Sister in her caftan, her cheeks very red, and Harry beautifully dressed for dinner, as always, with a jacket and tie. Mrs. Hale was taking care of them then, and undoubtedly she was in the kitchen making sure everything was perfect, from the fish chowder to her famous chocolate cake.

BUNNY WILLIAMS: I don't know when I've ever met a kinder man or a man who more personified being a gentleman than Mr. Parish. I remember once when I had gone up to Maine for the weekend, and Mrs. Parish had taken me off to see somebody's house that we were working on, the Rogers' or somebody's. I had to catch the ferry back and didn't have time to return to the house to say good-bye to Harry, who was very sick with emphysema. Harry

Sister and Harry.

(above) Sister and Harry at the Summer House at Christmastime.

(below) The Town House.

drove to the ferry station to say good-bye to me. That was just the way he was. I never saw him get angry; I never saw him behave in anything but the most charming way. The differences between the two of them were extreme, and yet, he adored her. They were very civil and respectful of each other until the day he died. I think they certainly had their ups and downs and it was very complicated, but they were devoted to each other. And the support, you know. There was tremendous caring there. They were best friends to each other, best buddies. I don't think she, as a woman, certainly at her age, could have been as successful alone.

MARK HAMPTON: Harry was very good-looking and he'd had this greatly handsome face as a young man. His speaking voice was deep and beautiful, with that perfectly lovely New York kind of accent that is so charming. He never raised his voice. He was really quite funny and very sarcastic.

I remember one Sunday on the front porch of the Summer House on my first trip to Dark Harbor. Sister was lamenting that she wished someone would be willing to drive the Humber back to New York. It was the car that she used for driving around the city, that funny little black four-door Humber.

I offered to drive it back. My wife, Duane, was working for *House & Garden,* and she had to get back to the city, but I was a graduate student and could afford a three-day weekend. So I stayed the afternoon and the evening. It was just hilarious. I think there were four of us on the porch. Barbara Drum was there. She and Sister were wonderful together, like a Katharine Hepburn movie. We started talking about wills. Harry said, "I suppose I have to leave everything to Sister." And she said, "I do expect to die before you do, but if I outlive you, what are you going to leave me? It's mine, all mine."

You didn't hear people with less of a sense of humor get into these hysterical topics. Kind of risky topics. The way she would say, with the hostess too near for comfort, "This is hideous." The other word she used all the time was *repellent.* She'd say, "Is that pretty? It's *repellent.*"

BILL HODGINS: Harry was such a gentleman. She never gave him enough credit, I think, but she never could have been the way she was if she hadn't had his strength behind her.

APPLE: The winter of 1977, the year Daddy died, was one of the coldest in memory. The Coast Guard cutter had to cut a path throught the ice for the ferry to have a clear way to and from the mainland. It was beautiful, but bitterly cold, and so quiet. Mummy and I would get on the ferry each morning to go to the hospital, always fearing the worst. Daddy was so brave until the end, just wanting to die peacefully. Emphysema is a terrible, terrible disease.

Daddy's funeral was a great tribute to him. Even though it was in Maine during the dead of winter, the church was packed with his friends from all over. The letters that Mum received recalled all the different phases of his life. There were letters from Wall Street, letters from Jackie Onassis and Marietta Tree, from friends in Maine, and from his favorite cause, the Lighthouse, which provides services for the blind. Mummy must have gotten three hundred letters, each with something touching and personal in it. Even now, more than twenty years later, people love to tell me what a wonderful and kind gentleman he was. I have always been proud to be his daughter.

RALPH GRAY (island resident): When Harry died, Mrs. Parish invited a group of us to come to the house. Harry was taken in by the year-round people. There was nothing put-on about him. She felt that he fit in with us, the locals. I used to carry Sister and Harry back and forth across the water when they missed the ferry. She was a good person and he was a kind and gentle man. Harry ran the rectory with me at the Episcopal church. He talked with me about what to do and what not to do.

SUSAN: I believe that after Harry died, Sister wore black for almost a year. She seemed to cope, but then after her son, Harry, died unexpectedly at age fifty, she really struggled with her sadness. In many ways, she never completely recovered. She threw herself into her work, but there was a lasting melancholy over her loss of "little Harry." The loss of the men in her family aged her enormously.

APPLE: My brother, Harry, was one of a kind. I remember people saying to me in awe, because he was such a remarkable person, "You're Harry Parish's sister?" He was probably the most artistic of my mother's three children. He was a painter, a sculptor, a collector, and an extremely good designer. His house in England had as much charm and good taste as any house Mummy ever helped with. When he first graduated from Harvard, he took a series of tests at Johnson-O'Connor to find out where his abilities lay. The results were conclusive that he should be in the design field. That wasn't the result he had in mind, but it certainly made sense. Instead, he went into banking. He and my mother were too much alike to have ever worked together, let alone be in the

Harry Parish III with his daughter, Jessica.

same room with each other for ten minutes without getting into an argument over something.

Harry lived in California when he was first married, and later he moved to London. He also bought a house in the English countryside. Wherever he lived, he had so many friends. Fancy people and the not so fancy—all were attracted to him. I remember hearing, years later, that he had telephoned a Boston friend of his to keep an eye on me, his sister.

His funeral was in the small stone English country church that he attended. Before the service, many of his friends came to arrange flowers on the altar. I remember delphiniums of all different shades of blues and purples, freshly cut from their gardens, standing in tall green buckets. Everyone was so considerate and caring. It had all been such a nightmare. I remember our Concorde fight to England from New York. We were hoping Harry would still be alive when we arrived.

Distance kept Harry apart from us all the last years of his life. We only really saw him when he came to Dark Harbor in the summer. He would stay in the Brown House Barn, which had originally belonged to Albert Hadley.

Harry Parish III.

His children, Michael and Jessica, would be there at the same time. He was a strict but caring father. It was unfortunate they always lived so far apart; it made it hard on all of them.

The passage of time has only served to remind me how kind he was to me. Whenever his name comes up, it is always with tales of his loyalty, friendship, and the good times we all had with him.

JESSICA PARISH: Sister called us all "pet," but, although I may be wrong, I think she did have her favorites. She definitely did feel something special for me. I don't know if that was because I was one of the youngest grandchildren or because I was her son's daughter. I think that Sister felt a special attachment toward me and my brother, Michael, particularly after my father died. I think that, as time went on, she was very proud of me and thought highly of me, but that didn't come easily. That took a long time to figure out. It wasn't something that was just given.

JOAN DILLON DE MOUCHY: Young Harry showed up in Luxembourg when Charlie died. The phone rang, and I said, "Oh, Harry, you are so nice to call. Thank you so much." And he said, "I'm downstairs." He'd come. I always felt that he turned up at crucial moments. He was terribly special. I wrote Sister and said that I thought I was the only girl in Harry's life who had never had a fling with him.

He ended up becoming very glamorous when he was in Britian. He was just relaxed and knew heaps of people.

VIRGINIA VALENTINE (family friend): Young Harry was a real homebody. He loved creating almost a nest for himself. He was very careful about which paintings he had and where he put them, saying, "Now use this and don't use that." He had excellent taste.

LANDON THOMAS (family friend): I was a little bit in awe of Harry Parish [III] because he was older than I, and just a year made a huge difference at that age. We all went to Harvard together and were in the Porcellian Club. Harry was a pretty overpowering personality, and in those days we all behaved badly, because everyone did. Everyone drank a lot. There were people on the fringe who, in retrospect, were alcoholics, but nobody knew that then.

I remember when I was about fifteen and staying on Kellogg's Island. Harry came over from Dark Harbor to spend the night. My sister, Nina, had a friend over from North Haven to spend the night also. Harry suggested that

D.B., Sister, and Apple heading out for the evening.

we hide out in their room. I don't remember how we got in, but somehow we did, and we hid in the closet. It was before the girls went to bed. They came in and were reading, and we were in the closet, and I didn't know what to do. Harry seemed quite sure of what he wanted to do. In the end, it turned out that we didn't do anything except sit there for a while. We were nervous, or at least I was. We gradually snuck out, and what that achieved, I don't know, but it was typical of Harry. That was the sort of thing we all did. It was immediately held up as a big coup.

RANDOLPH HARRISON (family friend): Harry and I were sandbox playmates in Far Hills; then we graduated to more grown-up activities in Dark Harbor. I guess I knew Harry about as long as I knew anybody. I think of him, remember him now, as the "Hawk," which was his sobriquet in college. The Hawk was smoother, much smoother, than the rest of us. He had great charm and an appeal that attracted "older" girls.

Today, after all these years, I can see Harry's face, hear his voice, his laughter, and visualize his expressions. He is unforgettable.

JOHN KRAMER (family friend): Harry III was an original, with a special talent for living that infected everyone he came in contact with. I remember one July night, when we were near Baltimore on a boat trip given by an environmental group I work with. We were startled to see Harry, who had flown over for a few days to show his support of the project. The surprise was succeeded by a marvelous evening in which he entertained us and made us feel good that he was on board and was our friend. There are very few people who touch your life in that way.

SUSAN: After her husband's and son's deaths, Sister looked more toward my mother and aunt for support. This brought them closer, and Sister became more of a friend to them and less of a domineering mother.

Following page: Sister on the porch in Maine.

Chapter Twenty-One

Maine

She loved Maine. I think it was her spiritual home.

MARION FRELINGHUYSEN

SUSAN: Originally known as Long Island, Islesboro lies near the center of Penobscot Bay in mid-coast Maine. Dark Harbor is located on the southern end of the island, which is approximately thirteen miles long and three miles wide. Neighboring Seven Hundred Acre Island, where Nancy Lancaster was a frequent visitor to her aunt and uncle, the Charles Dana Gibsons, is also part of the Dark Harbor social community.

I suspect that Dark Harbor was implanted in me that first summer. The smell of fir and pine, the feel of clean salt air, and the sound of the waves against the rocks were indelibly stamped into my psyche much the same way a spawning place is stamped into the Atlantic salmon. I'm sure that I return as much by instinct as by desire.

I have never spent a summer out of the sight of my grandparents' house and the harbor and the hills and our ocean neighbors: Vinalhaven, North Haven, Deer Isle, and the dozen little "picnic islands" that dot Penobscot Bay. The view never changes, the island never changes, and the people hardly ever change.

Dark Harbor is very special to me, and I owe a lot of what I am and what I do to that island. Here I went through all the ups and downs of childhood summers, lots of friends one day, no friends the next, then a new crush, then a falling-out, then sudden popularity again. Each and every one of us who grew up in Dark Harbor, who knew the beaches, the coves, the picnics, the little movie house, the only store, the dances in the Grand Ballroom, will never forget it. It has formed a bond between us. No words have to be spoken; it is just taken for granted that our life was special.

Learning to sail, understanding the power of the waters surrounding us, made us have respect for life in a boat, however small or large the boat. The races were serious; the competition made us try and try hard. The fight for first grew strong in us, and I suspect it became an important part of my everyday thinking. I clearly remember the day I learned to tie all the ship knots. They still hold tight in my memory, and I think that they have helped not just in keeping my boat fast but in keeping my life fast as well.

Even now I can smell the pines, feel the salt air, hear the waves lapping against the rocks. At night, wherever I am, I hear the seagulls calling, and sometimes in my dreams, it is so real that I wake up and feel that I must go, be off to Dark Harbor, and right away.

APPLE: About a week before actually getting into the car and driving to Maine, my apartment in Boston is a beehive of activity. I mention the name Maine and the dogs get into a frenzy. Things get boxed up and placed in front of the elevator—things you think you can't do without, although you can, in fact, perfectly well.

Leaving early is a must to miss the traffic out of Boston and to catch the ferry in Lincolnville before the lunch break, and don't go on a Thursday, as it's "pump-out day," which causes havoc to the ferry lines. Friends who say to me, "Oh, you must stop and see us on your way up to Dark Harbor" haven't a chance, nice as they are, as getting to the island is my only thought.

Finally, we get to Camden, with its one stop sign. We pass lots of antiques shops on a boring stretch of road and then, at last, we see out over a large, lush pasture, and glimpse the first sight of the islands. Each year, it seems more beautiful: the clearness, the crispness, the sharpness of the pine trees along the shore. Finally onto the ferry, past the buoy where one of my uncles stranded my mother for being so awful, past Warren Island and then onto our island. There the smell is of pine trees, sunshine or fog. Past Mummy's Brown House, now so spiffed up, past the Town House on the left, with the apple orchard planted by Mummy and Daddy—the trees bought years ago by them at Macy's department store in New York City, past the snug little Red House on the right. Then down through the village and Billy Warren's Dark Harbor Shop. Each place your eyes go is so familiar.

The Summer House is just the same. It's early, the porch waiting for plants, the lawn down to the water green, and the lattice garden still bare and unplanted. The bench in the garden, engraved with a poem almost completely covered with lichen, reminds me most of Mummy and Daddy and their house.

The kiss of the sun for pardon,
The song of the birds for mirth,
One is nearer God's heart in a garden
Than anywhere else on earth.

SAMUEL BELL: It would start out the day before: parking the car, getting the gas. Everything necessary so it would be a smooth transition. Then I would go home and lose a lot of sleep, knowing I had to drive twelve hours.

We started leaving about 6:00 in the morning. In the front hall, there would be everything: boxes of Christmas gifts, plants galore, packages, her little suitcases, which seemed never to die out. Tons of stuff. She would say, "Where are we going to sit?" I got it all in each time, and she would come to the car and say, "Hmmm. I didn't believe you could do it."

JESSICA PARISH: I would meet my father in New York or Boston and we would fly onto the island. I loved it. Somehow, it didn't seem as stressful to fly in. With the ferry, it was more stressful, arriving and then having to wait for the boat, sitting on the ferry, and running into people whom I did not recognize. Everyone of my parents' generation and my grandparents' generation all looked the same to me. And the kids. I knew some of the kids, but I was from the West Coast, and so I would arrive out there and definitely feel like I wasn't from the East Coast, and that I was a California kid.

I can remember arriving, driving up to the Summer House. I can hear the sound of the gravel now. I remember walking across the small bridge, with the little dog graves on the left, and feeling like I had two seconds to pull myself together, and then going around that corner, and there would be Poppop sitting on the porch.

LILY LEONARD GOODALE (family friend): I've been coming to Maine with my family since I was six months old. I wish I could be among the proud few who can boast never to have missed a summer. I can't, but I will tell you, it had to be a very good reason to keep me away.

My earliest memory is the excitement my brothers and sisters and I felt the night before our scheduled departure. We tossed and turned with anticipation of the early start the next morning. We always left at 4:00 A.M., as my grandmother's chauffeur liked to make the eleven o'clock ferry. I can remember the smell of balsam as we drove up Route 1, passing familiar landmarks along the way. We would hold our breath as we crested the hill between Camden and Lincolnville. All faces would be pressed against the right window, looking out over the bay, trying to judge the distance of the ferry, praying we would make it and not have to wait for the 1:00 P.M. Rare was the occasion my grandmother's chauffeur missed the early ferry.

He was a real regular on Islesboro, a friend to all the ferrymen, and a real ladies' man. We were greeted by familiar faces aboard the ferry, the same crew year after year. One of the most exciting things was to look for people you knew, friends and relatives. We would watch the cars that departed the boat and check out all of those that were in line. Even now, at forty, I look forward to seeing those whom I know. I watch all the cars as they load and unload. The ferry ride was always a thrill, but the wait to arrive on Islesboro was excruciating. The excitement grew as we approached our house, "The House in the Village." We were always greeted by warm smells from the kitchen, friendly cooks, familiar toys, books, and the smell of the old stuffed animals passed down from generation to generation.

DOUGLAS DILLON (family friend): I was just fourteen in 1923, and to travel to Dark Harbor, we boarded the Bar Harbor Express in New York in the evening. At about five o'clock in the morning, we would arrive in Portland, where there would be a great deal of banging about as the train was broken into two sections—one of which proceeded to Ellsworth for Bar Harbor by inland route, and the other section, which was ours, proceeded along the coast as far as Rockland, stopping many places along the way. I particularly remember crossing the Kennebec River, which occurred about nine o'clock in the morning. We had to cross by ferry, as there was no bridge. The train was broken into three sections, all of which were put on the ferry, which had three sets of parallel tracks. After we got across, another engine put the train together for the rest of the trip. It was fun for us youngsters to watch the proceedings. When we got to Rockland around noon, we went down to the steamer named *Pemaquid.* Her first stop was Dark Harbor, after which she went to Castine, with a possible stop at Pripet en route.

MRS. RAY HILL (family friend): On the Fourth of July, my mother would send the maids up to Dark Harbor. They arrived early with the trunks to open up the house. If you didn't own your house, you had to send up the linen, so the trunks were shipped up. Mother took seven people up to the island to help. We had the help of island people, too, like Mrs. Dodge.

We'd get on at Penn Station at night. The trip would take just a night. We'd have a stateroom. At night, there'd be someone like Mr. Boyer on the next car, wandering about with cocktails and dinner. You'd wake up in the morning and lift up the shade, and you'd be inching along. There was a steamer that would meet the train in Rockland and take us to Islesboro. I think it made two stops. That ferry left from the tip of Islesboro and went over to Belfast. Then there was a ferry that would take people, but not cars. I think it was in 1933 that we got cars.

SUSAN: The house to which Sister was taken by horse and carriage that first summer in 1910 was built by her uncle Gustav Kinnicutt as a wedding present for Sister's paternal grandparents, Francis and Eleanora Kinnicutt.

A 1907 *House & Garden* article on the summer houses of Isleboro described the Kinnicutt cottage:

> One very individual house is that of Dr. Francis P. Kinnicutt of New York. It is situated close to the water's edge, with pine trees protecting it on three sides; red tiled roof, white plastered walls, shuttered windows with heart-shaped openings, and white awnings make it an exact reproduction of a Devonshire cottage. Surrounded by a tiny strip of brilliant green lawn, and banked with flowers, it is quite ideal.

The Summer House.

After Harry and Sister were married, they bought a rambling yellow cottage for their family on the same point as her grandparents' house. It was perfectly situated, with a lawn gently rolling to the sea. They called it the Summer House.

We have a favorite poem in our family written by the poet Rachel Field. It begins, "But—once you have slept on an island / You'll never be quite the same." People who love islands share the delight of the "secret world" aspect of an island. It appeals to us that there is a little world unto itself, where the feeling of escape is intoxicating. You can see how Sister loved the idea of hidden worlds, as the Summer House is filled with them. Going down a dirt road, the first thing one sees of the house is a hand-painted sign warning motorists to beware of dogs and children. On the left is a circular gravel driveway with several apple trees in its grassy middle. Moving toward the house, one crosses a dark green bridge with an antique bell hanging from one of its posts. A visitor can casually announce his or her arrival, but it is usually small children who hang on the bellpull, jumping up and down. A pond with still, murky green water and a mass of cattails sits to the left of the bridge. As you pass over the bridge, you are hit with a surprise view of the ocean, which cannot be seen from the driveway. At this point, you face the front door of the original part of the house, which looks like a little Maine cottage, with its garden beds lining the foundation and creeping roses that straggle up its trellises.

Sister and Susan at a costume party. Sister is in a favorite blond wig and boa.

Around the corner, the lawn cascades down a hill to the ocean. At the bottom of the hill, there are two circular gardens and a green-lattice bathing gazebo. Looking back up the hill, you see the main part of the house, which is dominated by a large porch. A dark green lattice fence shields the house and its lawns from the road.

The secret world aspect of the Summer House extends to many of its rooms, which seem to be hidden, too. The upstairs, in the oldest part of the house, is at the top of a flight of stairs so steep that many guests won't even attempt them. It is made up of just two small rooms, built under the eaves, which Sister filled with child-sized furniture, and a tiny bathroom. The floors there are so slanted that you could roll down them. Everywhere color, patterns, and objects beckon the eye.

ELIZA CRATER (Sister's great-granddaughter, age nine): On a little island in Maine, there is a yellow house that used to belong to a sea captain. After the sea captain died, a wonderful lady named Poppop put a big addition on the yellow house, which I call the Summer House. When she did this, she put in two flower gardens and a huge vegetable garden. Little did we know she was a beautiful house decorator. She could make a closet look like a ballroom.

The youngest grandchildren: Alexander, Miles, Jessica, and Harry. Bayard Gilbert is missing.

HARRY BARTLETT (Sister's grandson): I came to know my grandmother better later in her life, during family vacations on Islesboro. Though she was often tired and ailing from old age, her mind was still sharp and she was filled with her notorious acid wit. She was a great admirer of the island's artistic heritage, frequently supporting local artists, myself among them. One peculiar memory of her artistic sensibility stands out. It happened while waiting for dinner guests to arrive at dusk one August night. After they arrived, forty-five minutes late, she lambasted them, not just for their tardiness but for consequently missing the spectacle of the shifting and elongating shadows that crossed the lawn.

BAYARD E. GILBERT (Sister's grandson): Poppop liked to lounge on the porch of her yellow Summer House, surrounded by white geraniums and joined by her family and Pekinese dogs, BumbleBee, HoneyBee, and Nanny, to watch fiery orange-and-blue sunsets over neighboring Seven Hundred Acre Island. Poppop used to enjoy a quick afternoon dip in the ocean before supper. She requested that her "Babykins" (me) join her, because I was the youngest grandchild. I recall that "Babykins" did not enjoy the cold Maine water as much as she did. I was more interested in searching for crabs under the rocks and slippery bubbled seaweed. Poppop would let me have my pick of wicker baskets to keep my pet crabs in. These brown wicker baskets, all shapes and sizes, were scattered throughout her houses and garages. I can remember barreling up the grass path between the Brown House and barn in her red station wagon. I was getting bounced between her dogs and the baskets of geraniums. I don't remember the objective of our mission, but she was probably looking for just the right pot or basket for her flowers.

CHARLIE BARTLETT (Sister's grandson): I typically saw my grandmother in Maine, where she had established a number of houses for her children and grandchildren to congregate every summer. She had a strong sense of how everything in the houses should look, and that went for her family's houses, too. I could have fun driving her crazy by saying "couch" instead of "sofa," which she insisted on.

As a kid, I wasn't supposed to touch anything, let alone sit down. I recall her caretaker, Wallace Leach, saying that he didn't like walking in the houses he was paid to maintain, for fear of breaking something.

I went to boarding school in the early seventies and grew up with role models like Jim Morrison, Jimi Hendrix, and Janis Joplin. This was quite a

Sister with Miles and Alexander Gilbert.

culture shock for my parents, though they were exposed to my style on a daily basis, and they finally acclimated themselves. In the seventies, those in the counterculture were called "freaks," even somewhat proudly by their own members, such as I. Poppop had a strong and assertive personality and tried to get me to conform. It was a constant and fruitless battle, which served only to create a gap between us. Poppop and I had little common ground, but the fact that she was attracted to nonconformists—particularly those who weren't her descendants or "charges"—kept us together. Even though she was seemingly straight and WASPy on the outside, many of her friends fell outside of the class that prides itself on being rigidly exclusive and isolated. We shared an interest in less orthodox types. Maybe that was because her extensive and challenging career allowed her to appreciate many elements of society. Also, maybe she was just bored with the same old monotony.

The other bridge between us was the allure of Islesboro. The island has everything I want and is as close to a perfect vacation place as I can imagine. For a long time, those two weeks on the island were the highlight of my year. Dark Harbor was the perfect place to overcome our differences. Poppop created that environment, and, for that, I am eternally grateful.

Sister with Apple, D.B., and grandchildren.

PETER GATES: Dark Harbor is a fifth-generation resort. Certainly it goes back to the 1850s. People there now are certainly connected umbilically. They marry among themselves, and it is certainly a world created for their own satisfactions. I think it has probably the most downscale yacht club and golf course in the world.

LAURA LEONARD AULT: In those days, we had night picnics that were very elaborate. Everything was taken down to the beach. They'd cook some of the food up at the house and take it down, or it would be cooked down there. It wasn't a bit like the type of picnics people have today. Perhaps eight people would help. It took the men two days to prepare, digging the pits and putting in all the rocks. A two-day performance to have everything just perfect. And it *was* perfect. Ruth Draper and Mrs. Howe used to do their monologues at picnics. They used to have separate fires and their own spots. They were marvelous.

Then we had picnics on boats. We used to do deep-sea fishing on the Marshall Fields' boat. They had three or four to crew and we'd go miles away. All the way to Matinicus. It was an all-day adventure. There were ocean liners in Camden Harbor—gigantic boats, big enough to cross the Atlantic. They were so glamorous, with these huge crews and people who lived on them. You knew everyone then. It was a different time.

People didn't feel they had to work in the summer during those days. They'd have a good time. There were a lot of girls and boys with not much to do, so they'd have these dances. The Islesboro Inn was an integral part of life then. People went down a steep flight of stairs and there were bathhouses where you could change your clothes. They had a little jetty that went out into the pool.

During the war, it was very hard to get around because nobody had gas. They would take the men up to play golf and then bring them back for lunch. They'd go up again in the afternoon. They didn't have tennis courts. Those were put in after the war. We spent months up there because we went up from New York much earlier than usual. We didn't have gas in New York and we couldn't get around, but up on Islesboro you could ride a bicycle. It was 1943 and all the men had gone away. The social life during the war wasn't much. There was no one to take care of the greens. We'd go back and forth for dinner and cards. Papa, Sally Gowen, and a lot of people from Philadelphia played cards—some domino game. Then we played canasta and gin rummy, and some people played bridge. That's how I got to know Sister. I'd be the fourth to play gin rummy or canasta because there weren't too many people and all the houses were closed. The ones that were open were operating on a reduced scale. We were rather all in one boat together. We had one radio and we'd all listen to that for news of the war, huddled around it, with the antennae way up. We could get Europe. Mama bought the best you could get for radios because my brother, Charlie, was stationed in India, and my sister, Jessie, was driving an ambulance in England.

NAT GOODALE (family friend): We'd off-load wicker picnic baskets and walk along a single path through pine scent and bay leaves to the sweeping beach and sloping sand of Jabez.

Our tasks were limited to gathering driftwood for the fire and keeping ourselves entertained. To us, the grown-ups were a blur (perhaps they felt the same, as cocktails were replenished). They did not swim, as we did, in sand-filled bathing suits on floating logs and beach-combed Styrofoam. I've come to know now how cold the water is, but then we were numbed and felt the chill only when we got out of the water and stood in the cool breeze. The adults drank and chatted while we stood in towels beside the fire. The billowing smoke always followed us and stung our eyes.

The picnic hampers were emptied of hamburgers and hot dogs and marshmallows and later refilled with dirty glasses and scraps of wax paper. My grandmother's favorite beach dessert was guava jelly on smoke-toasted bread. To this day, that taste still brings back all this innocence and the sight of my grandmother's skinny legs.

As the adventure concluded, we'd traipse barefoot on pine needles back to the Jeep in damp shorts, our hair tossed, not nearly as exuberant, and ready for a nap on top of the covers of our own beds beneath the swaying sun-soaked curtains and gentle afternoon sounds of distant boats coming through the open window.

Picnics represented the carefree calmness of summer. They still do. I've never left Penobscot Bay, and I still watch the parade of cousins, now with children of their own to play with my children. The coves and tides remain constant and we still scrape sand away, build fires, cook food, watch the children swim, and marvel at how they can stand the cold water.

JESSICA PARISH: Picnics were always an experience. We would go off on a picnic with Poppop on a boat we hired, or on somebody else's boat to Deer Isle or wherever. You'd arrive and there would be Susan and maybe Charlie, and all these older people. They'd be drinking Bloody Marys, and then they'd cook steaks for us on a rock. You'd heat a flat stone in a fire and put these really thinly sliced pieces of meat on it. First of all, I was a vegetarian for most of my teenage years, but I certainly did like Bloody Marys a lot. I also think that all they'd bring to drink were Bloody Marys. So I wouldn't eat the steak, and I'd drink the Bloody Marys, and by the time I got on the boat and got home, I was a total wreck.

VIRGINIA VALENTINE: Dark Harbor was a matriarchy. Well, I think that women learned to do a lot during World War II. It made it okay for a woman to be strong, and okay for a woman to be in control of something, and I think women changed society with their own behavior.

LILY LEONARD GOODALE: My grandmother, Mrs. Leonard, was called "Mama" (pronounced *MaMah*) and she was one of the grande dames. She lived in a huge Tudor house on a point; it was called Indian Head. She also owned the house we stayed in. Her house was big and scary inside. It was always dark and cool. She served tea on her sunporch every afternoon and everyone was invited. We spent hours swimming on her beach and rowing as far as we could in a boat that was usually kept tied to a tree. We had many picnics on her beach. She also owned a beach that was within walking distance, called "glass beach." It was a beach literally covered in sea glass.

MAISIE HOUGHTON: Maine appealed to women who wanted to build little empires. They could inherit the big old house or buy some land and set up little houses for their children.

JAMIE HOUGHTON: I'd never seen anything like the matriarchy here. It's just unbelievable. Not taking anything from the men, but I just think there was an extremely strong group of women here. I don't remember this being true in Marion, Massachusetts, down on the Cape where I grew up.

There was a little ritual that we had to go through when we first came. We used to go call on the grande dames. We'd call on Mrs. Leonard to start with, as she was the oldest grande dame around; then there was Sister, Irene (Kinnicutt), Ibbie Holmquist, and Ellie Choate. The minute we arrived, we had to make certain calls, and Sister was one of them.

SUSAN: Sister and her first cousin Ibbie were lifelong friends and rivals. They were both reigning Dark Harbor grande dames. Their mothers, May and Elizabeth Tuckerman, were sisters. They loved to fight, and both of them were very good at it. They said the most awful things to each other and would

Judges at the Dark Harbor Dog Show. Ibbie Holmquist at center, Lily Guest at right, Susan and Yummy in front.

vow never to speak again. The next day, one would invariably call the other to ask what she was going to wear that night. You have to understand how formidable these women were. You could not believe the bite of their words and the sheer power they wielded over their family and friends. Ibbie was an extraordinary painter, and I think she was always mad that Sister got more recognition, when she was probably just as talented. Many of her children and grandchildren are talented painters, as well. She had the most beautiful house in Maine. Her house, called Long Ledge, had great style.

CARL-PETER BRAESTRUP: I am the grandson of Sister's best friend and cousin, Elizabeth Elkins "Ibbie" Holmquist. I called her "Aunt Sister." Which is always funny, because when I'd talk about my aunt Sister, people would ask, "What's that about?" We are a family with names like "GaGa," which is what

I called my grandmother, Aunt Apple, Aunt Ev, Aunt D.B. A family of odd names. My own nickname is C.P.

In Dark Harbor, I was related to almost everyone, what with twenty first cousins who are all similar in appearance. One of the rituals of the summer was going around to greet the other grande dames, like Ellie Choate and Sister Parish. She always terrified me and I was very aware of everything I said, and whether I'd said the appropriate thing or if I had put my foot in it somehow.

GaGa and Aunt Sister were relatively young women when they were already in the role of grande dame and of Dark Harbor matriarchs. I can remember that for a couple of summers I did a sort of taxi service and picked up people at the airport, among them Aunt Sister and Albert Hadley and some other person. Aunt Sister had the worst cars. Her island car was a horrible, junky little four-door Chevette hatchback. I was so scared of Aunt Sister that not only did I get us lost on the way back from the airport in Bangor but I also didn't know the trick for getting the key out of the ignition. Well, I stripped the key and twisted the ignition, so it was spinning and spinning, and there was some question about whether I could get the car started. It was only by luck that I sort of jammed the key in and the engine turned over. I was quaking with fear that she would figure out that not only had I had broken the car but also that I would delay us. There were four adults in this small green clown car.

I used to stay at my grandmother's house, in the room she'd had as a child, and I used the bathroom she'd used as a child. On the walls was the same wallpaper, as the room hadn't been redone in fifty years, and on the wall in crayon was a list of my grandmother's friends. There at the top of the list is Dot, which was Sister's childhood name, Dot being short for Dorothy. And it's just amazing that it was always such a strong sign to me. Every summer, I would go and look at that list. Looking back, it's sort of strange, because I was fully aware of their back-and-forth arguments and the feud they had going on. So, as a model of friendship, it was hardly ideal. On the other hand, there was this longevity and this sense of devotion, despite all this turbulence and this constant uproar and upheaval: That's one thing you could count on in that relationship: Good or bad, it was there for life.

LAURA LEONARD AULT: We had marvelous costume parties at the old Islesboro Inn. The inn and the ballroom were attached, and at the ballroom, we all sat with the girls, separate from the boys. Then we'd all agonize, waiting for someone to come ask us to dance. If you became too unpopular, you'd pretend you had to go to the bathroom, and then you'd come back again. The inn was a great sprawling white thing, but they tore it down because it was too expensive to run. My father, Mr. Field, Mr. Dillon, and certain other people used to put up money to keep it going.

IRENE KINNICUTT: In Dark Harbor, it was grander a long time ago. Mr. Dillon, Ruth Field (Mrs. Marshall Field), and the Aldriches had huge parties. Everyone got dressed up. There were cocktail parties, and it was the same then as now, but less crowded. It was old money. It was who you were, not what you had. Things were more formal, but simpler. All well arranged, but not a big deal.

I love Dark Harbor. I have a seagull that has come for at least twenty-five years. When the house is opened for the summer, she flies around, and when she sees that I have arrived, she comes to me right away. When I drive up the driveway, she comes. I give her the same old crackers year after year. She always acts the same. When I am swimming, she hovers over me.

MAISIE HOUGHTON: The summer of 1969 was the first year I returned to the island. I was married to Jamie Houghton, and Sister was glad that newlyweds were coming back to the island. That was the last gasp of the old era, when people still wore black tie to dinner parties. Mr. Dillon was still giving his dances then.

The house in Dark Harbor, at the end of Kissel Point Road, where Irene Kinnicutt now lives, was the Kinnicutts' original house. During the flush days when Grandma and Grandpa Kinnicutt were rich, the Kinnicutts lived in the big house next door, which was torn down later. After my father died, my mother sold our house, so for ten years I didn't go back to Dark Harbor.

We bought that little yellow house on the road and moved in about 1971. A Maine house has everything in it—beds and bureaus—and you just move in.

JAMIE HOUGHTON: I adored Sister, but it took a little time. When you first meet her, you are a little scared. Here is this imposing woman, who is liable to say something extraordinarily insulting to you the first time that she meets you. It was either Sister or Aunt Ibbie who said, when I first came here, "Oh, well, you're better than we thought. We thought you were going to be blond and fat."

What I learned from very early on was that she loved to bully, and the way to get her was to bully right back—just to stand toe-to-toe and not to take it for a second. She'd throw an insult at me, and I'd throw one back at her. We just had this understanding. I never walked into a room but that she didn't look up and then the barb would come—*zoom*—and I would be ready with one to fling right back at her. Once she got the upper hand, she'd keep going. She'd bury you. I learned early on that if you let her bury you, then you could forget it. I'd talk about her ugly little dogs. I learned that was exactly the way to treat her. It was perfect, and I think we developed a great affection. Another thing I remember is that she would lie right through her teeth. Give you a few little lies to get the conversation going. Total exaggeration. After I had my accident, I was driving a golf cart around here. She came up to me and said, "You know, it's illegal to drive golf carts on the road here in Dark Harbor." The next day, I saw her in her golf cart on the road, so I said, "For Christ's sake, I thought you said it was illegal." She said, "I'm a ghost," and drove on.

When we first bought the yellow house, I wanted to cut a path down to the shore for the kids to use when they went swimming. I got into deep poison ivy and really had it badly. I was just a mess with the stuff. I remember Sister sitting there and saying, "That is ridiculous. There is *no* poison ivy on the island." I was almost dead. "There is *no* poison ivy in Dark Harbor." It didn't bother her at all.

APPLE: We had three ponies that we kept in Camden in the winter and in the yellow barn behind the Town House in the summer. Kangaroo, who was either a large pony or a small horse, detested children and used to pull Santa's sleigh in Camden every Christmas, biting every child in sight. Kangaroo was the type of animal Mummy liked—contrary. He had one green eye and one brown eye, and a mean glint in both of them. Mummy would hitch him up to an antique wicker cart called a "governess cart" and charge around the island with children bumping up and down beside her. She didn't know how to drive a cart, and Kangaroo definitely had a mind of his own. He hated that cart and he went absolutely anywhere he wanted.

One of Mummy's favorite pastimes was snooping around other people's houses. She liked to check on a new garden, a new porch, or any tiny improvement or addition. The ponies came in handy here. One day, she decided to check on my uncle Frankie's house in the village, which had recently been sold to some "new people." She and Kangaroo went down the main road,

(above) Sister driving
Kangaroo in the
Governess cart.

(left) Sister with Susan
and Charlie in the
Governess cart.

through the hedge outside of Frankie's house, and up the steps of the front porch, to the front door, and just as Mummy was stealing a peek inside, the girth slipped, flipping her under Kangaroo's side. Kangaroo became nervous and trotted out the front door, down the steps, back through the hedge, and deposited her in the village, at the center of town, at Mrs. Earles' gift shop. All the while, Mummy was trying to explain what had happened and to right herself, pride intact, though she had fallen off and broken her coccyx.

NANCY BREED (family friend): I remember going in the pony cart with Mrs. Parish, Susan and Harry, and sometimes Lily and Jessie. She would take us down the road by Mrs. Hale's cottage. I remember being warned that the pony kicked and bit and to stay away from both ends. Being in the governess cart was like sitting in a big wicker basket. You climbed in the back and sat on little benches. We'd trot and walk. She really made an event out of it.

WILHELMINA PENDLETON (island resident): Mrs. Parish had one good dog, named Ricky. He was so timid that the other dogs just had to look at him and he'd get out of the way. Mrs. Parish got him as a puppy. Ricky was one big knot, so she took him and got him clipped. When she got home, Mrs. Parish went into the house and left the dog in the car. She told me, "When you see Ricky, don't laugh at him. They pick up on these things."

They'd clipped him so that he had a ball on the end of his tail and a mane just like a lion. He looked at Nanny and the other dogs and just roared like a lion.

I told Mrs. Parish, "My God, Ricky went and got courage."

PAUL AND MARILYN PENDLETON (island residents): She had a sign down there that said BE ON THE LOOKOUT FOR DOGS AND CHILDREN. The word *dogs* came first.

APPLE: When houseguests of my friends come to the Dark Harbor dog show and refer to it jokingly as the "Woof Woof Show" or the "*Chien* Show," I completely lose my sense of humor and stare at them coldly, as I imagine my mother would have. I started the show with Phyllis and Fiona Field when I was ten years old. That was fifty-five years ago. Their wonderful maid, Kusi, made the ribbons. The Fields' chauffeur, Haslum, put up the ring. I'm sure in the beginning we just wanted to make some money. So instead of having lemonade stands, and as we were totally animal-crazy, a dog show seemed like a good idea. Obviously, Mummy and Daddy thought it best to give the proceeds to some good cause. The first year, the money went to fix the gutters at Christ Church; the next, to help purchase a font for christenings. As the years went by, we had a silent auction, which was extremely funny, with everyone bidding large amounts of money for local artwork—some very good and some really quite awful. One year, Mr. Douglas Dillon signed a one-hundred-dollar bill to be auctioned off. As he was then the secretary of the treasury, the bidding got very spirited, with his father, Mr. Clarence Dillon, upping the ante and then dropping out at the last moment.

The rules haven't changed—no adults in the ring, children only, with exceptions for enormous dogs being shown by very small children, and no dogs from off the island.

Preparations for the show itself start weeks before, when we get some responsible and hopefully enthusiastic children to help make the ribbons, draw or paint posters and put these in all public places, order the ice cream, and call the judges, announcer, and ticket takers.

The ring is always set up the night before, with American flags on each post. In the old days, it was placed in what was a field of Queen Anne's lace and daisies, but now that same field has become a manicured lawn—carefully taken care of and mowed—especially for the day of the dog show.

I remember Mum calling me every morning for about a week preceding the show to ask me if I had called Mr. Dillon to borrow his dog umbrella stand to put up at the gate. Had I called Aunt Ibbie to borrow her megaphone for the announcer? Had I called all the judges and ticket takers, and did I have enough ice-cream cones and napkins? She'd say, "And do you remember what a mess it was last year when you didn't have enough cones and people used napkins to hold their ice cream? It was disgusting. Don't let that happen ever again!"

It was my first day in South Africa, when I was feeling so lonely and lost. I knew that was the day of the dog show in Dark Harbor, and I thought of my wonderful Labrador, whom I just adored, YD, and I began to worry that my daughters had forgotten even to put him in a class. So I figured out the time difference and placed a call to the house in Dark Harbor. In those days, it was hard enough to get through to Dark Harbor from New York, but I happened to hit it on the nose. The moment I got through, I could hear clapping from the porch in Dark Harbor, and the clapping was for YD, who'd just won the grand championship. Imagine! Well . . . I burst into tears. That time, it was tears of joy.

ANNETTE DE LA RENTA: Remember the charm of the dog show and the trauma if your dog was asked to leave the ring? Remember Yummy? Every time he bit one of us, Sister would say how wonderful he was. Until I made it as a judge, it was just the worst thing in the whole world. I remember Mr. Dillon bought a drawing of mine at the auction. It was so exciting.

NANCY BREED: I had my dog, Penny and sometimes I would go in with various borrowed dogs. Some called them "borrowed," but others called them "stolen." We used to practice for the dog show, teaching them tricks. Remember Barnie, the minister's dog? He was one of the "stolen" dogs. Remember Bambie, the Chanlers' dog? She could dive for a rock in the water. That was in the trick class. It was one of the only times the entire dog show had to go down to the beach.

JESSIE LEONARD REID (family friend): At the dog show, Mrs. Parish would sit on the porch, watching everything. She looked happy, but she always made me nervous because she was very strict. All of the children looked perfect then, and they still do. When we were little, we were made to dress perfectly

Dark Harbor Dog Show.

in our clothes, which we bought in England. Even so, I remember going to see Mrs. Parish with Susan and not feeling quite right. As we got older, we wore T-shirts and shorts, and all of the older generation disapproved of us. My grandmother, Mama, and Mrs. Parish were friends, and they felt the same about our clothes. In Maine, we had our freedom, as our children do now.

SANDRA S. KRAMER (family friend): The summer of 1972 was the first summer my family and I spent on Islesboro. The Kramers were new members of the Tarrantine Club, and while we certainly were not the youngest club members, we were described as the "hippiest." John, my husband, had a twirling mustache, a huge belly, and drove a broken-down Buick convertible that the little boys loved. I wore long skirts and blue jeans and was in the midst of my most active women's movement work. I was on the telephone all day with my office in Washington, D.C., directing my staff. They were at the 1972 Republican Presidential Nominating Convention in Miami, Florida, working on women's political reform issues. I was exhausted from a yearlong national effort to get women delegates to both conventions. Thus, I didn't protest a lot when the boys did not always wear what I wanted them to wear, their white shorts and white polo shirts.

When we departed for the Dark Harbor Dog Show, I don't even remember looking at the boys' clothes. As we walked across Sister's beautiful lawn and took our seats on the grassy hill overlooking the show ring, I saw Sister approaching us. She was carrying her new Pekingese puppy. Before I could say hello, she went straight for Christopher, my oldest stepson, and thrust the Pekingese into his arms, commanding, "You are going to show Desmond." Christopher was speechless, and I was horrified. He was wearing the T-shirt from the Lobster Festival, with a huge wide-open mouth and a gigantic tongue protruding from the mouth. I don't remember what this bit of awfulness signified, but I do know that, for once, even my husband was aghast. Christopher was going to show Sister Parish's new puppy at the Dark Harbor dog show wearing a T-shirt with a huge tongue on it. Well, he did it. Around and around the ring with the adorable Pekingese he went. I can't remember whether or not the dog won or lost, but we do have wonderful photos of Christopher and Sister and her adorable puppy. She never said a word about Chris's T-shirt.

JAMIE HOUGHTON: If you described the dog show to anyone who didn't live here, they'd lock you up. I have always said that I do the easy part, because all

I do is the announcing. The judges are the ones who have to make the decisions. I think it's just a marvelous institution, and that it has lasted this long is just a wonderful tribute to Sister. It's just goes on and on, and gets stronger every year. I had such fun insulting her at every dog show. We always had such a wonderful time with that. Now she's gone and I can't tease her anymore.

SUSAN: Sister was the queen of Dark Harbor's gossip mill. When the Hollywood group arrived, so unlike the rest of Dark Harbor's summer people, and not entirely welcome to everyone, Sister was thrilled and made it a point to get to know them first. She loved new people. When Kirstie Alley and Parker Stevenson bought the old Islesboro Inn, Sister was one of the first people to be invited for dinner. Apparently, there were a number of actors staying there that weekend. One of them staggered down for cocktails the night she went and sat next to Sister. She asked him the traditional Dark Harbor question: "Well, what did you do today?" She meant which sport had he played or which beach had he sailed to. The famous actor looked at her, patting his wet hair as he spoke, and said, "Me? I just got up." To a seasoned member of the old guard, this was pure blasphemy.

When John Travolta and his wife, Kelly Preston, bought the Drexel cottage, Sister asked them over for drinks. Immediately, she wanted to know what they were all about. When John asked for juice instead of alcohol, she said, "John, there are so many things that I don't know about you. For example, why don't you take a drink?" John and Kelly totally charmed her and she delighted in making them welcome on the island, knowing they would be a great addition.

That is the way that Dark Harbor is run. The older generation has all of the information and they pass judgment based on that knowledge.

PARKER STEVENSON (actor and island summer resident): Kirstie Alley and I first bought property on an island in Maine in the spring of 1991. Sister played an irreplaceable role, not only in bringing life to our new home through work on one of our houses there but in also welcoming us to the community and making us feel a viable part of the activities and social life of the island.

Her wry humor and generous counsel eased our way and made us feel that we belonged. In addition to sponsoring our introduction to the community, Sister not only welcomed us into her own home but made us feel a welcome addendum to her own family. In time, I began to escort Sister to a weekly Sunday-morning church service. I remember Sister's comment after we endured a particularly endless and uninspiring sermon. She quipped, "That alone will guarantee that we get into heaven."

ALICE ROGERS: Sister had a real recognition of the year-round residents' place on this island, and that the rest of us were really just visitors or interlopers in a sense. She felt that certainly we had an investment here in terms of loving it and spending our time here and having our children grow up here in the summers, but nonetheless, she thought that the island truly belonged to the people who have lived here for generations. She knew about all the families.

APPLE: Mummy and Daddy were lucky to have wonderful friendships with the loyal year-round people on Islesboro. Daddy, of course, knew the island residents very well, as he lived there year-round at the end of his life. Mummy was a relentless taskmaster, but she loved the people of the island and she respected them. As a result, many, like Mildred Hale, were her lifelong friends. They added so much to Mummy and Daddy's life with their great humor, their island quirks, and a shared love of the island.

RALPH GRAY: I didn't do much for Mrs. Parish. Mostly, I put up with her. Just about everybody called her Sister, except for the people who worked for her. I knew her since the time we were both kids.

ANNETTE DE LA RENTA: Mrs. Hale cooked for us all the time, until Mummy and Daddy would arrive with their chef. Otherwise, it was Mrs. Hale and local people. I lived on Mrs. Hale's blueberry pie.

I remember laughing with Bernard Pendleton, the painter, and I've never had a garden as beautiful as the one Paul Pendleton did for me on the old tennis court. Never have I seen such a beautiful garden, with the delphinium ten feet tall. It was because of the island air. It was just a magical world.

WILHELMINA PENDLETON: I'll tell you about jacking up the bed. Mrs. Parish slept in a very high four-poster canopy bed and she had a beautiful pink-and-white rag rug on the floor underneath it. She wanted the rug turned over, because the sun shone in through the windows and it had faded. I told her that when I cleaned in the spring, I'd have Wallace help me pick up the bed. Well, I asked Wallace, and asked Wallace. Every day for a week, I asked Wallace and he said he'd be up in the morning, but he never came. So I said to my daughter, "There's got to be some goddamn way that you and I can turn that rug."

So I decided to get a car jack, and, sure enough, there was a bumper jack in my car. So I told my daughter to crawl under the bed and to shove it way back because the front legs weren't setting on the rug, only the back legs. So we hauled it down, jacked up the bed, and turned the rug over, then put everything back.

Mrs. Parish said, "Doesn't the rug look nice. Did you have any trouble?"

CAROLYN LEACH (island resident): Serving breakfast in bed to Mrs. Parish was my first job as a teenager. My cousin cooked and I served. Her breakfast was always supposed to be ready at seven o'clock, but being teenagers, we arrived at her house five minutes before it was due to be served and threw it together. If she reamed us out, we probably just laughed it off because we were kids. That first job was good training, though. She taught me a lot about setting up a breakfast tray and serving.

Years later, my husband, Wallace, became her caretaker. He did her flowers and her vegetables, as well as some of the carpentry and repairs to her different houses, for twenty years. They got along well. There were tense moments, but there were good moments, too. Mrs. Parish was a family person, and she treated everyone who worked for her like extended family.

JACK LEACH (island resident): Mrs. Parish called me once to go to the West Side of New York, to a place called the Painted Wagon, and pick up a load of furniture for Kirstie Alley. When I got back to the island and was unloading it, Mrs. Parish said, "I'll bet you ten dollars you didn't get the umbrella stand." I had, I told her. She said that she bet I hadn't. She bet me ten dollars that I hadn't.

I framed the check and the letter that she wrote me saying that I'd won the bet. I'll never cash that check. When she was busy, she was all business. She was tough and gruff and knew what she wanted. When she lost, she admitted it. She was as good as she was stubborn. That's what makes Islesboro tick, people like her.

DOREA ENGSTROM (island resident): You could hear her coming *putt-putt-putt* down the center of the road in her golf cart. She traveled right in the middle of the road.

Mrs. Parish was a lady who did not take no for an answer. I worked most of the time here for Mrs. Homans, and I had two or three other jobs. She called me and said, "Mrs. Homans told me that you'd close my house in the fall and open it back up in the spring." I said, "I can't. I'm too tired and I don't think that I have time."

"Well, you have to," she commanded. "You have to." Then she just hung up. She didn't know the meaning of the word *no,* so you didn't say no to her.

ALCE ROBERTSON: The best, most wonderful story I've got about Mrs. Parish, and the thing that I'll remember most about both of the Parishes, is when she asked me once which Broadway play I'd like to see. I told her *Camelot.* Next thing you know, she had all the arrangements made. She said, "Take that car and go to New York. Stop at my apartment and pick up the tickets. Your reservations are at Sardi's." The headwaiter was already tipped. She told me, "Just ask for Mrs. Dixon's table." Mrs. Dixon was the actress on TV who starred in *Playhouse 90.* She had a place here on the island at that time.

It was wonderful. She was a good friend, Mrs. Parish. She never called me without saying, "I love you." Just before she died, I went into her room. She took my hand and said, "I love you, Alce." We'd laughed so much, and it was all such good-hearted fun.

MARK HAMPTON: Is there anywhere more charming than Maine? Sister inaugurated these Columbus Day parties at Dark Harbor. Blue skies. Beautiful. We never had an ugly day, and we must have done it for five years. We'd go up, everyone from the office. One year, it was Bill Hodgins, Kevin McNamara, and Bunny, as well as some people I didn't know when I wasn't part of the staff. Sister would always stay at the Summer House and the rest of us were stashed around at the Town House or the Brown House, and then there were people like Ibbie Holmquist who would put someone up. The Brown House was the cutest thing you've ever seen. It was all sorts of rainbow colors: pale blue and shots of lavender and scarlet. A real color story. Albert owned the barn. He knew I loved to paint, and he loved to paint, so he'd laid in some paints and canvases. The living room had a lavender sofa. Well, honestly, have you ever seen a lavender sofa? And Albert had all that bone color and beige and white in the barn. That was just the most wonderful room. Everyone who likes houses has this fantasy, I think, about a room in a barn— the beams, the space, the airiness. There'd be people like Barbara Drum there, and I remember one year Mrs. Wells came, and there was always a fancy-dress night. Sometimes it was just fancy headdress. I'll never forget when Mrs. Wells came walking into that chintz room in that tiny house with those green

Sister and Gory dancing at the Parish-Hadley Columbus Day weekend costume party.

painted floors. She had on this incredible mauve caftan, with mauve satin shoes and a little mauve satin handbag. And diamond bracelets and two big emerald rings. Almost matching. Quite marvelous. She had this great tall headdress that nearly touched the ceiling. I don't know how she made it. All this sort of unexpected delight.

Then we'd sit down, dressed in our costumes, to that marvelous fish chowder with potatoes and pork rind. It's a marvelous soup. Dinner would be whatever it was and then a great pie. Then Mrs. Hale would come out of the kitchen and do her Dark Harbor stories, these little monologues, which were hilarious: "Lady with the Name of a Bird" and "Man with the Name of a Tree." It never failed to delight. It would just be better than the time before.

BUNNY WILLIAMS: Everyone went to the extreme at the costume parties. Mark Hampton came once as the Queen Mother.

You'd be on the floor, because there was no one funnier than Mrs. Parish was. It was the rubber nose; it was the pillow in the bosom. It was no costume . . . just the funny hat that she managed to put on backward or some blond wig she'd find. She was always, without a doubt, the most outrageous.

Mrs. Parish would always come to meet us at the ferry in an old pair of rolled-up khakis, L. L. Bean khakis, and her Top-Siders. And her hair—that perfect hair that was always beautiful—and here she had on a hair net. It was her Maine getup. That was the difference between her and someone like Diana Vreeland. Mrs. Parish could look very elegant and very New York, but when she went up to Maine, she looked like she belonged in Maine. She was not addicted to style. Mrs. Vreeland looked fantastic in New York, but, out of her element, she didn't know what to do. I remember one weekend when Mrs. Vreeland came to visit. It was so foggy, and she said, "Now I understand why they call it Dark Harbor." Diana was fine at night, when she could put on her caftan and jewelry, but during the day she was frightening, absolutely frightening.

MARIO BUATTA: I stayed in the Brown House. I was so thrilled to get up to Maine. I was with Dorothy Robinson, and we called Mrs. Parish and I said, "Guess who is on the island." She said, "I know. You had better come over." I said, "Maybe tomorrow." She said, "No. Right now."

So we went over and sat in the living room, where she was. We were there well over an hour, chatting, and when we got up to go, I said, "Sister, this is such a pretty house. I so look forward to seeing it." She took me to the door and said, "This is all you are seeing." She was up to her tricks. For the rest of the week, I didn't see her, and when I wanted to say good-bye, she received us in the guest room. She had had the vapors the entire time. So I got to see the guest room and that was it.

BILL HODGINS: We went up for the Fourth of July, Edward Cave and I. We had to ask Albert what kind of clothes we should take. Albert said to take a jacket and a tie. I asked, "Aren't we going to the country?" So we packed our bags and got on a plane up to Maine.

Then, of course, we spent the weekend changing clothes. We'd have breakfast, go out and play tennis, go to lunch, and then we'd go for a swim, and then we'd have tea, and then we'd have a nap, and then we'd get up and have dinner. On and on, the whole weekend. Sister took us out on a boat to go swimming. I have never been in such cold water in my life. The Great Lakes are warm compared to that. I got in and got back out. Practically bounced off the water and got back into the boat. I never swam again.

I remember another time, when Duane Hampton was on the chaise on the porch at the Summer House. I was just wandering around, and way off in the distance we heard a motorboat pulling someone on skis. Someone was screaming, "Hi, hi, hi." I looked at Duane, and she said, "That's probably Mark. He never stops." He was out in the bay. She kept right on reading.

HAROLD SIMMONS: What I will never forget is the time she took us for a ride in her speedboat. It was truly one of the most terrifying experiences of my life. She was a demon behind a wheel. She had a very heavy foot. There were four or five of us on the boat, and she took us out into the bay. She zoomed around at top speed and then, on the way back, she headed straight for the dock and didn't slow down. Everyone was screaming, "Stop! Stop!" We had totally ashen faces.

EDWARD LEE CAVE: We stayed at the little house in town. I remember going to Douglas Dillon's in black-tie. Which is so different from what you'd expect going to the beach. That's the way life is up there.

SUSAN: One of the things Sister loved to do most was swim in the ocean. Like many of her friends, she liked to do it every day, either in her cove or at Ruth Field's, whose saltwater pool was built into the rocks. Swimming is a tradition that separates the old guard from the more recent arrivals, who wouldn't dream of getting in the water.

At the Summer House, at the foot of the lawn, there is a dark green lattice gazebo, which is used as a kind of bathhouse. There, Sister kept her worn Porthault terry-cloth bathrobe with its faded pink initials, DMP, her white canvas Keds, which she used as swimming shoes, and her dark blue skirted bathing suit. She always went in the water backward, with her wrists first. If we were swimming with her, she would scrutinize our bathing suits to make sure we weren't wearing anything that she would categorize as "tacky," with loud colors or garish designs. She felt that certain things, like children's clothes or bathing suits, should be in appropriate muted colors, or, preferably, white. To avoid the freezing water was a sure sign that you were somehow ill-formed or "second rate." Frequently, Noelle and Regina, the French maids who came every summer, would also be there, their high-pitched voices shrieking, "Madame" as they dipped their toes into the water.

APPLE: She made me swim until I got married. Then I said I was never going to do it again.

DAVID KLEINBERG: I remember one time I was in Maine for the weekend, and she told me we were going swimming at one of her favorite watering holes. It was at Ruth Field's old house. I don't remember if she knew the people who bought the house or not, but it was your typical pull in, leave the car at the door, and shout, "Hoo-hoo" to say that she was there. I knew that I had to go in the water, which in Maine practically has ice cubes floating in it. I knew that it was a test and that I had to go or the weekend was over. We got there and she gave me some swimming trunks—I don't know whose—and told me to change in the bushes "over there." I did that and went down to the water, thinking, This is my death.

As I dove in, I pictured my heart attack and thought, When I start dying, that old lady on the beach certainly isn't going to save me. I swam around, got out, and she handed me a robe. Well, you know what it was. One of her old terry-cloth Porthault robes with pink roses on it. We got in the car and all she said was, "Those bushes are much skimpier than I thought."

KENNETH JAY LANE: I made these earrings, cascading down with a pearl shape, and they were a great success. I made them for Sister Parish, and she wore them very often, which was great. However, I think she wore them swimming in the cold, salty waters of the state of Maine. And the earrings became the worse for wear. I had a new pair made for her, in order to keep my reputation. But she would always appear wearing the originals, minus many stones. I presented her with a new pair, thinking perhaps the new earrings had been baptized as well. To no avail. The practically bald originals appeared again and again. I gave up.

NAT GOODALE: I spent summers on Seven Hundred Acre Island, off Islesboro, on the point that my great-grandfather Charles Dana Gibson bought in 1903.

My grandfather's caretaker, Lloyd Dyer, with his khaki cap tilting rakishly and his huge grip grasping my fingers, picked us up from the ferry landing in the thirty-foot power boat.

My father was an artist. Before we started school, we'd go to Maine in April and stay through Thanksgiving. My cousins were not so fortunate. I would watch their procession, coming and going, while we remained.

Seven Hundred Acre Island is removed from Islesboro by a mile of sheltered water across to the yacht club which we still refer to as the "Western Jetty." The separation was more than physical. We were in a world all our own and we mostly held to ourselves. There was always enough fascination with the tides, raft building, hunting for small crabs beneath draped seaweed, and, in the actual summer months, the parade of cousins.

Sister and Lily Guest lead children in a dance. The Town House is in the background.

It was a thrilling adventure to traverse the island on the dirt road to Jabez cove. We children would load onto the dilapidated army Jeep, which then bristled with little tanned arms and legs in short pants, all of us testing the edge by hanging off the side. The road would turn to a grassy rutted path and finally peter out.

MRS. WILLIAM CHANLER: I lived then on Seven Hundred Acre Island and Sister was from Dark Harbor. Once my husband, my son, Bayard, and I were having lunch with Sister on the porch. Her French cook, Noelle, made us a beautiful lunch. Sister was wearing a lovely straw hat trimmed in blue velvet. She looked so lovely, and when we left, I told her so. Sister smiled and said, "I can't help it." She had the most wonderful expression on her face.

SUSAN: After her swim, she would sit on the porch with its overflowing pots of flowers and flowering trees, stiff white-cushioned chairs, chaise longues, and dark green awning. The view from the porch was of the southernmost tip of Seven Hundred Acre Island, and sailboats moored off her cove in the distance.

From her chair, she conducted business by phone to the office. She spoke in whispered and dramatic expletives, her face pained with concern or impatience: "You can't paint it green—it would be fatal," or "I can't face it, Albert. You must fix it before I get back."

As Sister got older, she didn't swim as much with us, but her heart was in all of the activities that made up summer on the island. If she had what she called a "bum day," we would make sure to go and sit on the porch for a drink before supper. We would sit and sip our drinks with the sun setting and that pink glow settling over the water. "What did you do today, pet?" she would ask, and her memories and our stories would blend together.

Opposite page: Sunday lunch on the porch.

Chapter Twenty-Two

Continuity

The fog is closing in around me. I feel very alone. But I also feel content for the sense of continuity is still strong within me.

SISTER PARISH

I AM SITTING now on the porch at the Summer House in Dark Harbor. The shadows of the big maple trees are spreading across the gardens and on down the slope to the sea. The smell is of jasmine, lilies, foxglove, heliotrope, white petunias, looking like stars in their huge tubs. Hanging baskets of pink begonias fall from latticework arches. I turn my head to glance at a hummingbird reaching out at the pollen from the climbing clematis vines, purple, pink, and white. The ferns are in full glory hanging outside my bedroom door. The ducks are *taking an evening stroll toward me for a handful of bread. The sun is lowering behind the large fir trees and giant white birches. My memories are deep, thoughtful, sad, and contented, but I am always grateful for the happiness that this place has given me.*

I have had time, something that is rare. With time, I have had a moment to look at my own parlor. I am on my sofa covered with red-and-white cotton with a printed stitch the shape of diamonds. The sofa is seven feet long, filled with fluffy soft down and made to fill your dreams. I have a large woolen blanket of squares of every color crocheted with a black border and rainbow-colored tassels to crawl under with the sun pouring through the old glass windows. In front of the sofa is a boxlike stool, sitting on top of my work of art—a cat, black and white, with green eyes, on a pillow of needlework, orange and green. The walls are sky blue, with white woodwork; the floors bright red, with multicolored needlework rugs. My desk is between the two windows facing the village street. I hardly dare describe what it looks like and its contents. The desk is American and belonged to my mother—drop front and four drawers below, cubbyholes and a secret door. A clock with a loud tick sits on the shelf. It is painted with red curtains pulled back and a kitten on the windowsill. I bought it in London, only to find "Made in Portland" on the back. Two grinning (not noble-looking) lions tread with a pair of French brass candlesticks. Every little scrap I cherish. Memories so strong that tears well to a choked sob of happiness and sadness for things that I have had that are now gone. Opposite is the fireplace, the fire now burning away, making the brass shine. The smell of white birch fills the room.

I look toward the little white garden in memory of my mother, and my eyes are filled with tears, as Harry is not giving it its last little water for the day. He is ever present, as his love for this house and place was as strong as mine. Harry's last summer was here; he could look out and see what I have been telling you about. As he was growing increasingly ill, I would take him a little watering can filled with salt water and touch his forehead and hands with the water. He would smile and say, "This will make me well." Then he might add, "And do you remember—you brought that watering can back with you from France?"

There is not a thing in this house that doesn't have a complete story of our life together. Objects from our trips to Europe, England, and every antiques store as far north as Canada—all have a niche and home, loved and cherished. A pincushion of beads, in the shape of a butterfly; baskets from all over the world; a hundred pieces of golden oak that we bought with the house for one hundred dollars. Now they are painted white, decorated with roses, vines, pine trees, cats,

Sister's birthday fell in July so there was a party every summer. This was her
eighty-first, held in the Barn.

dogs, birds. The pictures on the walls range from depictions of strange lions and
tigers to garden scenes, samplers, embroidered pictures, special watercolors, family portraits, pastels of my brothers, a small pastel rose, needlework dogs, in
every possible shape, somehow always surrounded with flowers, a baby, and
something to eat. On the windowsills, I have photographs of the children, grandchildren, best friends that have died but have never been forgotten. Everywhere
there are presents from everyone over the many years. My birthday, July 15, has
brought lots of treasures, each one with deep memories. One special enamel box
inscribed "To my best friend." I have given that box to countless, endless people,
and when they are not looking, I bring it home again. That box has given such
pleasure, if only for brief moments.

In my own room, I sleep in a maple four-poster bed covered in white muslin,
with a fringe that I bought in Guatemala. I was born in that bed. The quilt is of
the finest stitching, the pattern of stars. It must have taken years to make, and I
always wish I could thank whoever made it. The highboy, a very good one, was
given to me by Ruth Draper. At this moment, by my side, is a new book of her
extraordinary life and achievements. A light on here and there to make me feel
I have a large staff turning down beds, bringing water, puffing up pillows,

Summer House front parlor.

setting breakfast trays with a sprig of flowers. Today, I am the staff, but I do it all. It is a wonderful feeling to know everything is in order. BumbleBee and HoneyBee, my Pekingese, are at my feet. Their eyes long to know if they can go with me or not. It is usually yes, much to most people's horror.

I reach the parlor, where one is born and then "laid out." That was taken for granted when the house was built, over two hundred years ago, by Mrs. Hale's ancestors. Even I think it is charming with its blue-and-white, pansy chintz curtains, dotted swiss ruffles peeking out from behind the suite of Victorian furniture sitting happily on the braided rug made by the blind. A Guatemalan striped rug near the door, a large painted hooped basket near the fire, a covered table with the most beautiful quilt falling on the floor. Chinese porcelain lamps with cutout shades, pinholes showing all the stars in the heaven. A wicker coffee table with the usual basket of roses from the garden. Sweet peas in another basket that we brought home from Italy. The mantel has a needlework scalloped border of blue and yellow roses—it took the place of the lace that had sadly been washed once too often. Here is our beautiful painted English desk—a magic desk because when it opens up, a mirror pops up behind, with a paper screen of birds and flowers. It has fretwork on the bottom that can be raised and lowered to hold small dogs. Needlework pillows of white roses against a sky blue background lean against the sofas. A small mahogany open bookcase contains the books that I have recently read or am about to read. Best of all, an ancient rocking chair of fine bamboo sits in front of the fire, and in the fire you see two iron cocks that Harry found, to be used as majestic andirons.

On the mantel are pictures of my grandmother's great-grandchildren, lined up backward in one picture, all with golden curly hair, and frontward in another, looking brown and healthy, with the world to face in front of them. Today, it is thirty years after those pictures were taken, and most of them are back here at this moment.

I pass the little staircase made by Captain Babidge, the old sea captain who also once lived here. It is a thing of wonder—an engineering feat that only a sea captain could accomplish. The stair goes straight up, pauses at a platform three feet wide, then goes straight up again. It takes you from the front hall to the upstairs hall, using the smallest-possible amount of space. The stairway carpet is needlework made by me, with all my favorite flowers on each step. The border is a scattered bunch of nasturtiums every few inches.

I won't go upstairs tonight, but I do glance back at the living room and dining room. The walls are white, with yellow linen curtains and painted valances, tassels, fringes, and bells. There is a large white sofa with the most exquisite patchwork silk pillows, and my father's wonderful chair, which has a book holder attached to it with a swinging brass arm. The rug is needlework, with two large lions under a palm tree. There is a modern wicker chaise, and the original golden oak dining table, which I covered in a matching chintz that has a long, thin fringe made of wood tassels. A portrait of a child watching a toy train crossing a bridge hangs on the wall. It was painted by Madeline Luca and was bought by my father on the quai d'Orsay many years ago. And there is the plant stand that looks like a bridge of steps, and a beautiful Regency painted bench with a yellow buttoned seat and decorated with garlands of flowers.

Beyond the early maple center table comes the dining room. The round table seating ten, also found in the house, is now a thing of wonder. It has been marbleized with a Chinese border copied from the screen by the pantry door. The chairs, then golden oak, are now white, with pads of chintz on the seats and backs. I keep a very large basket filled with mixed flowers, Queen Anne's lace, heads of lettuce, and overgrown onion heads, strong and bold, as if to say, I am not just an onion. The cabinet is filled with porcelain fruits—celery, asparagus, cabbage, turnips, tomatoes, lettuce, artichokes, melons—some old Chelsea, others new copies. Sometimes I have them on the table with the centerpiece—a very large head of lettuce. The tablecloth is mauve, with napkins in pale blue, yellow, pink, and raspberry. I might change this to a large swan with eight smaller swans making the round of the table on a pale, watery green cloth. I love doing the table if my energy holds out and my imagination is working full tilt. The lamps are of white plaster, painted, some of latticework, some of stars, all designed by our office. The shades are of tiny patterned chintz, with a small ruffle making the border.

In front of the table against the sliding doors is a large Aiken sofa with masses of colored pillows of the same yellow chintz. This is where I have my nap with Bumble and Honey. We dread the phone, as it is usually Sears Roebuck, saying that my guarantee on the icebox is now over.

Sister with her great-granddaughter Eliza.

I walk out the door facing the pond, where the frog is already croaking away, and the ducks are coming up the bank of hemlocks to say good night. It's hard to leave my little house, even for my special evening, but I look forward to my delicious bed, where I use the best of linen sheets given to me by Harry over the years.

My grandchildren are here, and when they come, they stay but a minute and then off to the boats, tennis courts, ice-cream cones, in the same spots where I struggled along to be popular and to play one game without shame. I feel proud of them, but I notice each year that they, too, have their inner problems, with life so unsure ahead of them. No matter what happens, I hope I can keep this house so that each and every one of them knows that his or her roots are here, given with pure love.

Time for a swim, with Bumble and Honey running down the waterfront. The fog is closing in around me. I feel very alone. But I also feel content, for the sense of continuity is still strong within me.

MARIAN FRELINGHUYSEN: When I used to visit Sister in Maine, she always took me to the graveyard at the church to show me the spot where she would be buried. She said, "Marian, I just want you to be sure to know where I'm going to be buried."

I always said, "Thank you, Sister. It must make you feel very secure knowing that." It meant a lot to her knowing where she would be.

JESSICA PARISH: The summer right before Poppop died, I had been working as a nurse for a couple of years and was used to being around sick people. I was aware of the fact that she wasn't going to live much longer. She seemed like someone who was in the process of dying. There was sort of a humility to her that summer. Toward the end of the summer, she started to get a little bit more disoriented. In the beginning, when I first arrived, her mind was still pretty clear and she still had a sense of humor. I remember someone arriving to give her a pedicure and that she always loved her feet. I like my feet, too, and we had that in common. She was very humble and very real that summer, and it was the first time I had ever seen her that way. I think Poppop was a very complicated woman. She wasn't a simple human being at all. There was a lot going on there, and that was one of the wonderful things about her.

SUSAN: Sister was very sick many times during my adult life. She had chronic back pain, insomnia, and a host of additional ailments that consistently plagued her. She drove herself tirelessly and, like many women of her generation, generally neglected her health. She preferred food saturated with cream and salt, loved vodka, and got no real exercise. Oftentimes, in her later years, she broke down with one of her more serious ailments and had to be hospitalized.

The circumstances of her illnesses were always highly dramatic and entailed midnight ferry runs from the island to the mainland hospital or terrible trips to a New York hospital emergency room. We were always afraid she would die, as it seemed close.

She was, without a doubt, one of the worst patients any hospital has ever encountered. She would sulk, sneer, and take swipes at whatever hospital worker crossed her path. I swear that to this day there is probably a sign over the entrance of PenBay Hospital in Rockland, Maine, with her name and an *X* over it banning her entry. I was told that a doctor informed her she was the worst patient he had ever had, and she shot back, "You are the worst doctor that I have ever had." We would cower in the corner as she assaulted the hospital staff. Usually, she would refuse all calls if we were not there to take messages. I remember one time when she was at PenBay Hospital and the nurse picked up the phone and turned to Sister, urging her to take the call. Poppop waved her away, her eyes closing in frustration. The nurse persisted, saying, "But you have to take it, Mrs. Parish. It's an Archbishop Buatta and he says he must speak to you." Sister smiled weakly and took Mario's call.

The last time she was sick was different. Her illnesses closed in on her, and her retreat from the world began. I kept hoping that it would be like her previous illnesses and that she would snap out of it. I kept wishing that the old Sister would come back and try to take charge of my life. I wanted her strong voice back, not the small, weak one that she had adopted. Even after she came home from the hospital, she was not the same. She had lost interest in things. She kept thinking that people who were dead were still alive. When I would take Eliza and Tucker to her apartment, Eliza would play make-believe games with Sister, who then really believed her four-year-old's rules. Eliza would tell her, "When I get back from the garden, the fairies will be here," and Sister would sometimes believe her.

Sister had been hospitalized in New York and had gone home to her apartment in the spring. It was heartbreaking for me to watch my mother and Aunt D.B., who were at her side constantly, and it became their crusade to get her to Maine. They repeatedly said, "If we can only get her to Dark Harbor, then everything will somehow be all right." Eventually, they did accomplish

Front view of the Summer House.

the move, when she was a little stronger, by hospital plane. This she was able to do with the help of her nurses, Mila and Lalee, who were with her during her last year. But when the sight of her gardens and the smell of ocean and pine didn't bring back her health even a little bit, we knew with a terrible certainty that this was the end. When Jessica and I said good-bye to her that August, we did not need to say that it would be the last time we would see her. We knew this, but it hurt too much to say.

On September 8, 1994, Sister died in the house that she loved on the island that meant so much to her. New York and Far Hills were part of her psyche, but Maine was part of her soul. When my mother called, I knew as I heard the phone ring that my grandmother was gone. Sister had finally found her peace, and I would only have her in my heart from that day on.

Following page: One of the views from the Summer House.

Chapter Twenty-Three

We Gathered in Dark Harbor: 1994

In the end, it all comes back to laughter. Sister was a very entertaining human being. Each of us has our own Sister story, but no one could tell a story better than she.

MAISIE HOUGHTON

SUSAN: A week after Sister died, we gathered in Dark Harbor to bury her. It was September, and fall was well under way. The light in Maine in the fall is filled with contrasts: the vibrant reds and oranges of the trees, the inky blue of the ocean, and the wide-open pale blue of the skies. The days are cool and breezy, but the sun is strong and bright. A friend of my mother calls them "navy blue days." In the winter, the light is starker, almost eerie, with that shadowy cast that Edward Hopper painted so well. It was quiet on the island. Most of the summer houses were boarded up for the winter, the ice-cream shop was closed for the season, and the roads were still and empty without the summer traffic.

There was a particular stillness in the air, as though we were literally caught between seasons, between generations. The head of the family, the matriarch, was gone and people's positions were shifting, resettling as things do after a storm. My mother and Aunt D.B. were now the elder generation, and my brothers, cousins, and I shifted into the middle position that they had vacated. Our children became "the kids," a category I had never wanted to leave. I felt as if it were my first day at a new school. I missed Sister and the security she had provided for me, but there was a certain feeling of freedom as well, as Sister had tried to keep a tight rein on those who would let her. We were now free to go out on our own, to make mistakes, and, we hoped, to make her proud as she looked down on us.

She wanted to be buried beside Harry in the cemetery next to the church. It is a cool and shady spot surrounded by an old stone wall covered with lichen. Moss grows between the gravestones and dappled light falls among the trees, hitting the gravestones. Uncle Gory and Uncle Harry are also buried there, along with many of Sister's closest friends. During her last months of sickness, she had longed for that place between her husband and her son. She had always been a frequent visitor to this little cemetery, bringing flowers and making sure all was well. She had often told me how happy she would be there.

We met at the cemetery to bury her before the funeral began. My mother had been worried that the grave would not be ready when we got there, but the man who digs the graves also works as the driver of the school bus, and as he passed my mother earlier that morning, he gave her the thumbs-up sign, assuring her that all had been taken care of. I will always remember looking at him as he stood on a rise of land, leaning against his shovel, as we said our last good-byes.

Sister had told Mom not to do the eulogy, as it would be too much for her. My mother has never risen to a challenge with such style and grace in her life. Her speech was not only heartfelt and moving but also spoken with such strength that there was a hush in the church when she was finished.

One of the islanders said it best when he later remarked, "Yes, sir, after hearing Apple at Mrs. Parish's funeral, everyone knew that torch had been passed."

The last hymn had been, at Sister's request, "America the Beautiful," and as I looked at the cast of people gathered on this tiny island off the coast of Maine, and thought of the turns Sister's life had taken, I was struck by how American her story really was.

After the funeral, everyone went back to the Summer House. It was my mother's house now. It seemed strange to be there without Sister on the porch to greet her friends. The island women had done their best and had made exactly what Sister would have wanted—huge hams and turkeys, tea sandwiches made of cucumber, smoked salmon, and chicken salad—all beautifully arranged on the dining room table.

People will tell you how painfully difficult it is to get to Dark Harbor. Typically, you have to take three forms of transportation: plane, car, and ferry. Though it is not an easy journey, somehow people simply appeared throughout the morning. They came by different routes, but they came. The liquor flowed, the tea sandwiches were passed, and we all told our Sister stories.

The following is the eulogy my mother gave for Sister in Dark Harbor.

I'm so glad to see you all here. Many things have been said about my mother, but she didn't understand many of them. She didn't understand why she was called a "living legend." She did not understand why she was called "The Grande Dame of American Decorators." She was very modest about her successes in life.

The only remark she really understood and appreciated was one that was made on the island, at the Village Market, where a group of men was having their morning coffee. One of them said, "That Sister Parish—she's a tough old turkey." I don't know who said it, but I know that she loved it.

And she *was* tough. She loved to be in control of things. When this was not always the case in the end, it made her mad and frustrated. In fact, one of the last things she said to her best friends Mela, Lallie, and Noelle, who had taken care of her, was, "I am the King of the Jungle. I am the Lord of the Jungle. I am the Lion."

She kept saying this over and over again, "I am the King of the Jungle. I am the Lord of the Jungle. I am the Lion."

After much thought, I think this is what she was saying to us: Ah. I am in control again. So I'm just going to slip away from my beloved island and be at peace.

And she did.

When I was a small child, I was afraid of storms—the thunder, the lightning, and the lashing of rains.

I was told, "Don't be afraid. It's just God and his buddies bowling in their private bowling alley in the stars."

Now, if one of my grandchildren is frightened, I will have something different to say.

"Don't be afraid," I'll say. "It is just your great-grandmother Poppop moving furniture around. She's just gotten another new job and will be hurling things around until it looks just right. Then there will be peace and quiet."

And when I see a beautiful sunset, I will say to myself, "Ah, Mother is at it again. She is putting the finishing touches on another beautiful room in the skies."

We will miss her.

SUSAN: My grandmother's memorial service in New York was very grand and solemn. It took place at St. James' Church, the old favorite for WASPs on the Upper East Side. Maisie Houghton spoke eloquently, and, like Mum, with style and grace. The most dramatic moment, which Sister, with her sense of theater, would have loved, was the ringing of the church bells eighty-four times, for each year of her life.

There was absolute silence as they rang, and I pictured the sound of those bells ringing out all over the East Side of New York, where she had worked and lived all of her life. I said good-bye not only to my grandmother but also to a whole generation and a way of life that we have lost forever.

This is the eulogy given by Maisie Houghton at Sister's memorial service in New York City.

About ten years ago, one Columbus Day weekend, I was staying in Dark Harbor in Sister's Red House—not to be confused with the Summer House, the Brown House, the Town House, or the Barn.

As Sister's niece, I have inherited the Kinnicutt magpie heart. We love to poke about antique shops, the dustier the better. We like to peek in forbidden windows.

So what was I doing there in Sister's Red House but rummaging. I sat at her old secretary, opening drawers, pretending to look for stamps, but really looking not so much for secrets *about* Sister, but more for the secret *of* Sister. What did I hope to find? The magic needle she used to prick her eggshell lampshades, the ribbon she used to thread through a fat pillow, or the scrap of paper the rest of us would throw away but Sister would seize upon for one of her collages?

I found, instead, this prayer, which I would like to read now. Copied out in her own hand, so I know it must have meant something to her; it is attributed to Saint Francis, surely a saint for Sister, with his roots in the worldly life, his affinity for animals, plants, and gardens. What I found is this: "You begin by loving and you go on loving and loving teaches you how to love. And the more you love, the more you learn to love."

So, for me, this prayer was a precious discovery, for it reminded me of how Sister treasured the mystery and power of love.

The prayer speaks of "learning to love," but I don't think Sister ever learned anything formally. She was born loving her family, her work, Dark Harbor, her dogs, and life itself.

I think she was unteachable. Everything she knew was already there in her heart, her bones, her quick, deft fingers. She learned as a child might learn—instinctively, eagerly, and irrevocably.

A child psychologist once told me, not Sister, the way to happiness for a child is to care passionately for something, to have at least one attachment and to know how to have fun.

For me, this description is the essence of Sister.

She had a child's vitality and energy, a child's willfulness. In describing herself in a sailboat race with a friend as crew, she admitted, "I got so mad, I bit him."

When she wondered what to give another beloved friend for her birthday, I said, "Oh, you can give her anything—anything from you she would love. Here, give her this," I added, pointing to a minute straw basket on her desk. "Oh, I couldn't bear to part with that," she replied. "I love it too much myself."

If she had a child's intense enthusiasm for life, she was a remarkably self-effacing, curious, and reserved grown woman, who had, as Apple said at the service in Dark Harbor, no idea what all the fuss was about over her success as a decorator. The praise was unimportant; she was on to her next job, the next perennial border, the extension of the porch.

The people she wanted to praise were her children, Harry, Apple, and D.B., her grandchildren and great-grandchildren. "I worship my daughters," she announced periodically and probably after behaving particularly outrageously toward them, but they were her heart and soul and they never, ever let her down.

As a teenager, I, too, had a whiff of Sister's parental authority when she shepherded me through a terrifying Far Hills coming-out party. Sister advanced on the stag line. "Dance with my niece," she commanded, while I cringed in the background. But, since one of those reluctant dancers ended up being my husband, Sister was, of course, again amazingly, maddeningly right.

She always got it right. The houses she created for her adored family were what drew us all to her. The iced tea or the stiff drink, the pots of primroses, the fire burning brightly, the soft throw on the end of the bed.

In the end, it all comes back to laughter. Sister was a very entertaining human being. Each of us has our own Sister story, but no one could tell a story better than she. Sometimes, often frequently, they were on other people, but also on herself.

Someone reminded me of one story she told of driving up to Maine by herself, when she began to plan her own funeral. She got herself so worked up and began crying so hard, worrying that no one would come, that she had to pull over to the side of the road to calm down.

I can't pin down exactly what was so funny about Sister's stories. It was the timing, her drawl of voice, those rolling black eyes. So I only remember looking forward to being with her, because with her, I knew I would laugh.

And what is laughter but loving life, keeping out the cold, embracing your family and your friends? All of which Sister did, so passionately and so triumphantly.

MY GRANDMOTHER HAS been gone for almost six years, but we talk frequently about what she would say or think. This is easy, because with Sister, everything was either fatal or marvelous. It was wonderful or it was ghastly. There was nothing in between. She was lavish in her praise—"Pet, you look lovely tonight"—or biting in her criticism—"If you don't do something about that hair, you will be ruined." Appearances and manners were her top priorities. She told us over and over again that neat hair, short, clean fingernails, and shined shoes were mandatory. She told me that these were her criteria for judging the young decorators at Parish-Hadley. Women, we were taught, should wear plenty of rouge and lipstick or fall into the category of looking "sickly," or, worse, "overtired." Being exactly on time, or at least five minutes early was also an expectation of Sister's. A lack of punctuality was a sure sign of moral weakness and bad breeding. She told me she had learned this from her mother. When I asked how her mother had managed so well, she replied, "She simply never undressed."

As she grew older, the dos and don'ts became less stringent and she became more of a friend than an authority figure. She was a wonderful grandmother because we had the luxury of distance a generation provided. I think she felt that having finished instilling in us the traditions and manners that were so important to her, we could now have fun. When Sister felt well, there was no one more fun.

Sister said that the theme of her life was continuity, so it was no coincidence that she excelled as a decorator. What is a house if not a receptacle for a family's footprint, memories, and traditions? Sister's message was not about the paintings, the furniture, or the house itself. It was about the desire to create a home, a special place for family to live and pass on their traditions with imagination and humor. She gave that to each of us. It was a simple message and she was a powerful messenger.

While putting this book together, we found a note she had written on a piece of scrap paper, expressing her wish to put together a book about her mother, who, along with her father, had made her childhood houses special places for her. We hope that we have written the book she would have wanted to write and so have fulfilled the wish expressed in her note.

Time has gone by, but the memory of my mother is still very vivid to me. I wonder if you could help me in writing a few words about her. What I would do is get as many small stories or quotes and descriptions of Ipswich, Far Hills, and New York. Short or long, it would help me make a tiny book to give to my children and grandchildren. I am writing this letter to the people that I remember Mother loved, but I am sure I have forgotten many, so please, if you could, mention it to anyone you think might be interested.

—SUSAN BARTLETT CRATER
Pelham, New York
September 1999

MUM WOULD BE pleased with the present state of her Summer House. It has a fresh coat of paint and new porch railings; the same standard yellow roses bloom and her agapanthus border the porch. Pansies and heliotrope fill antique planters in the porch corners, just as they always have.

Most of all, she would be happy to see how much the house is loved and used by her children, grandchildren, and great-grandchildren. She would be happy to know that all the things she loved have continued to be part of our summers.

Inside the house, nothing much has changed, as I have moved only a few things around. Canopy beds have made their way from one room to another, and now my granddaughter Eliza says she feels like she is sleeping in a princess's room.

People have said to me, "Oh, you are keeping the living room exactly the way it was when your mother was alive. It's almost like a shrine or a museum." This remark rather irritates me, as even if I wanted to change the room, there is no way to make it better than it is. Its white ruffled curtains, crisp chintz, rag rugs, and sour-apple green painted floors all look as fresh today as they did ten years ago.

It isn't that I don't have the confidence for change. My mother gave me that kind of courage years ago. When I had my first show of paintings she said, "Don't be afraid. Just do it." I did just that, and it worked.

I felt only marginally confident when I built a small house on the island, on land that Mum gave me years ago, and yet my new house has given me such happiness. I now wend my way down a path from the Summer House to my own small shingled house that sits among the pine trees. It looks very much like the Summer House once did, before it grew with all its additions.

I find myself, at this moment, sitting on my new porch, jotting notes down just as Mum did: ideas for next year's garden, the changes I am mentally making for moving furniture from one house to another—up from Boston, down from Maine, or vice versa—always creating something. I feel the excitement of just one small change, such as putting a colorful blanket on the back of a sofa. I make a small vignette on a table, composed of a robin's egg blue vase of wild asters with a china goat nibbling at them, beside a small bunch of faux asparagus tied together with raffia, and I know that this artistic gift I have inherited from my mother.

I think Mum would be pleased with the state of her beloved island. She was afraid that, without her, we wouldn't be able to keep everything going as she had wanted, but with Mum as our teacher, how could we fail?

The traditions that she cared about so much continue as before. Our lives are now as they were then; her gardens return as beautiful as she'd known them and her beloved dog show continues. My commitment to this island community is as strong as hers once was.

Though she is gone, I will always feel her presence around me in those things that she collected and loved. I can feel her here still, particularly on those days when I open a closet or a drawer and discover some funny little object stuffed way back in the corner. They remind me again of how lucky I was to have had such a mother, and such a friend.

APPLE PARISH BARTLETT
Dark Harbor, Maine
September 1999

The following are biographical notes and, in some cases, comments about Sister by the people who were interviewed for and contributed to this book. The majority were written by the contributors themselves.

A. JOHN ALBERTELLI works for John A. Weidl, Inc., in New Rochelle, New York. He was among the primary painters for Mrs. Parish.

SUSAN MARY ALSOP was married first to Bill Patten and then to Joseph Alsop, both of whom worshiped Sister. When Mrs. Alsop's first child was born in Paris in 1948, Sister attended his christening and made the party afterward a success. Now eighty-one years old, Mrs. Alsop lives a widow's quiet life in Washington, D.C.

BROOKE ASTOR has made countless contributions to New York City on behalf of the Vincent Astor Foundation, and is a well-known public figure. In addition to her work as a philanthropist, she is an accomplished author and has written many books, including *Footprints, Bluebird Is at Home,* and *A Patchwork Child.* She was a good friend of Mrs. Parish and a client of Parish-Hadley for many years. She presently lives in New York City.

KK AUCHINCLOSS was born in Boston. Mrs. Douglas Auchincloss first met Sister at an impossible interview instigated by Mrs. Wolcott Blair, who knew Sister was looking for a partner and strongly suggested she meet the then Mrs. John Simms Kelly. Although the interview was a miserable failure, it resulted in their lifelong friendship in New York, Dark Harbor, and various other places.

LAURA AULT was married to Lee Ault, an art collector, publisher of *Art in America,* and president of the Lee Ault Art Gallery in New York City. Laura was a lifelong friend and admirer of Sister. Their happy relationship spanned many summers, which they enjoyed on Maine's seacoast and islands, particularly Islesboro.

LETITIA BALDRIGE served as White House social secretary for Jacqueline Kennedy during the Kennedy administration. She has authored several etiquette books, including *Letitia Baldrige's Complete Guide to Executive Manners*. Her role since the 1970s has been "social arbiter for the nation."

SYBIL KINNICUTT BALDWIN is the eldest daughter of Frankie Kinnicutt, Sister's eldest brother.

CHARLES WILLIAM BARTLETT offers this limited biographical data. The oldest grandchild of Mrs. Parish, he doesn't act it, and he no doubt caused his grandmother the most amount of grief. He lives in Cambridge, Massachusetts, most of the time.

HENRY PARISH BARTLETT ("Harry") is one of Sister's grandsons. He said that he will always remember his grandmother's "welcome mat" at the Summer House. It said DON'T GO AWAY MAD. JUST GO AWAY. She liked to joust in her conversations. Sometimes she was playful, but when she played, she played to win. The welcome mat always reminded him of her chutzpahlike humor. An executive at Cadent.Com., an Internet development and design studio in Watertown, Massachusetts, he lives with his wife, Natalie, and their two children in Concord, Massachusetts.

JOSEPH W. BARTLETT is a partner at Morrison & Foerster, LLP, in New York City. A former undersecretary of commerce under Lyndon Johnson, law clerk to Chief Justice Earl Warren, and president of the Boston Bar Association, Mr. Bartlett graduated from Stanford Law School. He lives in New York City.

SAMUEL BELL was the driver for Parish-Hadley for fifteen years. He said his religion helped him in working for Mrs. Parish and the company.

GLENN BERNBAUM was born on April 5, 1922, in Philadelphia, Pennsylvania. For many years, he was the owner of Mortimer's, a restaurant frequented by New York's café society. He was a client of Parish-Hadley and a friend of Mrs. Parish. He died in 1998.

CARL-PETER BRAESTRUP received a B.A. in American studies from Yale University, then spent two years as a Peace Corps volunteer in Togo, Africa. Not content to bring home the shellacked coconut ice holders favored as souvenirs by other volunteers, he adopted a five-year-old boy, Bagna, now an energetic seventh grader. Today, they live in San Francisco, where Braestrup, a third-year law student, is planning to pursue a career in criminal prosecution.

MARCIE BRAGA began her decorating career at Parish-Hadley after graduating from Pratt Institute with a degree in design. She said Sister Parish's elegant style and attention to detail remain the greatest influence on her work.

NANCY BREED is an art historian and artist and lives on Long Island. Her mother was Mrs. Parish's friend and client in both Maine and New York—and had many fond memories of Sister, both personal and professional. Nancy formerly worked in costume and set design in the field of dance, and she feels that Mrs. Parish understood the theater of house decoration, considering the home a setting or stage for private life.

MARIO BUATTA, the well-known decorator, said that he cannot count all of the people from *AHlasskah* to *Allabaamhahh* (as Mrs. Parish would playfully have pronounced these names) who have been influenced by this godmother of chintz. Calling her "the original of the originals," he said Mrs. Parish's work looked like it had been there for a treasured lifetime. He used to phone her to ask what she had designed that he could copy. Her "bons," he said, were the best "mots" ever. One day, Sister asked him whether his career was in decorating, lecturing, personal and TV appearances, or designing furniture, wallpaper, and fabrics. His retort was, "All of the above," and he said that he owes a lot of it to her inspiration.

LIBBY CAMERON worked for Mrs. Parish at Parish-Hadley for fourteen years. In 1995, after Mrs. Parish's death, she left Parish-Hadley to establish her own decorating business in Larchmont, New York.

ALAN CAMPBELL served in the American Foreign Service (1951–1960), with posts in India, Naples, Tev Aviv, and Saigon, and subsequently worked for Rockefeller family organizations (1961–1975), where he was involved in setting up cultural exchanges with Asia relating to the visual and performing arts. In 1976, inspired by his exposure to Asian art and design, and the encouragement of Sister Parish and Albert Hadley, he started a fabric and wallpaper business, which flourished until he sold it and retired to northwest Connecticut.

CAROLE CAVALUZZO works in Parish-Hadley's accounting department. As an employee there since 1966, she was privileged, she said, to have had a professional relationship as well as a friendship with Mrs. Parish.

EDWARD LEE CAVE was born in Virginia, attended schools in New England and in Geneva, Switzerland, and then went to Columbia University. His all-important first job was with Mrs. Parish, where he was able to make use of his art history background, working on important assignments in the metropolitan area. From her office, he went to Sotheby's, where he was the first American hired when the company bought Parke Bernet in New York. In 1981, he started his own real estate company, which specializes in prestigious residential properties in Manhattan.

MRS. WILLIAM ASTOR CHANLER, JR., was a longtime resident of New York, but she now lives year-round with her husband in Camden, Maine. The Chanlers summered for many years in their cottage, Yellow Sands, on 700 Acre Island. A member of the Colony Club in New York and the Tarratine Club in Dark Harbor for many years, she was Sister's close friend and spent time with her in New York and Maine.

OATSIE CHARLES was in love for a long time with a derelict late Victorian house on the corner of R & Wisconsin streets in Georgetown. After several years, she bought and restored it, and though it was unique and wonderful, the interiors were a challenge. One day, Lily Guest called her to say she had asked Sister Parish to give her a ring. Sister did so, and, with Albert Hadley, made magic. From that time on she loved, enjoyed, and admired Sister.

PHYLLIS DILLON COLLINS said that her mother received a baby present from Sister when she was born. The attached note asked if Phyllis could marry Sister's son, Harry, when she was old enough to do so. Phyllis grew up in Far Hills and Dark Harbor with Harry, Apple, and D.B. She remembers their white goats. She also went to Foxcroft School with the Parish girls. Her mother and Mrs. Parish spoke with each other on the phone almost every day. She misses Sister's "Yoo-hoo," the greeting she called out when she arrived on surprise visits.

JUDY ANGELO COWEN said that back in the late forties it was a treat for her to peer in the window of Mrs. Henry Parish's little shop on East Sixty-ninth Street. When she got the nerve to enter the shop, she found that she and Mrs.

Parish were related by marriage. Sister's son was married to Judy's first cousin. They became good friends. Judy is a children's photographer and also shoots photos for authors' book jackets. One of her scarier assignments was photographing Sister's Pekingese dogs, but the pictures turned out well and got high marks from Sister.

DOUGLAS CRATER works in finance in New York City and lives with his wife, Susan, and their two children in a suburb of New York City. He knew Sister for the last fifteen years or so of her life. Aside from her obvious talents, Doug attributes Sister's success to the fact that she was just plain smart, knew how to handle people, and never took herself too seriously.

ELIZA APPLETON CRATER is Sister's great-granddaughter. She is nine years old and lives with her parents and brother, Tucker. She likes ballet, lacrosse, and art.

TILLIE TUCKERMAN CUTLER was fond of Sister, who was her cousin, and of Sister's husband, Harry. Mrs. Cutler's father, Bayard Tuckerman (Sister's uncle) said, after paying for her decoration of his apartment in Boston, that she was by far the most successful member of the family. She married George C. Cutler in 1940 and has five children and eight grandchildren.

JOAN TUCKERMAN DICK was born in Ipswich, Massachusetts, on April 21, 1891, and died on March 9, 1990. She married Evans Roger Dick in 1911. Mrs. Dick wrote movie reviews for the *Boston Herald*, as well as being a tireless advocate for a host of humanitarian causes. Mrs. Dick was Sister's aunt.

C. DOUGLAS DILLON served as secretary of the treasury from January 1961 to April 1965, and was ambassador to France from February 1953 to February 1957. He remembers that Sister called every year when she was fully ensconced in her house in Dark Harbor, insisting that he and Phyliss, and later he and Suzie, have dinner with her alone on the night they arrived for the summer—a warm and wonderful gesture, which they always appreciated.

DOREA ENGSTROM is a fifth-generation descendant of the first settler on Islesboro. She was an "overhomer," who came to the island first in 1951 as a guest, and later, in 1982, as a wife with a family. She sometimes worked for Mrs. Parish when Sister gave parties on the island. Dorea's children enjoyed the dog show every summer. Mrs Parish always waved as she tootled by in her car and, later, her golf cart. Dorea said Mrs. Parish was definitely the grande dame of Dark Harbor.

MARIAN FRELINGHUYSEN lives in Far Hills, New Jersey, and Northeast Harbor, Maine, and she and Sister were devoted friends for many years.

PETER GATES said that he had the good fortune to be born in time to witness the flowering of a remarkable generation, the last of the "beautiful people," the East Coast aristocracy, which went through the Depression, went to war, worked harder than, but drank as much as, their forebears, knew everyone worth knowing, and revered wit, style, taste, and charm. Eventually, they grew old and infirm, and most are now gone. Sister was a charter member of the group, as were his parents. He was a dazzled observer, a member of the comparatively charmless generation that followed. He misses Sister, and the other members of that generation. "Their like will not be seen again," he said.

BAYARD GILBERT is D.B. and Riley Gilbert's son and Mrs. Parish's grandson. A graduate of Louisiana State University, he works as a Thoroughbred jockey's agent at various racetracks in Arkansas, Louisiana, and Texas. He and his wife, Tobi, were married in December 1997. They reside in Hot Springs, Arkansas.

DOROTHY BAYARD PARISH GILBERT ("D.B.") lives in Hot Springs, Arkansas, with her husband, Riley. They have three children: Miles, Alexander, and Bayard.

ARCHIBALD GILLES has been president of the Andy Warhol Foundation for the Visual Arts since 1990. Prior to that, he headed the World Policy Institute, a research and policy-making organization in New York City. In the 1970s, he was president of the John Hay Whitney Foundation. He and his wife, Linda, summer in Dark Harbor, where they saw Mrs. Parish and enjoyed her wit, good cheer, and funny and always wise counsel.

LINDA GILLES has lived and worked in New York City since college. She was in the Drawings Department at the Metropolitan Museum and later—from 1974 to 1997—was director of the Vincent Astor Foundation. She is presently director of the new Chancellor's Office for Development at the New York City Board of Education. Linda said Sister was a wonderful and unique part of both her city and summer life.

JACQUELINE GONNET was an editor of *Vogue's Fashion in Living* from 1961 to 1963, and decorating editor of *House & Garden* from 1967 to 1993. She is now a public-relations consultant in New York City.

LILY AND NAT GOODALE summered in Islesboro as children and enjoyed it immensely, pushing the limits and testing their parents and friends. They believe they made a mark, and their shared memories of summers in Maine are deeply rooted ones. The Goodales reside in Maine full-time now, where they are raising hellions of their own and pursuing dreams on land, sea, and in the air. Their business, Island Picnics, caters picnics on island beaches.

RALPH GRAY knew Sister for almost seventy years, having met her first at Dudley Howe's house, where he was cooking lunch. Sister dropped in and was invited to stay for the meal. He never really worked for Mrs. Parish, but he occasionally took her out in his boat, the *Growler*, to run her to Lincolnville between scheduled ferry trips.

ALBERT HADLEY was born in Nashville, Tennessee. His early years in the South sparked his interest in design and all things related to a life lived with style and comfort. He left Nashville to serve in World War II and was stationed in London. After the war, he moved to New York to attend Parsons School of Design. After graduation, he stayed on to teach at Parsons; later he taught at the school's Paris campus. Returning to New York, he established his own design firm, then joined the firm of McMillen, Inc. In 1962, he began his legendary association with Mrs. Parish.

MARK HAMPTON was born in 1940 in Plainfield, Indiana. He graduated from Depauw University, attended Michigan University Law School, and received a degree in art history from Michigan School of Fine Arts. The *New York Times* described him as an "icon of American style and one of the nation's most sought after interior decorators." Among his well-heeled clients, he was most closely associated with President and Mrs. George Bush, for whom he decorated the White House. He was also an accomplished watercolorist and author. He died in the summer of 1998.

RANDOLPH HARRISON saw Mr. and Mrs. (Sister was always Mrs. Parish to him) Parish frequently at dinner parties, as his mother and Sister were good friends. He last saw their son, Harry, at his twenty-fifth college reunion, and later he was an usher at Harry's funeral. He was fascinated by Mrs. Parish's reminiscences, which, he found, were often revealing and enlightening about matters—frequently spicy—of which he was unaware.

MRS. RAY HILL worked for the American Red Cross on the front lines during

World War II and was at the Battle of the Bulge. She met her husband, Ray, in England and they were married in Paris. They lived in several cities in the United States and abroad, and with the exception of the war years, Jesse Hill never missed a summer in Dark Harbor, where she and Sister were close friends. She died in 1998.

MARI WATTS HITCHCOCK and Sister were friends for sixty years, beginning in 1934, when they were both bringing up children in the same town in New Jersey. Sister's husband, Harry, and Mari's husband, Jack Watts, were both in the navy during the war and were sent to the Pacific. Each summer, the Watts family lived in Islesboro, Maine, where they had a small farm up-island from Sister and Harry. Jack Watts died in 1981, and two years later, Mari sold their Islesboro home, Little Farm on the Water. In 1988, she married Ethan Allen Hitchcock. They live in Oldwick, New Jersey, where she still paints and works at the Magic Shop.

WILLIAM HODGINS said he had the good fortune to work with Mrs. Parish and Albert Hadley in the mid 1960s. He remembers them as teachers, respected friends, and cohorts. Sister, whom he called "Madame," was strict, caring, and had an inimitable sense of humor, he said.

MARY HOMANS was one of five children. She has been lucky enough to spend nearly all her summers in Dark Harbor. Since 1988, she has lived there year-round.

JAMIE HOUGHTON is married to Sister Parish's niece Maisie and lives in Corning, New York, and Islesboro, Maine. He claims his most noteworthy accomplishment was having been the master of ceremonies at the annual Dark Harbor Dog Show for many years. He was asked to take on this weighty role by Apple Bartlett, Sister's daughter and the creator of the dog show. Sister grudgingly accepted her daughter's decision, even though she knew how much Jamie detested her sniveling, barking Pekingese.

MAISIE KINNICUTT HOUGHTON was named after her paternal grandmother, May Tuckerman Kinnicutt, but she has always been called "Maisie." Sister Kinnicutt Parish, her aunt, told her parents, Frankie and Sybil Kinnicutt, to give her that nickname. She lives in Corning, New York, but spends much of her time in New York City and Dark Harbor, Maine, two places where she always looked forward to seeing her beloved aunt Sister.

KEITH IRVINE was born in Nairn, Scotland, in 1928, educated in England at Epsom College, served in Malaya in the Seaforth Highlanders, and then studied interior design at the Royal College of Art, London, under Sir Hugh Casson. This was followed by a five-year stint as an assistant to John Fowler, the eminence grise of decoration in the twentieth century. He was lent to Mrs. Parish ("as an indentured slave") in 1957 to work on the Engelhard house in Johannesburg, South Africa. At its successful conclusion, Mrs. Parish asked him to come work for her in New York. He was the first man ever to work for her firm, and he lasted a brief nine months, leaving to start his own decorating firm and the international fabric firm Clarence House.

ROBERT ISRAEL grew up in Seattle, then moved to New York after college to begin a career in advertising. Shortly after getting married, he was lured into the world of antiques by his brother-in-law, Fred Imberman. Together, they joined Fred's father at Kentshire Galleries, and over the next thirty years, they turned Kentshire into one of the preeminent sources for fine English antique furniture and decorative objects. He says that as head of her prestigious design firm, Mrs. Parish was indeed larger than life. They looked upon her visits to their gallery as "state visits."

ROBERT JACKSON was born in Toronto in 1931, educated at the University of Toronto, where his field was art and art history. He began his career as a decorative painter in London, where he lived from 1955 to 1965, specializing in murals and trompe l'oeil. He moved to New York in 1965 and worked with Parish-Hadley, Michael Greer, Mark Hampton, William Hodgins, and Mario Buatta, among others.

BERNARD KARR established Hyde Park Antiques, Ltd., in 1965. He is a leading specialist in eighteenth-century English furniture. He had a wonderful business relationship with Mrs. Parish.

ELIZABETH "TIZZIE" KINNICUTT is Sister's goddaughter and niece. Her father, Frankie Kinnicutt, was Sister's eldest brother.

IRENE KINNICUTT was born in Germany and grew up in France. After spending four years in South America during the war, she came to the United States with her young daughter, Lily. During that summer, she met her future husband, Gory Kinnicutt, and his sister and husband, the Parishes. She married Gory in 1948 in New York at Sister and Harry's apartment.

MICHAEL TUCKERMAN KINNICUTT is the son of Gustav Hermann Kinnicutt, Jr., and Irene Schultze-Jena. He was born in New York City on May 3, 1950, and, in true Kinnicutt tradition, spent his first summer in Dark Harbor. He attended the Buckley School, St. Mark's School ('68), and Harvard ('72). In 1984, he moved to Florence, Italy, the hometown of Laura Bonechi, whom he married in 1986. They have three children: Eleanora, Matteo, and Lorenzo. He is director of European communications for Pfizer, Inc., the pharmaceutical company.

DAVID KLEINBERG was born in Brooklyn and raised on Long Island. He got his B.A. at Trinity College in Hartford, Connecticut, and then went to work in the design field. He met Mrs. Parish in 1981, when he interviewed for a job at Parish-Hadley. The interview, he said, consisted mostly of small talk, including the subject of dogs. He worked happily at Parish-Hadley for the next sixteen years. He opened his own firm in May 1997, and credits Mrs. Parish for whatever good sense he has.

JOHN R. KRAMER was dean of Tulane Law School and associate dean of Georgetown Law Center. He was also counsel to a former Speaker of the U.S. House of Representatives, Thomas Foley, and president of the Marshall Field Foundation. He is chairman of the board of the Center for Budget and Policy Priorities in Washington, D.C., and is presently on the law faculty at Tulane Law School.

SANDRA S. KRAMER was an active participant in the women's movement during the late 1960s and the 1970s, directing the women's delegate selection political reform effort for both the 1972 Republican and Democratic nominating conventions. She founded the Women's Campaign Fund in 1974, and from 1974–1977, she staffed an advisory committee on women's rights and responsibilities. She is the current president of the Kramer Company and lives in New Orleans, Louisiana.

BARBARA ALLEN DE KWIATKOWSKI is a model, and she worked for Andy Warhol at *Interview* magazine. She also worked with Mrs. Parish on homes in Greenwich, Nassau, New York, and Kentucky.

KENNETH JAY LANE was born in Detroit; he attended the University of Michigan, then earned a degree in advertising from the Rhode Island School of Design. He worked in *Vogue*'s art department before joining Delman, and then Christian Dior. It was through his embellishing of shoes with rhinestone ornaments that he was motivated to begin experimenting with jewelry. Elegance, luxury, and good taste never go out of style, he said, and every woman has the right to live up to her potential to be glamorous. Sister once toasted him, as he sat at her right hand at her house in Dark Harbor: "When I first met Kenny Lane, I wasn't sure that I was his cup of tea." Kenny responded, "To Mrs. Parish, another man's poison!" Kenny said that Sister was right: She was not his cup of tea, but his cocktail.

CAROLYN LEACH and her husband, Wallace, grew up on Islesboro, went to school there, and raised their family there. Her first job was serving Mrs. Parish breakfast in bed when she was a teenager. Wallace worked as caretaker for Mrs. Parish's many houses for twenty years; he now works for Parker Stevenson, as does Carolyn from time to time.

JACK AND JACKIE LEACH owned the grocery store on Islesboro for many years, and now operate a trucking service on the island. They remember trips to New York to fetch things for Mrs. Parish.

RICHARD MANDER met Sister when she visited his cabinet shop to see the Hepplewhite twist-back chairs that he was making for Freddy Victoria. She asked him to make the same for her. After making custom furniture for Parish-Hadley for ten years, he was hired by Sister to supervise construction and custom furniture for another ten years. Since Sister's death, he has been in the restaurant business. His newest is called Helena's and is at 432 Lafayette Street in New York City. He also has a construction company in New York called CKC.

DUCHESSE JOAN DILLON DE MOUCHY misses Mrs. Parish, who, along with her children, was family to her and her sister, Phyllis. She hopes that her mother, her aunt Ibbie, Sister, and all the girls of that generation are up on cloud nine, having a ball.

BRIAN MURPHY is currently vice president of Parish-Hadley, where he has worked since 1987.

DIANTHA NYPE became director of public relations for the Kips Bay Boys and Girls Club in 1974; she worked on all their show houses until her retirement in 1998.

EDWARD CODMAN PARISH II is Harry Parish's younger brother:

Columbus sailed in 1492, but I arrived in 1912,
In this world to dig and delve.
Polio caught me in 1920, which taught me more than any school.
At age of eight, I knew life is great.
Thanks to parents who knew the same.
We crossed the continent, went to Europe
Did the things that I couldn't do, but did,
Like skiing in the Alps, and sailing boats
That flew, and riding horses at top gallop.
School came here and there.
Harvard helped me find a bride,
In junior class.
Dear Joan got me through and
Three children and 62 years later,
Rose to dance upon the stars.
Years of work and play
Have made me glad to
Be alive today.

JESSICA PARISH is one of Sister's granddaughters. She is currently living in Mill Valley, California, a town fifteen miles north of San Francisco. She works as a nurse practitioner, specializing in emergency medicine, and currently has two dogs. She said her grandmother taught her about the importance of surrounding herself with beauty, laughter, and family.

FRANCES E. PAUL and Sister were lifelong acquaintances. Sister's youngest brother, Bydie, and Frances's brother Louis Clark were best friends and roommates at St. Mark's School. They both died young. Frankie and Gory were also her longtime pals. They all gathered in Islesboro each summer during their teens and after, and had what Frances calls "idyllic fun" through the years. Now eighty-three, she lives on a Pennsylvania farm that has been in her family for five generations.

PAUL AND MARILYN PENDLETON have lived all their lives on Islesboro. Marilyn worked for the Parishes in the Town House when they were on the island during the winter. Her husband, Paul, credits Mrs. Parish with helping him to get a job as caretaker for Charlie Englehard's house on the island.

WILHELMINA PENDLETON always said that she's a native of Islesboro, but truthfully, she moved there when she was about eight, and she can't remember living anywhere else. She has always worked for the summer families. One fall, when Mrs. Parish returned to New York, Wilhelmina went with her, intending to stay with her at her apartment all winter, but she hated the city and missed the island, so she went home to Islesboro.

MRS. CHARLES PERCY is the wife of Senator Charles Percy. She lives in Washington, D.C., and Sister and she were good friends.

MARY JANE POOL was editor-in-chief of *House & Garden* for many years. She is the author of *The Gardens of Venice, The Gardens of Florence, The Angel Tree: A Christmas Celebration,* and *Gardens in the City: New York in Bloom.*

PATSY PRESTON has an active interest in and is on the boards of numerous educational and charitable organizations. She and Susan, Mrs. Parish's granddaughter, have been friends for many years.

JOHNNY AND NANCY PYNE knew Sister since the 1920s and they were all great friends. Sister's brother Bydie was Johnny Pyne's best friend. The Pynes were married in January 1950, have two wonderful children, and still live in Far Hills.

JESSIE LEONARD REID was a childhood friend of Susan Crater and spent summers on Islesboro. She lives in Ipswich, Massachusetts, with her husband and three boys. She is an herbologist and also makes different varieties of soap, which she sells at Apples in Dark Harbor.

ANNETTE ENGELHARD DE LA RENTA grew up in Far Hills, New Jersey, and knew Mrs. Parish since childhood, as Sister was a close friend of her parents. She spent many years in Dark Harbor, Maine, Cragwood, and New York City, all places that evoke fond memories of life with Mrs. Parish.

VOLNEY "TURKEY" RIGHTER was a lifelong friend of Sister and Harry Parish. He was a classmate of Harry's at St. Pauls School and Harvard. He is a founding partner of Harrington, Righter and Parsons, which is located in New York City, and represents TV stations nationwide. He presently lives in Bedford, New York.

ALCE ROBERTSON was born on Islesboro and, except for a time in New Jersey, has always lived there. She did domestic work for Mrs. Parish. She remembers Mrs. Parish's kindness. Alce said that when her son, Malcolm, was sick, the Parishes sent him to the Leahy Clinic in Boston and paid for everything.

ALICE ROGERS and Sister were friends for over thirty years. They shared a love for Islesboro, both thinking it the most beautiful place in the world. She raised her four children there and made it her family's home.

JOHN ROSSELLI is one of the institutions of the New York interior design world. The showrooms of Mr. Rosselli, a designer, artist, and antiques dealer, draw the top designers in the country.

JOSEPH SALZBERGER works for John A.Weidl, Inc. He was among the primary painters for Mrs. Parish.

HAROLD SIMMONS is a native of Mississippi, where he grew up on his family's cotton plantation. After graduating from the University of Mississippi, he spent a year as apprentice to a well-known Memphis decorator, then moved to New York and completed three years at Parsons School of Design. Next came a year and a half with the architectural firm of Alfred Easton Poor; he then settled into residential design at Mrs. Henry Parish II, Inc. (later to become Parish-Hadley). After twenty-one successful years with Parish-Hadley, he left in 1987 to join the firm of Peter Van Hattum Interiors. His partnership, Van Hattum & Simmons, Inc., continues to do residential design and decoration and has completed projects in various parts of the United States, England, and South America.

FORRESTER SMITH said that Mrs. Parish was a tiger, a tormentor, a teaser, and a tornado. He wonders how she has done over heaven.

PARKER STEVENSON was raised in Maine and New York. A graduate of Princeton University, he has been a film and television actor for over thirty years and is currently directing and producing. With his then wife, Kirstie Alley, he bought property on Islesboro in 1991.

EDWIN SUNDERLAND is a clergyman. He officiated at Sister's son's wedding and funeral. His mother, Dorothy Kissel, was a first cousin of Sister's father, Herman Kinnicutt.

LANDON THOMAS knew Sister Parish all his life, with most of their contact being in Dark Harbor, where he grew up with her children.

JOAN TILNEY and her husband, Robin, will never forget the surprise 7:00 A.M. "Yoo-hoo" on frequent Saturday mornings in Far Hills. Sister was already there in their farmhouse hall, with her two trailing Pekingese yapping madly at their bewildered black Labs. Sister always said, "I knew you would be up," as she made her way to their familiar kitchen. Sister said that Jane (Englehard) never appeared until noon and that she'd been awake since four o'clock. Sister performed miracles in transforming their old Far Hills house, and she is cherished in every nook.

FRANCIE TRAIN said that it wasn't until Sister died that she understood that, for her, two connections were not broken, but strengthened. She knew Sister from as far back as she can remember. They spent summers in Dark Harbor, where their parents were friends. Francie said that one could hardly be unaware of the magic and terror that Sister inspired. Only after Sister died did Francie realize that she and others in her generation had to become grown-ups, however reluctantly. Her new role fit badly, she said, like a wrong outfit at a wedding, but, to fill the space left by Sister, they had to try. The second connection, always there but now more focused, was the knowledge that she and Sister shared a profound appreciation and love for those wonderful friends, the native-born ladies and gentlemen of Islesboro, and the unspoiled beauty of the island. That, she said, is her inheritance from Sister and it will never fade.

VIRGINIA GUEST VALENTINE knew Sister from an early age because Sister was her mother's childhood friend. After her mother died, she was lucky enough to have Aunt Sister consider her a friend.

OLIVE WATSON called Sister after visiting a friend whose living room she loved. Sister helped her and her husband, Tom, over the next forty years. During this period, they also became good friends. Mrs. Watson said that she and her husband enjoyed many good times with Sister and that she truly misses her.

BUNNY WILLIAMS began her decorating career by joining the Parish-Hadley staff in 1967. She remained there for twenty-two years before opening her own design firm in 1988. Over those many years, she established a very strong personal as well as professional relationship with Mrs. Parish, a relationship she considers one of the most important in her life.

➤➤ ── ◄◄

Courtesy of Apple Parish Bartlett: family tree pp. xii–xiii, p. 1, p. 8, p. 11, p. 13, p. 14, p. 20, p. 22, p. 25, p. 29, p. 30, p. 32, p. 35, p. 37, p. 42, p. 45, p. 47, p. 49, p. 51, p. 60, p. 63, p. 67, p. 71, p. 77, p. 78, p. 83, p. 127, p. 159, p. 175, p. 181, p. 187, p. 192, p. 198, p. 201, p. 280, p. 282, p. 283, p. 284 (people), p. 288, p. 290, p. 292, p. 297, p. 298, p. 306, p. 310, p. 313, p. 319, p. 323, p. 325, p. 327, p. 328, p. 330, p. 333, p. 334; Courtesy of the *Boston Herald:* p. 6; Edward Cave: p. 120; Courtesy of Foxcroft School: p. 39; Horst*: p. 184; Courtesy of the John F. Kennedy Library, Boston: p. 87; Andre Kertész*: p. 53, p. 55, p. 56, p. 57, p. 59; Edward Parish: p. 284 (house); Courtesy of Parish-Hadley: p. 93, p. 94, p. 122, p. 125, p. 139, p. 164, p. 173, p. 178, p. 196, p. 203, p. 219, p. 236, p. 251, p. 258, p. 266, p. 273; Wilbur Pippin: p. ii.; Christian Reinhardt*: p. 114; Courtesy of Sotheby's, © 1999 Sotheby's Inc.: p. 134; William P. Steele: p. 236, p. 261; Nancy H. Stettinius: p. 287, p. 299, p. 301, p. 302

Color photo insert:

Harry Bartlett: p. 4 (Summer House); Condé Nast Archives*: p. 5; Oberto Gili*: p. 4 (Whitney bedroom); Mark Hampton: p. 1; Courtesy of the John F. Kennedy Library, Boston: p. 2, p. 3; Dennis Krukowski: p. 7 (front hall of Parish-Hadley); William P. Steele: p. 6, p. 7 (Kiluna Farm), p. 8

Black-&-white photo insert:

Edward Cave: p. 2, p. 6; Oberto Gili*: p. 5; Courtesy of Albert Hadley: p. 3; Anders Holmquist: p. 4; Courtesy of Parish-Hadley: p. 1; Courtesy of Sotheby's © 1999 Sotheby's Inc.: p. 7, p. 8

*Horst/*House & Garden*, 1976, Condé Nast Publications Inc.
Andre Kertész/*Vogue*, 1940, Condé Nast Publications Inc.
Christian Reinhardt/*House & Garden*, 1976, Condé Nast Publications Inc.
House & Garden, 1976, Condé Nast Archives
Oberto Gili/*House & Garden*, 1976, Condé Nast Publications Inc. (color insert)
Oberto Gili/*House & Garden*, 1976, Condé Nast Publications Inc. (b & w insert)